Learning PHP

*A Gentle Introduction to
the Web's Most Popular Language*

David Sklar

Beijing · Boston · Farnham · Sebastopol · Tokyo

Learning PHP

by David Sklar

Copyright © 2016 David Sklar. All rights reserved.

Printed in the United States of America.

Published by O'Reilly Media, Inc., 1005 Gravenstein Highway North, Sebastopol, CA 95472.

O'Reilly books may be purchased for educational, business, or sales promotional use. Online editions are also available for most titles (*http://safaribooksonline.com*). For more information, contact our corporate/institutional sales department: 800-998-9938 or *corporate@oreilly.com*.

Editor: Allyson MacDonald	**Indexer:** Ellen Troutman-Zaig
Production Editors: Colleen Lobner and Nicole Shelby	**Interior Designer:** David Futato
	Cover Designer: Randy Comer
Copyeditor: Gillian McGarvey	**Illustrator:** Rebecca Demarest
Proofreader: Rachel Head	

April 2016:   First Edition

Revision History for the First Edition

2016-04-07:   First Release

See *http://oreilly.com/catalog/errata.csp?isbn=9781491933572* for release details.

978-1-491-93357-2

[LSI]

To M and S: may you never stop learning.

Table of Contents

Preface

Boring websites are *static*. Interesting websites are *dynamic*—that is, their content changes. A giant static HTML page listing the names, pictures, descriptions, and prices of all 1,000 products a company has for sale is hard to use and takes forever to load. A dynamic web product catalog that lets you search and filter those products so you see only the six items that meet your price and category criteria is more useful, faster, and much more likely to close a sale.

The PHP programming language makes it easy to build dynamic websites. Whatever interactive excitement you want to create—whether it be as a product catalog, a blog, a photo album, or an event calendar—PHP is up to the task. And after reading this book, you'll be up to the task of building that dynamic website, too.

Who This Book Is For

This book will be useful for many different kinds of people:

- A hobbyist who wants to create an interactive website for himself, his family, or a nonprofit organization
- A website builder who wants to use the PHP setup provided by an ISP or hosting provider
- A developer or designer who needs to write a plugin or extension for a popular piece of software written in PHP, such as Drupal, WordPress, or MediaWiki
- A page designer who wants to communicate better with her developer co-workers
- A JavaScript whiz who wants to build server-side programs that complement her client-side code
- A Perl, Python, or Ruby programmer who wants to get up to speed with PHP
- Anybody who wants a straightforward, jargon-free introduction to one of the most popular programming languages for building interactive websites

PHP's gentle learning curve and approachable syntax make it an ideal "gateway" language for the nontechnical web professional. *Learning PHP* is aimed at this interested, intelligent, but not necessarily technical individual as well as at programmers familiar with another language who want to learn PHP.

If you are completely new to programming and embarking on your first interactive website, you've got the right book in your hands. The beginning chapters will give you a gentle introduction to the syntax of the PHP language and basic computer programming topics as they apply to PHP. Start at the beginning of the book and work your way forward.

If you are familiar with programming in another language but starting your first PHP project, you may want to start with the second section of the book and dip back into the first set of chapters when you have a specific question about syntax or how something basic is done in PHP.

Aside from basic computer literacy (knowing how to type, moving files around, surfing the Web), the only assumption that this book makes about you is that you're acquainted with HTML. You don't need to be an HTML wizard, but you should be comfortable with the HTML tags that populate a basic web page, such as <html>, <head>, <body>, <p>, <a>, and <br>. If you're not familiar with HTML, read *Head First HTML and CSS* by Elisabeth Robson and Eric Freeman (O'Reilly).

Contents of This Book

This book is designed so that you start at the beginning and work through the chapters in order. For the most part, each chapter depends on material in the previous chapters. Chapters 2 through 13 each end with exercises that test your understanding of the chapter's content.

Chapter 1 provides some general background on PHP and how it interacts with your web browser and a web server. It also shows some PHP programs and what they do, to give you an idea of what PHP programs look like. Especially if you're new to programming or building dynamic websites, it is important to read Chapter 1.

The next five chapters give you a grounding in the fundamentals of PHP. Before you can write great literature, you need to learn a little grammar and some vocabulary. That's what these chapters are for. (Don't worry—you'll learn enough PHP grammar and vocabulary right away to start writing some short programs, if not great literature.)

Chapter 2 shows you how to work with different kinds of data, such as pieces of text and numbers. This is important because the web pages that your PHP programs generate are just big pieces of text.

Chapter 3 describes the PHP commands that your programs can use to make decisions. These decisions are at the heart of the "dynamic" in *dynamic website*. The concepts in Chapter 3 are what you use, for example, to display only those items in a product catalog that fall between two prices a user enters in a web form.

Chapter 4 introduces *arrays*, which are collections of a bunch of individual numbers or pieces of text. Many frequent activities in PHP programs, such as processing submitted web form parameters or examining information pulled out of a database, involve using arrays.

As you write more complicated programs, you'll find yourself wanting to repeat similar tasks. *Functions*, discussed in Chapter 5, help you reuse pieces of your programs.

Chapter 6 shows how data and logic together are combined into *objects*. Objects are reusable bundles of code that help you structure your programs. Objects also allow you to integrate existing PHP add-ons and libraries into your code.

The next five chapters cover essential tasks in building a dynamic website: interacting with users, saving information, and interacting with other websites.

Chapter 7 supplies details on working with web forms, which are the primary way that users interact with your website.

Chapter 8 discusses databases. A database holds the information that your website displays, such as a product catalog or event calendar. This chapter shows you how to make your PHP programs talk to a database. With the techniques in Chapter 8, your website can do user-specific things such as display sensitive information only to authorized people or tell someone how many new message board posts have been created since she last logged in.

In addition to a database, you might also need to work with data stored in files. Chapter 9 explains to how read and write files from a PHP program.

Next, Chapter 10 details how to keep track of your users. This includes using cookies for transient data, but also users logging in to accounts and tracking session data such as a shopping cart of products.

The last chapter in this section, Chapter 11, delves into how your PHP program can interact with other websites and web services. You can retrieve the contents of other web pages or web APIs to use in your programs. Similarly, you can use PHP to serve up not just regular web pages but API responses to other clients.

Instead of new features you could incorporate into your programs, the next three chapters discuss things that help you be a better programmer.

Chapter 12 explains debugging: finding and fixing errors in your programs.

Chapter 13 shows how to write tests that exercise different parts of your program. These tests provide a way to make sure that your program does what you expect it to do.

Lastly, Chapter 14 talks about some aspects of software engineering that are not specific to PHP but that you should be familiar with as you work on projects with other developers.

The final section of the book is a collection of short explorations into a few common tasks and topics. These are not as fundamental as the material on the basic structure of PHP, or how to store information, but are still things that you're likely to run into as you spend time with PHP. These chapters give you the basics.

Chapter 15 shows PHP's powerful and comprehensive set of capabilities for working with dates and times. Chapter 16 discusses *package management*, with which you have a drop-dead simple way of incorporating useful libraries written by others into your code. Chapter 17 explains how to send email messages from your PHP program. Chapter 18 examines three popular PHP web application frameworks, which can jumpstart your project by eliminating a lot of common boilerplate code. Chapter 19 delves into using PHP from the command line (rather than from a web server), which can be a handy way to write simple utilities or test short programs. Finally, Chapter 20 lays out some techniques for successfully writing PHP programs that flawlessly handle text in different languages and character sets.

The two appendixes provide supplementary material. To run PHP programs, you need to have a copy of the PHP engine installed on your computer (or have an account with a web-hosting provider that supports PHP). Appendix A helps you get up and running, whether you are using Windows, OS X, or Linux.

Appendix B contains the answers to all the exercises in the book. No peeking until you've tried the exercises!

What's Not in This Book

This book is of finite length, so unfortunately it can't include everything there is to know about PHP. The primary goal of the book is to provide an introduction to PHP and to some of the basics of computer programming.

If you're already a PHP programmer and are primarily interested in what's new in PHP 7, *Upgrading to PHP 7* by Davey Shafik (O'Reilly) is a great place to look for all the details on what's new and different in this latest version of PHP. Bruno Skvorc's compilation of links and references at SitePoint (*http://bit.ly/skvorc-php7*) also has a lot of great detail.

Other Resources

The online annotated PHP Manual (*http://www.php.net/manual*) is a great resource for exploring PHP's extensive function library. Plenty of user-contributed comments offer helpful advice and sample code, too. Additionally, there are many PHP mailing lists covering installation, programming, extending PHP, and various other topics. You can learn about and subscribe to these mailing lists at *php.net*. Also worth exploring is the PHP Presentation System archive (*http://talks.php.net*). This is a collection of presentations about PHP that have been delivered at various conferences.

PHP The Right Way (*http://www.phptherightway.com*) is also a splendid resource for getting to know PHP, especially if you're familiar with another programming language.

After you're comfortable with the material in this book, the following books about PHP are good next steps:

- *Programming PHP* by Rasmus Lerdorf, Peter MacIntyre, and Kevin Tatroe (O'Reilly). A more detailed and technical look at how to write PHP programs. Includes information on security, XML, and generating graphics.
- *PHP Cookbook* by David Sklar and Adam Trachtenberg (O'Reilly). A comprehensive collection of common PHP programming problems and their solutions.
- *Modern PHP* by Josh Lockhart (O'Reilly). This book is not about syntax and specific PHP tasks. Instead, it helps you write PHP with consistent, high-quality style and understand good practices for software engineering with PHP: it covers issues such as code deployment, testing, and profiling.

These books are helpful for learning about databases, SQL, and MySQL:

- *Learning PHP, MySQL & JavaScript* by Robin Nixon (O'Reilly). Explains how to make PHP, MySQL and JavaScript sing in harmony to make a robust dynamic website.
- *SQL in a Nutshell* by Kevin E. Kline, Daniel Kline, and Brand Hunt (O'Reilly). Covers the essentials you need to know to write SQL queries, and covers the SQL dialects used by Microsoft SQL Server, MySQL, Oracle, and PostgreSQL.
- *MySQL Cookbook* by Paul DuBois (O'Reilly). A comprehensive collection of common MySQL tasks.
- *MySQL Reference Manual*. The ultimate source for information about MySQL's features and SQL dialect.

Conventions Used in This Book

The following programming and typesetting conventions are used in this book.

Programming Conventions

The code examples in this book are designed to work with PHP 7.0.0. They were tested with PHP 7.0.5, which was the most up-to-date version of PHP 7 available at the time of publication. Where the book references or uses features added in PHP 5.4.0 or later, there is generally a mention of which version the feature was added in.

Typographical Conventions

The following typographical conventions are used in this book:

Italic

> Indicates new terms, example URLs, example email addresses, filenames, file extensions, pathnames, and directories.

`Constant width`

> Indicates commands, options, switches, variables, attributes, keys, functions, types, classes, namespaces, methods, modules, properties, parameters, values, objects, events, event handlers, XML tags, HTML tags, macros, the contents of files, or the output from commands.

`Constant width italic`

> Shows text that should be replaced with user-supplied values.

 This icon signifies a tip, suggestion, or general note.

 This icon indicates a warning or caution.

Using Code Examples

Typing some of the example programs in the book yourself is instructive when you are getting started. However, if your fingers get weary, you can download all of the code examples from *https://github.com/oreillymedia/Learning_PHP*.

This book is here to help you get your job done. In general, you may use the code in this book in your programs and documentation. You do not need to contact the publisher for permission unless you're reproducing a significant portion of the code. For example, writing a program that uses several chunks of code from this book does not require permission. Selling or distributing a CD-ROM of examples from O'Reilly books does require permission. Answering a question by citing this book and quoting example code does not require permission. Incorporating a significant amount of example code from this book into your product's documentation does require permission.

We appreciate, but do not require, attribution. An attribution usually includes the title, author, publisher, and ISBN. For example: *Learning PHP* by David Sklar. Copyright 2016 David Sklar, 978-149-193357-2." If you feel your use of code examples falls outside fair use or the permission given above, feel free to contact the publisher at *permissions@oreilly.com*.

Safari® Books Online

 *Safari Books Online* is an on-demand digital library that delivers expert content in both book and video form from the world's leading authors in technology and business.

Technology professionals, software developers, web designers, and business and creative professionals use Safari Books Online as their primary resource for research, problem solving, learning, and certification training.

Safari Books Online offers a range of plans and pricing for enterprise, government, education, and individuals.

Members have access to thousands of books, training videos, and prepublication manuscripts in one fully searchable database from publishers like O'Reilly Media, Prentice Hall Professional, Addison-Wesley Professional, Microsoft Press, Sams, Que, Peachpit Press, Focal Press, Cisco Press, John Wiley & Sons, Syngress, Morgan Kaufmann, IBM Redbooks, Packt, Adobe Press, FT Press, Apress, Manning, New Riders, McGraw-Hill, Jones & Bartlett, Course Technology, and hundreds more. For more information about Safari Books Online, please visit us online.

Comments and Questions

Please address comments and questions concerning this book to the publisher:

O'Reilly Media, Inc.
1005 Gravenstein Highway
North Sebastopol, CA 95472
(800) 998-9938 (in the United States or Canada)
(707) 829-0515 (international or local)
(707) 829-0104 (fax)

There is a web page for this book, where we list errata, examples, and any additional information. You can access this page at *http://bit.ly/learning_php*.

To comment or ask technical questions about this book, send email to *bookquestions@oreilly.com*.

Or you can contact the author directly via his website, *http://www.sklar.com*.

For more information about our books, conferences, Resource Centers, and the O'Reilly Network, see our website at *http://www.oreilly.com*.

Acknowledgments

This book is the end result of the hard work of many people. Thank you to:

- The many programmers, testers, documentation writers, bug fixers, and other folks whose time, talent, and devotion have made PHP the first-class development platform that it is today. Without them, I'd have nothing to write about.
- My diligent reviewers: Thomas David Baker and Phil McCluskey. They caught plenty of mistakes, turned confusing explanations into clear ones, and otherwise made this book far better than it would have been without them.
- My diligent editor: Ally MacDonald. The author is just one of the many pieces it takes to make a book and Ally made sure everything that needed to happen with all of those pieces actually happened!

For a better fate than wisdom, thank you also to Susannah, with whom I continue to enjoy ignoring the syntax of things.

## CHAPTER 1

Orientation and First Steps

There are lots of great reasons to write computer programs in PHP. Maybe you want to learn PHP because you need to put together a small website that has some interactive elements. Perhaps PHP is being used where you work and you have to get up to speed. This chapter provides context for how PHP fits into the puzzle of website construction: what it can do and why it's so good at what it does. You'll also get your first look at the PHP language and see it in action.

PHP's Place in the Web World

PHP is a programming language that's used mostly for building websites. Instead of a PHP program running on a desktop computer for the use of one person, it typically runs on a web server and is accessed by lots of people using web browsers on their own computers. This section explains how PHP fits into the interaction between a web browser and a web server.

When you sit down at your computer and pull up a web page using a browser such as Safari or Firefox, you cause a little conversation to happen over the Internet between your computer and another computer. This conversation, and how it makes a web page appear on your screen, is illustrated in Figure 1-1.

Here's what's happening in the numbered steps of the diagram:

1. You type *www.example.com/catalog.html* into your browser's location bar.
2. The browser sends a message over the Internet to the computer named www.example.com asking for the */catalog.html* page.
3. Apache HTTP Server, a program running on the www.example.com computer, gets the message and reads the *catalog.html* file from its disk drive.

4. Apache sends the contents of the file back to your computer over the Internet as a response to the browser's request.

5. Your browser displays the page on your screen, following the instructions of the HTML tags in the page.

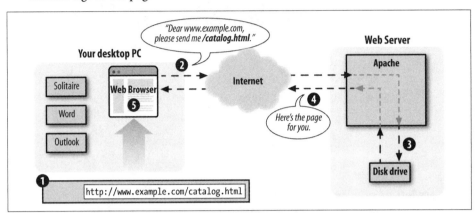

Figure 1-1. Client and server communication without PHP

Every time a browser asks for *http://www.example.com/catalog.html*, the web server sends back the contents of the same *catalog.html* file. The only time the response from the web server changes is if someone edits the file on the server.

When PHP is involved, however, the server does more work for its half of the conversation. Figure 1-2 shows what happens when a web browser asks for a page that is generated by PHP.

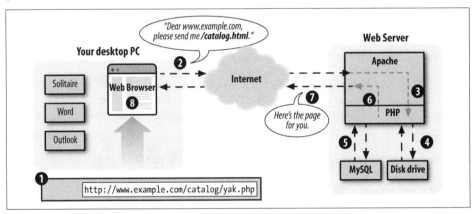

Figure 1-2. Client and server communication with PHP

Here's what's happening in the numbered steps of the PHP-enabled conversation:

1. You type *www.example.com/catalog/yak.php* into your browser's location bar.

2. Your browser sends a message over the Internet to the computer named www.example.com asking for the */catalog/yak.php* page.
3. Apache HTTP Server, a program running on the www.example.com computer, gets the message and asks the PHP engine, another program running on the www.example.com computer, "What does */catalog/yak.php* look like?"
4. The PHP engine reads the file *yak.php* from the disk drive.
5. The PHP engine runs the commands in *yak.php*, possibly exchanging data with a database program such as MySQL.
6. The PHP engine takes the *yak.php* program output and sends it back to Apache HTTP Server as an answer to "What does */catalog/yak.php* look like?"
7. Apache HTTP Server sends the page contents it got from the PHP engine back to your computer over the Internet in response to your browser's request.
8. Your browser displays the page on your screen, following the instructions of the HTML tags in the page.

PHP is a programming language. Something in the web server computer reads your PHP programs, which are instructions written in this programming language, and figures out what to do. The *PHP engine* follows your instructions. Programmers often say "PHP" when they mean either the programming language or the engine. In this book, just "PHP" means the programming language. "PHP engine" means the thing that follows the commands in the PHP programs you write and that generates web pages.

If PHP (the programming language) is like English (the human language), then the PHP engine is like an English-speaking person. The English language defines various words and combinations that, when read or heard by an English-speaking person, translate into various meanings that cause the person to do things such as feel embarrassed, go to the store to buy some milk, or put on pants. The programs you write in PHP (the programming language) cause the PHP engine to do things such as talk to a database, generate a personalized web page, or display an image.

This book is concerned with the details of writing those programs—i.e., what happens in step 5 of Figure 1-2 (although Appendix A contains details on configuring and installing the PHP engine on your own web server).

PHP is called a *server-side* language because, as Figure 1-2 illustrates, it runs on a web server. A language such as JavaScript can be used as a *client-side* language because, embedded in a web browser, it can cause that browser, while running on your desktop PC, to do something such as pop up a new window. Once the web server has sent the generated web page to the client (step 7 in Figure 1-2), PHP is out of the picture. If the page content contains some JavaScript, then that JavaScript runs on the client, but it is totally disconnected from the PHP program that generated the page.

A plain HTML web page is like the "sorry you found a cockroach in your soup" form letter you might get after dispatching an angry complaint to a bug-infested airline.

When your letter arrives at the airline's headquarters, the overburdened secretary in the customer service department pulls the "cockroach reply letter" out of the filing cabinet, makes a copy, and puts the copy in the mail back to you. Every similar request gets the exact same response.

In contrast, a dynamic page that PHP generates is like a postal letter you write to a friend across the globe. You can put whatever you like down on the page—doodles, diagrams, haikus, and tender stories of how unbearably cute your new baby is when she spatters mashed carrots all over the kitchen. The content of your letter is tailored to the specific person to whom it's being sent. Once you put that letter in the mailbox, however, you can't change it any more. It wings its way across the globe and is read by your friend. You don't have any way to modify the letter as your friend is reading it.

Now imagine you're writing a letter to an arts-and-crafts-inspired friend. Along with the doodles and stories you include instructions such as "Cut out the little picture of the frog at the top of the page and paste it over the tiny rabbit at the bottom of the page," and "Read the last paragraph on the page before any other paragraph." As your friend reads the letter, she also performs actions the letter instructs her to take. These actions are like JavaScript in a web page. They're set down when the letter is written and don't change after that. But when the reader of the letter follows the instructions, the letter itself can change. Similarly, a web browser obeys any JavaScript commands in a page and pops up windows, changes form menu options, or refreshes the page to a new URL.

What's So Great About PHP?

You may be attracted to PHP because it's free, because it's easy to learn, or because your boss told you that you need to start working on a PHP project next week. Since you're going to use PHP, you need to know a little bit about what makes it special. The next time someone asks you "What's so great about PHP?" use this section as the basis for your answer.

PHP Is Free (as in Money)

You don't have to pay anyone to use PHP. Whether you run the PHP engine on a beat-up 10-year-old PC in your basement or in a room full of million-dollar "enterprise-class" servers, there are no licensing fees, support fees, maintenance fees, upgrade fees, or any other kind of charge.

OS X and most Linux distributions come with PHP already installed. If yours doesn't, or you are using another operating system such as Windows, you can download PHP from *http://www.php.net*. Appendix A has detailed instructions on how to install PHP.

PHP Is Free (as in Speech)

As an open source project, PHP makes its innards available for anyone to inspect. If it doesn't do what you want, or you're just curious about why a feature works the way it does, you can poke around in the guts of the PHP engine (written in the C programming language) to see what's what. Even if you don't have the technical expertise to do that, you can get someone who does to do the investigating for you. Most people can't fix their own cars, but it's nice to be able to take your car to a mechanic who can pop open the hood and fix it.

PHP Is Cross-Platform

You can use PHP with a web server computer that runs Windows, Mac OS X, Linux, and many other versions of Unix. Plus, if you switch web server operating systems, you generally don't have to change any of your PHP programs. Just copy them from your Windows server to your Unix server, and they will still work.

While Apache is the most popular web server program used with PHP, you can also use nginx, Microsoft Internet Information Server (IIS), or any other web server that supports the CGI standard. PHP also works with a large number of databases, including MySQL, PostgreSQL, Oracle, Microsoft SQL Server, SQLite, Redis, and MongoDB.

If all the acronyms in the last paragraph freak you out, don't worry. It boils down to this: whatever system you're using, PHP probably runs on it just fine and works with whatever database you are already using.

PHP Is Widely Used

PHP is used on more than 200 million different websites, from countless tiny personal home pages to giants like Facebook, Wikipedia, Tumblr, Slack, and Yahoo. There are many books, magazines, and websites devoted to teaching PHP and exploring what you can do with it. There are companies that provide support and training for PHP. In short, if you are a PHP user, you are not alone.

PHP Hides Its Complexity

You can build powerful ecommerce engines in PHP that handle millions of customers. You can also build a small site that automatically maintains links to a changing list of articles or press releases. When you're using PHP for a simpler project, it doesn't get in your way with concerns that are only relevant in a massive system. When you need advanced features such as caching, custom libraries, or dynamic image generation, they are available. If you don't need them, you don't have to worry about them. You can just focus on the basics of handling user input and displaying output.

PHP Is Built for Web Programming

Unlike most other programming languages, PHP was created from the ground up for generating web pages. This means that common web programming tasks, such as accessing form submissions and talking to a database, are often easier in PHP. PHP comes with the capability to format HTML, manipulate dates and times, and manage web cookies—tasks that are often available only via add-on libraries in other programming languages.

PHP in Action

Ready for your first taste of PHP? This section contains a few program listings and explanations of what they do. If you don't understand everything going on in each listing, don't worry! That's what the rest of the book is for. Read these listings to get a sense of what PHP programs look like and an outline of how they work. Don't sweat the details yet.

When given a program to run, the PHP engine pays attention only to the parts of the program between PHP start and end tags. Whatever's outside those tags is printed with no modification. This makes it easy to embed small bits of PHP in pages that mostly contain HTML. The PHP engine runs the commands between <?php (the PHP start tag) and ?> (the PHP end tag). PHP pages typically live in files whose names end in *.php*. Example 1-1 shows a page with one PHP command.

Example 1-1. Hello, World!

```
<html>
<head><title>PHP says hello</title></head>
<body>
<b>
<?php
print "Hello, World!";
?>
</b>
</body>
</html>
```

The output of Example 1-1 is:

```
<html>
<head><title>PHP says hello</title></head>
<body>
<b>
Hello, World!</b>
</body>
</html>
```

In your web browser, this looks like Figure 1-3.

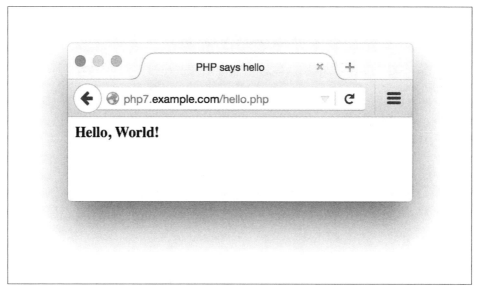

Figure 1-3. Saying hello with PHP

Printing a message that never changes is not a very exciting use of PHP, however. You could have included the "Hello, World!" message in a plain HTML page with the same result. More useful is printing dynamic data—i.e., information that changes. One of the most common sources of information for PHP programs is the user: the browser displays a form, the user enters information into that and hits the "submit" button, the browser sends that information to the server, and the server finally passes it on to the PHP engine where it is available to your program.

Example 1-2 is an HTML form with no PHP. The form consists simply of a text box named user and a Submit button. The form submits to *sayhello.php*, specified via the <form> tag's action attribute.

Example 1-2. HTML form for submitting data

```
<form method="POST" action="sayhello.php">
Your Name: <input type="text" name="user" />
<br/>
<button type="submit"">Say Hello</button>
</form>
```

Your web browser renders the HTML in Example 1-2 into the form shown in Figure 1-4.

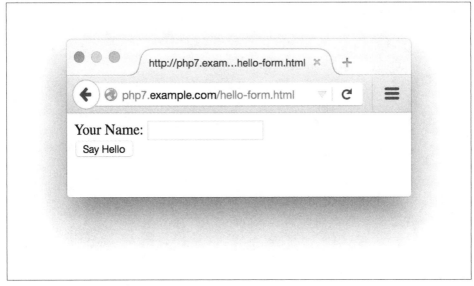

Figure 1-4. Printing a form

Example 1-3 shows the *sayhello.php* program that prints a greeting to whomever is named in the form's text box.

Example 1-3. Dynamic data

```
<?php
print "Hello, ";
// Print what was submitted in the form parameter called 'user'
print $_POST['user'];
print "!";
?>
```

If you type `Ellen` in the text box and submit the form, then Example 1-3 prints `Hello, Ellen!`. Figure 1-5 shows how your web browser displays that.

`$_POST` holds the values of submitted form parameters. In programming terminology, it is a *variable*, so called because you can change the values it holds. In particular, it is an *array* variable, because it can hold more than one value. This particular array is discussed in Chapter 7. Arrays in general are discussed in Chapter 4.

In this example, the line that begins with `//` is called a *comment line*. Comment lines are there for human readers of source code and are ignored by the PHP engine. Comments are useful for annotating your programs with information about how they work. "Comments" on page 15 discusses comments in more detail.

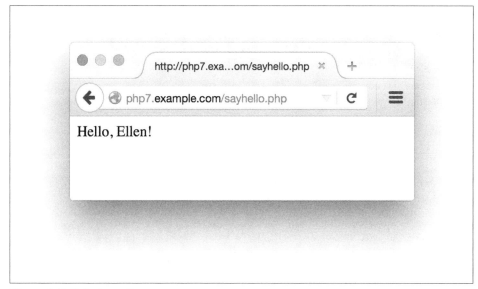

Figure 1-5. Printing a form parameter

You can also use PHP to print out the HTML form that lets someone submit a value for user. This is shown in Example 1-4.

Example 1-4. Printing a form

```php
<?php
print <<<_HTML_
<form method="post" action="$_SERVER[PHP_SELF]">
Your Name: <input type="text" name="user" />
<br/>
<button type="submit">Say Hello</button>
</form>
_HTML_;
?>
```

Example 1-4 uses a string syntax called a *here document*. Everything between the <<<_HTML_ and the _HTML_ is passed to the print command to be displayed. Just like in Example 1-3, a variable inside the string is replaced with its value. This time, the variable is $_SERVER[PHP_SELF]. This is a special PHP variable that contains the URL (without the protocol or hostname) of the current page. If the URL for the page in Example 1-4 is *http://www.example.com/users/enter.php*, then $_SERVER[PHP_SELF] contains /users/enter.php.

With $_SERVER[PHP_SELF] as the form action, you can put the code for printing a form and for doing something with the submitted form data in the same page. Example 1-5 combines Examples 1-3 and 1-4 into one page that displays a form and prints a greeting when the form is submitted.

Example 1-5. Printing a greeting or a form

```php
<?php
// Print a greeting if the form was submitted
if ($_POST['user']) {
    print "Hello, ";
    // Print what was submitted in the form parameter called 'user'
    print $_POST['user'];
    print "!";
} else {
    // Otherwise, print the form
    print <<<_HTML_
<form method="post" action="$_SERVER[PHP_SELF]">
Your Name: <input type="text" name="user" />
<br/>
<button type="submit">Say Hello</button>
</form>
_HTML_;
}
?>
```

Example 1-5 uses the if() construct to see whether the browser sent a value for the form parameter user. It uses that to decide which of two things to do: print a greeting or print a form. Chapter 3 talks about if(). Using $_SERVER[PHP_SELF] and processing forms are discussed in Chapter 7.

PHP has a huge library of internal functions that you can use in your programs. These functions help you accomplish common tasks. One built-in function is number_format(), which provides a formatted version of a number. Example 1-6 uses number_format() to print out a number.

Example 1-6. Printing a formatted number

```php
<?php print "The population of the US is about: ";
print number_format(320853904);
?>
```

Example 1-6 prints:

```
The population of the US is about: 320,853,904
```

Chapter 5 is about functions. It shows you how to write your own and explains the syntax for calling and handling the results of functions. Many functions, includ-

---

ing number_format(), have a *return value*. This is the result of running the function. In Example 1-6, the data the second print statement is given to print is the return value from number_format(). In this case, it's the comma-formatted population number.

One of the most common types of programs written in PHP is one that displays a web page containing information retrieved from a database. When you let submitted form parameters control what is pulled from the database, you open the door to a universe of interactivity on your website. Example 1-7 shows a PHP program that connects to a database server, retrieves a list of dishes and their prices based on the value of the form parameter meal, and prints those dishes and prices in an HTML table.

Example 1-7. Displaying information from a database

```php
<?php
// Use the SQLite database 'dinner.db'
$db = new PDO('sqlite:dinner.db');
// Define what the allowable meals are
$meals = array('breakfast','lunch','dinner');
// Check if submitted form parameter "meal" is one of
// "breakfast", "lunch", or "dinner"
if (in_array($_POST['meal'], $meals)) {
    // If so, get all of the dishes for the specified meal
    $stmt = $db->prepare('SELECT dish,price FROM meals WHERE meal LIKE ?');
    $stmt->execute(array($_POST['meal']));
    $rows = $stmt->fetchAll();
    // If no dishes were found in the database, say so
    if (count($rows) == 0) {
        print "No dishes available.";
    } else {
        // Print out each dish and its price as a row
        // in an HTML table
        print '<table><tr><th>Dish</th><th>Price</th></tr>';
        foreach ($rows as $row) {
            print "<tr><td>$row[0]</td><td>$row[1]</td></tr>";
        }
        print "</table>";
    }
} else {
    // This message prints if the submitted parameter "meal" isn't
    // "breakfast", "lunch", or "dinner"
    print "Unknown meal.";
}
?>
```

There's a lot going on in Example 1-7, but it's a testament to the simplicity and power of PHP that it takes only about 20 lines of code (without comments) to make this dynamic, database-backed web page. The following describes what happens in those 20 lines.

The `new PDO()` function at the top of the example sets up the connection to the SQLite database in a particular file. These functions, like the other database functions used in this example (`prepare()`, `execute()`, and `fetchAll()`), are explained in more detail in Chapter 8.

Things in the program that begin with a $, such as `$db`, `$_POST`, `$stmt`, and `$row`, are variables. Variables hold values that may change as the program runs or that are created at one point in the program and are saved to use later. Chapter 2 talks about variables.

After connecting to the database, the next task is to see what meal the user requested. The `$meals` array is initialized to hold the allowable meals: `breakfast`, `lunch`, and `dinner`. The statement `in_array($POST['meal'], $meals)` checks whether the submitted form parameter `meal` (the value of `$_POST['meal']`) is in the `$meals` array. If not, execution skips down to the end of the example, after the last `else`, and the program prints `Unknown meal`.

If an acceptable meal was submitted, `prepare()` and `execute()` send a query to the database. For example, if the meal is `breakfast`, the query that is sent is as follows:

```
SELECT dish,price FROM meals WHERE meal LIKE 'breakfast'
```

Queries to SQLite and most other relational databases are written in a language called Structured Query Language (SQL). Chapter 8 provides the basics of SQL. The `prepare()` function returns an identifier that we can use to get further information about the query.

The `fetchAll()` function uses that identifier to get all the matching meals the query found in the database. If there are no applicable meals, the program prints `No dishes available`. Otherwise, it displays information about the matching meals.

The program prints the beginning of the HTML table. Then, it uses the `foreach` construct to process each dish that the query found. The `print` statement uses elements of the array returned by `fetchAll()` to display one table row per dish.

Basic Rules of PHP Programs

This section lays out some ground rules about the structure of PHP programs. More foundational than basics such as "How do I print something?" or "How do I add two numbers?" these proto-basics are the equivalent of someone telling you that you should read pages in this book from top to bottom and left to right, or that what's important on the page are the black squiggles, not the large white areas.

If you've had a little experience with PHP already or you're the kind of person that prefers playing with all the buttons on your new Blu-Ray player before going back and reading in the manual about how the buttons actually work, feel free to skip ahead to Chapter 2 now and flip back here later. If you forge ahead to write some PHP programs of your own and they behave unexpectedly, or the PHP engine complains of "parse errors" when it tries to run your program, revisit this section for a refresher.

Start and End Tags

Each of the examples you've already seen in this chapter uses <?php as the PHP start tag and ?> as the PHP end tag. The PHP engine ignores anything outside of those tags. Text before the start tag or after the end tag is printed with no interference from the PHP engine. You can leave off the end tag at the end of a PHP file. If the PHP engine reaches the end of a file and doesn't see a PHP end tag, it acts as if there was one as the very last thing in the file. This is very useful for ensuring that invisible extra stuff (such as blank lines) after an end tag doesn't accidentally make it into your program output.

A PHP program can have multiple start and end tag pairs, as shown in Example 1-8.

Example 1-8. Multiple start and end tags

```
Five plus five is:
<?php print 5 + 5; ?>
<p>
Four plus four is:
<?php
 print 4 + 4;
?>
<p>
<img src="vacation.jpg" alt="My Vacation" />
```

The PHP source code inside each set of <?php ?> tags is processed by the PHP engine, and the rest of the page is printed as is. Example 1-8 prints:

```
Five plus five is:
10<p>
Four plus four is:
8<p>
<img src="vacation.jpg" alt="My Vacation" />
```

Some older PHP programs use <? as a start tag instead of <?php. The <? is called the *short open tag*, since it's shorter than <?php. It's usually better to use the regular <?php open tag since it's guaranteed to work on any server running the PHP engine. Support for the short tag can be turned on or off with a PHP configuration setting.

Appendix A shows you how to modify your PHP configuration to control which open tags are valid in your programs.

The rest of the examples in this chapter all begin with the `<?php` start tag and end with `?>`. In subsequent chapters, not all the examples have start and end tags—but remember, your programs need them in order for the PHP engine to recognize your code.

Whitespace and Case-Sensitivity

Like all PHP programs, the examples in this section consist of a series of statements, each of which ends with a semicolon. You can put multiple PHP statements on the same line of a program as long as they are separated with a semicolon. You can put as many blank lines between statements as you want. The PHP engine ignores them. The semicolon tells the engine that one statement is over and another is about to begin. No whitespace at all or lots and lots of whitespace between statements doesn't affect the program's execution. (*Whitespace* is programmer-speak for blank-looking characters such as spaces, tabs, and newlines.)

In practice, it's good style to put one statement on a line and blank lines between statements only when it improves the readability of your source code. The spacing in Examples 1-9 and 1-10 is bad. Instead, format your code as in Example 1-11.

Example 1-9. This PHP is too cramped

```php
<?php print "Hello"; print " World!"; ?>
```

Example 1-10. This PHP is too sprawling

```php
<?php

print "Hello";


print " World!";

?>
```

Example 1-11. This PHP is just right

```php
<?php
print "Hello";
print " World!";
?>
```

In addition to ignoring whitespace between lines, the PHP engine also ignores whitespace between language keywords and values. You can have zero spaces, one space, or a hundred spaces between `print` and `"Hello, World!"` and again between `"Hello, World!"` and the semicolon at the end of the line.

Good coding style is to put one space between `print` and the value being printed and then to follow the value immediately with a semicolon. Example 1-12 shows three lines, one with too much spacing, one with too little, and one with just the right amount.

Example 1-12. Spacing

```
<?php
print          "Too many spaces"              ;
print"Too few spaces";
print "Just the right amount of spaces";
?>
```

Language keywords (such as `print`) and function names (such as `number_format`) are not case-sensitive. The PHP engine doesn't care whether you use uppercase letters, lowercase letters, or both when you put these keywords and function names in your programs. The statements in Example 1-13 are identical from the engine's perspective.

Example 1-13. Keywords and function names are case-insensitive

```
<?php
// These four lines all do the same thing
print number_format(320853904);
PRINT Number_Format(320853904);
Print number_format(320853904);
pRiNt NUMBER_FORMAT(320853904);
?>
```

Comments

As you've seen in some of the examples in this chapter, comments are a way to explain to other people how your program works. Comments in source code are an essential part of any program. When you're coding, what you are writing may seem crystal clear to you at the time. A few months later, however, when you need to go back and modify the program, your brilliant logic may not be so obvious. That's where comments come in. By explaining in plain language how the programs work, comments make programs much more understandable.

Comments are even more important when the person who needs to modify the program isn't the original author. Do yourself and anyone else who might have occasion to read your source code a favor and fill your programs with a lot of comments.

Perhaps because they're so important, PHP provides many ways to put comments in your programs. One syntax you've seen already is to begin a line with //. This tells the PHP engine to treat everything on that line as a comment. After the end of the line, the code is treated normally. This style of comment is also used in other programming languages such as C++, JavaScript, and Java. You can also put // on a line after a statement to have the remainder of the line treated as a comment. PHP also supports the Perl- and shell-style single-line comments. These are lines that begin with #. You can use # to start a comment in the same places that you use //, but the modern style prefers // over #. Some single-line comments are shown in Example 1-14.

Example 1-14. Single-line comments with // or #

```php
<?php
// This line is a comment
print "Smoked Fish Soup ";
print 'costs $3.25.';

# Add another dish to the menu
print 'Duck with Pea Shoots ';
print 'costs $9.50.';
// You can put // or # inside single-line comments
// Using // or # somewhere else on a line also starts a comment
print 'Shark Fin Soup'; // I hope it's good!
print 'costs $25.00!'; # This is getting expensive!

# Putting // or # inside a string doesn't start a comment
print 'http://www.example.com';
print 'http://www.example.com/menu.php#dinner';
?>
```

For a multiline comment, start the comment with /* and end it with */. Everything between the /* and */ is treated as a comment by the PHP engine. Multiline comments are useful for temporarily turning off a small block of code. Example 1-15 shows some multiline comments.

Example 1-15. Multiline comments

```php
<?php
/* We're going to add a few things to the menu:
    - Smoked Fish Soup
    - Duck with Pea Shoots
    - Shark Fin Soup
*/
print 'Smoked Fish Soup, Duck with Pea Shoots, Shark Fin Soup ';
print 'Cost: 3.25 + 9.50 + 25.00';

/* This is the old menu:
```

```
The following lines are inside this comment so they don't get executed.
print 'Hamburger, French Fries, Cola ';
print 'Cost: 0.99 + 1.25 + 1.50';
*/
?>
```

There is no strict rule in PHP about which comment style is the best. Multiline comments are often the easiest to use, especially when you want to comment out a block of code or write a few lines describing a function. However, when you want to tack on a short explanation to the end of a line, a //-style comment fits nicely. Use whichever comment style you feel most comfortable with.

Chapter Summary

This chapter covered:

- PHP's usage by a web server to create a response or document to send back to the browser
- PHP as a server-side language, meaning it runs on the web server (this is in contrast to a client-side language such as JavaScript that is run inside of a web browser)
- What you sign up for when you decide to use PHP: it's free (in terms of money and speech), cross-platform, popular, and designed for web programming
- How PHP programs that print information, process forms, and talk to a database appear
- Some basics of the structure of PHP programs, such as the PHP start and end tags (<?php and ?>), whitespace, case-sensitivity, and comments

## CHAPTER 2

Data: Working with Text and Numbers

PHP can work with different types of data. In this chapter, you'll learn about individual values such as numbers and single pieces of text. You'll learn how to put text and numbers in your programs, as well as some of the limitations the PHP engine puts on those values and some common tricks for manipulating them.

Most PHP programs spend a lot of time handling text because they spend a lot of time generating HTML and working with information in a database. HTML is just a specially formatted kind of text; and information in a database, such as a username, a product description, or an address, is a piece of text, too. Slicing and dicing text easily means you can build dynamic web pages easily.

In Chapter 1, you saw variables in action, but this chapter teaches you more about them. A variable is a named container that holds a value. The value that a variable holds can change as a program runs. When you access data submitted from a form or exchange data with a database, you use variables. In real life, a variable is something such as your checking account balance. As time goes on, the value that the phrase "checking account balance" refers to fluctuates. In a PHP program, a variable might hold the value of a submitted form parameter. Each time the program runs, the value of the submitted form parameter can be different. But whatever the value, you can always refer to it by the same name. This chapter also explains in more detail what variables are: how you create them and do things such as change their values or print them.

Text

When they're used in computer programs, pieces of text are called *strings*. This is because they consist of individual items, strung together. Strings can contain letters, numbers, punctuation, spaces, tabs, or any other characters. Some examples of strings are I would like 1 bowl of soup, and "Is it too hot?" he asked, and There's no spoon!. A string can even contain the contents of a binary file, such as an image or a sound. The only limit to the length of a string in a PHP program is the amount of memory your computer has.

 Strings in PHP are sequences of *bytes*, not characters. If you're dealing only with English text then this distinction won't affect you. If you work with non-English text and need to make sure that your characters in other alphabets are handled properly, make sure to read Chapter 20, which discusses working with different character sets.

Defining Text Strings

There are a few ways to indicate a string in a PHP program. The simplest is to surround the string with single quotes:

```
print 'I would like a bowl of soup.';
print 'chicken';
print '06520';
print '"I am eating dinner," he growled.';
```

Since the string consists of everything inside the single quotes, that's what is printed:

```
I would like a bowl of soup.chicken06520"I am eating dinner," he growled.
```

Note that the output of those four print statements appears all on one line. No line breaks are added by print.[1]

The single quotes aren't part of the string. They are *delimiters*, which tell the PHP engine where the start and end of the string is. If you want to include a single quote inside a string surrounded with single quotes, put a backslash (\) before the single quote inside the string:

```
print 'We\'ll each have a bowl of soup.';
```

The \' sequence is turned into ' inside the string, so what is printed is:

```
We'll each have a bowl of soup.
```

The backslash tells the PHP engine to treat the following character as a literal single quote instead of the single quote that means "end of string." This is called *escaping*, and the backslash is called the *escape character*. An escape character tells the system to do something special with the character that comes after it. Inside a single-quoted

---

1 You may also see echo used in some PHP programs to print text. It works just like print.

string, a single quote usually means "end of string." Preceding the single quote with a backslash changes its meaning to a literal single quote character.

Curly Quotes and Text Editors

Word processors often automatically turn straight quotes like ' and " into curly quotes like ', ', ", and ". The PHP engine only understands straight quotes as string delimiters. If you're writing PHP programs in a word processor or text editor that puts curly quotes in your programs, you have two choices: tell your word processor to stop it or use a different one. A program such as Emacs, Vi, Sublime Text, or Windows Notepad leaves your quotes alone.

The escape character can itself be escaped. To include a literal backslash character in a string, put a backslash before it:

```
print 'Use a \\ to escape in a string';
```

This prints:

```
Use a \ to escape in a string
```

The first backslash is the escape character: it tells the PHP engine that something different is going on with the next character. This affects the second backslash: instead of the special action ("treat the next character literally"), a literal backslash is included in the string.

Note that these are backslashes that go from top left to bottom right, not forward slshes that go from bottom left to top right. Remember that two forward slashes in a PHP program (//) indicate a comment.

You can include whitespace such as newlines in single-quoted strings:

```
print '<ul>
<li>Beef Chow-Fun</li>
<li>Sauteed Pea Shoots</li>
<li>Soy Sauce Noodles</li>
</ul>';
```

This puts the HTML on multiple lines:

```
<ul>
<li>Beef Chow-Fun</li>
<li>Sauteed Pea Shoots</li>
<li>Soy Sauce Noodles</li>
</ul>
```

Since the single quote that marks the end of the string is immediately after the </ul>, there is no newline at the end of the string.

The only characters that get special treatment inside single-quoted strings are the backslash and single quote. Everything else is treated literally.

You can also delimit strings with double quotes. Double-quoted strings are similar to single-quoted strings, but they have more special characters. These special characters are listed in Table 2-1.

Table 2-1. Special characters in double-quoted strings

Character	Meaning
\n	Newline (ASCII 10)
\r	Carriage return (ASCII 13)
\t	Tab (ASCII 9)
\\	\
\$	$
\"	"
\0 .. \777	Octal (base 8) number
\x0 .. \xFF	Hexadecimal (base 16) number

The biggest difference between single-quoted and double-quoted strings is that when you include variable names inside a double-quoted string, the value of the variable is substituted into the string, which doesn't happen with single-quoted strings. For example, if the variable $user holds the value Bill, then 'Hi $user' is just that: Hi $user. However, "Hi $user" is Hi Bill. "Variables" on page 31 gets into this in more detail.

As mentioned in "PHP in Action" on page 6, you can also define strings with the *here document* syntax. A here document begins with <<< and a delimiter word. It ends with the same word at the beginning of a line. Example 2-1 shows a here document.

Example 2-1. Here document

```
<<<HTMLBLOCK
<html>
<head><title>Menu</title></head>
<body bgcolor="#fffed9">
<h1>Dinner</h1>
<ul>
  <li> Beef Chow-Fun
  <li> Sauteed Pea Shoots
  <li> Soy Sauce Noodles
  </ul>
</body>
</html>
HTMLBLOCK
```

In Example 2-1, the delimiter word is HTMLBLOCK. Here document delimiters can contain letters, numbers, and the underscore character. The first character of the delimiter must be a letter or underscore. It's a good idea to make all the letters in your here document delimiters uppercase to visually set off the here document. The delimiter that ends the here document must be alone on its line. The delimiter can't be indented and no whitespace, comments, or other characters are allowed after it. The only exception to this is that a semicolon is allowed immediately after the delimiter to end a statement. In that case, nothing can be on the same line after the semicolon. The code in Example 2-2 follows these rules to print a here document.

Example 2-2. Printing a here document

```
print <<<HTMLBLOCK
<html>
<head><title>Menu</title></head>
<body bgcolor="#fffed9">
<h1>Dinner</h1>
<ul>
  <li> Beef Chow-Fun
  <li> Sauteed Pea Shoots
  <li> Soy Sauce Noodles
  </ul>
</body>
</html>
HTMLBLOCK;
```

Here documents obey the same escape character and variable substitution rules as double-quoted strings. This makes them especially useful when you want to define or print a string that contains a lot of text or HTML with some variables mixed in. Later on in the chapter, Example 2-22 demonstrates this.

To combine two strings, use a . (period), the string concatenation operator. Here are some combined strings:

```
print 'bread' . 'fruit';
print "It's a beautiful day " . 'in the neighborhood.';
print "The price is: " . '$3.95';
print 'Inky' . 'Pinky' . 'Blinky' . 'Clyde';
```

The combined strings print as:

```
breadfruit
It's a beautiful day in the neighborhood.
The price is: $3.95
InkyPinkyBlinkyClyde
```

Manipulating Text

PHP has a number of built-in functions that are useful when working with strings. This section introduces the functions that are most helpful for two common tasks: validation and formatting. The "Strings" chapter of the online PHP Manual (*http:// www.php.net/strings*) has information on other built-in string handling functions.

Validating strings

Validation is the process of checking that input coming from an external source conforms to an expected format or meaning. It's making sure that a user really entered a zip code in the "zip Code" box of a form or a reasonable email address in the appropriate place. Chapter 7 delves into all the aspects of form handling, but since submitted form data is provided to your PHP programs as strings, this section discusses how to validate those strings.

The `trim()` function removes whitespace from the beginning and end of a string. Combined with `strlen()`, which tells you the length of a string, you can use this function to find out the length of a submitted value while ignoring any leading or trailing spaces. Example 2-3 shows you how. (Chapter 3 discusses in more detail the `if()` statement used in Example 2-3.)

Example 2-3. Checking the length of a trimmed string

```
// $_POST['zipcode'] holds the value of the submitted form parameter
// "zipcode"
$zipcode = trim($_POST['zipcode']);
// Now $zipcode holds that value, with any leading or trailing spaces
// removed
$zip_length = strlen($zipcode);
// Complain if the zip code is not 5 characters long
if ($zip_length != 5) {
    print "Please enter a zip code that is 5 characters long.";
}
```

Using `trim()` protects against someone who types a zip code of 732 followed by two spaces. Sometimes the extra spaces are accidental, and sometimes they are malicious. Whatever the reason, throw them away when appropriate to make sure that you're getting the string length you care about.

You can chain together the calls to `trim()` and `strlen()` for more concise code. Example 2-4 does the same thing as Example 2-3.

Example 2-4. Concisely checking the length of a trimmed string

```
if (strlen(trim($_POST['zipcode'])) != 5) {
    print "Please enter a zip code that is 5 characters long.";
}
```

Four things happen in the first line of Example 2-4. First, the value of the variable $_POST['zipcode'] is passed to the trim() function. Second, the return value of that function—$_POST['zipcode'] with leading and trailing whitespace removed—is handed off to the strlen() function, which then returns the length of the trimmed string. Third, this length is compared with 5. Last, if the length is not equal to 5 the print statement inside the if() block runs.

To compare two strings, use the equal operator (==), as shown in Example 2-5.

Example 2-5. Comparing strings with the equal operator

```
if ($_POST['email'] == 'president@whitehouse.gov') {
    print "Welcome, US President.";
}
```

The print statement in Example 2-5 runs only if the submitted form parameter email is the all-lowercase president@whitehouse.gov. When comparing strings with ==, case is important. The string president@whitehouse.GOV is not the same as President@Whitehouse.Gov or president@whitehouse.gov.

To compare strings without paying attention to case, use strcasecmp(). It compares two strings while ignoring differences in capitalization. If the two strings you provide to strcasecmp() are the same independent of any differences between upper- and lowercase letters, it returns 0. Example 2-6 shows how to use strcasecmp().

Example 2-6. Comparing strings case-insensitively

```
if (strcasecmp($_POST['email'], 'president@whitehouse.gov') == 0) {
    print "Welcome back, US President.";
}
```

The print statement in Example 2-6 runs if the submitted form parameter email is President@Whitehouse.Gov, PRESIDENT@WHITEHOUSE.GOV, presIDENT@white HOUSE.GoV, or any other capitalization of president@whitehouse.gov.

Formatting text

The printf() function gives you more control (compared to print) over how the output looks. You pass printf() a format string and a bunch of items to print. Each rule in the format string is replaced by one item. Example 2-7 shows `printf()` in action.

Example 2-7. Formatting a price with printf()

```
$price = 5; $tax = 0.075;
printf('The dish costs $%.2f', $price * (1 + $tax));
```

This prints:

```
The dish costs $5.38
```

In Example 2-7, the format rule `%.2f` is replaced with the value of `$price * (1 + $tax)` and formatted so that it has two decimal places.

Format string rules begin with `%` and then have some optional modifiers that affect what the rule does:

A padding character
　　If the string that is replacing the format rule is too short, this is used to pad it. Use a space to pad with spaces or a `0` to pad with zeros.

A sign
　　For numbers, a plus sign (+) makes `printf()` put a + before positive numbers (normally, they're printed without a sign.) For strings, a minus sign (-) makes `printf()` right-justify the string (normally, they're left-justified.)

A minimum width
　　This specifies the minimum size that the value replacing the format rule should be. If it's shorter, then the padding character is used to beef it up.

A period and a precision number
　　For floating-point numbers, this controls how many digits go after the decimal point. In Example 2-7, this is the only modifier present. The `.2` formats `$price * (1 + $tax)` with two decimal places.

After the modifiers come a mandatory character that indicates what kind of value should be printed. The three discussed here are `d` for decimal number, `s` for string, and `f` for floating-point number.

If this stew of percent signs and modifiers has you scratching your head, don't worry. The most frequent use of `printf()` is probably to format prices with the `%.2f` format rule as shown in Example 2-7. If you absorb nothing else about `printf()` for now, just remember that it's your go-to function when you want to format a decimal value.

But if you delve a little deeper, you can do some other handy things with it. For example, using the 0 padding character and a minimum width, you can format a date or zip code properly with leading zeros, as shown in Example 2-8.

Example 2-8. Zero-padding with printf()

```
$zip = '6520';
$month = 2;
$day = 6;
$year = 2007;

printf("ZIP is %05d and the date is %02d/%02d/%d", $zip, $month, $day, $year);
```

Example 2-8 prints:

```
ZIP is 06520 and the date is 02/06/2007
```

The sign modifier is helpful for explicitly indicating positive and negative values. Example 2-9 uses it to display some temperatures.

Example 2-9. Displaying signs with printf()

```
$min = -40;
$max = 40;
printf("The computer can operate between %+d and %+d degrees Celsius.", $min, $max);
```

Example 2-9 prints:

```
The computer can operate between -40 and +40 degrees Celsius.
```

To learn about other printf() format rules, visit *http://www.php.net/sprintf.*

Another kind of text formatting is to manipulate the case of strings. The functions strtolower() and strtoupper() make all-lowercase and all-uppercase versions, respectively, of a string. Example 2-10 shows strtolower() and strtoupper() at work.

Example 2-10. Changing case

```
print strtolower('Beef, CHICKEN, Pork, duCK');
print strtoupper('Beef, CHICKEN, Pork, duCK');
```

Example 2-10 prints:

```
beef, chicken, pork, duck
BEEF, CHICKEN, PORK, DUCK
```

The ucwords() function uppercases the first letter of each word in a string. This is useful when combined with strtolower() to produce nicely capitalized names when

they are provided to you in all uppercase. Example 2-11 shows how to combine `strto
lower()` and `ucwords()`.

Example 2-11. Prettifying names with ucwords()

```
print ucwords(strtolower('JOHN FRANKENHEIMER'));
```

Example 2-11 prints:

```
John Frankenheimer
```

With the `substr()` function, you can extract just part of a string. For example, you
may only want to display the beginnings of messages on a summary page.
Example 2-12 shows how to use `substr()` to truncate the submitted form parameter
`comments`.

Example 2-12. Truncating a string with substr()

```
// Grab the first 30 bytes of $_POST['comments']
print substr($_POST['comments'], 0, 30);
// Add an ellipsis
print '...';
```

If the submitted form parameter `comments` is:

```
The Fresh Fish with Rice Noodle was delicious, but I didn't like the Beef Tripe.
```

Example 2-12 prints:

```
The Fresh Fish with Rice Noodl...
```

The three arguments to `substr()` are the string to work with, the starting position of
the substring to extract, and the number of bytes to extract. The beginning of the
string is position 0, not 1, so `substr($_POST['comments'], 0, 30)` means "extract
30 bytes from `$_POST['comments']` starting at the beginning of the string."

When you give `substr()` a negative number for a start position, it counts back from
the end of the string to figure out where to start. A start position of `-4` means "start
four bytes from the end." Example 2-13 uses a negative start position to display just
the last four digits of a credit card number.

Example 2-13. Extracting the end of a string with substr()

```
print 'Card: XX';
print substr($_POST['card'],-4,4);
```

If the submitted form parameter `card` is `4000-1234-5678-9101`, Example 2-13 prints:

```
Card: XX9101
```

As a shortcut, use substr($_POST['card'],-4) instead of substr($_POST['card'], -4,4). When you leave out the last argument, substr() returns everything from the starting position (whether positive or negative) to the end of the string.

Instead of extracting a substring, the str_replace() function changes parts of a string. It looks for a substring and replaces the substring with a new string. This is useful for simple template-based customization of HTML. Example 2-14 uses str_replace() to set the class attribute of <span> tags.

Example 2-14. Using str_replace()

```
$html = '<span class="{class}">Fried Bean Curd<span>
<span class="{class}">Oil-Soaked Fish</span>';

print str_replace('{class}',$my_class,$html);
```

If $my_class has been set to lunch, then Example 2-14 prints:

```
<span class="lunch">Fried Bean Curd<span>
<span class="lunch">Oil-Soaked Fish</span>
```

Each instance of {class} (the first argument to str_replace()) is replaced by lunch (the value of $my_class) in the string that is the third argument passed to str_replace().

Numbers

Numbers in PHP are expressed using familiar notation, although you can't use commas or any other characters to group thousands. You don't have to do anything special to use a number with a decimal part as compared to an integer. Example 2-15 prints some valid numbers in PHP.

Example 2-15. Numbers

```
print 56;
print 56.3;
print 56.30;
print 0.774422;
print 16777.216;
print 0;
print -213;
print 1298317;
print -9912111;
print -12.52222;
print 0.00;
```

Using Different Kinds of Numbers

Internally, the PHP engine makes a distinction between numbers with a decimal part and those without one. The former are called *floating-point* numbers and the latter are called *integers*. Floating-point numbers take their name from the fact that the decimal point can "float" around to represent different amounts of precision.

The PHP engine uses the math facilities of your operating system to represent numbers, so the largest and smallest numbers you can use, as well as the number of decimal places you can have in a floating-point number, vary on different systems.

One distinction between the PHP engine's internal representation of integers and floating-point numbers is the exactness of how they're stored. The integer 47 is stored as exactly 47. The floating-point number 46.3 could be stored as 46.2999999. This affects the correct technique of how to compare numbers. "Building Complicated Decisions" on page 43 explains comparisons and shows how to properly compare floating-point numbers.

Arithmetic Operators

Doing math in PHP is a lot like doing math in elementary school, except it's much faster. Some basic operations between numbers are shown in Example 2-16.

Example 2-16. Math operations

```
print 2 + 2;
print 17 - 3.5;
print 10 / 3;
print 6 * 9;
```

The output of Example 2-16 is:

```
4
13.5
3.3333333333333
54
```

In addition to the plus sign (+) for addition, the minus sign (-) for subtraction, the forward slash (/) for division, and the asterisk (*) for multiplication, PHP also supports two asterisks (**) for exponentiation and the percent sign (%) for modulus division (returning the remainder of a division operation):

```
print 17 % 3;
```

This prints:

```
2
```

Since 17 divided by 3 is 5 with a remainder of 2, 17 % 3 equals 2. The modulus operator is useful for printing rows whose CSS class names alternate in an HTML table, as shown in Example 4-13.

 The exponentiation operator was introduced in PHP 5.6. If you're using an older version of PHP, use the pow( ) function.

The arithmetic operators, as well as the other PHP operators that you'll meet later in the book, fit into a strict precedence of operations. This is how the PHP engine decides in what order to do calculations if they are written ambiguously. For example, "3 + 4 * 2" could mean "add 3 and 4 and then multiply the result by 2," which results in 14. Or, it could mean "add 3 to the product of 4 and 2," which results in 11. In PHP (as well as the math world in general), multiplication has a higher precedence than addition, so the second interpretation is correct. First, the PHP engine multiplies 4 and 2, and then it adds 3 to the result.

The precedence table of all PHP operators is part of the online PHP Manual (*http:// www.php.net/language.operators.precedence*). You can avoid the need to memorize or repeatedly refer to this table, however, with a healthy dose of parentheses. Grouping operations inside parentheses unambiguously tells the PHP engine to do what's inside the parentheses first. The expression "(3 + 4) * 2" means "add 3 and 4 and then multiply the result by 2." The expression "3 + (4 * 2)" means "multiply 4 and 2 and then add 3 to the result."

Like in other modern programming languages, you don't have to do anything special to ensure that the results of your calculations are properly represented as integers or floating-point numbers. Dividing one integer by another produces a floating-point result if the two integers don't divide evenly. Similarly, if you do something to an integer that makes it larger than the maximum allowable integer or smaller than the minimum possible integer, the PHP engine converts the result into a floating-point number so you get the proper result for your calculation.

Variables

Variables hold the data that your program manipulates while it runs, such as user information that you've loaded from a database or entries that have been typed into an HTML form. In PHP, variables are denoted by a $ followed by the variable's name. To assign a value to a variable, use an equals sign (=). This is known as the *assignment operator*.

Here are a few examples:

```
$plates = 5;
$dinner = 'Beef Chow-Fun';
$cost_of_dinner = 8.95;
$cost_of_lunch = $cost_of_dinner;
```

Assignment works with here documents as well:

```
$page_header = <<<HTML_HEADER
<html>
<head><title>Menu</title></head>
<body bgcolor="#fffed9">
<h1>Dinner</h1>
HTML_HEADER;

$page_footer = <<<HTML_FOOTER
</body>
</html>
HTML_FOOTER;
```

Variable names may only include:

- Uppercase or lowercase Basic Latin letters (A-Z and a-z)
- Digits (0-9)
- Underscore (_)
- Any non-Basic Latin character (such as ç or ‍ᵢ or 🚌), if you're using a character encoding such as UTF-8 for your program file

Additionally, the first character of a variable name is not allowed to be a digit. Table 2-2 lists some allowable variable names.

Table 2-2. Allowable variable names

```
$size
$drinkSize
$SUPER_BIG_DRINK
$_d_r_i_n_k_y
$drink4you2
$напиток
$သောက်စရာ
$DRINK
$😀
```

Keep in mind that, despite the alluring aesthetic possibilities of variable names with emoticons in them, most PHP code sticks with digits, underscores, and Basic Latin letters.

Table 2-3 lists some disallowed variable names and what's wrong with them.

Table 2-3. Disallowed variable names

Variable name	Flaw
$2hot4u	Begins with a number
$drink-size	Unacceptable character: -
$drinkmaster@example.com	Unacceptable characters: @ and .
$drink!lots	Unacceptable character: !
$drink+dinner	Unacceptable character: +

Variable names are case-sensitive. This means that variables named $dinner, $Dinner, and $DINNER are separate and distinct, with no more in common than if they were named $breakfast, $lunch, and $supper. In practice, you should avoid using variable names that differ only by letter case. They make programs difficult to read and debug.

Operating on Variables

Arithmetic and string operators work on variables containing numbers or strings just like they do on literal numbers or strings. Example 2-17 shows some math and string operations at work on variables.

Example 2-17. Operating on variables

```
$price = 3.95;
$tax_rate = 0.08;
$tax_amount = $price * $tax_rate;
$total_cost = $price + $tax_amount;

$username = 'james';
$domain = '@example.com';
$email_address = $username . $domain;

print 'The tax is ' . $tax_amount;
print "\n"; // this prints a line break
print 'The total cost is ' .$total_cost;
print "\n"; // this prints a line break
print $email_address;
```

Example 2-17 prints:

```
The tax is 0.316
The total cost is 4.266
james@example.com
```

The assignment operator can be combined with arithmetic and string operators for a concise way to modify a value. An operator followed by the equals sign means "apply this operator to the variable." Example 2-18 shows two identical ways to add 3 to $price.

Example 2-18. Combined assignment and addition

```
// Add 3  the regular way
$price = $price + 3;
// Add 3 with the combined operator
$price += 3;
```

Combining the assignment operator with the string concatenation operator appends a value to a string. Example 2-19 shows two identical ways to add a suffix to a string. The advantage of the combined operators is that they are more concise.

Example 2-19. Combined assignment and concatenation

```
$username = 'james';
$domain = '@example.com';

// Concatenate $domain to the end of $username the regular way
$username = $username . $domain;
// Concatenate with the combined operator
$username .= $domain;
```

Incrementing and decrementing variables by 1 are so common that these operations have their own operators. The ++ operator adds 1 to a variable, and the -- operator subtracts 1. These operators are usually used in for() loops, which are detailed in Chapter 3. But you can use them on any variable holding a number, as shown in Example 2-20.

Example 2-20. Incrementing and decrementing

```
// Add 1 to $birthday
$birthday = $birthday + 1;
// Add another 1 to $birthday
++$birthday;

// Subtract 1 from $years_left
$years_left = $years_left - 1;
// Subtract another 1 from $years_left
--$years_left;
```

Putting Variables Inside Strings

Frequently, you print the values of variables combined with other text, such as when you display an HTML table with calculated values in the cells or a user profile page that shows a particular user's information in a standardized HTML template. Double-quoted strings and here documents have a property that makes this easy: you can *interpolate* variables into them. This means that if the string contains a variable name, the variable name is replaced by the value of the variable. In Example 2-21, the value of $email is interpolated into the printed string.

Example 2-21. Variable interpolation

```
$email = 'jacob@example.com';
print "Send replies to: $email";
```

Example 2-21 prints:

```
Send replies to: jacob@example.com
```

Here documents are especially useful for interpolating many variables into a long block of HTML, as shown in Example 2-22.

Example 2-22. Interpolating in a here document

```
$page_title = 'Menu';
$meat = 'pork';
$vegetable = 'bean sprout';
print <<<MENU
<html>
<head><title>$page_title</title></head>
<body>
<ul>
<li> Barbecued $meat
<li> Sliced $meat
<li> Braised $meat with $vegetable
</ul>
</body>
</html>
MENU;
```

Example 2-22 prints:

```
<html>
<head><title>Menu</title></head>
<body>
<ul>
<li> Barbecued pork
<li> Sliced pork
<li> Braised pork with bean sprout
</ul>
</body>
</html>
```

When you interpolate a variable into a string in a place where the PHP engine could be confused about the variable name, surround the variable with curly braces to remove the confusion. Example 2-23 needs curly braces so that `$preparation` is interpolated properly.

Example 2-23 Interpolating with curly braces

```php
$preparation = 'Braise';
$meat = 'Beef';
print "{$preparation}d $meat with Vegetables";
```

Example 2-23 prints:

```
Braised Beef with Vegetables
```

Without the curly braces, the `print` statement in Example 2-23 would be `print "$preparationd $meat with Vegetables";`. In that statement, it looks like the variable to interpolate is named `$preparationd`. The curly braces are necessary to indicate where the variable name stops and the literal string begins. The curly brace syntax is also useful for interpolating more complicated expressions and array values, discussed in Chapter 4.

Chapter Summary

This chapter covered:

- Defining strings in your programs in three different ways: with single quotes, with double quotes, and as a here document
- Escaping: what it is and what characters need to be escaped in each kind of string
- Validating a string by checking its length, removing leading and trailing whitespace from it, or comparing it to another string
- Formatting a string with `printf()`
- Manipulating the case of a string with `strtolower()`, `strtoupper()`, or `ucwords()`

- Selecting part of a string with `substr()`
- Changing part of a string with `str_replace()`
- Defining numbers in your programs
- Doing math with numbers
- Storing values in variables
- Naming variables appropriately
- Using combined operators with variables
- Using increment and decrement operators with variables
- Interpolating variables in strings

Exercises

1. Find the errors in this PHP program:
   ```
   <? php
   print 'How are you?';
   print 'I'm fine.';
   ??>
   ```

2. Write a PHP program that computes the total cost of this restaurant meal: two hamburgers at $4.95 each, one chocolate milkshake at $1.95, and one cola at 85 cents. The sales tax rate is 7.5%, and you left a pre-tax tip of 16%.

3. Modify your solution to the previous exercise to print out a formatted bill. For each item in the meal, print the price, quantity, and total cost. Print the pre-tax food and drink total, the post-tax total, and the total with tax and tip. Make sure that prices in your output are vertically aligned.

4. Write a PHP program that sets the variable `$first_name` to your first name and `$last_name` to your last name. Print out a string containing your first and last name separated by a space. Also print out the length of that string.

5. Write a PHP program that uses the increment operator (++) and the combined multiplication operator (*=) to print out the numbers from 1 to 5 and powers of 2 from 2 (2^1) to 32 (2^5).

6. Add comments to the PHP programs you've written for the other exercises. Try both single and multiline comments. After you've added the comments, run the programs to make sure they work properly and your comment syntax is correct.

## CHAPTER 3

Logic: Making Decisions and Repeating Yourself

Chapter 2 covered the basics of how to represent data in PHP programs. A program full of data is only half complete, though. The other piece of the puzzle is using that data to control how the program runs, taking actions such as:

- If an administrative user is logged in, print a special menu.
- Print a different page header if it's after three o'clock.
- Notify a user if new messages have been posted since she last logged in.

All of these actions have something in common: they make decisions about whether a certain logical condition involving data is true or false. In the first action, the logical condition is "Is an administrative user logged in?" If the condition is true (yes, an administrative user is logged in), then a special menu is printed. The same kind of thing happens in the next example. If the condition "Is it after three o'clock?" is true, then a different page header is printed. Likewise, if "Have new messages been posted since the user last logged in?" is true, then the user is notified.

When making decisions, the PHP engine boils down an expression into `true` or `false`. "Understanding true and false" on page 40 explains how the engine decides which expressions and values are `true` and which are `false`.

Those `true` and `false` values are used by language constructs such as `if()` to decide whether to run certain statements in a program. The ins and outs of `if()` are detailed in "Making Decisions" on page 41. Use `if()` and similar constructs any time the outcome of a program depends on some changing conditions.

While `true` and `false` are the cornerstones of decision making, usually you want to ask more complicated questions, such as "Is this user at least 21 years old?" or "Does this user have a monthly subscription to the website or enough money in his account to buy a daily pass?" "Building Complicated Decisions" on page 43 explains PHP's comparison and logical operators. These help you express whatever kinds of decisions you need to make in a program, such as seeing whether numbers or strings are greater than or less than each other. You can also chain together decisions into a larger decision that depends on its pieces.

Decision making is also used in programs when you want to repeatedly execute certain statements, and you need a way to indicate when the repetition should stop. Frequently, this is determined by a simple counter, such as "repeat 10 times." This is like asking the question "Have I repeated 10 times yet?" If so, then the program continues. If not, the action is repeated again. Determining when to stop can be more complicated, too—for example, "Show another math question to a student until six questions have been answered correctly." "Repeating Yourself" on page 51 introduces PHP's `while()` and `for()` constructs, which you can use to implement these kinds of loops.

Understanding true and false

Every expression in a PHP program has a truth value: `true` or `false`. Sometimes that truth value is important because you use it in a calculation, but sometimes you ignore it. Understanding how expressions evaluate to `true` or `false` is an important part of understanding PHP.

Most scalar values are `true`. All integers and floating-point numbers (except for 0 and 0.0) are `true`. All strings are `true` except for two: a string containing nothing at all and a string containing only the character 0. The special constants `false` and `null` also evaluate to `false`. These six values are `false`. Everything else is `true`.[1]

A variable equal to one of the `false` values, or a function that returns one of those values, also evaluates to `false`. Every other expression evaluates to `true`.

Figuring out the truth value of an expression has two steps. First, figure out the actual value of the expression. Then, check whether that value is `true` or `false`. Some expressions have common-sense values. The value of a mathematical expression is what you'd get by doing the math with paper and pencil. For example, 7 * 6 equals 42. Since 42 is `true`, the expression 7 * 6 is `true`. The expression 5 - 6 + 1 equals 0. Since 0 is `false`, the expression 5 - 6 + 1 is `false`.

---

1 An empty array is also `false`. This is discussed in Chapter 4.

The same is true with string concatenation. The value of an expression that concatenates two strings is the new combined string. The expression `'jacob'` . `'@example.com'` equals the string `jacob@example.com`, which is `true`.

The value of an assignment operation is the value being assigned. The expression `$price = 5` evaluates to 5, since that's what's being assigned to `$price`. Because assignment produces a result, you can chain assignment operations together to assign the same value to multiple variables:

```
$price = $quantity = 5;
```

This expression means "set `$price` equal to the result of setting `$quantity` equal to 5." When this expression is evaluated, the integer 5 is assigned to the variable `$quantity`. The result of that assignment expression is 5, the value being assigned. Then, that result (5) is assigned to the variable `$price`. Both `$price` and `$quantity` are set to 5.

Making Decisions

With the `if()` construct, you can have statements in your program that are only run if certain conditions are `true`. This lets your program take different actions depending on the circumstances. For example, you can check that a user has entered valid information in a web form before letting her see sensitive data.

The `if()` construct runs a block of code if its test expression is `true`. This is demonstrated in Example 3-1.

Example 3-1. Making a decision with if()

```
if ($logged_in) {
    print "Welcome aboard, trusted user.";
}
```

The `if()` construct finds the truth value of the expression inside its parentheses (the *test expression*). If the expression evaluates to `true`, then the statements inside the curly braces after the `if()` are run. If the expression isn't `true`, then the program continues with the statements after the curly braces. In this case, the test expression is just the variable `$logged_in`. If `$logged_in` is `true` (or has a value that evaluates to `true`, such as 5, -12.6, or Grass Carp), then `Welcome aboard, trusted user.` is printed.

You can have as many statements as you want in the code block inside the curly braces. However, you need to terminate each of them with a semicolon. This is the same rule that applies to code outside an `if()` statement. You don't, however, need a semicolon after the closing curly brace that encloses the code block. You also don't put a semicolon after the opening curly brace. Example 3-2 shows an if() clause that runs multiple statements when its test expression is `true`.

Example 3-2. Multiple statements in an if() code block

```
print "This is always printed.";
if ($logged_in) {
    print "Welcome aboard, trusted user.";
    print 'This is only printed if $logged_in is true.';
}
print "This is also always printed.";
```

To run different statements when the if() test expression is `false`, add an `else` clause to your if() statement. This is shown in Example 3-3.

Example 3-3. Using else with if()

```
if ($logged_in) {
    print "Welcome aboard, trusted user.";
} else {
    print "Howdy, stranger.";
}
```

In Example 3-3, the first `print` statement is only executed when the if() test expression (the variable `$logged_in`) is `true`. The second `print` statement, inside the `else` clause, is only run when the test expression is `false`.

The if() and `else` constructs are extended further with the `elseif()` construct. You can pair one or more `elseif()` clauses with an if() to test multiple conditions separately. Example 3-4 demonstrates `elseif()`.

Example 3-4. Using elseif()

```
if ($logged_in) {
    // This runs if $logged_in is true
    print "Welcome aboard, trusted user.";
} elseif ($new_messages) {
    // This runs if $logged_in is false but $new_messages is true
    print "Dear stranger, there are new messages.";
} elseif ($emergency) {
    // This runs if $logged_in and $new_messages are false
    // but $emergency is true
    print "Stranger, there are no new messages, but there is an emergency.";
}
```

If the test expression for the if() statement is `true`, the PHP engine executes the statements inside the code block after the if() and ignores the `elseif()` clauses and their code blocks. If the test expression for the if() statement is false, then the engine moves on to the first elseif() statement and applies the same logic. If that test expression is true, then it runs the code block for that elseif() statement. If it is false, then the engine moves on to the next elseif().

For a given set of if() and elseif() statements, at most one of the code blocks is run: the code block of the first statement whose test expression is true. If the test expression of the if() statement is true, none of the elseif() code blocks are run, even if their test expressions are true. Once one of the if() or elseif() test expressions is true, the rest are ignored. If none of the test expressions in the if() and elseif() statements are true, then none of the code blocks are run.

You can use else with elseif() to include a code block that runs if none of the if() or elseif() test expressions are true. Example 3-5 adds an else to the code in Example 3-4.

Example 3-5. elseif() with else

```
if ($logged_in) {
    // This runs if $logged_in is true
    print "Welcome aboard, trusted user.";
} elseif ($new_messages) {
    // This runs if $logged_in is false but $new_messages is true
    print "Dear stranger, there are new messages.";
} elseif ($emergency) {
    // This runs if $logged_in and $new_messages are false
    // but $emergency is true
    print "Stranger, there are no new messages, but there is an emergency.";
} else {
    // This runs if $logged_in, $new_messages, and
    // $emergency are all false
    print "I don't know you, you have no messages, and there's no emergency.";
}
```

All of the code blocks we've used so far have been surrounded by curly braces. Strictly speaking, you don't need to put curly braces around code blocks that contain just one statement. If you leave them out, the code still executes correctly. However, reading the code can be confusing if you leave out the curly braces, so it's always a good idea to include them. The PHP engine doesn't care, but humans who read your programs (especially you, reviewing code a few months after you've originally written it) will appreciate the clarity that the curly braces provide.

Building Complicated Decisions

The comparison and logical operators in PHP help you put together more complicated expressions on which an if() construct can decide. These operators let you compare values, negate values, and chain together multiple expressions inside one if() statement.

The equal operator is == (two equals signs). It returns true if the two values you test with it are equal. The values can be variables or literals. Some uses of the equal operator are shown in Example 3-6.

Example 3-6. The equal operator

```
if ($new_messages == 10) {
    print "You have ten new messages.";
}

if ($new_messages == $max_messages) {
    print "You have the maximum number of messages.";
}

if ($dinner == 'Braised Scallops') {
    print "Yum! I love seafood.";
}
```

Assignment Versus Comparison

Be careful not to use = when you mean ==. A single equals sign assigns a value and returns the value assigned. Two equals signs test for equality and return true if the values are equal. If you leave off the second equals sign, you usually get an if() test that is always true, as in the following:

```
if ($new_messages = 12) {
    print "It seems you now have twelve new messages.";
}
```

Instead of testing whether $new_messages equals 12, the code shown here sets $new_messages to 12. This assignment returns 12, the value being assigned. The if() test expression is always true, no matter what the value of $new_messages is. Additionally, the value of $new_messages is overwritten. One way to avoid using = instead of == is to put the variable on the right side of the comparison and the literal on the left side, as in the following:

```
if (12 == $new_messages) {
    print "You have twelve new messages.";
}
```

The test expression above may look a little funny, but it gives you some insurance if you accidentally use = instead of ==. With one equals sign, the test expression is 12 = $new_messages, which means "assign the value of $new_messages to 12." This doesn't make any sense: you can't change the value of 12. If the PHP engine sees this in your program, it reports a parse error and the program doesn't run. The parse error alerts you to the missing =. With the literal on the righthand side of the expression, the code is parseable by the engine, so it doesn't report an error.

The opposite of the equal operator is !=. It returns true if the two values that you test with it are not equal. See Example 3-7.

Example 3-7. The not-equal operator

```
if ($new_messages != 10) {
    print "You don't have ten new messages.";
}

if ($dinner != 'Braised Scallops') {
    print "I guess we're out of scallops.";
}
```

With the less-than operator (<) and the greater-than operator (>), you can compare amounts. Similar to < and > are <= ("less than or equal to") and >= ("greater than or equal to"). Example 3-8 shows how to use these operators.

Example 3-8. Less-than and greater-than (or equal to)

```
if ($age > 17) {
    print "You are old enough to download the movie.";
}
if ($age >= 65) {
    print "You are old enough for a discount.";
}
if ($celsius_temp <= 0) {
    print "Uh-oh, your pipes may freeze.";
}
if ($kelvin_temp < 20.3) {
    print "Your hydrogen is a liquid or a solid now.";
}
```

As mentioned in "Numbers" on page 29, floating-point numbers are stored internally in such a way that they could be slightly different than their assigned values. For example, 50.0 could be stored internally as 50.00000002. To test whether two floating-point numbers are equal, check whether the two numbers differ by less than some acceptably small threshold instead of using the equal operator. For example, if you are comparing currency amounts, then an acceptable threshold could be 0.00001. Example 3-9 demonstrates how to compare two floating-point numbers.

Example 3-9. Comparing floating-point numbers

```
if(abs($price_1 - $price_2) < 0.00001) {
    print '$price_1 and $price_2 are equal.';
} else {
    print '$price_1 and $price_2 are not equal.';
}
```

The `abs()` function used in Example 3-9 returns the absolute value of its argument. With `abs()`, the comparison works properly whether `$price_1` is larger than `$price_2` or `$price_2` is larger than `$price_1`.

The less-than and greater-than operators (and their "or equal to" partners) can be used with numbers or strings. Generally, strings are compared as if they were being looked up in a dictionary. A string that appears earlier in the dictionary is "less than" a string that appears later in the dictionary. Some examples of this are shown in Example 3-10.

Example 3-10. Comparing strings

```
if ($word < 'baa') {
    print "Your word isn't cookie.";
}
if ($word >= 'zoo') {
    print "Your word could be zoo or zymurgy, but not zone.";
}
```

String comparison can produce unexpected results, however, if the strings contain only numbers or start with numbers. When the PHP engine sees strings like this, it converts them to numbers for the comparison. Example 3-11 shows this automatic conversion in action.

Example 3-11. Comparing numbers and strings

```
// These values are compared using dictionary order
if ("x54321"> "x5678") {
    print 'The string "x54321" is greater than the string "x5678".';
} else {
    print 'The string "x54321" is not greater than the string "x5678".';
}

// These values are compared using numeric order
if ("54321" > "5678") {
    print 'The string "54321" is greater than the string "5678".';
} else {
    print 'The string "54321" is not greater than the string "5678".';
}

// These values are compared using dictionary order
```

```
if ('6 pack' < '55 card stud') {
    print 'The string "6 pack" is less than the string "55 card stud".';
} else {
    print 'The string "6 pack" is not less than the string "55 card stud".';
}

// These values are compared using numeric order
if ('6 pack' < 55) {
    print 'The string "6 pack" is less than the number 55.';
} else {
    print 'The string "6 pack" is not less than the number 55.';
}
```

The output of the four tests in Example 3-11 is:

```
The string "x54321" is not greater than the string "x5678".
The string "54321" is greater than the string "5678".
The string "6 pack" is not less than the string "55 card stud".
The string "6 pack" is less than the number 55.
```

In the first test, because both of the strings start with a letter, they are treated as regular strings and compared using dictionary order. Their first two characters (x5) are the same, but the third character of the first word (4) is less than the third character of the second word (6),[2] so the greater-than comparison returns false. In the second test, each string consists entirely of numerals, so the strings are compared as numbers. The number 54,321 is larger than the number 5,678, so the greater-than comparison returns true. In the third test, because both strings consist of numerals and other characters, they are treated as strings and compared using dictionary order. The numeral 6 comes after 5 in the engine's dictionary, so the less-than test returns false. In the last test, the PHP engine converts the string 6 pack to the number 6, and then compares it to the number 55 using numeric order. Since 6 is less than 55, the less-than test returns true.

If you want to ensure that the PHP engine compares strings using dictionary order without any converting to numbers behind the scenes, use the built-in function strcmp(). It always compares its arguments in dictionary order.

---

2 The "dictionary" that the PHP engine uses for comparing strings is the ASCII codes for characters. This puts numerals before letters, and orders the numerals from 0 to 9. It also puts uppercase letters before lowercase letters.

Comparing Non-ASCII Strings

Remember, strings in PHP are just sequences of bytes. If you need to compare strings whose letters wouldn't be found in a plain English dictionary, then the regular operators and string comparison functions may not do what you want. "Sorting and Comparing" on page 320 discusses the Collator class, which can compare and sort text in different character sets.

The strcmp() function takes two strings as arguments. It returns a positive number if the first string is greater than the second string or a negative number if the first string is less than the first string. "Greater than" and "less than" for strcmp() are defined by dictionary order. The function returns 0 if the strings are equal.

The same comparisons from Example 3-11 are shown using strcmp() in Example 3-12.

Example 3-12. Comparing strings with strcmp()

```
$x = strcmp("x54321","x5678");
if ($x > 0) {
    print 'The string "x54321" is greater than the string "x5678".';
} elseif ($x < 0) {
    print 'The string "x54321" is less than the string "x5678".';
}

$x = strcmp("54321","5678");
if ($x > 0) {
    print 'The string "54321" is greater than the string "5678".';
} elseif ($x < 0) {
    print 'The string "54321" is less than the string "5678".';
}

$x = strcmp('6 pack','55 card stud');
if ($x > 0) {
    print 'The string "6 pack" is greater than the string "55 card stud".';
} elseif ($x < 0) {
    print 'The string "6 pack" is less than the string "55 card stud".';
}

$x = strcmp('6 pack',55);
if ($x > 0) {
    print 'The string "6 pack" is greater than the number 55.';
} elseif ($x < 0) {
    print 'The string "6 pack" is less than the number 55.';
}
```

The output from Example 3-12 is as follows:

```
The string "x54321" is less than the string "x5678".
The string "54321" is less than the string "5678".
The string "6 pack" is greater than the string "55 card stud".
The string "6 pack" is greater than the number 55.
```

Using `strcmp()` and dictionary order produces different results than Example 3-11 for the second and fourth comparisons. In the second comparison, `strcmp()` computes that the string 54321 is less than 5678 because the second characters of the strings differ and 4 comes before 6. It doesn't matter to `strcmp()` that 5678 is shorter than 54321 or that it is numerically smaller. In dictionary order, 54321 comes before 5678. The fourth comparison turns out differently because `strcmp()` doesn't convert 6 pack to a number. Instead, it compares 6 pack and 55 as strings and computes that 6 pack is bigger because its first character, 6, comes later in the dictionary than the first character of 55.

The spaceship operator (`<=>`) does comparison similar to `strcmp()`, but for any data type. It evaluates to a negative number when its lefthand operand is less than the righthand operand, a positive number when the righthand operand is bigger, and 0 when they are equal. Example 3-13 shows the spaceship operator at work.

Example 3-13. Comparing data types with the spaceship operator

```
// $a is a negative number since 1 is less than 12.7
$a = 1 <=> 12.7;

// $b is a positive number since "c" comes after "b"
$b = "charlie" <=> "bob";

// Comparing numeric strings works like < and >, not like strcmp()
$x = '6 pack' <=> '55 card stud';
if ($x > 0) {
    print 'The string "6 pack" is greater than the string "55 card stud".';
} elseif ($x < 0) {
    print 'The string "6 pack" is less than the string "55 card stud".';
}

// Comparing numeric strings works like < and >, not like strcmp()
$x ='6 pack' <=> 55;
if ($x > 0) {
    print 'The string "6 pack" is greater than the number 55.';
} elseif ($x < 0) {
    print 'The string "6 pack" is less than the number 55.';
}
```

The spaceship operator was introduced in PHP 7. If you're using an older version of PHP, stick with the other comparison operators.

Example 3-13 prints:

```
The string "6 pack" is greater than the string "55 card stud".
The string "6 pack" is less than the number 55.
```

The spaceship operator follows the same rules about string and number conversion as the other comparison operators. It converts "numerical" strings to numbers just like ==, <, and the others.

To negate a truth value, use !. Putting ! before an expression is like testing to see whether the expression equals false. The two if() statements in Example 3-14 are equivalent.

Example 3-14. Using the negation operator

```
// The entire test expression ($finished == false)
// is true if $finished is false
if ($finished == false) {
    print 'Not done yet!';
}

// The entire test expression (! $finished)
// is true if $finished is false
if (! $finished) {
    print 'Not done yet!';
}
```

You can use the negation operator with any value. If the value is true, then the combination of it with the negation operator is false. If the value is false, then the combination of it with the negation operator is true. Example 3-15 shows the negation operator at work with a call to strcasecmp().

Example 3-15. The negation operator

```
if (! strcasecmp($first_name,$last_name)) {
    print '$first_name and $last_name are equal.';
}
```

In Example 3-15, the statement in the if() code block is executed only when the entire test expression is true. When the two strings provided to strcasecmp() are equal (ignoring capitalization), strcasecmp() returns 0, which is false. The test expression is the negation operator applied to this false value. The negation of false is true. So, the entire test expression is true when two equal strings are given to strcasecmp().

With logical operators, you can combine multiple expressions inside one if() statement. The logical AND operator (&&) tests whether one expression and another are both true. The logical OR operator (||) tests whether either one expression or another (or both) is true. These logical operators are used in Example 3-16.

Example 3-16. Logical operators

```
if (($age >= 13) && ($age < 65)) {
    print "You are too old for a kid's discount and too young for the senior's
discount.";
}

if (($meal == 'breakfast') || ($dessert == 'souffle')) {
    print "Time to eat some eggs.";
}
```

The first test expression in Example 3-16 is true when both of its subexpressions are true—when $age is at least 13 but not more than 65. The second test expression is true when at least one of its subexpressions is true: when $meal is breakfast or $dessert is souffle.

The admonition about operator precedence and parentheses from Chapter 2 holds true for logical operators in test expressions, too. To avoid ambiguity, surround each subexpression with parentheses inside a larger test expression.

Repeating Yourself

When a computer program does something repeatedly, it's called *looping*. This happens a lot—for example, when you want to retrieve a set of rows from a database, print rows of an HTML table, or print elements in an HTML <select> menu. The two looping constructs discussed in this section are while() and for(). Their specifics differ, but each requires you to specify the two essential attributes of any loop: what code to execute repeatedly and when to stop. The code to execute is a code block just like what goes inside the curly braces after an if() construct. The condition for stopping the loop is a logical expression just like an if() construct's test expression.

The while() construct is like a repeating if(). You provide an expression to while(), just like to if(). If the expression is true, then a code block is executed. Unlike if(), however, while() checks the expression again after executing the code block. If it's still true, then the code block is executed again (and again, and again, as long as the expression is true.) Once the expression is false, program execution continues with the lines after the code block. As you have probably guessed, your code block should do something that changes the outcome of the test expression so that the loop doesn't go on forever.

Example 3-17 uses `while()` to print an HTML form `<select>` menu with 10 choices.

Example 3-17. Printing a `<select>` menu with while()

```
$i = 1;
print '<select name="people">';
while ($i <= 10) {
    print "<option>$i</option>\n";
    $i++;
}
print '</select>';
```

Example 3-17 prints:

```
<select name="people"><option>1</option>
<option>2</option>
<option>3</option>
<option>4</option>
<option>5</option>
<option>6</option>
<option>7</option>
<option>8</option>
<option>9</option>
<option>10</option>
</select>
```

Before the `while()` loop runs, the code sets `$i` to 1 and prints the opening `<select>` tag. The test expression compares `$i` to `10`. As long as `$i` is less than or equal to `10`, the two statements in the code block are executed. The first prints an `<option>` tag for the `<select>` menu, and the second increments `$i`. If you didn't increment `$i` inside the `while()` loop, Example 3-17 would print out `<option>1</option>` forever.

After the code block prints `<option>10</option>`, the `$i++` line makes `$i` equal to 11. Then the test expression (`$i <= 10`) is evaluated. Since it's not `true` (11 is not less than or equal to `10`), the program continues past the `while()` loop's code block and prints the closing `</select>` tag.

The `for()` construct also provides a way for you to execute the same statements multiple times. Example 3-18 uses `for()` to print the same HTML form `<select>` menu as Example 3-17.

Example 3-18. Printing a <select> menu with for()

```
print '<select name="people">';
for ($i = 1; $i <= 10; $i++) {
    print "<option>$i</option>\n";
}
print '</select>';
```

Using for() is a little more complicated than using while(). Instead of one test expression in parentheses, there are three expressions separated with semicolons: the initialization expression, test expression, and iteration expression. Once you get the hang of it, however, for() is a more concise way to have a loop with easy-to-express initialization and iteration conditions.

The first expression in Example 3-18, $i = 1, is the *initialization expression*. It is evaluated once, when the loop starts. This is where you put variable initializations or other setup code. The second expression in Example 3-18, $i <= 10, is the test expression. It is evaluated once each time through the loop, before the statements in the loop body. If it's true, then the loop body is executed (print "<option> $i</option>"; in Example 3-18). The third expression in Example 3-18, $i++, is the *iteration expression*. It is run after each time the loop body is executed. In Example 3-18, the sequence of statements goes like this:

1. Initialization expression: $i = 1;
2. Test expression: $i <= 10 (true, $i is 1)
3. Code block: print "<option>$i</option>";
4. Iteration expression: $i++;
5. Test expression: $i <= 10 (true, $i is 2)
6. Code block: print "<option>$i</option>";
7. Iteration expression: $i++;
8. (Loop continues with incrementing values of $i)
9. Test expression: $i <= 10 (true, $i is 9)
10. Code block: print "<option>$i</option>";
11. Iteration expression: $i++;
12. Test expression: $i <= 10 (true, $i is 10)
13. Code block: print "<option>$i</option>";
14. Iteration expression: $i++;
15. Test expression: $i <= 10 (false, $i is 11)

You can combine multiple expressions in the initialization expression and the iteration expression of a for() loop by separating each of the individual expressions with a comma. This is usually done when you want to change more than one variable as the loop progresses. Example 3-19 applies this to the variables $min and $max.

Example 3-19. Multiple expressions in for()

```
print '<select name="doughnuts">';
for ($min = 1, $max = 10; $min < 50; $min += 10, $max += 10) {
    print "<option>$min - $max</option>\n";
}
print '</select>';
```

Each time through the loop, `$min` and `$max` are each incremented by 10. Example 3-19 prints:

```
<select name="doughnuts"><option>1 - 10</option>
<option>11 - 20</option>
<option>21 - 30</option>
<option>31 - 40</option>
<option>41 - 50</option>
</select>
```

Chapter Summary

This chapter covered:

- Evaluating an expression's truth value: `true` or `false`
- Making a decision with `if()`
- Extending `if()` with `else`
- Extending `if()` with `elseif()`
- Putting multiple statements inside an `if()`, `elseif()`, or `else` code block
- Using the equal (`==`) and not-equal (`!=`) operators in test expressions
- Distinguishing between assignment (`=`) and equality comparison (`==`)
- Using the less-than (`<`), greater-than (`>`), less-than-or-equal-to (`<=`), and greater-than-or-equal-to (`>=`) operators in test expressions
- Comparing two floating-point numbers with `abs()`
- Comparing two strings with operators
- Comparing two strings with `strcmp()` or `strcasecmp()`
- Comparing two values with the spaceship operator (`<=>`)
- Using the negation operator (`!`) in test expressions
- Using the logical operators (`&&` and `||`) to build more complicated test expressions
- Repeating a code block with `while()`
- Repeating a code block with `for()`

Exercises

1. Without using a PHP program to evaluate them, determine whether each of these expressions is `true` or `false`:

   a. `100.00 - 100`

   b. `"zero"`

   c. `"false"`

   d. `0 + "true"`

   e. `0.000`

   f. `"0.0"`

   g. `strcmp("false","False")`

   h. `0 <=> "0"`

2. Without running it through the PHP engine, figure out what this program prints:

```
$age = 12;
$shoe_size = 13;
if ($age > $shoe_size) {
    print "Message 1.";
} elseif (($shoe_size++) && ($age > 20)) {
    print "Message 2.";
} else {
    print "Message 3.";
}
print "Age: $age. Shoe Size: $shoe_size";
```

3. Use `while()` to print a table of Fahrenheit and Celsius temperature equivalents from –50 degrees F to 50 degrees F in 5-degree increments. On the Fahrenheit temperature scale, water freezes at 32 degrees and boils at 212 degrees. On the Celsius scale, water freezes at 0 degrees and boils at 100 degrees. So, to convert from Fahrenheit to Celsius, you subtract 32 from the temperature, multiply by 5, and divide by 9. To convert from Celsius to Fahrenheit, you multiply by 9, divide by 5, and then add 32.

4. Modify your answer to Exercise 3 to use `for()` instead of `while()`.

## CHAPTER 4

Groups of Data: Working with Arrays

Arrays are collections of related values, such as the data submitted from a form, the names of students in a class, or the populations of a list of cities. In Chapter 2, you learned that a variable is a named container that holds a value. An array is a container that holds multiple values.

This chapter shows you how to work with arrays. The next section, "Array Basics", goes over fundamentals such as how to create arrays and manipulate their elements. Frequently, you'll want to do something with each element in an array, such as print it or inspect it for certain conditions. "Looping Through Arrays" on page 62 explains how to do these things with the `foreach()` and `for()` constructs. "Modifying Arrays" on page 68 introduces the `implode()` and `explode()` functions, which turn arrays into strings and strings into arrays. Another kind of array modification is sorting, which is discussed in "Sorting Arrays" on page 70. Finally, "Using Multidimensional Arrays" on page 74 explores arrays that contain other arrays.

Working with arrays is a common PHP programming task. Chapter 7 shows you how to process form data, which the PHP engine automatically puts into an array for you. When you retrieve information from a database as described in Chapter 8, that data is often packaged into an array. Being comfortable with arrays makes it easy for you to manipulate these kinds of data.

Array Basics

An array is made up of *elements*. Each element has a *key* and a *value*. For example, an array holding information about the colors of vegetables has vegetable names for keys and colors for values, as shown in Figure 4-1.

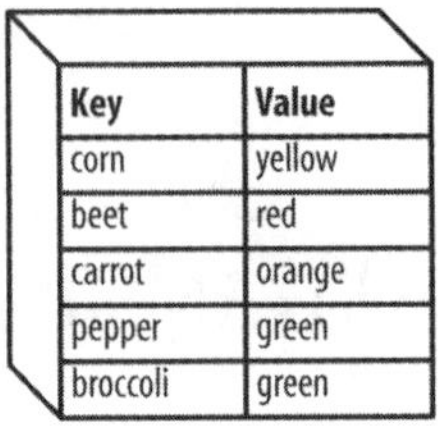

Figure 4-1. Keys and values in an array holding information about vegetable colors

An array can only have one element with a given key. In the vegetable color array, there can't be another element with the key corn even if its value is blue. However, the same value can appear many times in one array. You can have green peppers, green broccoli, and green celery.

Any string or number value can be an array element key, such as corn, 4, -36, or Salt Baked Squid. Arrays and other nonscalar[1] values can't be keys, but they can be element values. An element value can be anything: a string, a number, true, false, or a nonscalar type such as another array.

Creating an Array

To create an array, use the array() language construct. Specify a comma-delimited list of key/value pairs, with the key and the value separated by =>. This is shown in Example 4-1.

Example 4-1. Creating an array

```
$vegetables = array('corn' => 'yellow',
                    'beet' => 'red',
                    'carrot' => 'orange');

$dinner = array(0 => 'Sweet Corn and Asparagus',
                1 => 'Lemon Chicken',
                2 => 'Braised Bamboo Fungus');

$computers = array('trs-80' => 'Radio Shack',
                   2600 => 'Atari',
                   'Adam' => 'Coleco');
```

The array keys and values in Example 4-1 are strings (such as corn, Braised Bamboo Fungus, and Coleco) and numbers (such as 0, 1, and 2600). They are written just like

---

1 *Scalar* describes data that has a single value: a number, a piece of text, true, or false. Complex data types such as arrays, which hold multiple values, are not scalars.

other strings and numbers in PHP programs: with quotes around the strings but not around the numbers.

A shortcut for the array() language construct is a pair of square brackets (called the *short array syntax*). Example 4-2 creates the same arrays as Example 4-1 but with the short array syntax.

Example 4-2. Using short array syntax

```php
$vegetables = ['corn' => 'yellow', 'beet' => 'red', 'carrot' => 'orange'];

$dinner = [0 => 'Sweet Corn and Asparagus',
           1 => 'Lemon Chicken',
           2 => 'Braised Bamboo Fungus'];

$computers = ['trs-80' => 'Radio Shack', 2600 => 'Atari', 'Adam' => 'Coleco'];
```

 The short array syntax was introduced in PHP 5.4. If you're using an earlier version of PHP, you need to stick with array().

You can also add elements to an array one at a time by assigning a value to a particular array key. Example 4-3 builds the same arrays as the previous two examples but does it element by element.

Example 4-3. Creating an array element by element

```php
// An array called $vegetables with string keys
$vegetables['corn'] = 'yellow';
$vegetables['beet'] = 'red';
$vegetables['carrot'] = 'orange';

// An array called $dinner with numeric keys
$dinner[0] = 'Sweet Corn and Asparagus';
$dinner[1] = 'Lemon Chicken';
$dinner[2] = 'Braised Bamboo Fungus';

// An array called $computers with numeric and string keys
$computers['trs-80'] = 'Radio Shack';
$computers[2600] = 'Atari';
$computers['Adam'] = 'Coleco';
```

In Example 4-3, the square brackets after the array's variable name reference a particular key in the array. By assigning a value to that key, you create an element in the array.

Choosing a Good Array Name

Names for variables holding arrays follow the same rules as names for any other variables. Names for arrays and scalar variables come from the same pool of possible names, so you can't have an array called $vegetables and a scalar called $vegetables at the same time. If you assign a scalar value to an array (or vice versa), the old value is silently wiped out and the variable becomes the new value. In Example 4-4, $vegetables becomes a scalar, and $fruits becomes an array.

Example 4-4. Array and scalar collision

```
// This makes $vegetables an array
$vegetables['corn'] = 'yellow';

// This removes any trace of "corn" and "yellow" and makes $vegetables a scalar
$vegetables = 'delicious';

// This makes $fruits a scalar
$fruits = 283;

// This doesn't work -- $fruits stays 283 and the PHP engine
// issues a warning
$fruits['potassium'] = 'banana';

// But this overwrites $fruits and it becomes an array
$fruits = array('potassium' => 'banana');
```

In Example 4-1, the $vegetables and $computers arrays each store a list of relationships. The $vegetables array relates vegetables and colors, while the $computers array relates computer names and manufacturers. In the $dinner array, however, we just care about the names of dishes that are the array values. The array keys are just numbers that distinguish one element from another.

Creating a Numeric Array

PHP provides some shortcuts for working with arrays that have only numbers as keys. If you create an array with [] or array() by specifying only a list of values instead of key/value pairs, the PHP engine automatically assigns a numeric key to each value. The keys start at 0 and increase by one for each element. Example 4-5 uses this technique to create the $dinner array.

Example 4-5. Creating numeric arrays with array()

```
$dinner = array('Sweet Corn and Asparagus',
                'Lemon Chicken',
                'Braised Bamboo Fungus');
print "I want $dinner[0] and $dinner[1].";
```

Example 4-5 prints:

```
I want Sweet Corn and Asparagus and Lemon Chicken.
```

Internally, the PHP engine treats arrays with numeric keys and arrays with string keys (and arrays with a mix of numeric and string keys) identically. Because of the resemblance to features in other programming languages, programmers often refer to arrays with only numeric keys as "numeric," "indexed," or "ordered" arrays, and to string-keyed arrays as "associative" arrays. An *associative array*, in other words, is one whose keys signify something other than the positions of the values within the array. Each key is *associated* with its value.

PHP automatically uses incrementing numbers for array keys when you create an array or add elements to an array with the empty brackets syntax shown in Example 4-6.

Example 4-6. Adding elements with []

```
// Create $lunch array with two elements
// This sets $lunch[0]
$lunch[] = 'Dried Mushrooms in Brown Sauce';
// This sets $lunch[1]
$lunch[] = 'Pineapple and Yu Fungus';

// Create $dinner with three elements
$dinner = array('Sweet Corn and Asparagus', 'Lemon Chicken',
                'Braised Bamboo Fungus');
// Add an element to the end of $dinner
// This sets $dinner[3]
$dinner[] = 'Flank Skin with Spiced Flavor';
```

The empty brackets add an element to the array. The new element has a numeric key that's one more than the biggest numeric key already in the array. If the array doesn't exist yet, the empty brackets add an element with a key of 0.

 Making the first element have key 0, not key 1, is not in line with how normal humans (in contrast to computer programmers) think, so it bears repeating. The first element of an array with numeric keys is element 0, not element 1.

Finding the Size of an Array

The count() function tells you the number of elements in an array. Example 4-7 demonstrates count().

Example 4-7. Finding the size of an array

```
$dinner = array('Sweet Corn and Asparagus',
                'Lemon Chicken',
                'Braised Bamboo Fungus');

$dishes = count($dinner);

print "There are $dishes things for dinner.";
```

Example 4-7 prints:

```
There are 3 things for dinner.
```

When you pass it an empty array (that is, an array with no elements in it), `count()` returns 0. An empty array also evaluates to `false` in an `if()` test expression.

Looping Through Arrays

One of the most common things to do with an array is to consider each element in the array individually and process it in some way. This may involve incorporating it into a row of an HTML table or adding its value to a running total.

The easiest way to iterate through each element of an array is with `foreach()`. The `foreach()` construct lets you run a code block once for each element in an array. Example 4-8 uses `foreach()` to print an HTML table containing each element in an array.

Example 4-8. Looping with foreach()

```
$meal = array('breakfast' => 'Walnut Bun',
              'lunch' => 'Cashew Nuts and White Mushrooms',
              'snack' => 'Dried Mulberries',
              'dinner' => 'Eggplant with Chili Sauce');
print "<table>\n";
foreach ($meal as $key => $value) {
    print "<tr><td>$key</td><td>$value</td></tr>\n";
}
print '</table>';
```

Example 4-8 prints:

```
<table>
<tr><td>breakfast</td><td>Walnut Bun</td></tr>
<tr><td>lunch</td><td>Cashew Nuts and White Mushrooms</td></tr>
<tr><td>snack</td><td>Dried Mulberries</td></tr>
<tr><td>dinner</td><td>Eggplant with Chili Sauce</td></tr>
</table>
```

For each element in $meal, foreach() copies the key of the element into $key and the value into $value. Then, it runs the code inside the curly braces. In Example 4-8, the code prints $key and $value with some HTML to make a table row. You can use whatever variable names you want for the key and value inside the code block. If the variable names were in use before the foreach(), though, they're overwritten with values from the array.

When you're using foreach() to print out data in an HTML table, often you want to apply alternating CSS classes to each table row. This is easy to do when you store the alternating class names in a separate array. Then, switch a variable between 0 and 1 each time through the foreach() to print the appropriate class name. Example 4-9 alternates between the two class names in its $row_styles array.

Example 4-9. Alternating table row classes

```
$row_styles = array('even','odd');
$style_index = 0;
$meal = array('breakfast' => 'Walnut Bun',
              'lunch' => 'Cashew Nuts and White Mushrooms',
              'snack' => 'Dried Mulberries',
              'dinner' => 'Eggplant with Chili Sauce');
print "<table>\n";
foreach ($meal as $key => $value) {
    print '<tr class="' . $row_styles[$style_index] . '">';
    print "<td>$key</td><td>$value</td></tr>\n";
    // This switches $style_index between 0 and 1
    $style_index = 1 - $style_index;
}
print '</table>';
```

Example 4-9 prints:

```
<table>
<tr class="even"><td>breakfast</td><td>Walnut Bun</td></tr>
<tr class="odd"><td>lunch</td><td>Cashew Nuts and White Mushrooms</td></tr>
<tr class="even"><td>snack</td><td>Dried Mulberries</td></tr>
<tr class="odd"><td>dinner</td><td>Eggplant with Chili Sauce</td></tr>
</table>
```

Inside the foreach() code block, changing the values of loop variables like $key and $value doesn't affect the elements in the actual array. If you want to change the array element values, use the $key variable as an index into the array. Example 4-10 uses this technique to double each element in the array.

Example 4-10. Modifying an array with foreach()

```
$meals = array('Walnut Bun' => 1,
               'Cashew Nuts and White Mushrooms' => 4.95,
```

```
                    'Dried Mulberries' => 3.00,
                    'Eggplant with Chili Sauce' => 6.50);

foreach ($meals as $dish => $price) {
    // $price = $price * 2 does NOT work
    $meals[$dish] = $meals[$dish] * 2;
}

// Iterate over the array again and print the changed values
foreach ($meals as $dish => $price) {
    printf("The new price of %s is \$%.2f.\n",$dish,$price);
}
```

Example 4-10 prints:

```
The new price of Walnut Bun is $2.00.
The new price of Cashew Nuts and White Mushrooms is $9.90.
The new price of Dried Mulberries is $6.00.
The new price of Eggplant with Chili Sauce is $13.00.
```

There's a more concise form of foreach() for use with numeric arrays, shown in Example 4-11.

Example 4-11. Using foreach() with numeric arrays

```
$dinner = array('Sweet Corn and Asparagus',
                'Lemon Chicken',
                'Braised Bamboo Fungus');
foreach ($dinner as $dish) {
    print "You can eat: $dish\n";
}
```

Example 4-11 prints:

```
You can eat: Sweet Corn and Asparagus
You can eat: Lemon Chicken
You can eat: Braised Bamboo Fungus
```

With this form of foreach(), just specify one variable name after as, and each element value is copied into that variable inside the code block. However, you can't access element keys inside the code block.

To keep track of your position in the array with foreach(), you have to use a separate variable that you increment each time the foreach() code block runs. With for(), you get the position explicitly in your loop variable. The foreach() loop gives you the value of each array element, but the for() loop gives you the position of each array element. There's no loop structure that gives you both at once.

So, if you want to know what element you're on as you're iterating through a numeric array, use for() instead of foreach(). Your for() loop should depend on a loop variable that starts at 0 and continues up to one less than the number of elements in the array. This is shown in Example 4-12.

Example 4-12. Iterating through a numeric array with for()

```
$dinner = array('Sweet Corn and Asparagus',
                'Lemon Chicken',
                'Braised Bamboo Fungus');
for ($i = 0, $num_dishes = count($dinner); $i < $num_dishes; $i++) {
  print "Dish number $i is $dinner[$i]\n";
}
```

Example 4-12 prints:

```
Dish number 0 is Sweet Corn and Asparagus
Dish number 1 is Lemon Chicken
Dish number 2 is Braised Bamboo Fungus
```

When iterating through an array with for(), you have a running counter available of which array element you're on. Use this counter with the modulus operator (%) to alternate table row classes, as shown in Example 4-13.

Example 4-13. Alternating table row classes with for()

```
$row_styles = array('even','odd');
$dinner = array('Sweet Corn and Asparagus',
                'Lemon Chicken',
                'Braised Bamboo Fungus');
print "<table>\n";

for ($i = 0, $num_dishes = count($dinner); $i < $num_dishes; $i++) {
    print '<tr class="' . $row_styles[$i % 2] . '">';
    print "<td>Element $i</td><td>$dinner[$i]</td></tr>\n";
}
print '</table>';
```

Example 4-13 computes the correct table row class with $i % 2. This value alternates between 0 and 1 as $i alternates between even and odd. There's no need to use a separate variable, such as $style_index, as in Example 4-9, to hold the appropriate row class name. Example 4-13 prints:

```
<table>
<tr class="even"><td>Element 0</td><td>Sweet Corn and Asparagus</td></tr>
<tr class="odd"><td>Element 1</td><td>Lemon Chicken</td></tr>
<tr class="even"><td>Element 2</td><td>Braised Bamboo Fungus</td></tr>
</table>
```

When you iterate through an array using foreach(), the elements are accessed in the order in which they were added to the array. The first element added is accessed first, the second element added is accessed next, and so on. If you have a numeric array whose elements were added in a different order than how their keys would usually be ordered, this could produce unexpected results. Example 4-14 doesn't print array elements in numeric or alphabetic order.

Example 4-14. Array element order and foreach()

```
$letters[0] = 'A';
$letters[1] = 'B';
$letters[3] = 'D';
$letters[2] = 'C';

foreach ($letters as $letter) {
    print $letter;
}
```

Example 4-14 prints:

ABDC

To guarantee that elements are accessed in numerical key order, use for() to iterate through the loop:

```
for ($i = 0, $num_letters = count($letters); $i < $num_letters; $i++) {
    print $letters[$i];
}
```

This prints:

ABCD

If you're looking for a specific element in an array, you don't need to iterate through the entire array to find it. There are more efficient ways to locate a particular element. To check for an element with a certain key, use array_key_exists(), shown in Example 4-15. This function returns true if an element with the provided key exists in the provided array.

Example 4-15. Checking for an element with a particular key

```
$meals = array('Walnut Bun' => 1,
               'Cashew Nuts and White Mushrooms' => 4.95,
               'Dried Mulberries' => 3.00,
               'Eggplant with Chili Sauce' => 6.50,
               'Shrimp Puffs' => 0); // Shrimp Puffs are free!
$books = array("The Eater's Guide to Chinese Characters",
               'How to Cook and Eat in Chinese');

// This is true
if (array_key_exists('Shrimp Puffs',$meals)) {
    print "Yes, we have Shrimp Puffs";
}
// This is false
```

```
if (array_key_exists('Steak Sandwich',$meals)) {
    print "We have a Steak Sandwich";
}
// This is true
if (array_key_exists(1, $books)) {
    print "Element 1 is How to Cook and Eat in Chinese";
}
```

To check for an element with a particular value, use in_array(), as shown in Example 4-16.

Example 4-16. Checking for an element with a particular value

```
$meals = array('Walnut Bun' => 1,
               'Cashew Nuts and White Mushrooms' => 4.95,
               'Dried Mulberries' => 3.00,
               'Eggplant with Chili Sauce' => 6.50,
               'Shrimp Puffs' => 0);
$books = array("The Eater's Guide to Chinese Characters",
               'How to Cook and Eat in Chinese');

// This is true: key Dried Mulberries has value 3.00
if (in_array(3, $meals)) {
  print 'There is a $3 item.';
}
// This is true
if (in_array('How to Cook and Eat in Chinese', $books)) {
  print "We have How to Cook and Eat in Chinese";
}
// This is false: in_array() is case-sensitive
if (in_array("the eater's guide to chinese characters", $books)) {
  print "We have the Eater's Guide to Chinese Characters.";
}
```

The in_array() function returns true if it finds an element with the given value. It is case-sensitive when it compares strings. The array_search() function is similar to in_array(), but if it finds an element, it returns the element key instead of true. In Example 4-17, array_search() returns the name of the dish that costs $6.50.

Example 4-17. Finding an element with a particular value

```
$meals = array('Walnut Bun' => 1,
               'Cashew Nuts and White Mushrooms' => 4.95,
               'Dried Mulberries' => 3.00,
               'Eggplant with Chili Sauce' => 6.50,
               'Shrimp Puffs' => 0);

$dish = array_search(6.50, $meals);
if ($dish) {
```

```
    print "$dish costs \$6.50";
}
```

Example 4-17 prints:

```
Eggplant with Chili Sauce costs $6.50
```

Modifying Arrays

You can operate on individual array elements just like regular scalar variables, using arithmetic, logical, and other operators. Example 4-18 shows some operations on array elements.

Example 4-18. Operating on array elements

```
$dishes['Beef Chow Foon'] = 12;
$dishes['Beef Chow Foon']++;
$dishes['Roast Duck'] = 3;

$dishes['total'] = $dishes['Beef Chow Foon'] + $dishes['Roast Duck'];

if ($dishes['total'] > 15) {
    print "You ate a lot: ";
}

print 'You ate ' . $dishes['Beef Chow Foon'] . ' dishes of Beef Chow Foon.';
```

Example 4-18 prints:

```
You ate a lot: You ate 13 dishes of Beef Chow Foon.
```

Interpolating array element values in double-quoted strings or here documents is similar to interpolating numbers or strings. The easiest way is to include the array element in the string, but don't put quotes around the element key. This is shown in Example 4-19.

Example 4-19. Interpolating array element values in double-quoted strings

```
$meals['breakfast'] = 'Walnut Bun';
$meals['lunch'] = 'Eggplant with Chili Sauce';
$amounts = array(3, 6);

print "For breakfast, I'd like $meals[breakfast] and for lunch,\n";
print "I'd like $meals[lunch]. I want $amounts[0] at breakfast and\n";
print "$amounts[1] at lunch.";
```

Example 4-19 prints:

```
For breakfast, I'd like Walnut Bun and for lunch,
I'd like Eggplant with Chili Sauce. I want 3 at breakfast and
6 at lunch.
```

The interpolation in Example 4-19 works only with array keys that consist exclusively of letters, numbers, and underscores. If you have an array key that has whitespace or other punctuation in it, interpolate it with curly braces, as demonstrated in Example 4-20.

Example 4-20. Interpolating array element values with curly braces

```
$meals['Walnut Bun'] = '$3.95';
$hosts['www.example.com'] = 'website';

print "A Walnut Bun costs {$meals['Walnut Bun']}.\n";
print "www.example.com is a {$hosts['www.example.com']}.";
```

Example 4-20 prints:

```
A Walnut Bun costs $3.95.
www.example.com is a website.
```

In a double-quoted string or here document, an expression inside curly braces is evaluated and then its value is put into the string. In Example 4-20, the expressions used are lone array elements, so the element values are interpolated into the strings.

To remove an element from an array, use unset():

```
unset($dishes['Roast Duck']);
```

Removing an element with unset() is different than just setting the element value to 0 or the empty string. When you use unset(), the element is no longer there when you iterate through the array or count the number of elements in the array. Using unset() on an array that represents a store's inventory is like saying that the store no longer carries a product. Setting the element's value to 0 or the empty string says that the item is temporarily out of stock.

When you want to print all of the values in an array at once, the quickest way is to use the implode() function. It makes a string by combining all the values in an array, putting a string delimiter between each value. Example 4-21 prints a comma-separated list of dim sum choices.

Example 4-21. Making a string from an array with implode()

```
$dimsum = array('Chicken Bun','Stuffed Duck Web','Turnip Cake');
$menu = implode(', ', $dimsum);
print $menu;
```

Example 4-21 prints:

```
Chicken Bun, Stuffed Duck Web, Turnip Cake
```

To implode an array with no delimiter, use the empty string as the first argument to `implode()`:

```
$letters = array('A','B','C','D');
print implode('',$letters);
```

This prints:

```
ABCD
```

Use `implode()` to simplify printing HTML table rows, as shown in Example 4-22.

Example 4-22. Printing HTML table rows with implode()

```
$dimsum = array('Chicken Bun','Stuffed Duck Web','Turnip Cake');
print '<tr><td>' . implode('</td><td>',$dimsum) . '</td></tr>';
```

Example 4-22 prints:

```
<tr><td>Chicken Bun</td><td>Stuffed Duck Web</td><td>Turnip Cake</td></tr>
```

The `implode()` function puts its delimiter between each value, so to make a complete table row, you also have to print the opening tags that go before the first element and the closing tags that go after the last element.

The counterpart to `implode()` is called `explode()`. It breaks a string apart into an array. The delimiter argument to `explode()` is the string it should look for to separate array elements. Example 4-23 demonstrates `explode()`.

Example 4-23. Turning a string into an array with explode()

```
$fish = 'Bass, Carp, Pike, Flounder';
$fish_list = explode(', ', $fish);
print "The second fish is $fish_list[1]";
```

Example 4-23 prints:

```
The second fish is Carp
```

Sorting Arrays

There are several ways to sort arrays. Which function to use depends on how you want to sort your array and what kind of array it is.

The `sort()` function sorts an array by its element values. It should only be used on numeric arrays, because it resets the keys of the array when it sorts. Example 4-24 shows some arrays before and after sorting.

Example 4-24. Sorting with sort()

```
$dinner = array('Sweet Corn and Asparagus',
                'Lemon Chicken',
                'Braised Bamboo Fungus');
$meal = array('breakfast' => 'Walnut Bun',
              'lunch' => 'Cashew Nuts and White Mushrooms',
              'snack' => 'Dried Mulberries',
              'dinner' => 'Eggplant with Chili Sauce');

print "Before Sorting:\n";
foreach ($dinner as $key => $value) {
    print " \$dinner: $key $value\n";
}
foreach ($meal as $key => $value) {
    print "  \$meal: $key $value\n";
}

sort($dinner);
sort($meal);

print "After Sorting:\n";
foreach ($dinner as $key => $value) {
    print " \$dinner: $key $value\n";
}
foreach ($meal as $key => $value) {
    print "  \$meal: $key $value\n";
}
```

Example 4-24 prints:

```
Before Sorting:
 $dinner: 0 Sweet Corn and Asparagus
 $dinner: 1 Lemon Chicken
 $dinner: 2 Braised Bamboo Fungus
   $meal: breakfast Walnut Bun
   $meal: lunch Cashew Nuts and White Mushrooms
   $meal: snack Dried Mulberries
   $meal: dinner Eggplant with Chili Sauce
After Sorting:
 $dinner: 0 Braised Bamboo Fungus
 $dinner: 1 Lemon Chicken
 $dinner: 2 Sweet Corn and Asparagus
   $meal: 0 Cashew Nuts and White Mushrooms
   $meal: 1 Dried Mulberries
   $meal: 2 Eggplant with Chili Sauce
   $meal: 3 Walnut Bun
```

Both arrays have been rearranged in ascending order by element value. The first value in $dinner is now Braised Bamboo Fungus, and the first value in $meal is Cashew Nuts and White Mushrooms. The keys in $dinner haven't changed because it was a numeric array before we sorted it. The keys in $meal, however, have been replaced by numbers from 0 to 3.

To sort an associative array by element value, use asort(). This keeps keys together with their values. Example 4-25 shows the $meal array from Example 4-24 sorted with asort().

Example 4-25. Sorting with asort()

```
$meal = array('breakfast' => 'Walnut Bun',
              'lunch' => 'Cashew Nuts and White Mushrooms',
              'snack' => 'Dried Mulberries',
              'dinner' => 'Eggplant with Chili Sauce');

print "Before Sorting:\n";
foreach ($meal as $key => $value) {
    print "   \$meal: $key $value\n";
}

asort($meal);

print "After Sorting:\n";
foreach ($meal as $key => $value) {
    print "   \$meal: $key $value\n";
}
```

Example 4-25 prints:

```
Before Sorting:
   $meal: breakfast Walnut Bun
   $meal: lunch Cashew Nuts and White Mushrooms
   $meal: snack Dried Mulberries
   $meal: dinner Eggplant with Chili Sauce
After Sorting:
   $meal: lunch Cashew Nuts and White Mushrooms
   $meal: snack Dried Mulberries
   $meal: dinner Eggplant with Chili Sauce
   $meal: breakfast Walnut Bun
```

The values are sorted in the same way with asort() as with sort(), but this time, the keys stick around.

While sort() and asort() sort arrays by element value, you can also sort arrays by key with ksort(). This keeps key/value pairs together, but orders them by key. Example 4-26 shows $meal sorted with ksort().

Example 4-26. Sorting with ksort()

```
$meal = array('breakfast' => 'Walnut Bun',
              'lunch' => 'Cashew Nuts and White Mushrooms',
```

```
              'snack' => 'Dried Mulberries',
              'dinner' => 'Eggplant with Chili Sauce');

print "Before Sorting:\n";
foreach ($meal as $key => $value) {
    print "   \$meal: $key $value\n";
}

ksort($meal);

print "After Sorting:\n";
foreach ($meal as $key => $value) {
    print "   \$meal: $key $value\n";
}
```

Example 4-26 prints:

```
Before Sorting:
    $meal: breakfast Walnut Bun
    $meal: lunch Cashew Nuts and White Mushrooms
    $meal: snack Dried Mulberries
    $meal: dinner Eggplant with Chili Sauce
After Sorting:
    $meal: breakfast Walnut Bun
    $meal: dinner Eggplant with Chili Sauce
    $meal: lunch Cashew Nuts and White Mushrooms
    $meal: snack Dried Mulberries
```

The array is reordered so the keys are now in ascending alphabetical order. Each element is unchanged, so the value that went with each key before the sorting is still attached to the same key after the sorting. If you sort a numeric array with ksort(), then the elements are ordered so the keys are in ascending numeric order. This is the same order you start out with when you create a numeric array using array() or [ ].

The array-sorting functions sort(), asort(), and ksort() have counterparts that sort in descending order. The reverse-sorting functions are named rsort(), arsort(), and krsort(). They work exactly the same as sort(), asort(), and ksort(), except they sort the arrays so the largest (or alphabetically last) key or value is first in the sorted array, and subsequent elements are arranged in descending order. Example 4-27 shows arsort() in action.

Example 4-27. Sorting with arsort()

```
$meal = array('breakfast' => 'Walnut Bun',
              'lunch' => 'Cashew Nuts and White Mushrooms',
              'snack' => 'Dried Mulberries',
              'dinner' => 'Eggplant with Chili Sauce');

print "Before Sorting:\n";
foreach ($meal as $key => $value) {
```

```
        print "   \$meal: $key $value\n";
}

arsort($meal);

print "After Sorting:\n";
foreach ($meal as $key => $value) {
        print "   \$meal: $key $value\n";
}
```

Example 4-27 prints:

```
Before Sorting:
    $meal: breakfast Walnut Bun
    $meal: lunch Cashew Nuts and White Mushrooms
    $meal: snack Dried Mulberries
    $meal: dinner Eggplant with Chili Sauce
After Sorting:
    $meal: breakfast Walnut Bun
    $meal: dinner Eggplant with Chili Sauce
    $meal: snack Dried Mulberries
    $meal: lunch Cashew Nuts and White Mushrooms
```

The arsort() function keeps the association between key and value, just like asort(), but puts the elements in the opposite order (by value). The element whose value begins with W is now first, and the element whose value begins with C is last.

Using Multidimensional Arrays

As mentioned in "Array Basics" on page 57, the value of an array element can be another array. This is useful when you want to store data that has a more complicated structure than just a key and a single value. A standard key/value pair is fine for matching up a meal name (such as breakfast or lunch) with a single dish (such as Walnut Bun or Chicken with Cashew Nuts), but what about when each meal consists of more than one dish? Then, element values should be arrays, not strings.

Use the array() construct or the [] short array syntax to create arrays that have more arrays as element values, as shown in Example 4-28.

Example 4-28. Creating multidimensional arrays with array() and []

```
$meals = array('breakfast' => ['Walnut Bun','Coffee'],
               'lunch'     => ['Cashew Nuts', 'White Mushrooms'],
               'snack'     => ['Dried Mulberries','Salted Sesame Crab']);

$lunches = [ ['Chicken','Eggplant','Rice'],
             ['Beef','Scallions','Noodles'],
             ['Eggplant','Tofu'] ];
```

```
$flavors = array('Japanese' => array('hot' => 'wasabi',
                                      'salty' => 'soy sauce'),
                 'Chinese'  => array('hot' => 'mustard',
                                     'pepper-salty' => 'prickly ash'));
```

Access elements in these arrays of arrays by using more sets of square brackets to identify elements. Each set of square brackets goes one level into the entire array. Example 4-29 demonstrates how to access elements of the arrays defined in Example 4-28.

Example 4-29. Accessing multidimensional array elements

```
print $meals['lunch'][1];          // White Mushrooms
print $meals['snack'][0];          // Dried Mulberries
print $lunches[0][0];              // Chicken
print $lunches[2][1];              // Tofu
print $flavors['Japanese']['salty']; // soy sauce
print $flavors['Chinese']['hot'];  // mustard
```

Each level of an array is called a *dimension*. Before this section, all the arrays in this chapter have been *one-dimensional arrays*. They each have one level of keys. Arrays such as $meals, $lunches, and $flavors, shown in Example 4-29, are called *multidimensional arrays* because they each have more than one dimension.

You can also create or modify multidimensional arrays with the square bracket syntax. Example 4-30 shows some multidimensional array manipulation.

Example 4-30. Manipulating multidimensional arrays

```
$prices['dinner']['Sweet Corn and Asparagus'] = 12.50;
$prices['lunch']['Cashew Nuts and White Mushrooms'] = 4.95;
$prices['dinner']['Braised Bamboo Fungus'] = 8.95;

$prices['dinner']['total'] = $prices['dinner']['Sweet Corn and Asparagus'] +
                             $prices['dinner']['Braised Bamboo Fungus'];

$specials[0][0] = 'Chestnut Bun';
$specials[0][1] = 'Walnut Bun';
$specials[0][2] = 'Peanut Bun';
$specials[1][0] = 'Chestnut Salad';
$specials[1][1] = 'Walnut Salad';
// Leaving out the index adds it to the end of the array
// This creates $specials[1][2]
$specials[1][] = 'Peanut Salad';
```

To iterate through each dimension of a multidimensional array, use nested foreach() or for() loops. Example 4-31 uses foreach() to iterate through a multidimensional associative array.

Example 4-31. Iterating through a multidimensional array with foreach()

```
$flavors = array('Japanese' => array('hot' => 'wasabi',
                                      'salty' => 'soy sauce'),
                 'Chinese'  => array('hot' => 'mustard',
                                     'pepper-salty' => 'prickly ash'));

// $culture is the key and $culture_flavors is the value (an array)
foreach ($flavors as $culture => $culture_flavors) {
    // $flavor is the key and $example is the value
    foreach ($culture_flavors as $flavor => $example) {
        print "A $culture $flavor flavor is $example.\n";
    }
}
```

Example 4-31 prints:

```
A Japanese hot flavor is wasabi.
A Japanese salty flavor is soy sauce.
A Chinese hot flavor is mustard.
A Chinese pepper-salty flavor is prickly ash.
```

The first foreach() loop in Example 4-31 iterates through the first dimension of $flavors. The keys stored in $culture are the strings Japanese and Chinese, and the values stored in $culture_flavors are the arrays that are the element values of this dimension. The next foreach() iterates over those element value arrays, copying keys such as hot and salty into $flavor, and values such as wasabi and soy sauce into $example. The code block of the second foreach() uses variables from both foreach() statements to print out a complete message.

Just like nested foreach() loops iterate through a multidimensional associative array, nested for() loops iterate through a multidimensional numeric array, as shown in Example 4-32.

Example 4-32. Iterating through a multidimensional array with for()

```
$specials = array( array('Chestnut Bun', 'Walnut Bun', 'Peanut Bun'),
                   array('Chestnut Salad','Walnut Salad', 'Peanut Salad') );

// $num_specials is 2: the number of elements in the first dimension of $specials
for ($i = 0, $num_specials = count($specials); $i < $num_specials; $i++) {
    // $num_sub is 3: the number of elements in each subarray
    for ($m = 0, $num_sub = count($specials[$i]); $m < $num_sub; $m++) {
        print "Element [$i][$m] is " . $specials[$i][$m] . "\n";
    }
}
```

Example 4-32 prints:

```
Element [0][0] is Chestnut Bun
Element [0][1] is Walnut Bun
Element [0][2] is Peanut Bun
Element [1][0] is Chestnut Salad
Element [1][1] is Walnut Salad
Element [1][2] is Peanut Salad
```

In Example 4-32, the outer for() loop iterates over the two elements of $specials. The inner for() loop iterates over each element of the subarrays that hold the different strings. In the print statement, $i is the index in the first dimension (the elements of $specials), and $m is the index in the second dimension (the subarray).

To interpolate a value from a multidimensional array into a double-quoted string or here document, use the curly brace syntax from Example 4-20. Example 4-33 uses curly braces for interpolation to produce the same output as Example 4-32. In fact, the only different line in Example 4-33 is the print statement.

Example 4-33. Multidimensional array element value interpolation

```
$specials = array( array('Chestnut Bun', 'Walnut Bun', 'Peanut Bun'),
                   array('Chestnut Salad','Walnut Salad', 'Peanut Salad') );

// $num_specials is 2: the number of elements in the first dimension of $specials
for ($i = 0, $num_specials = count($specials); $i < $num_specials; $i++) {
    // $num_sub is 3: the number of elements in each subarray
    for ($m = 0, $num_sub = count($specials[$i]); $m < $num_sub; $m++) {
        print "Element [$i][$m] is {$specials[$i][$m]}\n";
    }
}
```

Chapter Summary

This chapter covered:

- Understanding the components of an array: elements, keys, and values
- Defining an array in your programs two ways: with array() and with the short array syntax
- Adding elements to an array with square brackets
- Understanding the shortcuts PHP provides for arrays with numeric keys
- Counting the number of elements in an array
- Visiting each element of an array with foreach()
- Alternating table row CSS class names with foreach() and an array of class names
- Modifying array element values inside a foreach() code block
- Visiting each element of a numeric array with for()

- Alternating table row CSS class names with `for()` and the modulus operator (%)
- Understanding the order in which `foreach()` and `for()` visit array elements
- Checking for an array element with a particular key
- Checking for an array element with a particular value
- Interpolating array element values in strings
- Removing an element from an array
- Generating a string from an array with `implode()`
- Generating an array from a string with `explode()`
- Sorting an array with `sort()`, `asort()`, or `ksort()`
- Sorting an array in reverse
- Defining a multidimensional array
- Accessing individual elements of a multidimensional array
- Visiting each element in a multidimensional array with `foreach()` or `for()`
- Interpolating multidimensional array elements in a string

Exercises

1. According to the US Census Bureau, the 10 largest American cities (by population) in 2010 were as follows:

   - New York, NY (8,175,133 people)
   - Los Angeles, CA (3,792,621)
   - Chicago, IL (2,695,598)
   - Houston, TX (2,100,263)
   - Philadelphia, PA (1,526,006)
   - Phoenix, AZ (1,445,632)
   - San Antonio, TX (1,327,407)
   - San Diego, CA (1,307,402)
   - Dallas, TX (1,197,816)
   - San Jose, CA (945,942)

   Define an array (or arrays) that holds this information about locations and populations. Print a table of locations and population information that includes the total population in all 10 cities.

2. Modify your solution to the previous exercise so that the rows in the result table are ordered by population. Then modify your solution so that the rows are ordered by city name.

3. Modify your solution to the first exercise so that the table also contains rows that hold state population totals for each state represented in the list of cities.

4. For each of the following kinds of information, state how you would store it in an array and then give sample code that creates such an array with a few elements. For example, for the first item, you might say, "An associative array whose key is

the student's name and whose value is an associative array of grade and ID number," as in the following:

```
$students = [ 'James D. McCawley' => [ 'grade' => 'A+','id' => 271231 ],
              'Buwei Yang Chao' => [ 'grade' => 'A', 'id' => 818211] ];
```

a. The grades and ID numbers of students in a class
b. How many of each item in a store inventory are in stock
c. School lunches for a week: the different parts of each meal (entrée, side dish, drink, etc.) and the cost for each day
d. The names of people in your family
e. The names, ages, and relationship to you of people in your family

## CHAPTER 5

Groups of Logic: Functions and Files

When you're writing computer programs, laziness is a virtue. Reusing code you've already written makes it easier to do as little work as possible. Functions are the key to code reuse. A *function* is a named set of statements that you can execute just by invoking the function name instead of retyping the statements. This saves time and prevents errors. Plus, functions make it easier to use code that other people have written (as you've discovered by using the built-in functions written by the authors of the PHP engine).

The basics of defining your own functions and using them are laid out in the next section, "Declaring and Calling Functions". When you call a function, you can hand it some values with which to operate. For example, if you wrote a function to check whether a user is allowed to access the current web page, you would need to provide the username and the current web page name to the function. These values are called *arguments*. "Passing Arguments to Functions" on page 83 explains how to write functions that accept arguments and how to use the arguments from inside the functions.

Some functions are one-way streets. You may pass them arguments, but you don't get anything back. A print_header() function that prints the top of an HTML page may take an argument containing the page title, but it doesn't give you any information after it executes. It just displays output. Most functions move information in two directions. The access control function mentioned previously is an example of this. The function gives you back a value: true (access granted) or false (access denied). This value is called the *return value*. You can use the return value of a function like any other value or variable. Return values are discussed in "Returning Values from Functions" on page 87.

The statements inside a function can use variables just like statements outside a function. However, the variables inside a function and outside a function live in two separate worlds. The PHP engine treats a variable called $name inside a function and a variable called $name outside a function as two unrelated variables. "Understanding Variable Scope" on page 92 explains the rules about which variables are usable in which parts of your programs. It's important to understand these rules—get them wrong and your code relies on uninitialized or incorrect variables. That's a bug that is hard to track down.

Because functions lend themselves so well to reuse, it's convenient to create separate files full of function definitions and then refer to those files from your programs. This lets different programs (and different parts of the same program) share the functions without duplication. "Running Code in Another File" on page 98 explains PHP's facilities for tying together multiple files in a program.

Declaring and Calling Functions

To create a new function, use the function keyword, followed by the function name and then, inside curly braces, the function body. Example 5-1 declares a new function called page_header().[1]

Example 5-1. Declaring a function

```
function page_header() {
    print '<html><head><title>Welcome to my site</title></head>';
    print '<body bgcolor="#ffffff">';
}
```

Function names follow the same rules as variable names: they must begin with a letter or an underscore, and the rest of the characters in the name can be letters, numbers, or underscores. The PHP engine doesn't prevent you from having a variable and a function with the same name, but you should avoid it if you can. Many things with similar names makes for programs that are hard to understand.

The page_header() function defined in Example 5-1 can be called just like a built-in function. Example 5-2 uses page_header() to print a complete page.

Example 5-2. Calling a function

```
page_header();
print "Welcome, $user";
print "</body></html>";
```

---

[1] Strictly speaking, the parentheses aren't part of the function name, but it's good practice to include them when referring to functions. Doing so helps you to distinguish functions from variables and other language constructs.

Functions can be defined before or after they are called. The PHP engine reads the entire program file and takes care of all the function definitions before it runs any of the commands in the file. The `page_header()` and `page_footer()` functions in Example 5-3 both execute successfully, even though `page_header()` is defined before it is called and `page_footer()` is defined after it is called.

Example 5-3. Defining functions before or after calling them

```
function page_header() {
    print '<html><head><title>Welcome to my site</title></head>';
    print '<body bgcolor="#ffffff">';
}

page_header();
print "Welcome, $user";
page_footer();

function page_footer() {
    print '<hr>Thanks for visiting.';
    print '</body></html>';
}
```

Passing Arguments to Functions

While some functions (such as `page_header()` in the previous section) always do the same thing, other functions operate on input that can change. The input values supplied to a function are called *arguments*. Arguments add to the power of functions because they make functions more flexible. You can modify `page_header()` to take an argument that holds the page color. The modified function declaration is shown in Example 5-4.

Example 5-4. Declaring a function with an argument

```
function page_header2($color) {
    print '<html><head><title>Welcome to my site</title></head>';
    print '<body bgcolor="#' . $color . '">';
}
```

In the function declaration, you add `$color` between the parentheses after the function name. This lets the code inside the function use a variable called `$color`, which holds the value passed to the function when it is called. For example, you can call the function like this:

```
page_header2('cc00cc');
```

This sets `$color` to `cc00cc` inside `page_header2()`, so it prints:

```
<html><head><title>Welcome to my site</title></head><body bgcolor="#cc00cc">
```

When you define a function that takes an argument as in Example 5-4, you must pass an argument to the function when you call it. If you call the function without a value for the argument, the PHP engine complains with a warning. For example, if you call page_header2() like this:

```
page_header2();
```

the engine prints a message that looks like this:

```
PHP Warning:  Missing argument 1 for page_header2()
```

To avoid this warning, define a function to take an optional argument by specifying a default in the function declaration. If a value is supplied when the function is called, then the function uses the supplied value. If a value is not supplied when the function is called, then the function uses the default value. To specify a default value, put it after the argument name. Example 5-5 sets the default value for $color to cc3399.

Example 5-5. Specifying a default value

```
function page_header3($color = 'cc3399') {
    print '<html><head><title>Welcome to my site</title></head>';
    print '<body bgcolor="#' . $color . '">';
}
```

Calling page_header3('336699') produces the same results as calling page_header2('336699'). When the body of each function executes, $color has the value 336699, which is the color printed for the bgcolor attribute of the <body> tag. But while page_header2() without an argument produces a warning, you can run page_header3() without an argument, with $color set to cc3399.

Default values for arguments must be literals, such as 12, cc3399, or Shredded Swiss Chard. They can't be variables. The following is not OK and will cause the PHP engine to stop running your program:

```
$my_color = '#000000';

// This is incorrect: the default value can't be a variable
function page_header_bad($color = $my_color) {
    print '<html><head><title>Welcome to my site</title></head>';
    print '<body bgcolor="#' . $color . '">';
}
```

To define a function that accepts multiple arguments, separate each argument with a comma in the function declaration. In Example 5-6, page_header4() takes two arguments: $color and $title.

Example 5-6. Defining a two-argument function

```
function page_header4($color, $title) {
    print '<html><head><title>Welcome to ' . $title . '</title></head>';
    print '<body bgcolor="#' . $color . '">';
}
```

To pass a function multiple arguments when you call it, separate the argument values by commas in the function call. Example 5-7 calls `page_header4()` with values for `$color` and `$title`.

Example 5-7. Calling a two-argument function

```
page_header4('66cc66','my homepage');
```

Example 5-7 prints:

```
<html><head><title>Welcome to my homepage</title></head><body bgcolor="#66cc66">
```

In Example 5-6, both arguments are mandatory. You can use the same syntax in functions that take multiple arguments to denote default argument values as you do in functions that take one argument. However, all of the optional arguments must come after any mandatory arguments. Example 5-8 shows the correct ways to define a three-argument function that has one, two, or three optional arguments.

Example 5-8. Multiple optional arguments

```
// One optional argument: it must be last
function page_header5($color, $title, $header = 'Welcome') {
    print '<html><head><title>Welcome to ' . $title . '</title></head>';
    print '<body bgcolor="#' . $color . '">';
    print "<h1>$header</h1>";
}
// Acceptable ways to call this function:
page_header5('66cc99','my wonderful page'); // uses default $header
page_header5('66cc99','my wonderful page','This page is great!'); // no defaults

// Two optional arguments: must be last two arguments
function page_header6($color, $title = 'the page', $header = 'Welcome') {
    print '<html><head><title>Welcome to ' . $title . '</title></head>';
    print '<body bgcolor="#' . $color . '">';
    print "<h1>$header</h1>";
}
// Acceptable ways to call this function:
page_header6('66cc99'); // uses default $title and $header
page_header6('66cc99','my wonderful page'); // uses default $header
page_header6('66cc99','my wonderful page','This page is great!'); // no defaults


// All optional arguments
```

```
function page_header7($color = '336699', $title = 'the page', $header = 'Welcome') {
    print '<html><head><title>Welcome to ' . $title . '</title></head>';
    print '<body bgcolor="#' . $color . '">';
    print "<h1>$header</h1>";
}
// Acceptable ways to call this function:
page_header7(); // uses all defaults
page_header7('66cc99'); // uses default $title and $header
page_header7('66cc99','my wonderful page'); // uses default $header
page_header7('66cc99','my wonderful page','This page is great!'); // no defaults
```

All of the optional arguments must be at the end of the argument list to avoid ambiguity. If page_header7() could be defined with a mandatory first argument of $color, an optional second argument of $title, and a mandatory third argument of $header, then what would page_header7('33cc66','Good Morning') mean? The 'Good Morning' argument could be a value for either $title or $header. Putting all optional arguments after any mandatory arguments avoids this confusion.

Any changes you make to a variable passed as an argument to a function don't affect the variable outside the function.[2] In Example 5-9, the value of $counter outside the function doesn't change.

Example 5-9. Changing argument values

```
function countdown($top) {
    while ($top > 0) {
        print "$top..";
        $top--;
    }
    print "boom!\n";
}

$counter = 5;
countdown($counter);
print "Now, counter is $counter";
```

Example 5-9 prints:

```
5..4..3..2..1..boom!
Now, counter is 5
```

Passing $counter as the argument to countdown() tells the PHP engine to copy the value of $counter into $top at the start of the function, because $top is the name of the argument. Whatever happens to $top inside the function doesn't affect $counter.

---

2 Except for objects. If you pass an object to a function, changes made to that object inside the function affect the object outside the function. Objects are discussed in Chapter 6.

Once the value of $counter is copied into $top, $counter is out of the picture for the duration of the function.

Modifying arguments doesn't affect variables outside the function even if the argument has the same name as a variable outside the function. If countdown() in Example 5-9 is changed so that its argument is called $counter instead of $top, the value of $counter outside the function doesn't change. The argument and the variable outside the function just happen to have the same name. They remain completely unconnected.

Returning Values from Functions

The header-printing function you've seen in this chapter takes action by displaying some output. In addition to an action such as printing data or saving information into a database, functions can also compute a value, called the *return value*, which can be used later in a program. To capture the return value of a function, assign the function call to a variable. Example 5-10 stores the return value of the built-in function number_format() in the variable $number_to_display.

Example 5-10. Capturing a return value

```
$number_to_display = number_format(321442019);
print "The population of the US is about: $number_to_display";
```

Just like Example 1-6, Example 5-10 prints:

```
The population of the US is about: 321,442,019
```

Assigning the return value of a function to a variable is just like assigning a string or number to a variable. The statement $number = 57 means "store 57 in the variable $number." The statement $number_to_display = number_format(321442019) means "call the number_format() function with the argument 321442019 and store the return value in $number_to_display." Once the return value of a function has been put into a variable, you can use that variable and the value it contains just like any other variable in your program.

To return values from functions you write, use the return keyword with a value to return. When a function is executing, as soon as it encounters the return keyword, it stops running and returns the associated value. Example 5-11 defines a function that returns the total amount of a restaurant check after adding tax and tip.

Example 5-11. Returning a value from a function

```
function restaurant_check($meal, $tax, $tip) {
    $tax_amount = $meal * ($tax / 100);
    $tip_amount = $meal * ($tip / 100);
```

```
    $total_amount = $meal + $tax_amount + $tip_amount;

    return $total_amount;
}
```

The value that `restaurant_check()` returns can be used like any other value in a program. Example 5-12 uses the return value in an `if()` statement.

Example 5-12. Using a return value in an if() statement

```
// Find the total cost of a $15.22 meal with 8.25% tax and a 15% tip
$total = restaurant_check(15.22, 8.25, 15);

print 'I only have $20 in cash, so...';
if ($total > 20) {
    print "I must pay with my credit card.";
} else {
    print "I can pay with cash.";
}
```

A particular `return` statement can only return one value. You can't return multiple values with something like `return 15, 23`. If you want to return more than one value from a function, you can put the different values into one array and then return the array.

Example 5-13 shows a modified version of `restaurant_check()` that returns a two-element array containing the total amount before the tip is added and after it is added.

Example 5-13. Returning an array from a function

```
function restaurant_check2($meal, $tax, $tip) {
    $tax_amount  = $meal * ($tax / 100);
    $tip_amount  = $meal * ($tip / 100);
    $total_notip = $meal + $tax_amount;
    $total_tip   = $meal + $tax_amount + $tip_amount;

    return array($total_notip, $total_tip);
}
```

Example 5-14 uses the array returned by `restaurant_check2()`.

Example 5-14. Using an array returned from a function

```
$totals = restaurant_check2(15.22, 8.25, 15);

if ($totals[0] < 20) {
    print 'The total without tip is less than $20.';
}
```

```
if ($totals[1] < 20) {
    print 'The total with tip is less than $20.';
}
```

Although you can only return a single value with a return statement, you can have more than one return statement inside a function. The first return statement reached by the program flow inside the function causes the function to stop running and return a value. This isn't necessarily the return statement closest to the beginning of the function. Example 5-15 moves the cash-or-credit-card logic from Example 5-12 into a new function that determines the appropriate payment method.

Example 5-15. Multiple return statements in a function

```
function payment_method($cash_on_hand, $amount) {
    if ($amount > $cash_on_hand) {
        return 'credit card';
    } else {
        return 'cash';
    }
}
```

Example 5-16 uses the new payment_method() function by passing it the result from restaurant_check().

Example 5-16. Passing a return value to another function

```
$total = restaurant_check(15.22, 8.25, 15);
$method = payment_method(20, $total);
print 'I will pay with ' . $method;
```

Example 5-16 prints the following:

```
I will pay with cash
```

This is because the amount restaurant_check() returns is less than 20. This is passed to payment_method() in the $total argument. The first comparison in payment_method(), between $amount and $cash_on_hand, is false, so the code in the else block inside payment_method() executes. This causes the function to return the string cash.

The rules about truth values discussed in Chapter 3 apply to the return values of functions just like other values. You can take advantage of this to use functions inside if() statements and other control flow constructs. Example 5-17 decides what to do by calling the restaurant_check() function from inside an if() statement's test expression.

Example 5-17. Using return values with if()

```
if (restaurant_check(15.22, 8.25, 15) < 20) {
    print 'Less than $20, I can pay cash.';
} else {
    print 'Too expensive, I need my credit card.';
}
```

To evaluate the test expression in Example 5-17, the PHP engine first calls the restaurant_check() function. The return value of the function is then compared with 20, just as it would be if it were a variable or a literal value. If restau rant_check() returns a number less than 20, which it does in this case, then the first print statement is executed. Otherwise, the second print statement runs.

A test expression can also consist of just a function call with no comparison or other operator. In such a test expression, the return value of the function is converted to true or false according to the rules outlined in "Understanding true and false" on page 40. If the return value is true, then the test expression is true. If the return value is false, so is the test expression. A function can explicitly return true or false to make it more obvious that it should be used in a test expression. The can_pay_cash() function in Example 5-18 does this as it determines whether we can pay cash for a meal.

Example 5-18. Functions that return true or false

```
function can_pay_cash($cash_on_hand, $amount) {
    if ($amount > $cash_on_hand) {
        return false;
    } else {
        return true;
    }
}

$total = restaurant_check(15.22,8.25,15);
if (can_pay_cash(20, $total)) {
    print "I can pay in cash.";
} else {
    print "Time for the credit card.";
}
```

In Example 5-18, the can_pay_cash() function compares its two arguments. If $amount is bigger, then the function returns true. Otherwise, it returns false. The if() statement outside the function single-mindedly pursues its mission as an if() statement—finding the truth value of its test expression. Since this test expression is a function call, it calls can_pay_cash() with the two arguments 20 and $total. The return value of the function is the truth value of the test expression and controls which message is printed.

Just like you can put a variable in a test expression, you can put a function's return value in a test expression. In any situation where you call a function that returns a value, you can think of the code that calls the function, such as restaurant_check(15.22,8.25,15), as being replaced by the return value of the function as the program runs.

One frequent shortcut is to use a function call with the assignment operator in a test expression and to rely on the fact that the result of the assignment is the value being assigned. This lets you call a function, save its return value, and check whether the return value is true all in one step. Example 5-19 demonstrates how to do this.

Example 5-19. Assignment and function call inside a test expression

```
function complete_bill($meal, $tax, $tip, $cash_on_hand) {
    $tax_amount = $meal * ($tax / 100);
    $tip_amount = $meal * ($tip / 100);
    $total_amount = $meal + $tax_amount + $tip_amount;
    if ($total_amount > $cash_on_hand) {
        // The bill is more than we have
        return false;
    } else {
        // We can pay this amount
        return $total_amount;
    }
}

if ($total = complete_bill(15.22, 8.25, 15, 20)) {
    print "I'm happy to pay $total.";
} else {
    print "I don't have enough money. Shall I wash some dishes?";
}
```

In Example 5-19, the complete_bill() function returns false if the calculated bill, including tax and tip, is more than $cash_on_hand. If the bill is less than or equal to $cash_on_hand, then the amount of the bill is returned. When the if() statement outside the function evaluates its test expression, the following things happen:

1. complete_bill() is called with arguments 15.22, 8.25, 15, and 20.
2. The return value of complete_bill() is assigned to $total.
3. The result of the assignment (which, remember, is the same as the value being assigned) is converted to either true or false and used as the end result of the test expression.

Understanding Variable Scope

As you saw in Example 5-9, changes inside a function to variables that hold arguments don't affect those variables outside of the function. This is because activity inside a function happens in a different *scope*. Variables defined outside of a function are called *global variables*. They exist in one scope. Variables defined inside of a function are called *local variables*. Each function has its own scope.

Imagine each function is one branch office of a big company, and the code outside of any function is the company headquarters. At the Philadelphia branch office, co-workers refer to each other by their first names: "Alice did great work on this report," or "Bob never puts the right amount of sugar in my coffee." These statements talk about the folks in Philadelphia (local variables of one function), and say nothing about an Alice or a Bob who works at another branch office (local variables of another function) or at the company headquarters (global variables).

Local and global variables work similarly. A variable called $dinner inside a function, whether or not it's an argument to that function, is completely disconnected from a variable called $dinner outside of the function and from a variable called $dinner inside another function. Example 5-20 illustrates the unconnectedness of variables in different scopes.

Example 5-20. Variable scope

```
$dinner = 'Curry Cuttlefish';

function vegetarian_dinner() {
    print "Dinner is $dinner, or ";
    $dinner = 'Sauteed Pea Shoots';
    print $dinner;
    print "\n";
}

function kosher_dinner() {
    print "Dinner is $dinner, or ";
    $dinner = 'Kung Pao Chicken';
    print $dinner;
    print "\n";
}

print "Vegetarian ";
vegetarian_dinner();
print "Kosher ";
kosher_dinner();
print "Regular dinner is $dinner";
```

Example 5-20 prints:

```
Vegetarian Dinner is , or Sauteed Pea Shoots
Kosher Dinner is , or Kung Pao Chicken
Regular dinner is Curry Cuttlefish
```

In both functions, before $dinner is set to a value inside the function, it has no value. The global variable $dinner has no effect inside the function. Once $dinner is set inside a function, though, it doesn't affect the global $dinner set outside any function or the $dinner variable in another function. Inside each function, $dinner refers to the local version of $dinner and is completely separate from a variable that happens to have the same name in another function.

Like all analogies, though, the analogy between variable scope and corporate organization is not perfect. In a company, you can easily refer to employees at other locations; the folks in Philadelphia can talk about "Alice at headquarters" or "Bob in Atlanta," and the overlords at headquarters can decide the futures of "Alice in Philadelphia" or "Bob in Charleston." With variables, however, you can access global variables from inside a function, but you can't access the local variables of a function from outside that function. This is equivalent to folks at a branch office being able to talk about people at headquarters but not anyone at the other branch offices, and to folks at headquarters not being able to talk about anyone at any branch office.

There are two ways to access a global variable from inside a function. The most straightforward is to look for them in a special array called $GLOBALS. Each global variable is accessible as an element in that array. Example 5-21 demonstrates how to use the $GLOBALS array.

Example 5-21. The $GLOBALS array

```
$dinner = 'Curry Cuttlefish';

function macrobiotic_dinner() {
    $dinner = "Some Vegetables";
    print "Dinner is $dinner";
    // Succumb to the delights of the ocean
    print " but I'd rather have ";
    print $GLOBALS['dinner'];
    print "\n";
}

macrobiotic_dinner();
print "Regular dinner is: $dinner";
```

Example 5-21 prints:

```
Dinner is Some Vegetables but I'd rather have Curry Cuttlefish
Regular dinner is: Curry Cuttlefish
```

Example 5-21 accesses the global $dinner from inside the function as $GLOBALS['dinner']. The $GLOBALS array can also modify global variables. Example 5-22 shows how to do that.

Example 5-22. Modifying a variable with $GLOBALS

```
$dinner = 'Curry Cuttlefish';

function hungry_dinner() {
    $GLOBALS['dinner'] .= ' and Deep-Fried Taro';
}

print "Regular dinner is $dinner";
print "\n";
hungry_dinner();
print "Hungry dinner is $dinner";
```

Example 5-22 prints:

```
Regular dinner is Curry Cuttlefish
Hungry dinner is Curry Cuttlefish and Deep-Fried Taro
```

Inside the hungry_dinner() function, $GLOBALS['dinner'] can be modified just like any other variable, and the modifications change the global variable $dinner. In this case, $GLOBALS['dinner'] has a string appended to it using the concatenation operator from Example 2-19.

The second way to access a global variable inside a function is to use the global keyword. This tells the PHP engine that further use of the named variable inside a function should refer to the global variable with the given name, not a local variable. This is called "bringing a variable into local scope." Example 5-23 shows the global keyword at work.

Example 5-23. The global keyword

```
$dinner = 'Curry Cuttlefish';

function vegetarian_dinner() {
    global $dinner;
    print "Dinner was $dinner, but now it's ";
    $dinner = 'Sauteed Pea Shoots';
    print $dinner;
    print "\n";
}

print "Regular Dinner is $dinner.\n";
vegetarian_dinner();
print "Regular dinner is $dinner";
```

Example 5-23 prints:

```
Regular Dinner is Curry Cuttlefish.
Dinner was Curry Cuttlefish, but now it's Sauteed Pea Shoots
Regular dinner is Sauteed Pea Shoots
```

The first `print` statement displays the unmodified value of the global variable `$dinner`. The `global $dinner` line in `vegetarian_dinner()` means that any use of `$dinner` inside the function refers to the global `$dinner`, not a local variable with the same name. So, the first `print` statement in the function prints the already-set global value, and the assignment on the next line changes the global value. Since the global value is changed inside the function, the last `print` statement outside the function prints the changed value as well.

The `global` keyword can be used with multiple variable names at once. Just separate each variable name with a comma. For example:

```
global $dinner, $lunch, $breakfast;
```

 Generally, use the `$GLOBALS` array to access global variables inside functions instead of the `global` keyword. Using `$GLOBALS` provides a reminder on every variable access that you're dealing with a global variable. Unless you're writing a very short function, it's easy to forget that you're dealing with a global variable with `global` and become confused as to why your code is misbehaving. Relying on the `$GLOBALS` array requires a tiny bit of extra typing, but it does wonders for your code's intelligibility.

You may have noticed something strange about the examples that use the `$GLOBALS` array. These examples use `$GLOBALS` inside a function, but don't bring `$GLOBALS` into local scope with the `global` keyword. The `$GLOBALS` array, whether used inside or outside a function, is always in scope. This is because `$GLOBALS` is a special kind of predefined variable, called an *auto-global*. Auto-globals are variables that can be used anywhere in your PHP programs without anything required to bring them into scope. They're like a well-known employee that everyone, at headquarters or a branch office, refers to by his first name.

The auto-globals are always arrays that are automatically populated with data. They contain things such as submitted form data, cookie values, and session information. Chapters 7 and 10 each describe specific auto-global variables that are useful in different contexts.

Enforcing Rules on Arguments and Return Values

Unless you tell the PHP engine otherwise, function arguments and return values don't have any constraints on their types or values. The countdown() function in Example 5-9 assumes that its argument is a number, but you could pass a string such as "Caramel" as an argument and the PHP engine wouldn't complain.

Type declarations are a way to express constraints on argument values. These tell the PHP engine what kind of value is allowed for an argument so it can warn you when the wrong kind is provided. Table 5-1 shows the different kinds of declarations the PHP engine understands and what version of PHP introduced support for them.

Table 5-1. Type declarations

Declaration	Argument rule	Minimum PHP version
array	Must be an array	5.1.0
bool	Must be boolean: true or false	7.0.0
callable	Must be something representing a function or method that can be called[a]	5.4.0
float	Must be a floating-point number	7.0.0
int	Must be an integer	7.0.0.
string	Must be a string	7.0.0.
Name of a class	Must be an instance of that class (see Chapter 6 for more information about classes and instances).	5.0.0

[a] This can be a string containing a valid function name, a two-element array where the first element is an object instance and the second is a string holding a method name, or a few other things. See *http://www.php.net/language.types.callable* for all the details.

When defining a function, the type declaration goes before the argument name. Example 5-24 shows the function from Example 5-9 with the appropriate int type declaration in place.

Example 5-24. Declaring an argument type

```php
function countdown(int $top) {
    while ($top > 0) {
        print "$top..";
        $top--;
    }
    print "boom!\n";
}

$counter = 5;
countdown($counter);
print "Now, counter is $counter";
```

The only difference between Example 5-9 and Example 5-24 is the `int` after `countdown(` and before `$top`. When `countdown()` is passed a valid integer (such as 5), the code runs just fine. If another type of value is passed, then the PHP engine complains. For example, if you call `countdown("grunt");` when using PHP 7, then you get an error message similar to:

```
PHP Fatal error:  Uncaught TypeError: Argument 1 passed to countdown()
must be of the type integer, string given, called in decl-error.php
on line 2 and defined in countdown.php:2
Stack trace:
#0 decl-error.php(2): countdown('grunt')
#1 {main}
  thrown in countdown.php on line 2
```

In the error message, the PHP engine tells you about a `TypeError`, indicating which argument (1) passed to which function (`countdown()`) had a type mismatch, including what the argument type was supposed to be (`integer`) and what the argument type actually was (`string`). You also get information about where the problematic function call is and where the called function is defined.

In PHP 7, that `TypeError` is an exception that can be caught with an exception handler. "Indicating a Problem with Exceptions" on page 108 provides details on how to catch exceptions in your program.[3]

PHP 7 also supports type declarations for the kind of value a function returns. To enforce checking of the return type of a function, put a `:` after the `)` that closes the argument list, and then the return type declaration. For example, Example 5-25 shows the `restaurant_check()` function from Example 5-26 augmented with a return type declaration.

Example 5-25. Declaring a return type

```
function restaurant_check($meal, $tax, $tip): float {
    $tax_amount = $meal * ($tax / 100);
    $tip_amount = $meal * ($tip / 100);
    $total_amount = $meal + $tax_amount + $tip_amount;

    return $total_amount;
}
```

---

3 In earlier versions of PHP, type declaration violations are reported as the paradoxically named `Catchable fatal error`. These errors cause your program to stop running unless you handle them yourself in a special error handler. *http://www.php.net/set_error_handler* describes how to implement your own error handler for this situation.

If the function in Example 5-25 returns anything but a `float`, the PHP engine generates a `TypeError`.

For scalar type declarations in PHP 7, the enforcement of the declarations is not absolutely strict by default.

Even with type declarations, PHP 7 attempts to convert the type of an argument or return value that doesn't *actually* match a type declaration but *could* match it. Numeric values get silently converted to strings, and strings that contain numbers get silently converted to the appropriate numeric type.

You can turn off this loosey-goosey default in a particular file by putting `declare(strict_types=1);` at the top of the file. Then, the arguments and return values of any function calls in that file must match the type declarations (but you can still pass an integer as an argument declared as `float`).

You can't enforce strict typing globally. You have to declare it in each file for which you want to use it.

Running Code in Another File

The PHP code examples we've seen so far are mostly self-contained individual files. Any variables or functions that are used are also defined in the same file. As your programs grow, they are easier to manage when you can split the code into different files. The `require` directive tells the PHP engine to load code located in a different file, making it easy to reuse that code in many places.

For example, consider some of the functions defined earlier in this chapter. We could combine them into one file and save it as *restaurant-functions.php*, as shown in Example 5-26.

Example 5-26. Defining functions in their own file

```php
<?php

function restaurant_check($meal, $tax, $tip) {
    $tax_amount = $meal * ($tax / 100);
    $tip_amount = $meal * ($tip / 100);
    $total_amount = $meal + $tax_amount + $tip_amount;

    return $total_amount;
}

function payment_method($cash_on_hand, $amount) {
    if ($amount > $cash_on_hand) {
        return 'credit card';
```

```
    } else {
        return 'cash';
    }
}

?>
```

Assuming Example 5-26 is saved as *restaurant-functions.php*, then another file could reference it, as shown in Example 5-27, with `require 'restaurant-functions.php';`.

Example 5-27. Referencing a separate file

```
require 'restaurant-functions.php';

/* $25 check, plus 8.875% tax, plus 20% tip */
$total_bill = restaurant_check(25, 8.875, 20);

/* I've got $30 */
$cash = 30;

print "I need to pay with " . payment_method($cash, $total_bill);
```

The `require 'restaurant-functions.php';` line in Example 5-27 tells the PHP engine to stop reading the commands in the file it's currently reading, go read all the commands in the *restaurant-functions.php* file, and then come back to the first file and keep going. In this example, *restaurant-functions.php* just defines some functions, but a file loaded with `require` can contain any valid PHP code. If that loaded file contains `print` statements, then the PHP engine will print whatever it's told to print out.

If the `require` statement can't find the file it's told to load, or it does find the file but it doesn't contain valid PHP code, the PHP engine stops running your program. The `include` statement also loads code from another file, but will keep going if there's a problem with the loaded file.

How the PHP Engine Finds Files

If `require` or `include` is given an absolute pathname—one that starts with / on OS X or Linux or with a drive letter or \ on Windows—then the PHP engine just looks in that specific place for the file.

Similarly, if a relative path is provided—starting with ./ for the current directory or ../ for the parent of the current directory—then the PHP only looks in that place for the file.

However, for other filenames or pathnames provided, the PHP engine consults the configuration directive `include_path`. Its value is a list of directories to look in when

---

requiring or including files. If the file can't be found in any of those directories, the PHP engine checks the directory that contains the file doing the requiring or including.

Because organizing your code in separate files makes it easy to reuse common functions and definitions, this book relies on it frequently in subsequent chapters. Using `require` and `include` also opens the door to easily using code libraries written by other people, which is discussed in Chapter 16.

Chapter Summary

This chapter covered:

- Defining functions and calling them in your programs
- Defining a function with mandatory arguments
- Defining a function with optional arguments
- Returning a value from a function
- Understanding variable scope
- Using global variables inside a function
- Understanding type declarations
- Using argument type declarations
- Using return type declarations
- Organizing PHP code in separate files

Exercises

1. Write a function to return an HTML `<img />` tag. The function should accept a mandatory argument of the image URL and optional arguments for `alt` text, `height`, and `width`.

2. Modify the function in the previous exercise so that only the filename is passed to the function in the URL argument. Inside the function, prepend a global variable to the filename to make the full URL. For example, if you pass *photo.png* to the function, and the global variable contains `/images/`, then the `src` attribute of the returned `<img>` tag would be `/images/photo.png`. A function like this is an easy way to keep your image tags correct, even if the images move to a new path or server. Just change the global variable—for example, from `/images/` to `http://images.example.com/`.

3. Put your function from the previous exercise in one file. Then make another file that loads the first file and uses it to print out some `<img />` tags.

4. What does the following code print out?

```php
<?php

function restaurant_check($meal, $tax, $tip) {
    $tax_amount = $meal * ($tax / 100);
    $tip_amount = $meal * ($tip / 100);
    return $meal + $tax_amount + $tip_amount;
}

$cash_on_hand = 31;
$meal = 25;
$tax = 10;
$tip = 10;

while(($cost = restaurant_check($meal,$tax,$tip)) < $cash_on_hand) {
    $tip++;
    print "I can afford a tip of $tip% ($cost)\n";
}

?>
```

5. Web colors such as #ffffff and #cc3399 are made by concatenating the hexa-decimal color values for red, green, and blue. Write a function that accepts deci-mal red, green, and blue arguments and returns a string containing the appropriate color for use in a web page. For example, if the arguments are 255, 0, and 255, then the returned string should be #ff00ff. You may find it helpful to use the built-in function dechex(), which is documented at *http://www.php.net/dechex*.

## CHAPTER 6

Data and Logic Together: Working with Objects

The basics of data and logic that you've seen so far are enough to get lots of things done in PHP. An additional concept—*object-oriented programming*, which combines data with the logic that operates on it—helps to organize your code. In particular, objects are great for making reusable bundles of code, so being familiar with how they work will make it easier to use lots of existing PHP add-ons and libraries.

In the programming world, an *object* is a structure that combines data about a thing (such as the ingredients in an entrée) with actions on that thing (such as determining if a certain ingredient is in the entrée). Using objects in a program provides an organizational structure for grouping related variables and functions together.

Here are some basic terms to know when working with objects:

Class

A template or recipe that describes the variables and functions for a kind of object. For example, an `Entree` class would contain variables that hold its name and ingredients. The functions in an `Entree` class would be for things such as cooking the entrée, serving it, and determining whether a particular ingredient is in it.

Method
A function defined in a class.

Property
A variable defined in a class.

Instance

An individual usage of a class. If you are serving three entrées for dinner in your program, you would create three instances of the Entree class. While each of these instances is based on the same class, they differ internally by having different property values. The methods in each instance contain the same instructions, but probably produce different results because they each rely on the particular property values in their instance. Creating a new instance of a class is called "instantiating an object."

Constructor

A special method that is automatically run when an object is instantiated. Usually, constructors set up object properties and do other housekeeping that makes the object ready for use.

Static method

A special kind of method that can be called without instantiating a class. Static methods don't depend on the property values of a particular instance.

Object Basics

Example 6-1 defines an Entree class to represent an entrée.

Example 6-1. Defining a class

```
class Entree {
    public $name;
    public $ingredients = array();

    public function hasIngredient($ingredient) {
        return in_array($ingredient, $this->ingredients);
    }
}
```

In Example 6-1, the class definition starts with the special keyword class followed by the name we're giving to the class. After the class name, everything between the curly braces is the definition of the class—the properties and methods of the class. This class has two properties ($name and $ingredients) and one method (hasIngredient()). The public keyword tells the PHP engine which parts of your program are allowed to access the particular property or method the keyword is attached to. We'll get into that later, in "Property and Method Visibility" on page 113.

The hasIngredient() method looks mostly like a regular function definition, but its body contains something new: $this. This is a special variable that refers to whatever instance of a class is calling the function. Example 6-2 shows this in action with two different instances.

Example 6-2. Creating and using objects

```
// Create an instance and assign it to $soup
$soup = new Entree;
// Set $soup's properties
$soup->name = 'Chicken Soup';
$soup->ingredients = array('chicken', 'water');

// Create a separate instance and assign it to $sandwich
$sandwich = new Entree;
// Set $sandwich's properties
$sandwich->name = 'Chicken Sandwich';
$sandwich->ingredients = array('chicken', 'bread');


foreach (['chicken','lemon','bread','water'] as $ing) {
    if ($soup->hasIngredient($ing)) {
        print "Soup contains $ing.\n";
    }
    if ($sandwich->hasIngredient($ing)) {
        print "Sandwich contains $ing.\n";
    }
}
```

The new operator returns a new Entree object, so in Example 6-2, $soup and $sandwich each refer to different instances of the Entree class.

The arrow operator (->), composed of a hyphen and a greater-than sign, is your road to the properties (variables) and methods (functions) inside an object. To access a property, put the arrow after the object's name and put the property after the arrow. To call a method, put the method name after the arrow, followed by the parentheses that indicate a function call.

Note that the arrow operator used to access properties and methods is different from the operator that separates array keys and values in array() or foreach(). The array arrow has an equals sign: =>. The object arrow has a hyphen: ->.

Assigning a value to a property works just like assigning a value to any other variable, but with the arrow syntax to indicate the property name. The expression $soup->name means "the name property inside the object instance that the $soup variable holds," and the expression $sandwich->ingredients means "the ingredients property inside the object instance that the $sandwich variable holds."

Inside the foreach() loop, each object's hasIngredient() method gets called. The method is passed the name of an ingredient, and it returns whether or not that ingredient is in the object's ingredient list. Here you can see how the special $this variable works. When $soup->hasIngredient() is called, $this refers to $soup inside the body of hasIngredient(). When $sandwich->hasIngredient() is called, $this refers to $sandwich. The $this variable doesn't always refer to the same object instance, but instead refers to the instance the method is being called on. This means that when Example 6-2 runs, it prints:

```
Soup contains chicken.
Sandwich contains chicken.
Sandwich contains bread.
Soup contains water.
```

In Example 6-2, when $ing is chicken, then both $soup->hasIngredient($ing) and $sandwich->hasIngredient($ing) return true. Both objects' $ingredients properties contain an element with the value chicken. But only $soup->ingredients has water and only $sandwich->ingredients has bread. Neither object has lemon in its $ingredients property.

Classes can also contain static methods. These methods cannot use the $this variable since they do not get run in the context of a specific object instance, but on the class itself. Static methods are useful for behavior that is relevant to what the class is for, but not to any one object. Example 6-3 adds a static method to Entree that returns a list of possible entrée sizes.

Example 6-3. Defining a static method

```
class Entree {
    public $name;
    public $ingredients = array();

    public function hasIngredient($ingredient) {
        return in_array($ingredient, $this->ingredients);
    }

    public static function getSizes() {
        return array('small','medium','large');
    }
}
```

The declaration of the static method in Example 6-3 is similar to other method definitions, with the addition of the static keyword before function. To call a static method, you put :: between the class name and the method name instead of ->, as shown in Example 6-4.

Example 6-4. Calling a static method

```
$sizes = Entree::getSizes();
```

Constructors

A class can have a special method, called a *constructor*, which is run when the object is created. Constructors typically handle setup and housekeeping tasks that make the object ready to use. For example, we can change the Entree class and give it a constructor. This constructor accepts two arguments: the name of the entrée and the ingredient list. By passing those values to the constructor, we avoid having to set the properties after the object is created. In PHP, the constructor method of a class is always called __construct(). Example 6-5 shows the changed class with its constructor method.

Example 6-5. Initializing an object with a constructor

```php
class Entree {
    public $name;
    public $ingredients = array();

    public function __construct($name, $ingredients) {
        $this->name = $name;
        $this->ingredients = $ingredients;
    }

    public function hasIngredient($ingredient) {
        return in_array($ingredient, $this->ingredients);
    }
}
```

In Example 6-5, you can see that the __construct() method accepts two arguments and assigns their values to the properties of the class. The fact that the argument names match the property names is just a convenience—the PHP engine doesn't require that they match. Inside a constructor, the $this keyword refers to the specific object instance being constructed.

To pass arguments to the constructor, treat the class name like a function name when you invoke the new operator by putting parentheses and argument values after it. Example 6-6 shows our class with the constructor in action by creating $soup and $sandwich objects identical to what we've used previously.

Example 6-6. Calling constructors

```php
// Some soup with name and ingredients
$soup = new Entree('Chicken Soup', array('chicken', 'water'));

// A sandwich with name and ingredients
$sandwich = new Entree('Chicken Sandwich', array('chicken', 'bread'));
```

The constructor is invoked by the new operator as part of what the PHP engine does to create a new object, but the constructor itself doesn't create the object. This means that the constructor function doesn't return a value and can't use a return value to signal that something went wrong. That is a job for *exceptions*, discussed in the next section.

Indicating a Problem with Exceptions

In Example 6-5, what happens if something other than an array is passed in as the $ingredients argument? As the code is written in Example 6-5, nothing! $this->ingredients is assigned the value of $ingredients no matter what it is. But if it's not an array, this causes problems when hasIngredient() is called—that method assumes the $ingredients property is an array.

Constructors are great for verifying that supplied arguments are the right type or otherwise appropriate. But they need a way to complain if there is a problem. This is where an *exception* comes in. An exception is a special object that can be used to indicate that something exceptional has happened. Creating an exception interrupts the PHP engine and sets it on a different code path.

Example 6-7 modifies the Entree constructor to throw an exception if the $ingredients argument is not an array. ("Throwing" an exception means you use an exception tell the PHP engine that something went wrong.)

Example 6-7. Throwing an exception

```
class Entree {
    public $name;
    public $ingredients = array();

    public function __construct($name, $ingredients) {
        if (! is_array($ingredients)) {
            throw new Exception('$ingredients must be an array');
        }
        $this->name = $name;
        $this->ingredients = $ingredients;
    }

    public function hasIngredient($ingredient) {
        return in_array($ingredient, $this->ingredients);
    }
}
```

Exceptions are represented by the Exception class. The first argument to Exception's constructor is a string describing what went wrong. So, the line throw new

Exception('$ingredients must be an array'); creates a new `Exception` object and then hands it to the `throw` construct in order to interrupt the PHP engine.

If `$ingredients` is an array, then the code runs just as before. If it's not an array, then the exception is thrown. Example 6-8 shows the creation of an `Entree` object with a bad `$ingredients` argument.

Example 6-8. Causing an exception to be thrown

```
$drink = new Entree('Glass of Milk', 'milk');
if ($drink->hasIngredient('milk')) {
    print "Yummy!";
}
```

Example 6-8 displays an error message like this (assuming the code is in a file named *exception-use.php* and the `Entree` class definition is in a file named *construct-exception.php*):

```
PHP Fatal error:  Uncaught Exception: $ingredients must be an array
in construct-exception.php:9
Stack trace:
#0 exception-use.php(2): Entree->__construct('Glass of Milk', 'milk')
#1 {main}
  thrown in construct-exception.php on line 9
```

In that error output, there are two separate things to recognize. The first is the error message from the PHP engine: `PHP Fatal error: Uncaught exception 'Exception' with message '$ingredients must be an array' in construct-exception.php:9`. This means that in line 9 of *construct-exception.php* (the file defining the `Entree` class), an exception was thrown. Because there was no additional code to deal with that exception (we'll see how to do that shortly), it's called "uncaught" and causes the PHP engine to come to a screaming halt—a "fatal" error that stops program execution immediately.

The second thing in that error output is a *stack trace*: a list of all the functions that were active when the PHP engine stopped. Here there's just one: the `Entree` constructor that got called from `new Entree`. The `{main}` line in the stack trace represents the first level of program execution before anything else runs. You'll always see that at the bottom of any stack trace.

It's good that we prevented `hasIngredient()` from getting called so it doesn't operate on a non-array of ingredients, but completely stopping the program with such a harsh error message is overkill. The flip side of throwing exceptions is *catching* them —grabbing the exception before the PHP engine gets it and bails out.

To handle an exception yourself, do two things:

1. Put the code that might throw an exception inside a `try` block.
2. Put a `catch` block after the potentially exception-throwing code in order to handle the problem.

Example 6-9 adds `try` and `catch` blocks to deal with the exception.

Example 6-9. Handling an exception

```
try {
    $drink = new Entree('Glass of Milk', 'milk');
    if ($drink->hasIngredient('milk')) {
        print "Yummy!";
    }
} catch (Exception $e) {
    print "Couldn't create the drink: " . $e->getMessage();
}
```

In Example 6-9, the `try` and `catch` blocks work together. Each of the statements inside the `try` block is run, stopping if an exception is encountered. If that happens, the PHP engine jumps down to the `catch` block, setting the variable $e to hold the `Exception` object that was created. The code inside the `catch` block uses the `Exception` class's `getMessage()` method to retrieve the text of the message given to the exception when it was created. Example 6-9 prints:

```
Couldn't create the drink: $ingredients must be an array
```

Extending an Object

One of the aspects of objects that make them so helpful for organizing your code is the notion of *subclassing*, which lets you reuse a class while adding some custom functionality. A subclass (sometimes called a *child class*) starts with all the methods and properties of an existing class (the *parent class*), but then can change them or add its own.

For example, consider an entrée that is not just a single dish but a combination of a few, such as a bowl of soup and a sandwich together. Our existing `Entree` class would be forced to model this either by treating "soup" and "sandwich" as ingredients or by enumerating all of the soup ingredients and sandwich ingredients as ingredients of this combo. Neither solution is ideal: soup and sandwich themselves are not ingredients, and reenumerating all the ingredients would mean we would need to update multiple places when any ingredient changed.

We can solve the problem more cleanly by making a subclass of `Entree` that expects to be given `Entree` object instances as ingredients and then modifying the subclass's `hasIngredient()` method to inspect those object instances for ingredients. The code for this `ComboMeal` class is shown in Example 6-10.

Example 6-10. Extending the Entree class

```
class ComboMeal extends Entree {

    public function hasIngredient($ingredient) {
        foreach ($this->ingredients as $entree) {
            if ($entree->hasIngredient($ingredient)) {
                return true;
            }
        }
        return false;
    }
}
```

In Example 6-10, the class name, `ComboMeal`, is followed by `extends Entree`. This tells the PHP engine that the `ComboMeal` class should inherit all of the methods and properties of the `Entree` class. To the PHP engine, it's as if you retyped the definition of `Entree` inside the definition of `ComboMeal`, but you get that without actually having to do all that tedious typing. Then, the only things that need to be inside the curly braces of `ComboMeal`'s definition are changes or additions. In this case, the only change is a new `hasIngredient()` method. Instead of examining `$this->ingredients` as an array, it treats it as an array of `Entree` objects and calls the `hasIngredient()` method on each of those objects. If any of those calls return `true`, it means that one of the entrées in the combo has the specified ingredient, so `Combo Meal`'s `hasIngredient()` method returns `true`. If, after iterating through all of the entrées, nothing has returned `true`, then the method returns `false`, which means that no entrée has the ingredient in it. Example 6-11 shows the subclass at work.

Example 6-11. Using a subclass

```
// Some soup with name and ingredients
$soup = new Entree('Chicken Soup', array('chicken', 'water'));

// A sandwich with name and ingredients
$sandwich = new Entree('Chicken Sandwich', array('chicken', 'bread'));

// A combo meal
$combo = new ComboMeal('Soup + Sandwich', array($soup, $sandwich));

foreach (['chicken','water','pickles'] as $ing) {
    if ($combo->hasIngredient($ing)) {
        print "Something in the combo contains $ing.\n";
    }
}
```

Because both the soup and the sandwich contain chicken, the soup contains water, but neither contains pickles, Example 6-11 prints:

```
Something in the combo contains chicken.
Something in the combo contains water.
```

This works well, but we don't have any guarantee that the items passed to ComboMeal's constructor are really Entree objects. If they're not, then invoking hasIngredient() on them could cause an error. To fix this, we need to add a custom constructor to ComboMeal that checks this condition and also invokes the regular Entree constructor so that the properties are set properly. A version of ComboMeal with this constructor is shown in Example 6-12.

Example 6-12. Putting a constructor in a subclass

```
class ComboMeal extends Entree {

    public function __construct($name, $entrees) {
        parent::__construct($name, $entrees);
        foreach ($entrees as $entree) {
            if (! $entree instanceof Entree) {
                throw new Exception('Elements of $entrees must be Entree objects');
            }
        }
    }

    public function hasIngredient($ingredient) {
        foreach ($this->ingredients as $entree) {
            if ($entree->hasIngredient($ingredient)) {
                return true;
            }
        }
        return false;
    }
}
```

The constructor in Example 6-12 uses the special syntax parent::__construct() to refer to the constructor in Entree. Just as $this has a special meaning inside of object methods, so does parent. It refers to the class of which the current class is a subclass. Because ComboMeal extends Entree, parent inside of ComboMeal refers to Entree. So, parent::__construct() inside of ComboMeal refers to the __construct() method inside the Entree class.

In subclass constructors, it is important to remember that you have to call the parent constructor explicitly. If you leave out the call to parent::__construct(), the parent constructor never gets called and its presumably important behavior never gets executed by the PHP engine. In this case, Entree's constructor makes sure that $ingredients is an array and sets the $name and $ingredients properties.

After the call to `parent::__construct()`, ComboMeal's constructor ensures that each provided ingredient of the combo is itself an Entree object. It uses the instanceof operator for this. The expression `$entree instanceof Entree` evaluates to true if $entree refers to an object instance of the Entree class.[1] If any of the provided ingredients (which, for a ComboMeal, are really entrées) are not Entree objects, then the code throws an exception.

Property and Method Visibility

The ComboMeal constructor in Example 6-12 does a great job of ensuring that a ComboMeal is only given instances of Entree to be its ingredients. But what happens after that? Subsequent code could change the value of the $ingredients property to anything—an array of non-Entrees, a number, or even false.

We prevent this problem by changing the *visibility* of the properties. Instead of public, we can label them as private or protected. These other visibility settings don't change what code inside the class can do—it can always read or write its own properties. The private visibility prevents any code outside the class from accessing the property. The protected visibility means that the only code outside the class that can access the property is code in subclasses.

Example 6-13 shows a modified version of the Entree class in which the $name property is private and the $ingredients property is protected.

Example 6-13. Changing property visibility

```
class Entree {
    private $name;
    protected $ingredients = array();

    /* Since $name is private, this provides a way to read it */
    public function getName() {
        return $this->name;
    }

    public function __construct($name, $ingredients) {
        if (! is_array($ingredients)) {
            throw new Exception('$ingredients must be an array');
        }
        $this->name = $name;
        $this->ingredients = $ingredients;
    }
```

---

1 The instanceof operator also evaluates to true if the provided object is a subclass of the provided class name. This code will work, for example, with combo meals made up of other combo meals.

```
    public function hasIngredient($ingredient) {
        return in_array($ingredient, $this->ingredients);
    }
}
```

Because $name is `private` in Example 6-13, there is no way to read or change it from code outside `Entree`. The added `getName()` method provides a way for non-`Entree` code to get the value of $name, though. This kind of method is called an *accessor*. It provides access to a property that would otherwise be forbidden. In this case, the combination of `private` visibility and an accessor that returns the property value lets any code read the value of $name, but nothing outside of `Entree` can change $name's value once it's been set.

The $ingredients property, on the other hand, is `protected`, which allows access to $ingredients from subclasses. This ensures that the `hasIngredient()` method in `ComboMeal` works properly.

The same visibility settings apply equally to methods as well as properties. Methods marked `public` may be invoked by any code. Methods marked `private` may be invoked only by other code inside the same class. Methods marked `protected` may be invoked only by other code inside the same class or inside subclasses.

Namespaces

Beginning with version 5.4, the PHP engine lets you organize your code into *namespaces*. Namespaces provide a way to group related code and ensure that names of classes that you've written don't collide with identically named classes written by someone else.[2]

Getting comfortable with namespaces is important so you can incorporate packages written by others into your programs. Chapter 16 goes into detail about using the Composer package management system. This section familiarizes you with the syntax of namespaces.

Think of a namespace as a container that can hold class definitions or other namespaces. It's a syntactic convenience, rather than providing new functionality. When you see the `namespace` keyword or some backslashes in what appears to be a class name, you've encountered a PHP namespace.

To define a class inside a particular namespace, use the `namespace` keyword at the top of a file with a namespace name. Then, a class definition later in the file will define

---

2 Namespaces cover functions and some other things that are not classes, but this section just explores namespaces with classes.

the class inside that namespace. Example 6-14 defines a Fruit class inside the Tiny namespace.

Example 6-14. Defining a class in a namespace

```
namespace Tiny;

class Fruit {
    public static function munch($bite) {
      print "Here is a tiny munch of $bite.";
    }
}
```

To use a class defined in a namespace, you need to incorporate the namespace into how you refer to the class. The most unambiguous way to do this is to begin with \ (the top-level namespace), then write the name of the namespace the class is in, then add another \, then write the class name. For example, to invoke munch() on the Fruit class defined in Example 6-14, write:

```
\Tiny\Fruit::munch("banana");
```

Namespaces can also hold other namespaces. If Example 6-14 began with namespace Tiny\Eating;, then you'd refer to the class as \Tiny\Eating\Fruit.

Without that leading \, how a reference to a class gets resolved depends on the *current namespace*—whatever namespace is active at the time of the reference. In a PHP file with no namespace declaration at the top, the current namespace is the top-level namespace. Class names behave like regular class names that you've encountered so far without namespaces. The namespace keyword, however, changes the current namespace. A declaration of namespace Tiny; changes the current namespace to Tiny. That's why the class Fruit definition in Example 6-14 puts the Fruit class inside the Tiny namespace.

However, this also means that any *other* class name reference in that file is resolved relative to the Tiny namespace. A method inside the Tiny\Fruit class that contains the code $soup = new Entree('Chicken Soup', array('chicken','water')); tells the PHP engine to look for an Entree class *inside* the Tiny namespace. It's as if the code were written as $soup = new \Tiny\Entree('Chicken Soup', array('chicken','water'));. To unambiguously refer to a class in the top-level namespace, you need a leading \ before the class name.

Typing all those backslashes and namespace names over and over again is painful. The PHP engine gives you the use keyword to simplify things. Example 6-15 shows how to use use.

Example 6-15. Using the use keyword

```php
use Tiny\Eating\Fruit as Snack;

use Tiny\Fruit;

// This calls \Tiny\Eating\Fruit::munch();
Snack::munch("strawberry");

// This calls \Tiny\Fruit::munch();
Fruit::munch("orange");
```

Writing use Tiny\Eating\Fruit as Snack; tells the PHP engine, "For the rest of this file, when I say Snack as a class name, I really mean \Tiny\Eating\Fruit." Without the as, the PHP engine infers the "nickname" for the class from the last element of what is given to use. So, use Tiny\Fruit; tells the PHP engine, "For the rest of this file, when I say Fruit as a class name, I really mean \Tiny\Fruit."

These kinds of use declarations are especially helpful with many modern PHP frameworks that put their various classes into namespaces and subnamespaces. With a few use lines at the top of your file, you can transform verbose incantations such as \Symfony\Component\HttpFoundation\Response to a more concise Response.

Chapter Summary

This chapter covered:

- Understanding how objects help you organize your code
- Defining a class with methods and properties
- Creating an object with the new operator
- Accessing methods and properties with the arrow operator
- Defining and calling a static method
- Initializing an object with a constructor
- Throwing an exception to indicate a problem
- Catching an exception to handle the problem
- Extending a class with a subclass
- Controlling access to properties and methods by changing visibility
- Organizing code into namespaces

Exercises

1. Create a class called `Ingredient`. Each instance of this class represents a single ingredient. The instance should keep track of an ingredient's name and its cost.
2. Add a method to your `IngredientCost` class that changes the cost of an ingredient.
3. Make a subclass of the `Entree` class used in this chapter that accepts `Ingredient` objects instead of string ingredient names to specify the ingredients. Give your `Entree` subclass a method that returns the total cost of the entrée.
4. Put your `Ingredient` class into its own namespace and modify your other code that uses `IngredientCost` to work properly.

## CHAPTER 7

Exchanging Information with Users: Making Web Forms

Form processing is an essential component of almost any web application. *Forms* are how users communicate with your server: signing up for a new account, searching a forum for all the posts about a particular subject, retrieving a lost password, finding a nearby restaurant or shoemaker, or buying a book.

Using a form in a PHP program is a two-step activity. Step one is to display the form. This involves constructing HTML that has tags for the appropriate user-interface elements in it, such as text boxes, checkboxes, and buttons. If you're not familiar with the HTML required to create forms, the "HTML Forms" chapter in Elisabeth Robson and Eric Freeman's *Head First HTML and CSS* (O'Reilly) is a good place to start.

When a user sees a page with a form in it, she inputs the requested information into the form and then clicks a button or hits Enter to send the form information back to your server. Processing that submitted form information is step two of the operation.

Example 7-1 is a page that says "Hello" to a user. If the page is loaded in response to a form submission, then it displays a greeting. Otherwise, the page displays a form with which a user can submit her name.

Example 7-1. Saying "Hello"

```
if ('POST' == $_SERVER['REQUEST_METHOD']) {
    print "Hello, ". $_POST['my_name'];
} else {
    print<<<_HTML_
<form method="post" action="$_SERVER[PHP_SELF]">
 Your name: <input type="text" name="my_name" >
<br>
<input type="submit" value="Say Hello">
```

```
</form>
_HTML_;
}
```

Remember the client and server communication picture from Chapter 1? Figure 7-1 shows the client and server communication necessary to display and process the form in Example 7-1. The first request-and-response pair causes the browser to display the form. In the second request-and-response pair, the server processes the submitted form data and the browser displays the results.

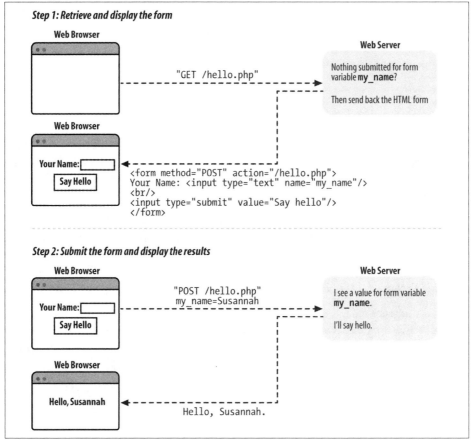

Figure 7-1. Displaying and processing a simple form

The response to the first request is some HTML for a form. Figure 7-2 shows what the browser displays when it receives that response.

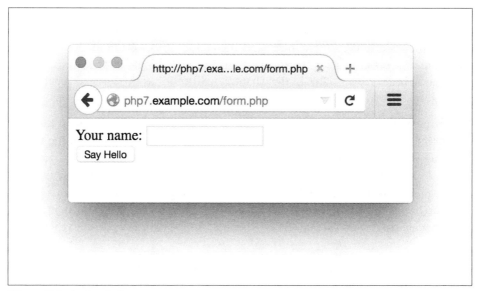

Figure 7-2. A simple form

The response to the second request is the result of processing the submitted form data. Figure 7-3 shows the output when the form is submitted with Susannah typed in the text box.

Figure 7-3. The form, submitted

The pattern in Example 7-1 of "if form data has been submitted, process it; otherwise, print out a form" is common in simple programs. When you're building a basic form, putting the code to display the form and the code to process the form in the same page makes it easier to keep the form and its associated logic in sync. As we get to more complicated forms later in this chapter, we'll split out the form to separate the display and the processing logic into separate files.

The form submission is sent back to the same URL that was used to request the form in the first place. This is because of the special variable that is the value of the `action` attribute in the `<form>` tag: `$_SERVER['PHP_SELF']`. The `$_SERVER` auto-global array holds a variety of information about your server and the current request the PHP engine is processing. The `PHP_SELF` element of `$_SERVER` holds the pathname part of the current request's URL. For example, if a PHP script is accessed at *http:// www.example.com/store/catalog.php*, `$_SERVER['PHP_SELF']` is `/store/catalog.php`[1] in that page.

The simple form also makes use of `$_SERVER['REQUEST_METHOD']`. This array element is the HTTP method that the web browser used to request the current page. For regular web pages, it is almost always either `GET` or `POST`. A `GET` usually means a regular page retrieval and a `POST` is a form submission. The value of `$_SERVER['REQUEST_METHOD']` is always uppercase, no matter how the value of the `action` attribute in the `<form>` tag is written.

So, testing whether `$_SERVER['REQUEST_METHOD']` is `POST` lets us check whether the form was submitted or it was a regular page request.

The `$_POST` array is an auto-global variable that holds submitted form data. The keys in `$_POST` are the form element names, and the corresponding values in `$_POST` are the values of the form elements. Typing your name into the text box in Example 7-1 and clicking the submit button makes the value of `$_POST['my_name']` whatever you typed into the text box because the `name` attribute of the text box is `my_name`.

The structure of Example 7-1 is the kernel of the form processing material in this chapter. However, it has a flaw: printing unmodified external input—as `print "Hello, ". $_POST['my_name'];` does with the value of the `my_name` form parameter —is dangerous. Data that comes from outside of your program, such as a submitted form parameter, can contain embedded HTML or JavaScript. "HTML and JavaScript" on page 138 explains how to make your program safer by cleaning up external input.

---

1 As discussed in Example 4-19, the array element `$_SERVER['PHP_SELF']` goes in the here document without quotes around the key for its value to be interpolated properly.

The rest of this chapter provides details about the various aspects of form handling. "Accessing Form Parameters" on page 124 dives into the specifics of handling different kinds of form input, such as form parameters that can submit multiple values. "Form Processing with Functions" on page 127 lays out a flexible, function-based structure for working with forms that simplifies some form maintenance tasks. This function-based structure also lets you check the submitted form data to make sure it doesn't contain anything unexpected. "Validating Data" on page 129 explains the different ways you can check submitted form data. "Displaying Default Values" on page 142 demonstrates how to supply default values for form elements and preserve user-entered values when you redisplay a form. Finally, "Putting It All Together" on page 144 shows a complete form that incorporates everything in the chapter: function-based organization, validation and display of error messages, defaults and preserving user input, and processing submitted data.

Useful Server Variables

In addition to `PHP_SELF` and `REQUEST_METHOD`, the `$_SERVER` auto-global array contains a number of useful elements that provide information on the web server and the current request. Table 7-1 lists some of them.

Table 7-1. Entries in $_SERVER

Element	Example	Description
QUERY_STRING	category=kitchen&price=5	The part of the URL after the question mark where the URL parameters live. The example query string shown is for the URL *http://www.example.com/catalog/store.php?category=kitchen&price=5*.
PATH_INFO	/browse	Extra path information tacked onto the end of the URL after a slash. This is a way to pass information to a script without using the query string. The example PATH_INFO shown is for the URL *http://www.example.com/catalog/store.php/browse*.
SERVER_NAME	www.example.com	The name of the website on which the PHP engine is running. If the web server hosts many different virtual domains, this is the name of the particular virtual domain that is being accessed.
DOCUMENT_ROOT	/usr/local/htdocs	The directory on the web server computer that holds the documents available on the website. If the document root is */usr/local/htdocs* for the website *http://www.example.com*, then a request for *http://www.example.com/catalog/store.php* corresponds to the file */usr/local/htdocs/catalog/store.php*.
REMOTE_ADDR	175.56.28.3	The IP address of the user making the request to your web server.

Element	Example	Description
REMOTE_HOST	pool0560.cvx.dialup.verizon.net	If your web server is configured to translate user IP addresses into hostnames, this is the hostname of the user making the request to your web server. Because this address-to-name translation is relatively expensive (in terms of computational time), most web servers do not do it.
HTTP_REFERER[a]	http://shop.oreilly.com/product/0636920029335.do	If someone clicked on a link to reach the current URL, HTTP_REFERER contains the URL of the page that contained the link. This value can be faked, so don't use it as your sole criterion for giving access to private web pages. It can, however, be useful for finding out who's linking to you.
HTTP_USER_AGENT	Mozilla/5.0 (Macintosh; Intel Mac OS X 10.10; rv: 37.0) Gecko/20100101 Firefox/37.0	The web browser that retrieved the page. The example value is the signature of Firefox 37 running on OS X. Like with HTTP_REFERER, this value can be faked, but is useful for analysis.

[a] The correct spelling is HTTP_REFERRER. But it was misspelled in an early Internet specification document, so you frequently see the three-R version when web programming.

Accessing Form Parameters

At the beginning of every request, the PHP engine sets up some auto-global arrays that contain the values of any parameters submitted in a form or passed in the URL. URL and form parameters from GET method forms are put into $_GET. Form parameters from POST method forms are put into $_POST.

The URL *http://www.example.com/catalog.php?product_id=21&category=fryingpan* puts two values into $_GET:

- $_GET['product_id'] is set to 21
- $_GET['category'] is set to fryingpan

Submitting the form in Example 7-2 causes the same values to be put into $_POST, assuming 21 is entered in the text box and Frying Pan is selected from the menu.

Example 7-2. A two-element form

```
<form method="POST" action="catalog.php">
<input type="text" name="product_id">
<select name="category">
<option value="ovenmitt">Pot Holder</option>
<option value="fryingpan">Frying Pan</option>
<option value="torch">Kitchen Torch</option>
</select>
<input type="submit" name="submit">
</form>
```

Example 7-3 incorporates the form in Example 7-2 into a complete PHP program that prints the appropriate values from $_POST after displaying the form. Because the action attribute of the <form> tag in Example 7-3 is catalog.php, you need to save the program in a file called *catalog.php* on your web server. If you save it in a file with a different name, adjust the action attribute accordingly.

Example 7-3. Printing submitted form parameters

```
<form method="POST" action="catalog.php">
<input type="text" name="product_id">
<select name="category">
<option value="ovenmitt">Pot Holder</option>
<option value="fryingpan">Frying Pan</option>
<option value="torch">Kitchen Torch</option>
</select>
<input type="submit" name="submit">
</form>
Here are the submitted values:

product_id: <?php print $_POST['product_id'] ?? '' ?>
<br/>
category: <?php print $_POST['category'] ?? '' ?>
```

To avoid a warning message from PHP when no POST variables have been submitted, Example 7-3 uses ??, the *null coalesce* operator.

The code $_POST['product_id'] ?? '' evaluates to whatever's in $_POST['product_id'] if there's something there, or the empty string ('') otherwise. Without it, you'd see messages like PHP Notice: Undefined index: product_id when the page is retrieved by the GET method and no POST variables have been set up.

 The null coalesce operator was introduced in PHP 7. If you're using an older version of PHP, use isset() instead:

```
if (isset($_POST['product_id'])) {
    print $_POST['product_id'];
}
```

A form element that can have multiple values needs to have a name that ends in []. This tells the PHP engine to treat the multiple values as array elements. The <select> menu in Example 7-4 has its submitted values put into $_POST['lunch'].

Example 7-4. Multiple-valued form elements

```
<form method="POST" action="eat.php">
<select name="lunch[]" multiple>
<option value="pork">BBQ Pork Bun</option>
```

```
<option value="chicken">Chicken Bun</option>
<option value="lotus">Lotus Seed Bun</option>
<option value="bean">Bean Paste Bun</option>
<option value="nest">Bird-Nest Bun</option>
</select>
<input type="submit" name="submit">
</form>
```

If the form in Example 7-4 is submitted with `Chicken Bun` and `Bird-Nest Bun` selected, then `$_POST['lunch']` becomes a two-element array, with element values `chicken` and `nest`. Access these values using the regular multidimensional array syntax. Example 7-5 incorporates the form from Example 7-4 into a complete program that prints out each value selected in the menu. (The same rule applies here to the filename and the `action` attribute. Save the code in Example 7-5 in a file called *eat.php* or adjust the `action` attribute of the `<form>` tag to the correct filename.)

Example 7-5. Accessing multiple submitted values

```
<form method="POST" action="eat.php">
<select name="lunch[]" multiple>
<option value="pork">BBQ Pork Bun</option>
<option value="chicken">Chicken Bun</option>
<option value="lotus">Lotus Seed Bun</option>
<option value="bean">Bean Paste Bun</option>
<option value="nest">Bird-Nest Bun</option>
</select>
<input type="submit" name="submit">
</form>
Selected buns:
<br/>
<?php
if (isset($_POST['lunch'])) {
    foreach ($_POST['lunch'] as $choice) {
        print "You want a $choice bun. <br/>";
    }
}
?>
```

With `Chicken Bun` and `Bird-Nest Bun` selected in the menu, Example 7-5 prints (after the form):

```
Selected buns:
You want a chicken bun.
You want a nest bun.
```

You can think of a form element named `lunch[]` as translating into the following PHP code when the form is submitted (assuming the submitted values for the form element are `chicken` and `nest`):

```
$_POST['lunch'][] = 'chicken';
$_POST['lunch'][] = 'nest';
```

As you saw in Example 4-6, this syntax adds an element to the end of an array.

Form Processing with Functions

The basic form in Example 7-1 can be made more flexible by putting the display code and the processing code in separate functions. Example 7-6 is a version of Example 7-1 with functions.

Example 7-6. Saying "Hello" with functions

```
// Logic to do the right thing based on
// the request method
if ($_SERVER['REQUEST_METHOD'] == 'POST') {
    process_form();
} else {
    show_form();
}

// Do something when the form is submitted
function process_form() {
    print "Hello, ". $_POST['my_name'];
}

// Display the form
function show_form() {
    print<<<_HTML_
<form method="POST" action="$_SERVER[PHP_SELF]">
Your name: <input type="text" name="my_name">
<br/>
<input type="submit" value="Say Hello">
</form>
_HTML_;
}
```

To change the form or what happens when it's submitted, change the body of `process_form()` or `show_form()`.

Breaking up the form processing and display into functions also makes it easy to add a data validation stage. Data validation, covered in detail in "Validating Data" on page 129, is an essential part of any web application that accepts input from a form. Data should be validated after a form is submitted, but before it is processed. Example 7-7 adds a validation function to Example 7-6.

Example 7-7. Validating form data

```
// Logic to do the right thing based on
// the request method
if ($_SERVER['REQUEST_METHOD'] == 'POST') {
    if (validate_form()) {
        process_form();
    } else {
        show_form();
    }
} else {
    show_form();
}

// Do something when the form is submitted
function process_form() {
    print "Hello, ". $_POST['my_name'];
}

// Display the form
function show_form() {
    print<<<_HTML_
<form method="POST" action="$_SERVER[PHP_SELF]">
Your name: <input type="text" name="my_name">
<br/>
<input type="submit" value="Say Hello">
</form>
_HTML_;
}

// Check the form data
function validate_form() {
    // Is my_name at least 3 characters long?
    if (strlen($_POST['my_name']) < 3) {
        return false;
    } else {
        return true;
    }
}
```

The validate_form() function in Example 7-7 returns false if $_POST['my_name'] is less than three characters long, and returns true otherwise. At the top of the page, validate_form() is called when the form is submitted. If it returns true, then process_form() is called. Otherwise, show_form() is called. This means that if you submit the form with a name that's at least three characters long, such as Bob or Bartholomew, the same thing happens as in previous examples: a Hello, Bob or Hello, Bartholomew message is displayed. If you submit a short name such as BJ or leave the text box blank, then validate_form() returns false and process_form() is never called. Instead show_form() is called and the form is redisplayed.

Example 7-7 doesn't tell you what's wrong if you enter a name that doesn't pass the test in `validate_form()`. Ideally, when someone submits data that fails a validation test, you should explain the error when you redisplay the form and, if appropriate, redisplay the value entered inside the appropriate form element. The following section shows you how to display error messages, and "Displaying Default Values" on page 142 explains how to safely redisplay user-entered values.

Validating Data

Data validation is one of the most important parts of a web application. Weird, wrong, and damaging data shows up where you least expect it. Users can be careless, malicious, and fabulously more creative (often accidentally) than you may ever imagine when you are designing your application. Even a a *Clockwork Orange*–style forced viewing of a filmstrip on the dangers of unvalidated data would not over-emphasize how crucial it is that you stringently validate any piece of data coming into your application from an external source. Some of these external sources are obvious: most of the input to your application is probably coming from a web form. But there are lots of other ways data can flow into your programs as well: databases that you share with other people or applications, web services and remote servers, even URLs and their parameters.

As mentioned earlier, Example 7-7 doesn't indicate what's wrong with the form if the check in `validate_form()` fails. Example 7-8 alters `validate_form()` and `show_form()` to manipulate and print an array of possible error messages.

Example 7-8. Displaying error messages with the form

```
// Logic to do the right thing based on
// the request method
if ($_SERVER['REQUEST_METHOD'] == 'POST') {
    // If validate_form() returns errors, pass them to show_form()
    if ($form_errors = validate_form()) {
        show_form($form_errors);
    } else {
        process_form();
    }
} else {
    show_form();
}

// Do something when the form is submitted
function process_form() {
    print "Hello, ". $_POST['my_name'];
}

// Display the form
function show_form($errors = ) {
```

```
    // If some errors were passed in, print them out
    if ($errors) {
        print 'Please correct these errors: <ul><li>';
        print implode('</li><li>', $errors);
        print '</li></ul>';
    }

    print<<<_HTML_
<form method="POST" action="$_SERVER[PHP_SELF]">
Your name: <input type="text" name="my_name">
<br/>
<input type="submit" value="Say Hello">
</form>
_HTML_;
}

// Check the form data
function validate_form() {
    // Start with an empty array of error messages
    $errors = array();

    // Add an error message if the name is too short
    if (strlen($_POST['my_name']) < 3) {
        $errors[ ] = 'Your name must be at least 3 letters long.';
    }

    // Return the (possibly empty) array of error messages
    return $errors;
}
```

The code in Example 7-8 takes advantage of the fact that an empty array evaluates to false. The line if ($form_errors = validate_form()) decides whether to call show_form() again and pass it the error array, or to call process_form(). The array that validate_form() returns is assigned to $form_errors. The truth value of the if() test expression is the result of that assignment, which, as you saw in "Understanding true and false" on page 40, is the value being assigned. So, the if() test expression is true if $form_errors has some elements in it, and false if $form_errors is empty. If validate_form() encounters no errors, then the array it returns is empty.

It is a good idea to do validation checks on all of the form elements in one pass, instead of redisplaying the form immediately when you find a single element that isn't valid. A user should find out all of his errors when he submits a form instead of having to submit the form over and over again, with a new error message revealed on each submission. The validate_form() function in Example 7-8 does this by adding an element to $errors for each problem with a form element. Then, show_form() prints out a list of the error messages.

The validation methods shown here all go inside the `validate_form()` function. If a form element doesn't pass the test, then a message is added to the `$errors` array.

Required Elements

To make sure something has been entered into a required element, check the element's length with `strlen()`, as in Example 7-9.

Example 7-9. Verifying a required element

```
if (strlen($_POST['email']) == 0) {
    $errors[] = "You must enter an email address.";
}
```

It is important to use `strlen()` when checking a required element instead of testing the value itself in an `if()` statement. A test such as `if (! $_POST['quantity'])` treats a value that evaluates to `false` as an error. Using `strlen()` lets users enter a value such as 0 into a required element.

Numeric or String Elements

To ensure that a submitted value is an integer or floating-point number, use `filter_input()` function with an appropriate filter. With `filter_input`, you tell PHP what kind of input to operate on, the name of the submitted value in the input, and what rule you want the value to conform to. The `FILTER_VALIDATE_INT` and `FILTER_VALIDATE_FLOAT` filters check for integers and floating-point numbers, respectively.

Example 7-10 shows the integer filter in use.

Example 7-10. Filtering integer input

```
$ok = filter_input(INPUT_POST, 'age', FILTER_VALIDATE_INT);
if (is_null($ok) || ($ok === false)) {
    $errors[] = 'Please enter a valid age.';
}
```

In Example 7-10, `filter_input(INPUT_POST, 'age', FILTER_VALIDATE_INT)` tells the PHP engine to examine submitted form data (`INPUT_POST`), specifically the form field named `age`, and check it against the integer validation filter (`FILTER_VALIDATE_INT`). The `filter_input()` function gets told where to look (`INPUT_POST`) and what field to check (`age`) rather than being given an entry in an array such as `$_POST['age']` so that it can properly handle missing values and avoid being confused if your PHP program changes values in `$_POST`.

If `filter_input()` sees that the specified input element is valid, it returns the value. If the specified input element is missing, it returns `null`. If the specified input element is present but not valid according to the filter, the function returns `false`. In the `if()` test expression in Example 7-10, `$ok` is compared to `false` with `===` (three equals signs). This is called the *identity operator*. It compares values and evaluates to `true` if the two values are the same and have the same type. As you saw in Example 3-11, when you compare two values of different types (such as string and integer, or integer and boolean), the PHP engine may change the type of the values to compare them. In this case, if the value of the submitted input was 0, which is a valid integer, `$ok` would be 0. Then the regular equality comparison between `$ok` and `false` would be `true`, since 0 evaluates to `false`. With the identity operator, the comparison is `false`, because the types don't match.

This means that the `$errors` array gets an error message added to it if the `age` form element is either not present (`is_null($ok)`) or not an integer (`$ok === false`).

Filtering floating-point numbers works similarly, as shown in Example 7-11.

Example 7-11. Filtering floating-point input

```
$ok = filter_input(INPUT_POST, 'price', FILTER_VALIDATE_FLOAT);
if (is_null($ok) || ($ok === false)) {
    $errors[] = 'Please enter a valid price.';
}
```

When validating elements (particularly string elements), it is often helpful to remove leading and trailing whitespace with the `trim()` function. You can combine this with the `strlen()` test for required elements to disallow an entry of just whitespace characters. The combination of `trim()` and `strlen()` is shown in Example 7-12.

Example 7-12. Combining trim() and strlen()

```
if (strlen(trim($_POST['name'])) == 0) {
    $errors[] = "Your name is required.";
}
```

All URL and submitted form data arrives at the PHP engine as strings. The `filter_input()` function, if given a numeric filter (and a valid value), returns the value converted to an integer or floating-point number. Like working with a whitespace-trimmed string, using these converted values rather than `$_POST` directly is often convenient in your program. A good way to accomplish that is to have your validation function build an array of converted values to work with. This is shown in Example 7-13.

Example 7-13. Building an array of modified input data

```
function validate_form() {
    $errors = array();
    $input = array();

    $input['age'] = filter_input(INPUT_POST, 'age', FILTER_VALIDATE_INT);
    if (is_null($input['age']) || ($input['age'] === false)) {
        $errors[] = 'Please enter a valid age.';
    }

    $input['price'] = filter_input(INPUT_POST, 'price', FILTER_VALIDATE_FLOAT);
    if (is_null($input['price']) || ($input['price'] === false)) {
        $errors[] = 'Please enter a valid price.';
    }

    // Use the null coalesce operator in case $_POST['name'] isn't set
    $input['name'] = trim($_POST['name'] ?? '');
    if (strlen($input['name']) == 0) {
        $errors[] = "Your name is required.";
    }

    return array($errors, $input);
}
```

The validate_form() function in Example 7-13 builds up the $input array, putting values into it as they are checked. It also builds up the $errors array if there are any problems. Having created both arrays, it needs to return both so that the rest of the program can use $input, not just $errors. To do that, it bundles them up into a two-element array and returns that.

If validate_form() is returning both input and errors, the code calling it must be modified to take that into account. Example 7-14 shows a modified version of the beginning of Example 7-8 that handles both arrays returned from validate_form().

Example 7-14. Handling errors and modified input data

```
// Logic to do the right thing based on the request method
if ($_SERVER['REQUEST_METHOD'] == 'POST') {
    // If validate_form() returns errors, pass them to show_form()
    list($form_errors, $input) = validate_form();
    if ($form_errors) {
        show_form($form_errors);
    } else {
        process_form($input);
    }
} else {
    show_form();
}
```

In Example 7-14, the list() construct is used to *destructure* the return value from validate_form(). Because we know that validate_form() will always return an array with two elements (the first element is the possibly empty array of error messages and the second element is the array of modified input data), list($form_errors, $input) tells the PHP engine to put the first element of that returned array into the $form_errors variable and the second element into $input. Having those separate arrays in separate variables makes the code easier to read.

Once the returned arrays are properly handled, the logic is similar. If the $errors array is not empty, then show_form() is called with the $errors array as an argument. Otherwise, the form processing function is called. One slight difference is that now the form processing function is passed the array of modified input values to use. This means that process_form() should now refer to $input['my_name'] rather than $_POST['my_name'] to find values to print.

Number Ranges

To check whether an integer falls within a certain range, use the min_range and max_range options of the FILTER_VALIDATE_INT filter. The options get passed as a fourth argument to filter_input(), as shown in Example 7-15.

Example 7-15. Checking an integer range

```
$input['age'] = filter_input(INPUT_POST, 'age', FILTER_VALIDATE_INT,
                             array('options' => array('min_range' => 18,
                                                      'max_range' => 65)));
if (is_null($input['age']) || ($input['age'] === false)) {
    $errors[] = 'Please enter a valid age between 18 and 65.';
}
```

Notice that the array of options and their values are not themselves the fourth argument to filter_input(). That argument is a one-element array with a key of options and a value of the actual array of options and their values.

The FILTER_VALIDATE_FLOAT filter doesn't support the min_range and max_range options, so you need to do the comparisons yourself:

```
$input['price'] = filter_input(INPUT_POST, 'price', FILTER_VALIDATE_FLOAT);
if (is_null($input['price']) || ($input['price'] === false) ||
    ($input['price'] < 10.00) || ($input['price'] > 50.00)) {
    $errors[] = 'Please enter a valid price between $10 and $50.';
}
```

To test a date range, convert the submitted date value into a DateTime object and then check that its value is appropriate (for more information on DateTime objects and the checkdate() functions used in Example 7-16, see Chapter 15). Because DateTime objects encapsulate all the bits of information necessary to represent a point in time, you don't have to do anything special when using a range that spans a month or year boundary. Example 7-16 checks to see whether a supplied date is less than six months old.

Example 7-16. Checking a date range

```
// Make a DateTime object for 6 months ago
$range_start = new DateTime('6 months ago');
// Make a DateTime object for right now
$range_end   = new DateTime();

// 4-digit year is in $_POST['year']
// 2-digit month is in $_POST['month']
// 2-digit day is is $_POST['day']
$input['year'] = filter_input(INPUT_POST, 'year', FILTER_VALIDATE_INT,
                              array('options' => array('min_range' => 1900,
                                                       'max_range' => 2100)));
$input['month'] = filter_input(INPUT_POST, 'month', FILTER_VALIDATE_INT,
                              array('options' => array('min_range' => 1,
                                                       'max_range' => 12)));
$input['day'] = filter_input(INPUT_POST, 'day', FILTER_VALIDATE_INT,
                              array('options' => array('min_range' => 1,
                                                       'max_range' => 31)));
// No need to use === to compare to false since 0 is not a valid
// choice for year, month, or day. checkdate() makes sure that
// the number of days is valid for the given month and year.
if ($input['year'] && input['month'] && input['day'] &&
    checkdate($input['month'], $input['day'], $input['year'])) {
    $submitted_date = new DateTime(strtotime($input['year'] . '-' .
                                             $input['month'] . '-' .
                                             $input['day']));
    if (($range_start > $submitted_date) || ($range_end < $submitted_date)) {
        $errors[] = 'Please choose a date less than six months old.';
    }
} else {
    // This happens if someone omits one of the form parameters or submits
    // something like February 31.
    $errors[] = 'Please enter a valid date.';
}
```

Email Addresses

Checking an email address is arguably the most common form validation task. There is, however, no perfect one-step way to make sure an email address is valid, since "valid" could mean different things depending on your goal. If you truly want to make sure that someone is giving you a working email address, and that the person providing it controls that address, you need to do two things. First, when the email address is submitted, send a message containing a random string to that address. In the message, tell the user to submit the random string in a form on your site. Or, you can include a URL in the message that the user can just click on, which has the code embedded into it. If the code is submitted (or the URL is clicked on), then you know that the person who received the message and controls the email address submitted it to your site (or at least is aware of and approves of the submission).

If you don't want to go to all the trouble of verifying the email address with a separate message, there is still an easy syntax check you can do in your form validation code to weed out mistyped addresses. The FILTER_VALIDATE_EMAIL filter checks strings against the rules for valid email addresses, as shown in Example 7-17.

Example 7-17. Checking the syntax of an email address

```
$input['email'] = filter_input(INPUT_POST, 'email', FILTER_VALIDATE_EMAIL);
if (! $input['email']) {
    $errors[] = 'Please enter a valid email address';
}
```

In Example 7-17, the simpler validity check if (! $input['email']) is fine because any submitted strings that would evaluate to false (such as the empty string or 0) are also invalid email addresses.

<select> Menus

When you use a <select> menu in a form, you need to ensure that the submitted value for the menu element is one of the permitted choices in the menu. Although a user can't submit an off-menu value using a mainstream, well-behaved browser such as Firefox or Chrome, an attacker can construct a request containing any arbitrary value without using a browser.

To simplify display and validation of <select> menus, put the menu choices in an array. Then, iterate through that array to display the <select> menu inside the show_form() function. Use the same array in validate_form() to check the submitted value. Example 7-18 shows how to display a <select> menu with this technique.

Example 7-18. Displaying a <select> menu

```
$sweets = array('Sesame Seed Puff','Coconut Milk Gelatin Square',
                'Brown Sugar Cake','Sweet Rice and Meat');

function generate_options($options) {
    $html = '';
    foreach ($options as $option) {
        $html .= "<option>$option</option>\n";
    }
    return $html;
}
```

```
// Display the form
function show_form() {
    $sweets = generate_options($GLOBALS['sweets']);
    print<<<_HTML_
<form method="post" action="$_SERVER[PHP_SELF]">
Your Order: <select name="order">
$sweets
</select>
<br/>
<input type="submit" value="Order">
</form>
_HTML_;
}
```

The HTML that show_form() in Example 7-18 prints is:

```
<form method="post" action="order.php">
Your Order: <select name="order">
<option>Sesame Seed Puff</option>
<option>Coconut Milk Gelatin Square</option>
<option>Brown Sugar Cake</option>
<option>Sweet Rice and Meat</option>

</select>
<br/>
<input type="submit" value="Order">
</form>
```

Inside validate_form(), use the array of <select> menu options like this:

```
$input['order'] = $_POST['order'];
if (! in_array($input['order'], $GLOBALS['sweets'])) {
    $errors[] = 'Please choose a valid order.';
}
```

If you want a <select> menu with different displayed choices and option values, you need to use a more complicated array. Each array element key is a value attribute for one option. The corresponding array element value is the displayed choice for that option. In Example 7-19, the option values are puff, square, cake, and ricemeat. The displayed choices are Sesame Seed Puff, Coconut Milk Gelatin Square, Brown Sugar Cake, and Sweet Rice and Meat.

Example 7-19. A <select> menu with different choices and values

```
$sweets = array('puff' => 'Sesame Seed Puff',
                'square' => 'Coconut Milk Gelatin Square',
                'cake' => 'Brown Sugar Cake',
                'ricemeat' => 'Sweet Rice and Meat');

function generate_options_with_value ($options) {
```

```
    $html = '';
    foreach ($options as $value => $option) {
        $html .= "<option value=\"$value\">$option</option>\n";
    }
    return $html;
}


// Display the form
function show_form() {
    $sweets = generate_options_with_value($GLOBALS['sweets']);
    print<<<_HTML_
<form method="post" action="$_SERVER[PHP_SELF]">
Your Order: <select name="order">
$sweets
</select>
<br/>
<input type="submit" value="Order">
</form>
_HTML_;
}
```

The form displayed by Example 7-19 is as follows:

```
<form method="post" action="order.php">
Your Order: <select name="order">
<option value="puff">Sesame Seed Puff</option>
<option value="square">Coconut Milk Gelatin Square</option>
<option value="cake">Brown Sugar Cake</option>
<option value="ricemeat">Sweet Rice and Meat</option>

</select>
<br/>
<input type="submit" value="Order">
</form>
```

The submitted value for the <select> menu in Example 7-19 should be puff, square, cake, or ricemeat. Example 7-20 shows how to verify this in validate_form().

Example 7-20. Checking a <select> menu submission value

```
$input['order'] = $_POST['order'];
if (! array_key_exists($input['order'], $GLOBALS['sweets'])) {
    $errors[] = 'Please choose a valid order.';
}
```

HTML and JavaScript

Submitted form data that contains HTML or JavaScript can cause big problems. Consider a simple blog application that lets users submit comments on a blog post page and then displays a list of those comments below the blog post. If users behave nicely and enter only comments containing plain text, the page remains benign. One user submits `Cool page! I like how you list the different ways to cook fish.` When you come along to browse the page, that's what you see.

The situation is more complicated when the submissions are not just plain text. If an enthusiastic user submits `This page <b>rules!!!!</b>` as a comment, and it is redisplayed verbatim by the application, then you see `rules!!!!` in bold when you browse the page. Your web browser can't tell the difference between HTML tags that come from the application itself (perhaps laying out the comments in a table or a list) and HTML tags that happen to be embedded in the comments that the application is printing.

Although seeing bold text instead of plain text is a minor annoyance, displaying unfiltered user input leaves the application open to giving you a much larger headache. Instead of `<b></b>` tags, one user's submission could contain a malformed or unclosed tag (such as `<a href="` with no ending `"` or `>`) that prevents your browser from displaying the page properly. Even worse, that submission could contain Java-Script code that, when executed by your web browser as you look at the page, does nasty stuff such as send a copy of your cookies to a stranger's email box or surreptitiously redirect you to another web page.

The application acts as a facilitator, letting a malicious user upload some HTML or JavaScript that is later run by an unwitting user's browser. This kind of problem is called a *cross-site scripting attack* because the poorly written blog application allows code from one source (the malicious user) to masquerade as coming from another place (the application hosting the comments).

To prevent cross-site scripting attacks in your programs, never display unmodified external input. Either remove suspicious parts (such as HTML tags) or encode special characters so that browsers don't act on embedded HTML or JavaScript. PHP gives you two functions that make these tasks simple. The `strip_tags()` function removes HTML tags from a string, and the `htmlentities()` function encodes special HTML characters.

Example 7-21 demonstrates `strip_tags()`.

Example 7-21. Stripping HTML tags from a string

```
// Remove HTML from comments
$comments = strip_tags($_POST['comments']);
// Now it's OK to print $comments
print $comments;
```

If `$_POST['comments']` contains

```
I
<b>love</b> sweet <div
class="fancy">rice</div> &
tea.
```

then Example 7-21 prints:

```
I love sweet rice & tea.
```

All HTML tags and their attributes are removed, but the plain text between the tags is left intact. The `strip_tags()` function is very convenient, but it behaves poorly with mismatched < and > characters. For example, it turns I <3 Monkeys into I . It starts stripping once it sees that < and never stops because there's no corresponding <.

Encoding instead of stripping the tags often gives better results. Example 7-22 demonstrates encoding with `htmlentities()`.

Example 7-22. Encoding HTML entities in a string

```
$comments = htmlentities($_POST['comments']);
// Now it's OK to print $comments
print $comments;
```

If `$_POST['comments']` contains

```
I
<b>love</b> sweet <div
class="fancy">rice</div> &
tea
```

then Example 7-22 prints:

```
I &lt;b&gt;love&lt;/b&gt; sweet &lt;div class=&quot;fancy
&quot;&gt;rice&lt;/div&gt; &amp; tea.
```

The characters that have a special meaning in HTML (<, >, &, and ") have been changed into their entity equivalents:

- < to <
- > to >
- & to &
- " to "

When a browser sees <, it prints out a < character instead of thinking "OK, here comes an HTML tag." This is the same idea (but with a different syntax) as escaping a " or $ character inside a double-quoted string, as you saw in "Text" on page 19. Figure 7-4 shows what the output of Example 7-22 looks like in a web browser.

In most applications, you should use htmlentities() to sanitize external input. This function doesn't throw away any content, and it also protects against cross-site scripting attacks. A discussion board where users post messages, for example, about HTML ("What does the <div> tag do?") or algebra ("If x<y, is 2x>z?") wouldn't be very useful if those posts were run through strip_tags(). The questions would be printed as "What does the tag do?" and "If xz?"

Figure 7-4. Displaying entity-encoded text

Beyond Syntax

Most of the validation strategies discussed in this chapter so far check the syntax of a submitted value. They make sure that what's submitted matches a certain format. However, sometimes you want to make sure that a submitted value has not just the correct syntax, but an acceptable meaning as well. The <select> menu validation does this. Instead of just assuring that the submitted value is a string, it matches it against a specific array of values. The confirmation-message strategy for checking email addresses is another example of checking for more than syntax. If you ensure only that a submitted email address has the correct form, a mischievous user can provide an address such as president@whitehouse.gov that almost certainly doesn't belong to her. The confirmation message makes sure that the meaning of the address —i.e., "this email address belongs to the user providing it"—is correct.

Displaying Default Values

Sometimes, you want to display a form with a value already in a text box or with pre-selected checkboxes, radio buttons, or `<select>` menu items. Additionally, when you redisplay a form because of an error, it is helpful to preserve any information that a user has already entered. Example 7-23 shows the code to do this. It belongs at the beginning of `show_form()` and makes `$defaults` the array of values to use with the form elements.

Example 7-23. Building an array of defaults

```
if ($_SERVER['REQUEST_METHOD'] == 'POST') {
    $defaults = $_POST;
} else {
    $defaults = array('delivery'  => 'yes',
                      'size'      => 'medium',
                      'main_dish' => array('taro','tripe'),
                      'sweet'     => 'cake');
}
```

If `$_SERVER['REQUEST_METHOD']` is POST, that means the form has been submitted. In that case, the defaults should come from whatever the user submitted. Otherwise, you can set your own defaults. For most form parameters, the default is a string or a number. For form elements that can have more than one value, such as the multivalued `<select>` menu `main_dish`, the default value is an array.

After setting the defaults, provide the appropriate value from `$defaults` when printing out the HTML tag for the form element. Remember to encode the defaults with `htmlentities()` when necessary in order to prevent cross-site scripting attacks. Because of the structure of the HTML tags, you need to treat text boxes, `<select>` menus, text areas, and checkboxes/radio buttons differently.

For text boxes, set the `value` attribute of the `<input>` tag to the appropriate element of `$defaults`. Example 7-24 shows how to do this.

Example 7-24. Setting a default value in a text box

```
print '<input type="text" name="my_name" value="' .
    htmlentities($defaults['my_name']). '">';
```

For multiline text areas, put the entity-encoded value between the `<textarea>` and `</textarea>` tags, as shown in Example 7-25.

Example 7-25. Setting a default value in a multiline text area

```
print '<textarea name="comments">';
print htmlentities($defaults['comments']);
print '</textarea>';
```

For <select> menus, add a check to the loop that prints out the <option> tags so that it prints a selected attribute when appropriate. Example 7-26 contains the code to do this for a single-valued <select> menu.

Example 7-26. Setting a default value in a <select> menu

```
$sweets = array('puff' => 'Sesame Seed Puff',
                'square' => 'Coconut Milk Gelatin Square',
                'cake' => 'Brown Sugar Cake',
                'ricemeat' => 'Sweet Rice and Meat');

print '<select name="sweet">';
// > is the option value, $label is what's displayed
foreach ($sweets as $option => $label) {
    print '<option value="' .$option .'"';
    if ($option == $defaults['sweet']) {
        print ' selected';
    }
    print "> $label</option>\n";
}
print '</select>';
```

To set defaults for a multivalued <select> menu, you need to convert the array of defaults into an associative array in which each key is a choice that should be selected. Then, print the selected attribute for the options found in that associative array. Example 7-27 demonstrates how to do this.

Example 7-27. Setting defaults in a multivalued <select> menu

```
$main_dishes = array('cuke' => 'Braised Sea Cucumber',
                     'stomach' => "Sauteed Pig's Stomach",
                     'tripe' => 'Sauteed Tripe with Wine Sauce',
                     'taro' => 'Stewed Pork with Taro',
                     'giblets' => 'Baked Giblets with Salt',
                     'abalone' => 'Abalone with Marrow and Duck Feet');

print '<select name="main_dish[]" multiple>';

$selected_options = array();
foreach ($defaults['main_dish'] as $option) {
    $selected_options[$option] = true;
}
```

```
// print out the <option> tags
foreach ($main_dishes as $option => $label) {
    print '<option value="' . htmlentities($option) . '"';
    if (array_key_exists($option, $selected_options)) {
        print ' selected';
    }
    print '>' . htmlentities($label) . '</option>';
    print "\n";
}
print '</select>';
```

For checkboxes and radio buttons, add a `checked` attribute to the `<input>` tag. The syntax for checkboxes and radio buttons is identical except for the `type` attribute. Example 7-28 prints a default-aware checkbox named `delivery` and three default-aware radio buttons, each named `size` and each with a different value.

Example 7-28. Setting defaults for checkboxes and radio buttons

```
print '<input type="checkbox" name="delivery" value="yes"';
if ($defaults['delivery'] == 'yes') { print ' checked'; }
print '> Delivery?';

$checkbox_options = array('small' => 'Small',
                          'medium' => 'Medium',
                          'large' => 'Large');

foreach ($checkbox_options as $value => $label) {
    print '<input type="radio" name="size" value="'.$value.'"';
    if ($defaults['size'] == $value) { print ' checked'; }
    print '> $label ";
}
```

Putting It All Together

Turning the humble web form into a feature-packed application with data validation, printing default values, and processing the submitted results might seem like an intimidating task. To ease your burden, this section contains a complete example of a program that does it all:

- Displaying a form, including default values
- Validating the submitted data
- Redisplaying the form with error messages and preserved user input if the submitted data isn't valid
- Processing the submitted data if it is valid

The do-it-all example relies on a class containing some helper functions to simplify form element display and processing. This class is listed in Example 7-29.

Example 7-29. Form element display helper class

```
class FormHelper {
    protected $values = array();

    public function __construct($values = array()) {
        if ($_SERVER['REQUEST_METHOD'] == 'POST') {
            $this->values = $_POST;
        } else {
            $this->values = $values;
        }
    }

    public function input($type, $attributes = array(), $isMultiple = false) {
        $attributes['type'] = $type;
        if (($type == 'radio') || ($type == 'checkbox')) {
            if ($this->isOptionSelected($attributes['name'] ?? null,
                                        $attributes['value'] ?? null)) {
                $attributes['checked'] = true;
            }
        }
        return $this->tag('input', $attributes, $isMultiple);
    }

    public function select($options, $attributes = array()) {
        $multiple = $attributes['multiple'] ?? false;
        return
            $this->start('select', $attributes, $multiple) .
            $this->options($attributes['name'] ?? null, $options) .
            $this->end('select');
    }

    public function textarea($attributes = array()) {
        $name = $attributes['name'] ?? null;
        $value = $this->values[$name] ?? '';
        return $this->start('textarea', $attributes) .
                htmlentities($value) .
                $this->end('textarea');
    }

    public function tag($tag, $attributes = array(), $isMultiple = false) {
        return "<$tag {$this->attributes($attributes, $isMultiple)} />";
    }
    public function start($tag, $attributes = array(), $isMultiple = false) {
        // <select> and <textarea> tags don't get value attributes on them
        $valueAttribute = (! (($tag == 'select')||($tag == 'textarea')));
        $attrs = $this->attributes($attributes, $isMultiple, $valueAttribute);
        return "<$tag $attrs>";
```

```php
    }
    public function end($tag) {
        return "</$tag>";
    }

    protected function attributes($attributes, $isMultiple,
                                  $valueAttribute = true) {
        $tmp = array();
        // If this tag could include a value attribute and it
        // has a name and there's an entry for the name
        // in the values array, then set a value attribute
        if ($valueAttribute && isset($attributes['name']) &&
            array_key_exists($attributes['name'], $this->values)) {
            $attributes['value'] = $this->values[$attributes['name']];
        }
        foreach ($attributes as $k => $v) {
            // True boolean value means boolean attribute
            if (is_bool($v)) {
                if ($v) { $tmp[] = $this->encode($k); }
            }
            // Otherwise k=v
            else {
                $value = $this->encode($v);
                // If this is an element that might have multiple values,
                // tack [] onto its name
                if ($isMultiple && ($k == 'name')) {
                    $value .= '[]';
                }
                $tmp[] = "$k=\"$value\"";
            }
        }
        return implode(' ', $tmp);
    }

    protected function options($name, $options) {
        $tmp = array();
        foreach ($options as $k => $v) {
            $s = "<option  value=\"{$this->encode($k)}\"";
            if ($this->isOptionSelected($name, $k)) {
                $s .= ' selected';
            }
            $s .= ">{$this->encode($v)}</option>";
            $tmp[] = $s;
        }
        return implode('', $tmp);
    }

    protected function isOptionSelected($name, $value) {
        // If there's no entry for $name in the values array,
        // then this option can't be selected
        if (! isset($this->values[$name])) {
            return false;
```

```
        }
        // If the entry for $name in the values array is itself
        // an array, check if $value is in that array
        else if (is_array($this->values[$name])) {
            return in_array($value, $this->values[$name]);
        }
        // Otherwise, compare $value to the entry for $name
        // in the values array
        else {
            return $value == $this->values[$name];
        }
    }

    public function encode($s) {
        return htmlentities($s);
    }
}
```

Methods in Example 7-29 incorporate the appropriate logic discussed in "Displaying Default Values" on page 142 for particular kinds of form elements. Because the form code in Example 7-30 has a number of different elements, it's easier to put the element display code in functions that are called repeatedly than to duplicate the code each time you need to print a particular element.

The FormHelper constructor should be passed an associative array of default values for arguments. If the request method is not POST, it uses this array to figure out appropriate defaults. Otherwise, it uses the submitted data as the basis for defaults.

FormHelper's input() method generates appropriate HTML for any <input/> element. Its required first argument is the type of the element (such as submit, radio, or text). The optional second argument is an associative array of element attributes (such as ['name' => 'meal']). The optional third argument should be true if you're generating HTML for an element that can have multiple values, such as a checkbox.

The select() method generates HTML for a <select> menu. Its first argument is an array of options for the menu and its optional second argument is an associative array of attributes for the <select> tag. For a multivalued <select> menu, make sure to include 'multiple' => true in the array of attributes passed as the second argument.

The textarea() method generates HTML for a <textarea>. It just takes a single argument: an associative array of attributes for the tag.

Those three methods should take care of the majority of your form display needs, but in case you need other tags or special treatment, you can use the tag(), start(), and end() methods.

The `tag()` method produces HTML for an entire self-closing HTML tag such as `<input/>`. Its arguments are the name of the tag, an optional array of attributes, and `true` if the tag can accept multiple values. The `input()` method uses `tag()` to actually generate the proper HTML.

The `start()` and `end()` methods are for elements with separate start and end tags. The `start()` method generates the element start tag, accepting the familiar trio of tag name, attributes, and multiple flag as arguments. The `end()` method just accepts a tag name for an argument and returns the closing tag HTML. For example, if you're using an HTML tag such as `<fieldset>`, you could call `start('fieldset',['name' => 'adjustments'])`, then emit HTML that should be inside the field set, then call `end('fieldset')`.

The rest of the class is devoted to methods that help to generate the HTML and are not meant to be called from outside the class. The `attributes()` method formats a set of attributes to be appropriately included inside an HTML tag. Using the defaults set up in the object, it inserts an appropriate `value` attribute when necessary. It also takes care of appending `[]` to the element name if the element can accept multiple values and assures that all attribute values are appropriately encoded with HTML entities.

The `options()` method handles formatting the `<option>` tags for a `<select>` menu. With the help of `isOptionSelected()`, it figures out which options should be marked as `selected` and does proper HTML entity encoding.

The `encode()` method is a wrapper for PHP's built-in `htmlentities()` method. It's `public` so that other code can use it to make your entity encoding consistent.

The code in Example 7-30 relies on the `FormHelper` class and displays a short food-ordering form. When the form is submitted correctly, it shows the results in the browser and emails them to an address defined in `process_form()` (presumably to the chef, so he can start preparing your order). Because the code jumps in and out of PHP mode, it includes the `<?php` start tag at the beginning of the example and the `?>` closing tag at the end to make things clearer.

Example 7-30. A complete form: display with defaults, validation, and processing

```php
<?php

// This assumes FormHelper.php is in the same directory as
// this file.
require 'FormHelper.php';

// Set up the arrays of choices in the select menus.
// These are needed in display_form(), validate_form(),
// and process_form(), so they are declared in the global scope.
```

```php
$sweets = array('puff' => 'Sesame Seed Puff',
                'square' => 'Coconut Milk Gelatin Square',
                'cake' => 'Brown Sugar Cake',
              . 'ricemeat' => 'Sweet Rice and Meat');

$main_dishes = array('cuke' => 'Braised Sea Cucumber',
                     'stomach' => "Sauteed Pig's Stomach",
                     'tripe' => 'Sauteed Tripe with Wine Sauce',
                     'taro' => 'Stewed Pork with Taro',
                     'giblets' => 'Baked Giblets with Salt',
                     'abalone' => 'Abalone with Marrow and Duck Feet');

// The main page logic:
// - If the form is submitted, validate and then process or redisplay
// - If it's not submitted, display
if ($_SERVER['REQUEST_METHOD'] == 'POST') {
    // If validate_form() returns errors, pass them to show_form()
    list($errors, $input) = validate_form();
    if ($errors) {
        show_form($errors);
    } else {
        // The submitted data is valid, so process it
        process_form($input);
    }
} else {
    // The form wasn't submitted, so display
    show_form();
}

function show_form($errors = array()) {
    $defaults = array('delivery' => 'yes',
                      'size'     => 'medium');
    // Set up the $form object with proper defaults
    $form = new FormHelper($defaults);

    // All the HTML and form display is in a separate file for clarity
    include 'complete-form.php';
}

function validate_form() {
    $input = array();
    $errors = array();

    // name is required
    $input['name'] = trim($_POST['name'] ?? '');
    if (! strlen($input['name'])) {
        $errors[] = 'Please enter your name.';
    }
    // size is required
    $input['size'] = $_POST['size'] ?? '';
    if (! in_array($input['size'], ['small','medium','large'])) {
        $errors[] = 'Please select a size.';
```

```
    }
    // sweet is required
    $input['sweet'] = $_POST['sweet'] ?? '';
    if (! array_key_exists($input['sweet'], $GLOBALS['sweets'])) {
        $errors[] = 'Please select a valid sweet item.';
    }
    // exactly two main dishes required
    $input['main_dish'] = $_POST['main_dish'] ?? array();
    if (count($input['main_dish']) != 2) {
        $errors[] = 'Please select exactly two main dishes.';
    } else {
        // we know there are two main dishes selected, so make sure they are
        // both valid
        if (! (array_key_exists($input['main_dish'][0], $GLOBALS['main_dishes']) &&
                array_key_exists($input['main_dish'][1], $GLOBALS['main_dishes']))) {
            $errors[] = 'Please select exactly two valid main dishes.';
        }
    }
    // if delivery is checked, then comments must contain something
    $input['delivery'] = $_POST['delivery'] ?? 'no';
    $input['comments'] = trim($_POST['comments'] ?? '');
    if (($input['delivery'] == 'yes') && (! strlen($input['comments']))) {
        $errors[] = 'Please enter your address for delivery.';
    }

    return array($errors, $input);
}

function process_form($input) {
    // look up the full names of the sweet and the main dishes in
    // the $GLOBALS['sweets'] and $GLOBALS['main_dishes'] arrays
    $sweet = $GLOBALS['sweets'][ $input['sweet'] ];
    $main_dish_1 = $GLOBALS['main_dishes'][ $input['main_dish'][0] ];
    $main_dish_2 = $GLOBALS['main_dishes'][ $input['main_dish'][1] ];
    if (isset($input['delivery']) && ($input['delivery'] == 'yes')) {
        $delivery = 'do';
    } else {
        $delivery = 'do not';
    }
    // build up the text of the order message
    $message=<<<_ORDER_
Thank you for your order, {$input['name']}.
You requested the {$input['size']} size of $sweet, $main_dish_1, and $main_dish_2.
You $delivery want delivery.
_ORDER_;
    if (strlen(trim($input['comments']))) {
        $message .= 'Your comments: '.$input['comments'];
    }

    // send the message to the chef
    mail('chef@restaurant.example.com', 'New Order', $message);
    // print the message, but encode any HTML entities
```

```
    // and turn newlines into <br/> tags
    print nl2br(htmlentities($message, ENT_HTML5));
}
?>
```

There are four parts to the code in Example 7-30: the code in the global scope at the top of the example, the show_form() function, the validate_form() function, and the process_form() function.

The global scope code does three things. The first is that it loads the FormHelper class from its separate file. Then, it sets up two arrays that describe the choices in the form's two <select> menus. Because these arrays are used by each of the show_form(), validate_form(), and process_form() functions, they need to be defined in the global scope. The global code's last task is to process the if() statement that decides what to do: display, validate, or process the form.

Displaying the form is accomplished by show_form(). First, the function makes $defaults an array of default values. This array is passed to FormHelper's constructor, so the $form object uses the right default values. Then, show_form() hands off control to another file, *complete-form.php*, which contains the actual HTML and PHP code to display the form. Putting the HTML in a separate file for a big program like this makes it easier to digest everything and also easier for the two files to be changed independently. The contents of *complete-form.php* are shown in Example 7-31.

Example 7-31. PHP and HTML generating a form

```
<form method="POST" action="<?= $form->encode($_SERVER['PHP_SELF']) ?>">
<table>
    <?php if ($errors) { ?>
        <tr>
            <td>You need to correct the following errors:</td>
            <td><ul>
                <?php foreach ($errors as $error) { ?>
                    <li><?= $form->encode($error) ?></li>
                <?php } ?>
            </ul></td>
    <?php }  ?>

    <tr><td>Your Name:</td><td><?= $form->input('text', ['name' => 'name']) ?>
    </td></tr>

    <tr><td>Size:</td>
        <td><?= $form->input('radio',['name' => 'size', 'value' => 'small']) ?>
        Small <br/>
            <?= $form->input('radio',['name' => 'size', 'value' => 'medium']) ?>
            Medium <br/>
            <?= $form->input('radio',['name' => 'size', 'value' => 'large']) ?>
            Large <br/>
```

```
        </td></tr>

    <tr><td>Pick one sweet item:</td>
        <td><?= $form->select($GLOBALS['sweets'], ['name' => 'sweet']) ?></td>
    </tr>

    <tr><td>Pick two main dishes:</td>
        <td><?= $form->select($GLOBALS['main_dishes'], ['name' => 'main_dish',
                                                'multiple' => true]) ?></td>
    </tr>

    <tr><td>Do you want your order delivered?</td>
        <td><?= $form->input('checkbox',['name' => 'delivery',
                                         'value' => 'yes'])
        ?> Yes </td></tr>

    <tr><td>Enter any special instructions.<br/>
        If you want your order delivered, put your address here:</td>
        <td><?= $form->textarea(['name' => 'comments']) ?></td></tr>

    <tr><td colspan="2" align="center">
    <?=$form->input('submit', ['value' => 'Order']) ?>
    </td></tr>

</table>
</form>
```

The code in *complete-form.php* executes as if it were part of the show_form() function. This means that local variables in the function, such as $errors and $form, are available in *complete-form.php*. Like all included files, *complete-form.php* starts outside of any PHP tags, so it can print some plain HTML and then jump into PHP mode when it needs to call methods or use PHP logic. The code here uses the special *short echo tag* (<?=) as a concise way to display the results of various method calls. Starting a PHP block with <?= means exactly the same thing as starting a PHP block with <php echo. Since our various FormHelper methods return HTML that should be displayed, this makes a handy way to build up the HTML for the form.

Back in the main file, the validate_form() function builds an array of error messages if the submitted form data doesn't meet appropriate criteria. Note that the checks for size, sweet, and main_dish don't just look to see whether something was submitted for those parameters, but also that what was submitted is a valid value for the particular parameter. For size, this means that the submitted value must be small, medium, or large. For sweet and main_dish, this means that the submitted values must be keys in the global $sweets or $main_dishes arrays. Even though the form contains default values, it's still a good idea to validate the input. Someone trying to break into your website could bypass a regular web browser and construct a request with an arbitrary value that isn't a legitimate choice for the `<select>` menu or radio button set.

Lastly, `process_form()` takes action when the form is submitted with valid data. It builds a string, `$message`, that contains a description of the submitted order. Then it emails `$message` to chef@restaurant.example.com and prints it. The built-in `mail()` function sends the email message. Before printing `$message`, `process_form()` passes it through two functions. The first is `htmlentities()`, which, as you've already seen, encodes any special characters as HTML entities. The second is `nl2br()`, which turns any newlines in `$message` into HTML `<br>` tags. Turning newlines into `<br>` tags makes the line breaks in the message display properly in a web browser.

Chapter Summary

This chapter covered:

- Understanding the conversation between the web browser and web server that displays a form, processes the submitted form parameters, and then displays a result
- Making the connection between the `<form>` tag's `action` attribute and the URL to which form parameters are submitted
- Using values from the `$_SERVER` auto-global array
- Accessing submitted form parameters in the `$_GET` and `$_POST` auto-global arrays
- Accessing multivalued submitted form parameters
- Using the `show_form()`, `validate_form()`, and `process_form()` functions to modularize form handling
- Displaying error messages with a form
- Validating form elements: required elements, integers, floating-point numbers, strings, date ranges, email addresses, and `<select>` menus
- Defanging or removing submitted HTML and JavaScript before displaying it
- Displaying default values for form elements
- Using helper functions to display form elements

Exercises

1. What does `$_POST` look like when the following form is submitted with the third option in the Braised Noodles menu selected, the first and last options in the Sweet menu selected, and 4 entered into the text box?

```
<form method="POST" action="order.php">
Braised Noodles with: <select name="noodle">
<option>crab meat</option>
<option>mushroom</option>
```

```
<option>barbecued pork</option>
<option>shredded ginger and green onion</option>
</select>
<br/>
Sweet: <select name="sweet[]" multiple>
<option value="puff"> Sesame Seed Puff
<option value="square"> Coconut Milk Gelatin Square
<option value="cake"> Brown Sugar Cake
<option value="ricemeat"> Sweet Rice and Meat
</select>
<br/>
Sweet Quantity: <input type="text" name="sweet_q">
<br/>
<input type="submit" name="submit" value="Order">
</form>
```

2. Write a `process_form()` function that prints out all submitted form parameters and their values. You can assume that form parameters have only scalar values.

3. Write a program that does basic arithmetic. Display a form with text box inputs for two operands and a `<select>` menu to choose an operation: addition, subtraction, multiplication, or division. Validate the inputs to make sure that they are numeric and appropriate for the chosen operation. The processing function should display the operands, the operator, and the result. For example, if the operands are 4 and 2 and the operation is multiplication, the processing function should display something like 4 * 2 = 8.

4. Write a program that displays, validates, and processes a form for entering information about a package to be shipped. The form should contain inputs for the from and to addresses for the package, dimensions of the package, and weight of the package. The validation should check (at least) that the package weighs no more than 150 pounds and that no dimension of the package is more than 36 inches. You can assume that the addresses entered on the form are both US addresses, but you should check that a valid state and a zip code with valid syntax are entered. The processing function in your program should print out the information about the package in an organized, formatted report.

5. (Optional) Modify your `process_form()` function that enumerates all submitted form parameters and their values so that it correctly handles submitted form parameters that have array values. Remember, those array values could themselves contain arrays.

## CHAPTER 8

Remembering Information: Databases

The HTML and CSS that give your website its pretty face reside in individual files on your web server. So does the PHP code that processes forms and performs other dynamic wizardry. There's a third kind of information necessary to a web application, though: data. And while you can store data such as user lists and product information in individual files, most people find it easier to use databases, which are the focus of this chapter.

Lots of information falls under the broad umbrella of *data*:

- Who your users are, such as their names and email addresses
- What your users do, such as message board posts and profile information
- The "stuff" that your site is about, such as a list of record albums, a product catalog, or what's for dinner

There are three big reasons why this kind of data belongs in a database instead of in files: convenience, simultaneous access, and security. A database program makes it much easier to search for and manipulate individual pieces of information. With a database program, you can do things such as change the email address for user Duck29 to ducky@ducks.example.com in one step. If you put usernames and email addresses in a file, changing an email address would be much more complicated: you'd have to read the old file, search through each line until you find the one for Duck29, change the line, and write the file back out. If, at same time, one request updates Duck29's email address and another updates the record for user Piggy56, one update could be lost, or (worse) the data file could be corrupted. Database software manages the intricacies of simultaneous access for you.

In addition to searchability, database programs usually provide you with a different set of access control options compared to files. It is an exacting process to set things up properly so that your PHP programs can create, edit, and delete files on your web server without opening the door to malicious attackers who could abuse that setup to alter your PHP scripts and data files. A database program makes it easier to arrange the appropriate levels of access to your information. It can be configured so that your PHP programs can read and change some information, but only read other information. However the database access control is set up, it doesn't affect how files on the web server are accessed. Just because your PHP program can change values in the database doesn't give an attacker an opportunity to change your PHP programs and HTML files themselves.

The word *database* is used in a few different ways when talking about web applications. A database can be a pile of structured information, a program (such as MySQL or Oracle) that manages that structured information, or the computer on which that program runs. This book uses "database" to mean the pile of structured information. The software that manages the information is a *database program*, and the computer that the database program runs on is a *database server*.

Most of this chapter uses the PHP Data Objects (PDO) database program abstraction layer. This is a part of PHP that simplifies communication between your PHP program and your database program. With PDO, you can use the same functions in PHP to talk to many different kinds of database programs. Without PDO, you need to rely on other PHP functions to talk to your database program. The appropriate set of functions varies with each database program. Some of the more exotic features of your database program may only be accessible through the database-specific functions.

Organizing Data in a Database

Information in your database is organized in *tables*, which have rows and columns. (Columns are also sometimes referred to as *fields*.) Each column in a table is a category of information, and each row is a set of values for each column. For example, a table holding information about dishes on a menu would have columns for each dish's ID, name, price, and whether or not it's spicy. Each row in the table is the group of values for one particular dish—for example, "1," "Fried Bean Curd," "5.50," and "0" (meaning not spicy).

You can think of a table as being organized like a simple spreadsheet, with column names across the top, as shown in Figure 8-1.

One important difference between a spreadsheet and a database table, however, is that the rows in a database table have no inherent order. When you want to retrieve data from a table with the rows arranged in a particular way (e.g., in alphabetic order by student name), you need to explicitly specify that order when you ask the database for the data. The "SQL Lesson: ORDER BY and LIMIT" sidebar in this chapter describes how to do this.

ID	Name	Price	Is spicy?
1	Fried Bean Curd	5.50	0
2	Braised Sea Cucumber	9.95	0
3	Walnut Bun	1.00	0
4	Eggplant with Chili Sauce	6.50	1

Figure 8-1. Data organized in a table

Structured Query Language (SQL) is a language used to ask questions of and give instructions to the database program. Your PHP program sends SQL queries to a database program. If the query retrieves data in the database (for example, "Find me all spicy dishes"), then the database program responds with the set of rows that match the query. If the query changes data in the database (for example, "Add this new dish" or "Double the prices of all nonspicy dishes"), then the database program replies with whether or not the operation succeeded.

SQL is a mixed bag when it comes to case-sensitivity. SQL keywords are not case-sensitive, but in this book they are always written in uppercase to distinguish them from the other parts of the queries. Names of tables and columns in your queries generally are case-sensitive. All of the SQL examples in this book use lowercase column and table names to help you distinguish them from the SQL keywords. Any literal values that you put in queries are case-sensitive. Telling the database program that the name of a new dish is `fried bean curd` is different than telling it that the new dish is called `FRIED Bean Curd`.

Almost all of the SQL queries that you write to use in your PHP programs will rely on one of four SQL commands: `INSERT`, `UPDATE`, `DELETE`, or `SELECT`. Each of these commands is described in this chapter. "Creating a Table" on page 160 describes the `CREATE TABLE` command, which you use to make new tables in your database.

To learn more about SQL, read *SQL in a Nutshell*, by Kevin E. Kline (O'Reilly). It provides an overview of standard SQL as well as the SQL extensions in MySQL, Oracle, PostgreSQL, and Microsoft SQL Server. For more in-depth information about working with PHP and MySQL, read *Learning PHP, MySQL & JavaScript*, by Robin Nixon (O'Reilly). *MySQL Cookbook* by Paul DuBois (O'Reilly) is also an excellent source for answers to lots of SQL and MySQL questions.

Connecting to a Database Program

To establish a connection to a database program, create a new PDO object. You pass the PDO constructor a string that describes the database you are connecting to, and it returns an object that you use in the rest of your program to exchange information with the database program.

Example 8-1 shows a call to new PDO() that connects to a database named restaurant in a MySQL server running on db.example.com, using the username penguin and the password top^hat.

Example 8-1. Connecting with a PDO object

```
$db = new PDO('mysql:host=db.example.com;dbname=restaurant','penguin','top^hat');
```

The string passed as the first argument to the PDO constructor is called a *data source name* (DSN). It begins with a prefix indicating what kind of database program to connect to, then has a :, then some semicolon-separated *key=value* pairs providing information about how to connect. If the database connection needs a username and password, these are passed as the second and third arguments to the PDO constructor.

The particular *key=value* pairs you can put in a DSN depend on what kind of database program you're connecting to. Although the PHP engine has the capability to connect to many different databases with PDO, that connectivity has to be enabled when the engine is built and installed on your server. If you get a could not find driver message when creating a PDO object, it means that your PHP engine installation does not incorporate support for the database you're trying to use.

Table 8-1 lists the DSN prefixes and options for some of the most popular database programs that work with PDO.

Table 8-1. PDO DSN prefixes and options

Database program	DSN prefix	DSN options	Notes
MySQL	mysql	host, port, dbname, unix_socket, charset	unix_socket is for local MySQL connections. Use it or host and port, but not both.
PostgreSQL	pgsql	host, port, dbname, user, password, others	The whole connection string is passed to an internal PostgreSQL connection function, so you can use any of the options listed in the PostgreSQL documentation (*http://bit.ly/pgsql-param*).
Oracle	oci	dbname, charset	The value of dbname should either be an Oracle Instant Client connection URI of the form //hostname:port/database or an address name defined in your *tnsnames.ora* file.

Database program	DSN prefix	DSN options	Notes
SQLite	sqlite	None	After the prefix, the entire DSN must be either a path to an SQLite database file, or the string :memory: to use a temporary in-memory database.
ODBC	odbc	DSN, UID, PWD	The value for the DSN key inside the DSN string should either be a name defined in your ODBC catalog or a full ODBC connection string.
MS SQL Server or Sybase	mssql, sybase, dblib	host, dbname, charset, appname	The appname value is a string that the database program uses to describe your connection in its statistics. The mssql prefix is for when the PHP engine is using Microsoft's SQL Server libraries; the sybase prefix is for when the engine is using Sybase CT-Lib libraries; the dblib prefix is for when the engine is using the FreeTDS libraries.

The host and port DSN options, as seen in Example 8-1, specify the host and net-work port of the database server. The charset option, available with some database programs, specifies how the database program should handle non-English characters. The user and password options for PostgreSQL and the UID and PWD options for ODBC provide a way to put the connection username and password in the DSN string. If they are used, their values override any username or password passed as additional arguments to the PDO constructor.

If all goes well with new PDO(), it returns an object that you use to interact with the database. If there is a problem connecting, it throws a PDOException exception. Make sure to catch exceptions that could be thrown from the PDO constructor so you can verify that the connection succeeded before going forward in your program. Example 8-2 shows how to do this.

Example 8-2. Catching connection errors

```
try {
    $db = new PDO('mysql:host=localhost;dbname=restaurant','penguin','top^hat');
    // Do some stuff with $db here
} catch (PDOException $e) {
    print "Couldn't connect to the database: " . $e->getMessage();
}
```

In Example 8-2, if the PDO constructor throws an exception, then any code inside the try block after the call to new PDO() doesn't execute. Instead, the PHP engine jumps ahead to the catch block, where an error is displayed.

For example, if top^hat is the wrong password for user penguin, Example 8-2 prints something like:

```
Couldn't connect to the database: SQLSTATE[HY000] [1045] Access denied
for user 'penguin'@'client.example.com'
(using password: YES)
```

Creating a Table

Before you can put any data into or retrieve any data from a database table, you must create the table. This is usually a one-time operation. You tell the database program to create a new table once. Your PHP program that uses the table may read from or write to that table every time it runs, but it doesn't have to re-create the table each time. If a database table is like a spreadsheet, then creating a table is like making a new spreadsheet file. After you create the file, you can open it many times to read or change it.

The SQL command to create a table is CREATE TABLE. You provide the name of the table and the names and types of all the columns in the table. Example 8-3 shows the SQL command to create the dishes table pictured in Figure 8-1.

Example 8-3. Creating the dishes table

```
CREATE TABLE dishes (
    dish_id INTEGER PRIMARY KEY,
    dish_name VARCHAR(255),
    price DECIMAL(4,2),
    is_spicy INT
)
```

Example 8-3 creates a table called dishes with four columns. The dishes table looks like the one pictured in Figure 8-1. The columns in the table are dish_id, dish_name, price, and is_spicy. The dish_id and is_spicy columns are integers. The price column is a decimal number. The dish_name column is a string.

After the literal CREATE TABLE comes the name of the table. Then, between the parentheses, is a comma-separated list of the columns in the table. The phrase that defines each column has two parts: the column name and the column type. In Example 8-3, the column names are dish_id, dish_name, price, and is_spicy. The column types are INTEGER, VARCHAR(255), DECIMAL(4,2), and INT.

Additionally, the dish_id column's type has PRIMARY KEY after it. This tells the database program that the values for this column can't be duplicated in this table. Only one row can have a particular dish_id value at a time. Additionally, this lets SQLite, the database program used in this chapter's examples, automatically assign new unique values to this column when we insert data. Other database programs have different syntax for automatically assigning unique integer IDs. For example, MySQL uses the AUTO_INCREMENT keyword, PostgreSQL uses serial types, and Oracle uses sequences.

INT and INTEGER can generally be used interchangeably. However, a quirk of SQLite is that in order to get the automatic assign-new-unique-values behavior with PRIMARY KEY, you need to specify the column type INTEGER exactly.

Some column types include length or formatting information in parentheses. For example, VARCHAR(255) means "a variable-length character column that is at most 255 characters long." The type DECIMAL(4,2) means "a decimal number with two digits after the decimal place and four digits total." Table 8-2 lists some common types for database table columns.

Table 8-2. Common database table column types

Column type	Description
VARCHAR(*length*)	A variable-length string up to *length* characters long
INT	An integer
BLOB[a]	Up to 64 KB of string or binary data
DECIMAL(*total_digits,decimal_places*)	A decimal number with a total of *total_digits* digits and *decimal_places* digits after the decimal point
DATETIME[b]	A date and time, such as 1975-03-10 19:45:03 or 2038-01-18 22:14:07

[a] PostgreSQL calls this BYTEA instead of BLOB.

[b] Oracle calls this DATE instead of DATETIME.

Different database programs support different column types, although all database programs should support the types listed in Table 8-2. The maximum and minimum numbers that the database can handle in numeric columns and the maximum size of text columns varies based on what database program you are using. For example, MySQL allows VARCHAR columns to be up to 255 characters long, but Microsoft SQL Server allows VARCHAR columns to be up to 8,000 characters long. Check your database manual for the specifics that apply to you.

To actually create the table, you need to send the CREATE TABLE command to the database. After connecting with new PDO(), use the exec() function to send the command as shown in Example 8-4.

Example 8-4. Sending a CREATE TABLE command to the database program

```
try {
    $db = new PDO('sqlite:/tmp/restaurant.db');
    $db->setAttribute(PDO::ATTR_ERRMODE, PDO::ERRMODE_EXCEPTION);
    $q = $db->exec("CREATE TABLE dishes (
```

```
        dish_id INT,
        dish_name VARCHAR(255),
        price DECIMAL(4,2),
        is_spicy INT
)");
} catch (PDOException $e) {
    print "Couldn't create table: " . $e->getMessage();
}
```

The next section explains exec() in much more detail. The call to $db->setAttribute() in Example 8-4 ensures that PDO throws exceptions if there are problems with queries, not just a problem when connecting. Error handling with PDO is also discussed in the next section.

The opposite of CREATE TABLE is DROP TABLE. It removes a table and the data in it from a database. Example 8-5 shows the syntax of a query that removes the dishes table.

Example 8-5. Removing a table

```
DROP TABLE dishes
```

Once you've dropped a table, it's gone for good, so be careful with DROP TABLE!

Putting Data into the Database

Assuming the connection to the database succeeds, the object returned by new PDO() provides access to the data in your database. Calling that object's functions lets you send queries to the database program and access the results. To put some data into the database, pass an INSERT statement to the object's exec() method, as shown in Example 8-6.

Example 8-6. Inserting data with exec()

```
try {
    $db = new PDO('sqlite:/tmp/restaurant.db');
    $db->setAttribute(PDO::ATTR_ERRMODE, PDO::ERRMODE_EXCEPTION);
    $affectedRows = $db->exec("INSERT INTO dishes (dish_name, price, is_spicy)
                                    VALUES ('Sesame Seed Puff', 2.50, 0)");
} catch (PDOException $e) {
    print "Couldn't insert a row: " . $e->getMessage();
}
```

The exec() method returns the number of rows affected by the SQL statement that was sent to the database server. In this case, inserting one row returns 1 because one row (the row you inserted) was affected.

If something goes wrong with INSERT, an exception is thrown. Example 8-7 attempts an INSERT statement that has a bad column name in it. The dishes table doesn't contain a column called dish_size.

Example 8-7. Checking for errors from exec()

```
try {
    $db = new PDO('sqlite:/tmp/restaurant.db');
    $db->setAttribute(PDO::ATTR_ERRMODE, PDO::ERRMODE_EXCEPTION);
    $affectedRows = $db->exec("INSERT INTO dishes (dish_size, dish_name,
                                        price, is_spicy)
                            VALUES ('large', 'Sesame Seed Puff', 2.50, 0)");
} catch (PDOException $e) {
    print "Couldn't insert a row: " . $e->getMessage();
}
```

Because the call to $db->setAttribute() tells PDO to throw an exception any time there's an error, Example 8-7 prints:

```
Couldn't insert a row: SQLSTATE[HY000]: General error: 1 table dishes
has no column named dish_size
```

PDO has three error modes: exception, silent, and warning. The exception error mode, which is activated by calling $db->setAttribute(PDO::ATTR_ERRMODE, PDO::ERRMODE_EXCEPTION), is the best for debugging and is the mode that makes it easiest to ensure you don't miss a database problem. If you don't handle an exception that PDO generates, your program stops running.

The other two error modes require you to check the return values from your PDO function calls to determine if there is an error and then use additional PDO methods to find information about the error.

The silent mode is the default. Like other PDO methods, if exec() fails at its task, it returns false. Example 8-8 checks exec()'s return value and then uses PDO's errorInfo() method to get details of the problem.

Example 8-8. Working with the silent error mode

```
// The constructor always throws an exception if it fails
try {
    $db = new PDO('sqlite:/tmp/restaurant.db');
} catch (PDOException $e) {
    print "Couldn't connect: " . $e->getMessage();
}
$result = $db->exec("INSERT INTO dishes (dish_size, dish_name, price, is_spicy)
                        VALUES ('large', 'Sesame Seed Puff', 2.50, 0)");
if (false === $result) {
    $error = $db->errorInfo();
    print "Couldn't insert!\n";
```

```
    print "SQL Error={$error[0]}, DB Error={$error[1]}, Message={$error[2]}\n";
}
```

Example 8-8 prints:

```
Couldn't insert!
SQL Error=HY000, DB Error=1, Message=table dishes has no column named dish_size
```

In Example 8-8, the return value from exec() is compared with false using the triple-equals-sign identity operator to distinguish between an actual error (false) and a successful query that just happened to affect zero rows. Then, errorInfo() returns a three-element array with error information. The first element is an SQLSTATE error code. These are error codes that are mostly standardized across different database programs. In this case, HY000 is a catch-all for general errors. The second element is an error code specific to the particular database program in use. The third element is a textual message describing the error.

The warning mode is activated by setting the PDO::ATTR_ERRMODE attribute to PDO::ERRMODE_WARNING, as shown in Example 8-9. In this mode, functions behave as they do in silent mode—no exceptions, returning false on error—but the PHP engine also generates a warning-level error message. Depending on how you've configured error handling, this message may get displayed on screen or in a log file. "Controlling Where Errors Appear" on page 249 shows how to control where error messages appear.

Example 8-9. Working with the warning error mode

```
// The constructor always throws an exception if it fails
try {
    $db = new PDO('sqlite:/tmp/restaurant.db');
} catch (PDOException $e) {
    print "Couldn't connect: " . $e->getMessage();
}
$db->setAttribute(PDO::ATTR_ERRMODE, PDO::ERRMODE_WARNING);
$result = $db->exec("INSERT INTO dishes (dish_size, dish_name, price, is_spicy)
                     VALUES ('large', 'Sesame Seed Puff', 2.50, 0)");
if (false === $result) {
    $error = $db->errorInfo();
    print "Couldn't insert!\n";
    print "SQL Error={$error[0]}, DB Error={$error[1]}, Message={$error[2]}\n";
}
```

Example 8-9 produces the same output as Example 8-8 but also generates the following error message:

```
PHP Warning:  PDO::exec(): SQLSTATE[HY000]: General error: 1 table dishes
has no column named dish_size in error-warning.php on line 10
```

SQL Lesson: INSERT

The INSERT command adds a row to a database table. Example 8-10 shows the syntax of INSERT.

Example 8-10. Inserting data

```
INSERT INTO table (column1[, column2, column3, ...])
    VALUES (value1[, value2, value3, ...])
```

The INSERT query in Example 8-11 adds a new dish to the dishes table.

Example 8-11. Inserting a new dish

```
INSERT INTO dishes (dish_id, dish_name, price, is_spicy)
    VALUES (1, 'Braised Sea Cucumber', 6.50, 0)
```

String values such as Braised Sea Cucumber have to have single quotes around them when used in an SQL query. Because single quotes are used as string delimiters, you need to escape single quotes (by putting two single quotes in a row) when they appear inside of a query. Example 8-12 shows how to insert a dish named General Tso's Chicken into the dishes table.

Example 8-12. Quoting a string value

```
INSERT INTO dishes (dish_id, dish_name, price, is_spicy)
    VALUES (2, 'General Tso''s Chicken', 6.75, 1)
```

The number of columns enumerated in the parentheses before VALUES must match the number of values in the parentheses after VALUES. To insert a row that contains values only for some columns, just specify those columns and their corresponding values, as shown in Example 8-13.

Example 8-13. Inserting without all columns

```
INSERT INTO dishes (dish_name, is_spicy)
    VALUES ('Salt Baked Scallops', 0)
```

As a shortcut, you can eliminate the column list when you're inserting values for all columns. Example 8-14 performs the same INSERT as Example 8-11.

Example 8-14. Inserting with values for all columns

```
INSERT INTO dishes
    VALUES (1, 'Braised Sea Cucumber', 6.50, 0)
```

Use the exec() function to change data with UPDATE. Example 8-15 shows some UPDATE statements.

Example 8-15. Changing data with exec()

```
try {
    $db = new PDO('sqlite:/tmp/restaurant.db');
    $db->setAttribute(PDO::ATTR_ERRMODE, PDO::ERRMODE_EXCEPTION);
    // Eggplant with Chili Sauce is spicy
    // If we don't care how many rows are affected,
    // there's no need to keep the return value from exec()
    $db->exec("UPDATE dishes SET is_spicy = 1
               WHERE dish_name = 'Eggplant with Chili Sauce'");
    // Lobster with Chili Sauce is spicy and pricy
    $db->exec("UPDATE dishes SET is_spicy = 1, price=price * 2
               WHERE dish_name = 'Lobster with Chili Sauce'");
} catch (PDOException $e) {
    print "Couldn't insert a row: " . $e->getMessage();
}
```

Also use the exec() function to delete data with DELETE. Example 8-16 shows exec() with two DELETE statements.

Example 8-16. Deleting data with exec()

```
try {
    $db = new PDO('sqlite:/tmp/restaurant.db');
    $db->setAttribute(PDO::ATTR_ERRMODE, PDO::ERRMODE_EXCEPTION);
    // remove expensive dishes
    if ($make_things_cheaper) {
        $db->exec("DELETE FROM dishes WHERE price > 19.95");
    } else {
        // or, remove all dishes
        $db->exec("DELETE FROM dishes");
    }
} catch (PDOException $e) {
    print "Couldn't delete rows: " . $e->getMessage();
}
```

SQL Lesson: UPDATE

The UPDATE command changes data already in a table. Example 8-17 shows the syntax of UPDATE.

Example 8-17. Updating data

```
UPDATE tablename SET column1=value1[, column2=value2,
    column3=value3, ...] [WHERE where_clause]
```

The value that a column is changed to can be a string or number, as shown in Example 8-18. The lines in Example 8-18 that begin with ; are SQL comments.

Example 8-18. Setting a column to a string or number

```
; Change price to 5.50 in all rows of the table
UPDATE dishes SET price = 5.50

; Change is_spicy to 1 in all rows of the table
UPDATE dishes SET is_spicy = 1
```

The value can also be an expression that includes column names. The query in Example 8-19 doubles the price of each dish.

Example 8-19. Using a column name in an UPDATE expression

```
UPDATE dishes SET price = price * 2
```

The UPDATE queries shown so far change all rows in the dishes table. To only change some rows with an UPDATE query, add a WHERE clause. This is a logical expression that describes which rows you want to change. The changes in the UPDATE query then happen only in rows that match the WHERE clause. Example 8-20 contains two UPDATE queries, each with a WHERE clause.

Example 8-20. Using a WHERE clause with UPDATE

```
; Change the spicy status of Eggplant with Chili Sauce
UPDATE dishes SET is_spicy = 1
             WHERE dish_name = 'Eggplant with Chili Sauce'

; Decrease the price of General Tso's Chicken
UPDATE dishes SET price = price - 1
             WHERE dish_name = 'General Tso's Chicken'
```

The WHERE clause is explained in more detail in the sidebar "SQL Lesson: SELECT" on page 175.

Remember that exec() returns the number of rows changed or removed by an UPDATE or DELETE statement. Use the return value to find out how many rows that query affected. Example 8-21 reports how many rows have had their prices changed by an UPDATE query.

Example 8-21. Finding how many rows an UPDATE or DELETE affects

```
// Decrease the price of some dishes
$count = $db->exec("UPDATE dishes SET price = price + 5 WHERE price > 3");
print 'Changed the price of ' . $count . ' rows.';
```

If there are two rows in the dishes table whose price is more than 3, then Example 8-21 prints:

```
Changed the price of 2 rows.
```

SQL Lesson: DELETE

The DELETE command removes rows from a table. Example 8-22 shows the syntax of DELETE.

Example 8-22. Removing rows from a table

```
DELETE FROM tablename [WHERE where_clause]
```

Without a WHERE clause, DELETE removes all the rows from the table. Example 8-23 clears out the dishes table.

Example 8-23. Removing all rows from a table

```
DELETE FROM dishes
```

With a WHERE clause, DELETE removes the rows that match the WHERE clause. Example 8-24 shows two DELETE queries with WHERE clauses.

Example 8-24. Removing some rows from a table

```
; Delete rows in which price is greater than 10.00
DELETE FROM dishes WHERE price > 10.00

; Delete rows in which dish_name is exactly "Walnut Bun"
DELETE FROM dishes WHERE dish_name = 'Walnut Bun'
```

There is no SQL UNDELETE command, so be careful with your DELETEs.

Inserting Form Data Safely

As "HTML and JavaScript" on page 138 explained, printing unsanitized form data can leave you and your users vulnerable to a cross-site scripting attack. Using unsanitized form data in SQL queries can cause a similar problem, called an "SQL injection attack." Consider a form that lets a user suggest a new dish. The form contains a text element called new_dish_name into which the user can type the name of a new dish. The call to exec() in Example 8-25 inserts the new dish into the dishes table, but is vulnerable to an SQL injection attack.

Example 8-25. Unsafe insertion of form data

```
$db->exec("INSERT INTO dishes (dish_name)
       VALUES ('$_POST[new_dish_name]')");
```

If the submitted value for new_dish_name is reasonable, such as Fried Bean Curd, then the query succeeds. PHP's regular double-quoted string interpolation rules make the query INSERT INTO dishes (dish_name) VALUES ('Fried Bean Curd'), which is valid and respectable. A query with an apostrophe in it causes a problem, though. If the submitted value for new_dish_name is General Tso's Chicken, then the query becomes INSERT INTO dishes (dish_name) VALUES ('General Tso's Chicken'). This makes the database program confused. It thinks that the apostrophe between Tso and s ends the string, so the s Chicken' after the second single quote is an unwanted syntax error.

What's worse, a user who really wants to cause problems can type in specially constructed input to wreak havoc. Consider this unappetizing input:

```
x'); DELETE FROM dishes; INSERT INTO dishes (dish_name) VALUES ('y.
```

When that gets interpolated, the query becomes:

```
INSERT INTO DISHES (dish_name) VALUES ('x');
DELETE FROM dishes; INSERT INTO dishes (dish_name) VALUES ('y')
```

Some databases let you pass multiple queries separated by semicolons in one call of exec(). On those databases, the previous input will cause the dishes table to be demolished: a dish named x is inserted, all dishes are deleted, and a dish named y is inserted.

By submitting a carefully built form input value, a malicious user can inject arbitrary SQL statements into your database program. To prevent this, you need to escape special characters (most importantly, the apostrophe) in SQL queries. PDO provides a helpful feature called *prepared statements* that makes this a snap.

With prepared statements, you separate your query execution into two steps. First, you give PDO's prepare() method a version of your query with a ? in the SQL in each place you want a value to go. This method returns a PDOStatement object. Then, you call execute() on your PDOStatement object, passing it an array of values to be substituted for the placeholding ? characters. The values are appropriately quoted before they are put into the query, protecting you from SQL injection attacks. Example 8-26 shows the safe version of the query from Example 8-25.

Example 8-26. Safe insertion of form data

```
$stmt = $db->prepare('INSERT INTO dishes (dish_name) VALUES (?)');
$stmt->execute(array($_POST['new_dish_name']));
```

You don't need to put quotes around the placeholder in the query. PDO takes care of that for you, too. If you want to use multiple values in a query, put multiple placeholders in the query and in the value array. Example 8-27 shows a query with three placeholders.

Example 8-27. Using multiple placeholders

```
$stmt = $db->prepare('INSERT INTO dishes (dish_name,price,is_spicy) VALUES (?,?,?)');
$stmt->execute(array($_POST['new_dish_name'], $_POST['new_price'],
                     $_POST['is_spicy']));
```

A Complete Data Insertion Form

Example 8-28 combines the database topics covered so far in this chapter with the form-handling code from Chapter 7 to build a complete program that displays a form, validates the submitted data, and then saves the data into a database table. The form displays input elements for the name of a dish, the price of a dish, and whether the dish is spicy. The information is inserted into the dishes table.

The code in Example 8-28 relies on the FormHelper class defined in Example 7-29. Instead of repeating it in this example, the code assumes it has been saved into a file called *FormHelper.php* and then loads it with the require 'FormHelper.php' line at the top of the program.

Example 8-28. Program for inserting records into dishes

```php
<?php

// Load the form helper class
require 'FormHelper.php';

// Connect to the database
try {
    $db = new PDO('sqlite:/tmp/restaurant.db');
} catch (PDOException $e) {
    print "Can't connect: " . $e->getMessage();
    exit();
}
// Set up exceptions on DB errors
$db->setAttribute(PDO::ATTR_ERRMODE, PDO::ERRMODE_EXCEPTION);

// The main page logic:
// - If the form is submitted, validate and then process or redisplay
// - If it's not submitted, display
if ($_SERVER['REQUEST_METHOD'] == 'POST') {
    // If validate_form() returns errors, pass them to show_form()
    list($errors, $input) = validate_form();
    if ($errors) {
```

```
            show_form($errors);
        } else {
            // The submitted data is valid, so process it
            process_form($input);
        }
    } else {
        // The form wasn't submitted, so display
        show_form();
    }

    function show_form($errors = array()) {
        // Set our own defaults: price is $5
        $defaults = array('price' => '5.00');

        // Set up the $form object with proper defaults
        $form = new FormHelper($defaults);

        // All the HTML and form display is in a separate file for clarity
        include 'insert-form.php';
    }

    function validate_form() {
        $input = array();
        $errors = array();

        // dish_name is required
        $input['dish_name'] = trim($_POST['dish_name'] ?? '');
        if (! strlen($input['dish_name'])) {
            $errors[] = 'Please enter the name of the dish.';
        }

        // price must be a valid floating-point number and
        // more than 0
        $input['price'] = filter_input(INPUT_POST, 'price', FILTER_VALIDATE_FLOAT);
        if ($input['price'] <= 0) {
            $errors[] = 'Please enter a valid price.';
        }

        // is_spicy defaults to 'no'
        $input['is_spicy'] = $_POST['is_spicy'] ?? 'no';

        return array($errors, $input);
    }

    function process_form($input) {
        // Access the global variable $db inside this function
        global $db;

        // Set the value of $is_spicy based on the checkbox
        if ($input['is_spicy'] == 'yes') {
            $is_spicy = 1;
        } else {
```

```
        $is_spicy = 0;
    }

    // Insert the new dish into the table
    try {
        $stmt = $db->prepare('INSERT INTO dishes (dish_name, price, is_spicy)
                              VALUES (?,?,?)');
        $stmt->execute(array($input['dish_name'], $input['price'],$is_spicy));
        // Tell the user that we added a dish
        print 'Added ' . htmlentities($input['dish_name']) . ' to the database.';
    } catch (PDOException $e) {
        print "Couldn't add your dish to the database.";
    }
}

?>
```

Example 8-28 has the same basic structure as the form examples from Chapter 7: functions for displaying, validating, and processing the form with some global logic that determines which function to call. The two new pieces are the global code that sets up the database connection and the database-related activities in process_form().

The database setup code comes after the require statements and before the if ($_SERVER['REQUEST_METHOD'] == 'POST'). The new PDO() call establishes a database connection, and the next few lines check to make sure the connection succeeded and then set up exception mode for error handling.

The show_form() function displays the form HTML defined in the *insert-form.php* file. This file is shown in Example 8-29.

Example 8-29. Form for inserting records into dishes

```
<form method="POST" action="<?= $form->encode($_SERVER['PHP_SELF']) ?>">
<table>
    <?php if ($errors) { ?>
        <tr>
            <td>You need to correct the following errors:</td>
            <td><ul>
                <?php foreach ($errors as $error) { ?>
                    <li><?= $form->encode($error) ?></li>
                <?php } ?>
            </ul></td>
    <?php } ?>

    <tr>
        <td>Dish Name:</td>
        <td><?= $form->input('text', ['name' => 'dish_name']) ?></td>
    </tr>
    <tr>
```

```
        <td>Price:</td>
        <td><?= $form->input('text', ['name' => 'price']) ?></td>
    </tr>

    <tr>
        <td>Spicy:</td>
        <td><?= $form->input('checkbox',['name' => 'is_spicy',
                                         'value' => 'yes']) ?> Yes</td>
    </tr>

    <tr><td colspan="2" align="center">
        <?= $form->input('submit',['name' => 'save','value' => 'Order']) ?>
    </td></tr>

</table>
</form>
```

Aside from connecting, all of the other interaction with the database is in the `process_form()` function. First, the `global $db` line lets you refer to the database connection variable inside the function as `$db` instead of the clumsier `$GLOBALS['db']`. Then, because the `is_spicy` column of the table holds a `1` in the rows of spicy dishes and a `0` in the rows of nonspicy dishes, the `if()` clause in `process_form()` assigns the appropriate value to the local variable `$is_spicy` based on what was submitted in `$input['is_spicy']`.

After that come the calls to `prepare()` and `execute()` that actually put the new information into the database. The `INSERT` statement has three placeholders that are filled by the variables `$input['dish_name']`, `$input['price']`, and `$is_spicy`. No value is necessary for the `dish_id` column because SQLite populates that automatically. Lastly, `process_form()` prints a message telling the user that the dish was inserted. The `htmlentities()` function protects against any HTML tags or JavaScript in the dish name. Because `prepare()` and `execute()` are inside a `try` block, if anything goes wrong, an alternate error message is printed.

Retrieving Data from the Database

Use the `query()` method to retrieve information from the database. Pass it an SQL query for the database. It returns a `PDOStatement` object that provides access to the retrieved rows. Each time you call the `fetch()` method of this object, you get the next row returned from the query. When there are no more rows left, `fetch()` returns a value that evaluates to `false`, making it perfect to use in a `while()` loop. This is shown in Example 8-30.

Example 8-30. Retrieving rows with query() and fetch()

```
$q = $db->query('SELECT dish_name, price FROM dishes');
while ($row = $q->fetch()) {
    print "$row[dish_name], $row[price] \n";
}
```

Example 8-30 prints:

```
Walnut Bun, 1
Cashew Nuts and White Mushrooms, 4.95
Dried Mulberries, 3
Eggplant with Chili Sauce, 6.5
```

The first time through the while() loop, fetch() returns an array containing Walnut Bun and 1. This array is assigned to $row. Since an array with elements in it evaluates to true, the code inside the while() loop executes, printing the data from the first row returned by the SELECT query. This happens three more times. On each trip through the while() loop, fetch() returns the next row in the set of rows returned by the SELECT query. When it has no more rows to return, fetch() returns a value that evaluates to false, and the while() loop is done.

By default, fetch() returns an array with both numeric and string keys. The numeric keys, starting at 0, contain each column's value for the row. The string keys do as well, with key names set to column names. In Example 8-30, the same results could be printed using $row[0] and $row[1].

If you want to find out how many rows a SELECT query has returned, your only fool-proof option is to retrieve all the rows and count them. The PDOStatement object provides a rowCount() method, but it doesn't work with all databases. If you have a small number of rows and you're going to use them all in your program, use the fetchAll() method to put them into an array without looping, as shown in Example 8-31.

Example 8-31. Retrieving all rows without a loop

```
$q = $db->query('SELECT dish_name, price FROM dishes');
// $rows will be a four-element array; each element is
// one row of data from the database
$rows = $q->fetchAll();
```

If you have so many rows that retrieving them all is impractical, ask your database program to count the rows for you with SQL's COUNT() function. For example, SELECT COUNT(*) FROM dishes returns one row with one column whose value is the number of rows in the entire table.

SQL Lesson: SELECT

The SELECT command retrieves data from the database. Example 8-32 shows the syntax of SELECT.

Example 8-32. Retrieving data

```
SELECT column1[, column2, column3, ...] FROM tablename
```

The SELECT query in Example 8-33 retrieves the dish_name and price columns for all the rows in the dishes table.

Example 8-33. Retrieving dish_name and price

```
SELECT dish_name, price FROM dishes
```

As a shortcut, you can use * instead of a list of columns. This retrieves all columns from the table. The SELECT query in Example 8-34 retrieves everything from the dishes table.

*Example 8-34. Using * in a SELECT query*

```
SELECT * FROM dishes
```

To restrict a SELECT statement so that it matches only certain rows, add a WHERE clause to it. Only rows that meet the tests listed in the WHERE clause are returned by the SELECT statement. The WHERE clause goes after the table name, as shown in Example 8-35.

Example 8-35. Restricting the rows returned by SELECT

```
SELECT column1[, column2, column3, ...] FROM tablename
      WHERE where_clause
```

The *where_clause* part of the query is a logical expression that describes which rows you want to retrieve. Example 8-36 shows some SELECT queries with WHERE clauses.

Example 8-36. Retrieving certain dishes

```
; Dishes with price greater than 5.00
SELECT dish_name, price FROM dishes WHERE price > 5.00

; Dishes whose name exactly matches "Walnut Bun"
SELECT price FROM dishes WHERE dish_name = 'Walnut Bun'

; Dishes with price more than 5.00 but less than or equal to 10.00
SELECT dish_name FROM dishes WHERE price > 5.00 AND price <= 10.00

; Dishes with price more than 5.00 but less than or equal to 10.00,
; or dishes whose name exactly matches "Walnut Bun" (at any price)
```

```
SELECT dish_name, price FROM dishes WHERE (price > 5.00 AND price <= 10.00)
    OR dish_name = 'Walnut Bun'
```

Table 8-3 lists some operators that you can use in a WHERE clause.

Table 8-3. SQL WHERE clause operators

Operator	Description
=	Equal to (like == in PHP)
<>	Not equal to (like != in PHP)
>	Greater than
<	Less than
>=	Greater than or equal to
<=	Less than or equal to
AND	Logical AND (like && in PHP)
OR	Logical OR (like || in PHP)
( )	Grouping

If you are expecting only one row to be returned from a query, you can chain your fetch() call onto the end of query(). Example 8-37 uses a chained fetch() to display the least expensive item in the dishes table. The ORDER BY and LIMIT parts of the query in Example 8-37 are explained in the sidebar "SQL Lesson: ORDER BY and LIMIT" on page 176.

Example 8-37. Retrieving a row with a chained fetch()

```
$cheapest_dish_info = $db->query('SELECT dish_name, price
                                FROM dishes ORDER BY price LIMIT 1')->fetch();
print "$cheapest_dish_info[0], $cheapest_dish_info[1]";
```

Example 8-37 prints:

```
Walnut Bun, 1
```

SQL Lesson: ORDER BY and LIMIT

As mentioned in "Organizing Data in a Database" on page 156, rows in a table don't have any inherent order. A database server doesn't have to return rows from a SELECT query in any particular pattern. To force a certain order on the returned rows, add an ORDER BY clause to your SELECT. Example 8-38 returns all the rows in the dishes table ordered by price, lowest to highest.

Example 8-38. Ordering rows returned from a SELECT query

```
SELECT dish_name FROM dishes ORDER BY price
```

To order from highest to lowest value, add `DESC` (descending) after the column that the results are ordered by. Example 8-39 returns all the rows in the `dishes` table ordered by price, highest to lowest.

Example 8-39. Ordering from highest to lowest

```
SELECT dish_name FROM dishes ORDER BY price DESC
```

You can specify multiple columns to order by. If two rows have the same value for the first `ORDER BY` column, they are sorted by the second. The query in Example 8-40 orders rows in `dishes` by price (highest to lowest). If multiple rows have the same price, then they are ordered alphabetically by name.

Example 8-40. Ordering by multiple columns

```
SELECT dish_name FROM dishes ORDER BY price DESC, dish_name
```

Using `ORDER BY` doesn't change the order of the rows in the table itself (remember, they don't really have any set order), but rearranges the results of the query. This affects only the answer to the query. If you hand someone a menu and ask him to read you the appetizers in alphabetical order, it doesn't affect the printed menu—just the response to your query ("Read me all the appetizers in alphabetical order").

Normally, a `SELECT` query returns all rows that match the `WHERE` clause (or all rows in a table if there is no `WHERE` clause). Sometimes it's helpful to just get a certain number of rows back. You may want to find the lowest-priced dish available or just print 10 search results. To restrict the results to a specific number of rows, add a `LIMIT` clause to the end of the query. Example 8-41 returns the row from `dishes` with the lowest price.

Example 8-41. Limiting the number of rows returned by SELECT

```
SELECT * FROM dishes ORDER BY price LIMIT 1
```

Example 8-42 returns the first (sorted alphabetically by dish name) 10 rows from `dishes`.

Example 8-42. Still limiting the number of rows returned by SELECT

```
SELECT dish_name, price FROM dishes ORDER BY dish_name LIMIT 10
```

In general, you should only use `LIMIT` in a query that also has an `ORDER BY` clause. If you leave out `ORDER BY`, the database program can return rows in any order. So, the "first" row one time a query is executed might not be the "first" row another time the same query is executed.

Changing the Format of Retrieved Rows

So far, fetch() has been returning rows from the database as combined numerically and string-indexed arrays. This makes for concise and easy interpolation of values in double-quoted strings—but it can also be problematic. Trying to remember, for example, which column from the SELECT query corresponds to element 6 in the result array can be difficult and error-prone. Some string column names might require quoting to interpolate properly. And having the PHP engine set up numeric indexes and string indexes is wasteful if you don't need them both. Fortunately, PDO lets you specify that you'd prefer to have each result row delivered in a different way. Pass an alternate *fetch style* to fetch() or fetchAll() as a first argument and you get your row back as only a numeric array, only a string array, or an object.

To get a row back as an array with only numeric keys, pass PDO::FETCH_NUM as the first argument to fetch() or fetchAll(). To get an array with only string keys, use PDO::FETCH_ASSOC (remember that string-keyed arrays are sometimes called "associative" arrays).

To get a row back as an object instead of an array, use PDO::FETCH_OBJ. The object that's returned for each row has property names that correspond to column names.

Example 8-43 shows these alternate fetch styles in action.

Example 8-43. Using a different fetch style

```
// With numeric indexes only, it's easy to join the values together
$q = $db->query('SELECT dish_name, price FROM dishes');
while ($row = $q->fetch(PDO::FETCH_NUM)) {
    print implode(', ', $row) . "\n";
}

// With an object, property access syntax gets you the values
$q = $db->query('SELECT dish_name, price FROM dishes');
while ($row = $q->fetch(PDO::FETCH_OBJ)) {
    print "{$row->dish_name} has price {$row->price} \n";
}
```

If you want to use an alternate fetch style repeatedly, you can set the default for a particular statement for all queries you issue on a given connection. To set the default for a statement, call setFetchMode() on your PDOStatement object, as shown in Example 8-44.

Example 8-44. Setting a default fetch style on a statement

```
$q = $db->query('SELECT dish_name, price FROM dishes');
// No need to pass anything to fetch(); setFetchMode()
// takes care of it
```

```
$q->setFetchMode(PDO::FETCH_NUM);
while($row = $q->fetch()) {
    print implode(', ', $row) . "\n";
}
```

To set the default fetch style for everything, use `setAttribute()` to set the `PDO::ATTR_DEFAULT_FETCH_MODE` attribute on your database connection, like this:

```
// No need to call setFetchMode() or pass anything to fetch();
// setAttribute() takes care of it
$db->setAttribute(PDO::ATTR_DEFAULT_FETCH_MODE, PDO::FETCH_NUM);

$q = $db->query('SELECT dish_name, price FROM dishes');
while ($row = $q->fetch()) {
    print implode(', ', $row) . "\n";
}

$anotherQuery = $db->query('SELECT dish_name FROM dishes WHERE price < 5');
// Each subarray in $moreDishes is numerically indexed, too
$moreDishes = $anotherQuery->fetchAll();
```

Retrieving Form Data Safely

It's possible to use placeholders with SELECT statements just as you do with INSERT, UPDATE, or DELETE statements. Instead of using query() directly, use prepare() and execute(), but give prepare() a SELECT statement.

However, when you use submitted form data or other external input in the WHERE clause of a SELECT, UPDATE, or DELETE statement, you must take extra care to ensure that any SQL wildcards are appropriately escaped. Consider a search form with a text element called dish_search into which the user can type the name of a dish she's looking for. The call to execute() in Example 8-45 uses placeholders to guard against confounding single quotes in the submitted value.

Example 8-45. Using a placeholder in a SELECT statement

```
$stmt = $db->prepare('SELECT dish_name, price FROM dishes
                      WHERE dish_name LIKE ?');
$stmt->execute(array($_POST['dish_search']));
while ($row = $stmt->fetch()) {
    // ... do something with $row ...
}
```

Whether dish_search is Fried Bean Curd or General Tso's Chicken, the placeholder interpolates the value into the query appropriately. However, what if dish_search is %chicken%? Then, the query becomes SELECT dish_name, price FROM dishes WHERE dish_name LIKE '%chicken%'. This matches all rows that contain the string chicken, not just rows in which dish_name is exactly %chicken%.

SQL Lesson: Wildcards

Wildcards are useful for matching text inexactly, such as finding strings that end with .edu or that contain @. SQL has two wildcards: the underscore (_) matches one character and the percent sign (%) matches any number of characters (including zero characters). The wildcards are active inside strings used with the LIKE operator in a WHERE clause.

Example 8-46 shows two SELECT queries that use LIKE and wildcards.

Example 8-46. Using wildcards with SELECT

```
; Retrieve all rows in which dish name begins with D
SELECT * FROM dishes WHERE dish_name LIKE 'D%'

; Retrieve rows in which dish name is Fried Cod, Fried Bod,
; Fried Nod, and so on.
SELECT * FROM dishes WHERE dish_name LIKE 'Fried _od'
```

Wildcards are active in the WHERE clauses of UPDATE and DELETE statements, too. The query in Example 8-47 doubles the prices of all dishes that have chili in their names.

Example 8-47. Using wildcards with UPDATE

```
UPDATE dishes SET price = price * 2 WHERE dish_name LIKE '%chili%'
```

The query in Example 8-48 deletes all rows whose dish_name ends with Shrimp.

Example 8-48. Using wildcards with DELETE

```
DELETE FROM dishes WHERE dish_name LIKE '%Shrimp'
```

To match against a literal % or _ when using the LIKE operator, put a backslash before the % or _. The query in Example 8-49 finds all rows whose dish_name contains 50% off.

Example 8-49. Escaping wildcards

```
SELECT * FROM dishes WHERE dish_name LIKE '%50\% off%'
```

Without the backslash, the query in Example 8-49 would match rows whose dish_name contains 50 and then has a space and off somewhere later in the name, such as Spicy 50 shrimp with shells off salad or Famous 500 offer duck.

To prevent SQL wildcards in form data from taking effect in queries, you must forgo the comfort and ease of the placeholder and rely on two other functions: quote() in PDO and PHP's built-in strtr() function. First, call quote() on the submitted value.

This does the same quoting operation that the placeholder does. For example, it turns `General Tso's Chicken` into `'General Tso''s Chicken'`. The next step is to use `strtr()` to backslash-escape the SQL wildcards `%` and `_`. The quoted and wildcard-escaped value can then be used safely in a query.

Example 8-50 shows how to use `quote()` and `strtr()` to make a submitted value safe for a `WHERE` clause.

Example 8-50. Not using a placeholder in a SELECT statement

```
// First, do normal quoting of the value
$dish = $db->quote($_POST['dish_search']);
// Then, put backslashes before underscores and percent signs
$dish = strtr($dish, array('_' => '\_', '%' => '\%'));
// Now, $dish is sanitized and can be interpolated right into the query
$stmt = $db->query("SELECT dish_name, price FROM dishes
                    WHERE dish_name LIKE $dish");
```

You can't use a placeholder in this situation because the escaping of the SQL wildcards has to happen after the regular quoting. The regular quoting puts a backslash before single quotes, but also before backslashes. If `strtr()` processes the string first, a submitted value such as `%chicken%` becomes `\%chicken\%`. Then, the quoting (whether by `quote()` or the placeholder processing) turns `\%chicken\%` into `'\\%chicken\\%'`. This is interpreted by the database to mean a literal backslash, followed by the "match any characters" wildcard, followed by `chicken`, followed by another literal backslash, followed by another "match any characters" wildcard. However, if `quote()` goes first, `%chicken%` is turned into `'%chicken%'`. Then, `strtr()` turns it into `'\%chicken\%'`. This is interpreted by the database as a literal percent sign, followed by `chicken`, followed by another percent sign, which is what the user entered.

Not quoting wildcard characters has an even more drastic effect in the `WHERE` clause of an `UPDATE` or `DELETE` statement. Example 8-51 shows a query incorrectly using placeholders to allow a user-entered value to control which dishes have their prices set to $1.

Example 8-51. Incorrect use of placeholders in an UPDATE statement

```
$stmt = $db->prepare('UPDATE dishes SET price = 1 WHERE dish_name LIKE ?');
$stmt->execute(array($_POST['dish_name']));
```

If the submitted value for `dish_name` in Example 8-51 is `Fried Bean Curd`, then the query works as expected: the price of that dish only is set to 1. But if `$_POST['dish_name']` is `%`, then all dishes have their price set to 1! The `quote()` and strtr() technique prevents this problem. The right way to do the update is in Example 8-52.

Example 8-52. Correct use of quote() and strtr() with an UPDATE statement

```
// First, do normal quoting of the value
$dish = $db->quote($_POST['dish_name']);
// Then, put backslashes before underscores and percent signs
$dish = strtr($dish, array('_' => '\_', '%' => '\%'));
// Now, $dish is sanitized and can be interpolated right into the query
$db->exec("UPDATE dishes SET price = 1 WHERE dish_name LIKE $dish");
```

A Complete Data Retrieval Form

Example 8-53 is another complete database and form program. It presents a search form and then prints an HTML table of all rows in the dishes table that match the search criteria. Like Example 8-28, it relies on the form helper class being defined in a separate *FormHelper.php* file.

Example 8-53. Program for searching the dishes table

```
<?php

// Load the form helper class
require 'FormHelper.php';

// Connect to the database
try {
    $db = new PDO('sqlite:/tmp/restaurant.db');
} catch (PDOException $e) {
    print "Can't connect: " . $e->getMessage();
    exit();
}
// Set up exceptions on DB errors
$db->setAttribute(PDO::ATTR_ERRMODE, PDO::ERRMODE_EXCEPTION);

// Set up fetch mode: rows as objects
$db->setAttribute(PDO::ATTR_DEFAULT_FETCH_MODE, PDO::FETCH_OBJ);

// Choices for the "spicy" menu in the form
$spicy_choices = array('no','yes','either');

// The main page logic:
// - If the form is submitted, validate and then process or redisplay
// - If it's not submitted, display
if ($_SERVER['REQUEST_METHOD'] == 'POST') {
    // If validate_form() returns errors, pass them to show_form()
    list($errors, $input) = validate_form();
    if ($errors) {
```

```
            show_form($errors);
    } else {
        // The submitted data is valid, so process it
        process_form($input);
    }
} else {
    // The form wasn't submitted, so display
    show_form();
}


function show_form($errors = array()) {
    // Set our own defaults
    $defaults = array('min_price' => '5.00',
                      'max_price' => '25.00');

    // Set up the $form object with proper defaults
    $form = new FormHelper($defaults);

    // All the HTML and form display is in a separate file for clarity
    include 'retrieve-form.php';
}

function validate_form() {
    $input = array();
    $errors = array();

    // Remove any leading/trailing whitespace from submitted dish name
    $input['dish_name'] = trim($_POST['dish_name'] ?? '');

    // Minimum price must be a valid floating-point number
    $input['min_price'] = filter_input(INPUT_POST,'min_price',
                                       FILTER_VALIDATE_FLOAT);
    if ($input['min_price'] === null || $input['min_price'] === false) {
        $errors[] = 'Please enter a valid minimum price.';
    }

    // Maximum price must be a valid floating-point number
    $input['max_price'] = filter_input(INPUT_POST,'max_price',
                                       FILTER_VALIDATE_FLOAT);
    if ($input['max_price'] === null || $input['max_price'] === false) {
        $errors[] = 'Please enter a valid maximum price.';
    }

    // Minimum price must be less than the maximum price
    if ($input['min_price'] >= $input['max_price']) {
        $errors[] = 'The minimum price must be less than the maximum price.';
    }

    $input['is_spicy'] = $_POST['is_spicy'] ?? '';
    if (! array_key_exists($input['is_spicy'], $GLOBALS['spicy_choices'])) {
        $errors[] = 'Please choose a valid "spicy" option.';
```

```
    }
    return array($errors, $input);
}

function process_form($input) {
    // Access the global variable $db inside this function
    global $db;

    // Build up the query
    $sql = 'SELECT dish_name, price, is_spicy FROM dishes WHERE
            price >= ? AND price <= ?';

    // If a dish name was submitted, add to the WHERE clause.
    // We use quote() and strtr() to prevent user-entered wildcards from working.
    if (strlen($input['dish_name'])) {
        $dish = $db->quote($input['dish_name']);
        $dish = strtr($dish, array('_' => '\_', '%' => '\%'));
        $sql .= " AND dish_name LIKE $dish";
    }

    // If is_spicy is "yes" or "no", add appropriate SQL
    // (if it's "either", we don't need to add is_spicy to the WHERE clause)
    $spicy_choice = $GLOBALS['spicy_choices'][ $input['is_spicy'] ];
    if ($spicy_choice == 'yes') {
        $sql .= ' AND is_spicy = 1';
    } elseif ($spicy_choice == 'no') {
        $sql .= ' AND is_spicy = 0';
    }

    // Send the query to the database program and get all the rows back
    $stmt = $db->prepare($sql);
    $stmt->execute(array($input['min_price'], $input['max_price']));
    $dishes = $stmt->fetchAll();

    if (count($dishes) == 0) {
        print 'No dishes matched.';
    } else {
        print '<table>';
        print '<tr><th>Dish Name</th><th>Price</th><th>Spicy?</th></tr>';
        foreach ($dishes as $dish) {
            if ($dish->is_spicy == 1) {
                $spicy = 'Yes';
            } else {
                $spicy = 'No';
            }
            printf('<tr><td>%s</td><td>$%.02f</td><td>%s</td></tr>',
                    htmlentities($dish->dish_name), $dish->price, $spicy);
        }
    }
}
?>
```

Example 8-53 is a lot like Example 8-28: it uses the standard display/validate/process form structure with global code for database setup and database interaction inside process_form(). The show_form() function displays the form HTML defined in the *retrieve-form.php* file. This file is shown in Example 8-54.

Example 8-54. Form for retrieving information about dishes

```
<form method="POST" action="<?= $form->encode($_SERVER['PHP_SELF']) ?>">
<table>
    <?php if ($errors) { ?>
        <tr>
            <td>You need to correct the following errors:</td>
            <td><ul>
                <?php foreach ($errors as $error) { ?>
                    <li><?= $form->encode($error) ?></li>
                <?php } ?>
            </ul></td>
    <?php }  ?>

    <tr>
        <td>Dish Name:</td>
        <td><?= $form->input('text', ['name' => 'dish_name']) ?></td>
    </tr>

    <tr>
        <td>Minimum Price:</td>
        <td><?= $form->input('text',['name' => 'min_price']) ?></td>
    </tr>

    <tr>
        <td>Maximum Price:</td>
        <td><?= $form->input('text',['name' => 'max_price']) ?></td>
    </tr>

    <tr>
        <td>Spicy:</td>
        <td><?= $form->select($GLOBALS['spicy_choices'], ['name' => 'is_spicy']) ?>
        </td>
    </tr>

    <tr>
        <td colspan="2" align="center">
            <?= $form->input('submit', ['name' => 'search',
                                        'value' => 'Search']) ?></td>
    </tr>
</table>
</form>
```

One difference in Example 8-53 is an additional line in its database setup code: a call to `setAttribute()` that changes the fetch mode. Since `process_form()` is going to retrieve information from the database, the fetch mode is important.

The `process_form()` function builds up a SELECT statement, sends it to the database with `execute()`, retrieves the results with `fetchAll()`, and prints the results in an HTML table. Up to four factors go into the WHERE clause of the SELECT statement. The first two are the minimum and maximum price. These are always in the query, so they get placeholders in `$sql`, the variable that holds the SQL statement.

Next comes the dish name. That's optional, but if it's submitted, it goes into the query. A placeholder isn't good enough for the `dish_name` column, though, because the submitted form data could contain SQL wildcards. Instead, `quote()` and `strtr()` prepare a sanitized version of the dish name, and it's added directly onto the WHERE clause.

The last possible column in the WHERE clause is `is_spicy`. If the submitted choice is yes, then `AND is_spicy = 1` goes into the query so that only spicy dishes are retrieved. If the submitted choice is no, then `AND is_spicy = 0` goes into the query so that only nonspicy dishes are found. If the submitted choice is `either`, then there's no need to have `is_spicy` in the query—rows should be picked regardless of their spiciness.

After the full query is constructed in `$sql`, it's prepared with `prepare()` and sent to the database program with `execute()`. The second argument to `execute()` is an array containing the minimum and maximum price values so that they can be substituted for the placeholders. The array of rows that `fetchAll()` returns is stored in `$dishes`.

The last step in `process_form()` is printing some results. If there's nothing in `$dishes`, `No dishes matched` is displayed. Otherwise, a `foreach()` loop iterates through `dishes` and prints out an HTML table row for each dish, using `printf()` to format the price properly and `htmlentities()` to encode any special characters in the dish name. An `if()` clause turns the database-friendly `is_spicy` values of 1 or 0 into the human-friendly values of Yes or No.

Chapter Summary

This chapter covered:

- Figuring out what kinds of information belong in a database
- Understanding how data is organized in a database
- Establishing a database connection
- Creating a table in the database
- Removing a table from the database

- Using the SQL INSERT command
- Inserting data into the database with exec()
- Checking for database errors by handling exceptions
- Changing the error mode with setAttribute()
- Using the SQL UPDATE and DELETE commands
- Changing or deleting data with exec()
- Counting the number of rows affected by a query
- Using placeholders to insert data safely
- Using the SQL SELECT command
- Retrieving data from the database with query() and fetch()
- Counting the number of rows retrieved by query()
- Using the SQL ORDER BY and LIMIT keywords with SELECT
- Retrieving rows as string-keyed arrays or objects
- Using the SQL wildcards with LIKE: % and _
- Escaping SQL wildcards in SELECT statements
- Saving submitted form parameters in the database
- Using data from the database in form elements

Exercises

The following exercises use a database table called dishes with the following structure:

```
CREATE TABLE dishes (
    dish_id     INT,
    dish_name   VARCHAR(255),
    price       DECIMAL(4,2),
    is_spicy    INT
)
```

Here is some sample data to put into the dishes table:

```
INSERT INTO dishes VALUES (1,'Walnut Bun',1.00,0)
INSERT INTO dishes VALUES (2,'Cashew Nuts and White Mushrooms',4.95,0)
INSERT INTO dishes VALUES (3,'Dried Mulberries',3.00,0)
INSERT INTO dishes VALUES (4,'Eggplant with Chili Sauce',6.50,1)
INSERT INTO dishes VALUES (5,'Red Bean Bun',1.00,0)
INSERT INTO dishes VALUES (6,'General Tso''s Chicken',5.50,1)
```

1. Write a program that lists all of the dishes in the table, sorted by price.
2. Write a program that displays a form asking for a price. When the form is submitted, the program should print out the names and prices of the dishes whose price is at least the submitted price. Don't retrieve from the database any rows or columns that aren't printed in the table.

3. Write a program that displays a form with a `<select>` menu of dish names. Create the dish names to display by retrieving them from the database. When the form is submitted, the program should print out all of the information in the table (ID, name, price, and spiciness) for the selected dish.

4. Create a new table that holds information about restaurant customers. The table should store the following information about each customer: customer ID, name, phone number, and the ID of the customer's favorite dish. Write a program that displays a form for putting a new customer into the table. The part of the form for entering the customer's favorite dish should be a `<select>` menu of dish names. The customer's ID should be generated by your program, not entered in the form.

## CHAPTER 9

Working with Files

The data storage destination of choice for a web application is a database. That doesn't mean that you're completely off the hook from dealing with regular old files, though. Plain text files are still a handy, universal way to exchange some kinds of information.

You can do easy customization of your website by storing HTML templates in text files. When it's time to generate a specialized page, load the text file, substitute real data for the template elements, and print it. Example 9-2 shows you how to do this.

Files are also good for exchanging tabular data between your program and a spreadsheet. In your PHP programs, you can easily read and write the CSV (comma-separated value) files with which spreadsheet programs work.

This chapter shows you how to work with files from your PHP programs: dealing with *file permissions*, which your computer uses to enforces rules about which files your programs can read and write; reading data from and writing data to files; and handling errors that may occur with file-related operations.

Understanding File Permissions

To read or write a file with any of the functions you'll learn about in this chapter, the PHP engine must have permission from the operating system to do so. Every program that runs on a computer, including the PHP engine, runs with the privileges of a particular user account. Most of the user accounts correspond to people. When you log in to your computer and start up your word processor, that word processor runs with the privileges that correspond to your account: it can read files that you are allowed to see and write files that you are allowed to change.

Some user accounts on a computer, however, aren't for people but for system processes such as web servers. When the PHP interpreter runs inside of a web server, it has the privileges that the web server's "account" has. So if the web server is allowed to read a certain file or directory, then the PHP engine (and therefore your PHP program) can read that file or directory. If the web server is allowed to change a certain file or write new files in a particular directory, then so can the PHP engine and your PHP program.

Usually, the privileges extended to a web server's account are more limited than the privileges that go along with a real person's account. The web server (and the PHP engine) need to be able to read all of the PHP program files that make up your website, but they shouldn't be able to change them. If a bug in the web server or an insecure PHP program lets an attacker break in, the PHP program files should be protected against being changed by that attacker.

In practice, what this means is that your PHP programs shouldn't have too much trouble reading most files that you need to read. (Of course, if you try to read another user's private files, you may run into a problem—but that's as it should be!) However, the files that your PHP program can change and the directories into which your program can write new files are limited. If you need to create lots of new files in your PHP programs, work with your system administrator to make a special directory that you can write to but that doesn't compromise system security. "Inspecting File Permissions" on page 198 shows you how to determine which files and directories your programs are allowed to read and write.

Reading and Writing Entire Files

This section shows you how to work with an entire file at once, as opposed to manipulating just a few lines of a file. PHP provides special functions for reading or writing a whole file in a single step.

Reading a File

To read the contents of a file into a string, use `file_get_contents()`. Pass it a filename, and it returns a string containing everything in the file. Example 9-2 reads the file in Example 9-1 with `file_get_contents()`, modifies it with `str_replace()`, and then prints the result.

Example 9-1. page-template.html for Example 9-2

```
<html>
<head><title>{page_title}</title></head>
<body bgcolor="{color}">

<h1>Hello, {name}</h1>
```

```
</body>
</html>
```

Example 9-2. Using file_get_contents() with a page template

```php
// Load the template file from the previous example
$page = file_get_contents('page-template.html');

// Insert the title of the page
$page = str_replace('{page_title}', 'Welcome', $page);

// Make the page blue in the afternoon and
// green in the morning
if (date('H' >= 12)) {
    $page = str_replace('{color}', 'blue', $page);
} else {
    $page = str_replace('{color}', 'green', $page);
}

// Take the username from a previously saved session
// variable
$page = str_replace('{name}', $_SESSION['username'], $page);

// Print the results
print $page;
```

 Every time you use a file access function, you need to check that it didn't encounter an error because of a lack of disk space, permission problem, or other failure. Error checking is discussed in detail in "Checking for Errors" on page 199. The examples in the next few sections don't have error-checking code, so you can see the actual file access function at work without other new material getting in the way. Real programs that you write always need to check for errors after calling a file access function.

With $_SESSION['username'] set to Jacob, Example 9-2 prints:

```html
<html>
<head><title>Welcome</title></head>
<body bgcolor="green">

<h1>Hello, Jacob</h1>

</body>
</html>
```

Writing a File

The counterpart to reading the contents of a file into a string is writing a string to a file. And the counterpart to file_get_contents() is file_put_contents(). Example 9-3 extends Example 9-2 by saving the HTML to a file instead of printing it.

Example 9-3. Saving a file with file_put_contents()

```
// Load the template file we used earlier
$page = file_get_contents('page-template.html');

// Insert the title of the page
$page = str_replace('{page_title}', 'Welcome', $page);

// Make the page blue in the afternoon and
// green in the morning
if (date('H' >= 12)) {
    $page = str_replace('{color}', 'blue', $page);
} else {
    $page = str_replace('{color}', 'green', $page);
}

// Take the username from a previously saved session
// variable
$page = str_replace('{name}', $_SESSION['username'], $page);

// Write the results to page.html
file_put_contents('page.html', $page);
```

Example 9-3 writes the value of $page (the HTML) to the file *page.html*. The first argument to file_put_contents() is the filename to write to, and the second argument is what to write to the file.

Reading and Writing Parts of Files

The file_get_contents() and file_put_contents() functions are fine when you want to work with an entire file at once. But when it's time for precision work, use the file() function to access each line of a file. Example 9-4 reads a file in which each line contains a name and an email address and then prints an HTML-formatted list of that information.

Example 9-4. Accessing each line of a file

```
foreach (file('people.txt') as $line) {
    $line = trim($line);
    $info = explode('|', $line);
    print '<li><a href="mailto:' . $info[0] . '">' . $info[1] ."</li>\n";
}
```

Suppose *people.txt* contains what's listed in Example 9-5.

Example 9-5. people.txt for Example 9-4

```
alice@example.com|Alice Liddell
bandersnatch@example.org|Bandersnatch Gardner
charles@milk.example.com|Charlie Tenniel
dodgson@turtle.example.com|Lewis Humbert
```

Then, Example 9-4 prints:

```
<li><a href="mailto:alice@example.com">Alice Liddell</li>
<li><a href="mailto:bandersnatch@example.org">Bandersnatch Gardner</li>
<li><a href="mailto:charles@milk.example.com">Charlie Tenniel</li>
<li><a href="mailto:dodgson@turtle.example.com">Lewis Humbert</li>
```

The `file()` function returns an array. Each element of that array is a string containing one line of the file, newline included. So, the `foreach()` loop in Example 9-4 visits each element of the array, putting the string in `$line`. The `trim()` function removes the trailing newline, `explode()` breaks apart the line into what's before the | and what's after it, and then `print` outputs the HTML list elements.

Although `file()` is very convenient, it can be problematic with very large files. It reads the whole file to build the array of lines—and with a file that contains lots of lines, that may use up too much memory. In that case, you need to read the file line-by-line, as shown in Example 9-6.

Example 9-6. Reading a file one line at a time

```
$fh = fopen('people.txt','rb');
while ((! feof($fh)) && ($line = fgets($fh))) {
    $line = trim($line);
    $info = explode('|', $line);
    print '<li><a href="mailto:' . $info[0] . '">' . $info[1] ."</li>\n";
}
fclose($fh);
```

The four file access functions in Example 9-6 are `fopen()`,`fgets()`, `feof()`, and `fclose()`. They work together as follows:

- The `fopen()` function opens a connection to the file and returns a variable that's used for subsequent access to the file in the program. (This is conceptually similar to the database connection variable returned by `new PDO()` that you saw in Chapter 8.)
- The `fgets()` function reads a line from the file and returns it as a string.
- The PHP engine keeps a bookmark of where its current position in the file is. The bookmark starts at the beginning of the file, so the first time that `fgets()` is

called, the first line of the file is read. After that line is read, the bookmark is updated to the beginning of the next line.

- The feof() function returns true if the bookmark is past the end of the file ("eof" stands for "end of file").
- The fclose() function closes the connection to the file.

The while() loop in Example 9-6 keeps executing as long as two things are true:

- feof($fh) returns false.
- The $line value that fgets($fh) returns evaluates to true.

Each time fgets($fh) runs, the PHP engine grabs a line from the file, advances its bookmark, and returns the line. When the bookmark is pointing at the very last spot in the file, feof($fh) still returns false. At that point, however, fgets($fh) returns false because it tries to read a line and can't. So, both of those checks are necessary to make the loop end properly.

Example 9-6 uses trim() on $line because the string that fgets() returns includes the trailing newline at the end of the line. The trim() function removes the newline, which makes the output look better.

The first argument to fopen() is the name of the file that you want to access. As with other PHP file access functions, use forward slashes (/) instead of backslashes (\) here, even on Windows. Example 9-7 opens a file in the Windows system directory.

Example 9-7. Opening a file on Windows

```
$fh = fopen('c:/windows/system32/settings.txt','rb');
```

Because backslashes have a special meaning (escaping, which you saw in "Defining Text Strings" on page 20) inside strings, it's easier to use forward slashes in filenames. The PHP engine does the right thing in Windows and loads the correct file.

The second argument to fopen() is the *file mode*. This controls what you're allowed to do with the file once it's opened: reading, writing, or both. The file mode also affects where the PHP engine's file position bookmark starts, whether the file's contents are cleared out when it's opened, and how the PHP engine should react if the file doesn't exist. Table 9-1 lists the different modes that fopen() understands.

Table 9-1. File modes for fopen()

Mode	Allowable actions	Position bookmark starting point	Clear contents?	If the file doesn't exist?
rb	Reading	Beginning of file	No	Issue a warning, return false.
rb+	Reading, Writing	Beginning of file	No	Issue a warning, return false.
wb	Writing	Beginning of file	Yes	Try to create it.

Mode	Allowable actions	Position bookmark starting point	Clear contents?	If the file doesn't exist?
wb+	Reading, writing	Beginning of file	Yes	Try to create it.
ab	Writing	End of file	No	Try to create it.
ab+	Reading, writing	End of file	No	Try to create it.
xb	Writing	Beginning of file	No	Try to create it; if the file does exist, issue a warning and return `false`.
xb+	Reading, writing	Beginning of file	No	Try to create it; if the file does exist, issue a warning and return `false`.
cb	Writing	Beginning of file	No	Try to create it.
cb+	Reading, writing	Beginning of file	No	Try to create it.

Once you've opened a file in a mode that allows writing, use the `fwrite()` function to write something to the file. Example 9-8 uses the `wb` mode with `fopen()` and uses `fwrite()` to write information retrieved from a database table to the file *dishes.txt*.

Example 9-8. Writing data to a file

```
try {
    $db = new PDO('sqlite:/tmp/restaurant.db');
} catch (Exception $e) {
    print "Couldn't connect to database: " . $e->getMessage();
    exit();
}

// Open dishes.txt for writing
$fh = fopen('dishes.txt','wb');

$q = $db->query("SELECT dish_name, price FROM dishes");
while($row = $q->fetch()) {
    // Write each line (with a newline on the end) to
    // dishes.txt
    fwrite($fh, "The price of $row[0] is $row[1] \n");
}
fclose($fh);
```

The `fwrite()` function doesn't automatically add a newline to the end of the string you write. It just writes exactly what you pass to it. If you want to write a line at a time (such as in Example 9-8), be sure to add a newline (`\n`) to the end of the string that you pass to `fwrite()`.

Working with CSV Files

One type of text file gets special treatment in PHP: the CSV file. It can't handle graphs or charts, but excels at sharing tables of data among different programs. To read a line of a CSV file, use `fgetcsv()` instead of `fgets()`. It reads a line from the CSV file and returns an array containing each field in the line. Example 9-9 is a CSV file of information about restaurant dishes. Example 9-10 uses `fgetcsv()` to read the file and insert the information in it into the `dishes` database table from Chapter 8.

Example 9-9. dishes.csv

```
"Fish Ball with Vegetables",4.25,0
"Spicy Salt Baked Prawns",5.50,1
"Steamed Rock Cod",11.95,0
"Sauteed String Beans",3.15,1
"Confucius ""Chicken""",4.75,0
```

Example 9-10. Inserting CSV data into a database table

```
try {
    $db = new PDO('sqlite:/tmp/restaurant.db');
} catch (Exception $e) {
    print "Couldn't connect to database: " . $e->getMessage();
    exit();
}
$fh = fopen('dishes.csv','rb');
$stmt = $db->prepare('INSERT INTO dishes (dish_name, price, is_spicy)
                                  VALUES (?,?,?)');
while ((! feof($fh)) && ($info = fgetcsv($fh))) {
    // $info[0] is the dish name    (the  first field in a line of dishes.csv)
    // $info[1] is the price        (the second field)
    // $info[2] is the spicy status (the  third field)
    // Insert a row into the database table
    $stmt->execute($info);
    print "Inserted $info[0]\n";
}
// Close the file
fclose($fh);
```

Example 9-10 prints:

```
Inserted Fish Ball with Vegetables
Inserted Spicy Salt Baked Prawns
Inserted Steamed Rock Cod
Inserted Sauteed String Beans
Inserted Confucius "Chicken"
```

Writing a CSV-formatted line is similar to reading one. The `fputcsv()` function takes a file handle and an array of values as arguments and writes those values, formatted as proper CSV, to the file. Example 9-11 uses `fputcsv()` along with `fopen()` and `fclose()` to retrieve information from a database table and write it to a CSV file.

Example 9-11. Writing CSV-formatted data to a file

```
try {
    $db = new PDO('sqlite:/tmp/restaurant.db');
} catch (Exception $e) {
    print "Couldn't connect to database: " . $e->getMessage();
    exit();
}

// Open the CSV file for writing
$fh = fopen('dish-list.csv','wb');

$dishes = $db->query('SELECT dish_name, price, is_spicy FROM dishes');
while ($row = $dishes->fetch(PDO::FETCH_NUM)) {
    // Write the data in $row as a CSV-formatted string. fputcsv()
    // adds a newline at the end.
    fputcsv($fh, $row);
}
fclose($fh);
```

To send a page that consists only of CSV-formatted data back to a web client, you need to tell fputcsv() to write the data to the regular PHP output stream (instead of a file). You also have to use PHP's header() function to tell the web client to expect a CSV document instead of an HTML document. Example 9-12 shows how to call the header() function with the appropriate arguments.

Example 9-12. Changing the page type to CSV

```
// Tell the web client to expect a CSV file
header('Content-Type: text/csv');
// Tell the web client to view the CSV file in a separate program
header('Content-Disposition: attachment; filename="dishes.csv"');
```

Example 9-13 contains a complete program that sends the correct CSV header, retrieves rows from a database table, and prints them. Its output can be loaded directly into a spreadsheet program from a user's web browser.

Example 9-13. Sending a CSV file to the browser

```
try {
    $db = new PDO('sqlite:/tmp/restaurant.db');
} catch (Exception $e) {
    print "Couldn't connect to database: " . $e->getMessage();
    exit();
}

// Tell the web client that a CSV file called "dishes.csv" is coming
header('Content-Type: text/csv');
header('Content-Disposition: attachment; filename="dishes.csv"');
```

```
// Open a file handle to the output stream
$fh = fopen('php://output','wb');

// Retrieve the info from the database table and print it
$dishes = $db->query('SELECT dish_name, price, is_spicy FROM dishes');
while ($row = $dishes->fetch(PDO::FETCH_NUM)) {
    fputcsv($fh, $row);
}
```

In Example 9-13, the first argument to `fputcsv()` is `php://output`. This is a special built-in file handle which sends data to the same place that `print` sends it to.

To generate more complicated spreadsheets that include formulas, formatting, and images, use the PHPOffice PHPExcel package (*https://packagist.org/packages/phpof fice/phpexcel*).

 See Chapter 16 for details on how to install packages.

Inspecting File Permissions

As mentioned at the beginning of the chapter, your programs can only read and write files when the PHP engine has permission to do so. You don't have to cast about blindly and rely on error messages to figure out what those permissions are, however. PHP gives you functions with which you can determine what your program is allowed to do.

To check whether a file or directory exists, use `file_exists()`. Example 9-14 uses this function to report whether a directory's index file has been created.

Example 9-14. Checking the existence of a file

```
if (file_exists('/usr/local/htdocs/index.html')) {
    print "Index file is there.";
} else {
    print "No index file in /usr/local/htdocs.";
}
```

To determine whether your program has permission to read or write a particular file, use `is_readable()` or `is_writeable()`. Example 9-15 checks that a file is readable before retrieving its contents with `file_get_contents()`.

Example 9-15. Testing for read permission

```
$template_file = 'page-template.html';
if (is_readable($template_file)) {
    $template = file_get_contents($template_file);
} else {
    print "Can't read template file.";
}
```

Example 9-16 verifies that a file is writeable before appending a line to it with `fopen()` and `fwrite()`.

Example 9-16. Testing for write permission

```
$log_file = '/var/log/users.log';
if (is_writeable($log_file)) {
    $fh = fopen($log_file,'ab');
    fwrite($fh, $_SESSION['username'] . ' at ' . strftime('%c') . "\n");
    fclose($fh);
} else {
    print "Cant write to log file.";
}
```

Checking for Errors

So far, the examples in this chapter have been shown without any error checking in them. This keeps them shorter, so you can focus on the file manipulation functions such as `file_get_contents()`, `fopen()`, and `fgetcsv()`. It also makes them somewhat incomplete. Just like talking to a database program, working with files means interacting with resources external to your program. This means you have to worry about all sorts of things that can cause problems, such as operating system file permissions or a disk running out of free space.

In practice, to write robust file-handling code, you should check the return value of each file-related function. They each generate a warning message and return `false` if there is a problem. If the configuration directive `track_errors` is on, the text of the error message is available in the global variable `$php_errormsg`.

Example 9-17 shows how to check whether `fopen()` or `fclose()` encounters an error.

Example 9-17. Checking for an error from fopen() or fclose()

```
try {
    $db = new PDO('sqlite:/tmp/restaurant.db');
} catch (Exception $e) {
    print "Couldn't connect to database: " . $e->getMessage();
    exit();
}
```

```
// Open dishes.txt for writing
$fh = fopen('/usr/local/dishes.txt','wb');
if (! $fh) {
    print "Error opening dishes.txt: $php_errormsg";
} else {
    $q = $db->query("SELECT dish_name, price FROM dishes");
    while($row = $q->fetch()) {
        // Write each line (with a newline on the end) to
        // dishes.txt
        fwrite($fh, "The price of $row[0] is $row[1] \n");
    }
    if (! fclose($fh)) {
        print "Error closing dishes.txt: $php_errormsg";
    }
}
```

If your program doesn't have permission to write into the */usr/local* directory, then fopen() returns false, and Example 9-17 prints:

```
Error opening dishes.txt: failed to open stream: Permission denied
```

It also generates a warning message that looks like this:

```
Warning: fopen(/usr/local/dishes.txt): failed to open stream: Permission denied
in dishes.php on line 5
```

"Controlling Where Errors Appear" on page 249 talks about how to control where the warning message is shown.

The same thing happens with fclose(). If it returns false, then the Error closing dishes.txt message is printed. Sometimes operating systems buffer data written with fwrite() and don't actually save the data to the file until you call fclose(). If there's no space on the disk for the data you're writing, the error might show up when you call fclose(), not when you call fwrite().

Checking for errors from the other file-handling functions (such as fgets(), fwrite(), fgetcsv(), file_get_contents(), and file_put_contents()) is a little trickier. This is because you have to do something special to distinguish the value they return when an error happens from the data they return when everything goes OK.

If something goes wrong with fgets(), file_get_contents(), or fgetcsv(), they each return false. However, it's possible that these functions could succeed and still return a value that evaluates to false in a comparison. If file_get_contents() reads a file that just consists of the one character 0, then it returns a one-character string, 0. Remember from "Understanding true and false" on page 40, though, that such a string is considered false.

To get around this, be sure to use the identity operator to check the function's return value. That way, you can compare the value with `false` and know that an error has happened only if the function actually returns `false`, not a string that evaluates to `false`.

Example 9-18 shows how to use the identity operator to check for an error from `file_get_contents()`.

Example 9-18. Checking for an error from file_get_contents()

```
$page = file_get_contents('page-template.html');
// Note the three equals signs in the test expression
if ($page === false) {
    print "Couldn't load template: $php_errormsg";
} else {
    // ... process template here
}
```

Use the same technique with `fgets()` or `fgetcsv()`. Example 9-19 correctly checks for errors from `fopen()`, `fgets()`, and `fclose()`.

Example 9-19. Checking for an error from fopen(), fgets(), or fclose()

```
$fh = fopen('people.txt','rb');
if (! $fh) {
    print "Error opening people.txt: $php_errormsg";
} else {
    while (! feof($fh)) {
        $line = fgets($fh);
        if ($line !== false) {
            $line = trim($line);
            $info = explode('|', $line);
            print '<li><a href="mailto:' . $info[0] . '">' . $info[1] ."</li>\n";
        }
    }
    if (! fclose($fh)) {
        print "Error closing people.txt: $php_errormsg";
    }
}
```

When `fwrite()`, `fputcsv()`, and `file_put_contents()` succeed, they return the number of bytes they've written. When `fwrite()` or `fputcsv()` fails, it returns `false`, so you can use the identity operator with it just like with `fgets()`. The `file_put_contents()` function is a little different. Depending on what goes wrong, it either returns `false` or -1, so you need to check for both possibilities. Example 9-20 shows how to check for errors from `file_put_contents()`.

Example 9-20. Checking for an error from file_put_contents()

```
// Load the file from Example 9-1
$page = file_get_contents('page-template.html');

// Insert the title of the page
$page = str_replace('{page_title}', 'Welcome', $page);

// Make the page blue in the afternoon and
// green in the morning
if (date('H' >= 12)) {
    $page = str_replace('{color}', 'blue', $page);
} else {
    $page = str_replace('{color}', 'green', $page);
}

// Take the username from a previously saved session
// variable
$page = str_replace('{name}', $_SESSION['username'], $page);

$result = file_put_contents('page.html', $page);
// Need to check if file_put_contents() returns false or -1
if (($result === false) || ($result == -1)) {
    print "Couldn't save HTML to page.html";
}
```

Sanitizing Externally Supplied Filenames

Just as data submitted in a form or URL can cause problems when it is displayed (cross-site scripting attack) or put in an SQL query (SQL injection attack), it can also cause problems when it is used as a filename or as part of a filename. This problem doesn't have a fancy name like those other attacks, but it can be just as devastating.

The cause of the problem is the same: there are special characters that must be escaped so they lose their special meaning. In filenames, the special characters are / (which separates parts of filenames), and the two-character sequence .. (which means "go up one directory" in a filename).

For example, the funny-looking filename */usr/local/data/../../../etc/passwd* doesn't point to a file in the */usr/local/data* directory but instead to the location of the file */etc/passwd*, which, on most Unix systems, contains a list of user accounts. The filename */usr/local/data/../../../etc/passwd* means "from the directory */usr/local/data*, go up one level (to */usr/local*), then go up another level (to */usr*), then go up another level (to /, the top level of the filesystem), then down into */etc*, then stop at the file *passwd*."

How could this be a problem in your PHP programs? When you use data from a form in a filename, you are vulnerable to an attack that enables a user to gain access to areas of your filesystem that you may not have intended, unless you sanitize the submitted form data. Example 9-21 takes the approach of removing all forward slashes and .. sequences from a submitted form parameter before incorporating the parameter into a filename.

Example 9-21. Cleaning up a form parameter that goes in a filename

```
// Remove slashes from user
$user = str_replace('/', '', $_POST['user']);
// Remove .. from user
$user = str_replace('..', '', $user);

if (is_readable("/usr/local/data/$user")) {
    print 'User profile for ' . htmlentities($user) .': <br/>';
    print file_get_contents("/usr/local/data/$user");
}
```

If a malicious user supplies ../../../etc/passwd as the user form parameter in Example 9-21, that is translated into etcpasswd before being interpolated into the filename used with file_get_contents().

Another helpful technique for getting rid of user-entered nastiness is to use realpath(). It translates an obfuscated filename that contains .. sequences into the ..-less version of the filename that more directly indicates where the file is. For example, realpath('/usr/local/data/../../../etc/passwd') returns the string /etc/passwd. You can use realpath() as in Example 9-22 to see whether filenames, after incorporating form data, are acceptable.

Example 9-22. Cleaning up a filename with realpath()

```
$filename = realpath("/usr/local/data/$_POST[user]");

// Make sure that $filename is under /usr/local/data
if (('/usr/local/data/' == substr($filename, 0, 16)) &&
    is_readable($filename)) {
    print 'User profile for ' . htmlentities($_POST['user']) .': <br/>';
    print file_get_contents($filename);
} else {
    print "Invalid user entered.";
}
```

In Example 9-22, if $_POST['user'] is james, then $filename is set to /usr/local/data/james and the if() code block runs. However, if $_POST['user'] is something suspicious such as ../secrets.txt, then $filename is set to /usr/local/secrets.txt, and the if() test fails, so Invalid user entered. is printed.

Chapter Summary

This chapter covered:

- Understanding where the PHP engine's file access permissions come from
- Reading entire files with `file_get_contents()`
- Writing entire files with `file_put_contents()`
- Reading each line of a file with `file()`
- Opening and closing files with `fopen()` and `fclose()`
- Reading a line of a file with `fgets()`
- Using `feof()` and a `while()` loop to read each line in a file
- Using forward slashes in filenames with all operating systems
- Providing different file modes to `fopen()`
- Writing data to a file with `fwrite()`
- Reading a line of a CSV file with `fgetcsv()`
- Writing a line of a CSV file with `fputcsv()`
- Using the `php://output` stream to display output
- Determining whether a file exists with `file_exists()`
- Inspecting file permissions with `is_readable()` and `is_writeable()`
- Checking for errors returned from file access functions
- Understanding when to check a return value with the identity operator (`===`)
- Removing potentially dangerous parts of externally supplied filenames

Exercises

1. Outside of the PHP engine, create a new template file in the style of Example 9-1. Write a program that uses `file_get_contents()` and `file_put_contents()` to read the HTML template file, substitute values for the template variables, and save the new page to a separate file.
2. Outside of the PHP engine, create a file that contains some email addresses, one per line. Make sure a few of the addresses appear more than once in the file. Call that file *addresses.txt*. Then, write a PHP program that reads each line in *addresses.txt* and counts how many times each address appears. For each distinct address in *addresses.txt*, your program should write a line to another file, *addresses-count.txt*. Each line in *addresses-count.txt* should consist of the number of times an address appears in *addresses.txt*, a comma, and the email address. Write the lines to *addresses-count.txt* in sorted order from the address that occurs the most times in *addresses.txt* to the address that occurs the fewest times in *addresses.txt*.

3. Display a CSV file as an HTML table. If you don't have a CSV file (or spreadsheet program) handy, use the data from Example 9-9.

4. Write a PHP program that displays a form that asks a user for the name of a file underneath the web server's document root directory. If that file exists on the server, is readable, and is underneath the web server's document root directory, then display the contents of the file. For example, if the user enters *article.html*, display the file *article.html* in the document root directory. If the user enters *catalog/show.php*, display the file *show.php* in the directory *catalog* under the document root directory. Table 7-1 tells you how to find the web server's document root directory.

5. Modify your solution to the previous exercise so that the program displays only files whose names end in *.html*. Letting users look at the PHP source code of any page on your site can be dangerous if those pages have sensitive information in them such as database usernames and passwords.

## CHAPTER 10

Remembering Users: Cookies and Sessions

A web server is a lot like a clerk at a busy deli full of pushy customers. The customers at the deli shout requests: "I want a half pound of corned beef!" and "Give me a pound of pastrami, sliced thin!" The clerk scurries around slicing and wrapping to satisfy the requests. Web clients electronically shout requests ("Give me */catalog/ yak.php*!" or "Here's a form submission for you!"), and the server, with the PHP engine's help, electronically scurries around constructing responses to satisfy the requests.

The deli clerk has an advantage that the web server doesn't, though: a memory. She naturally ties together all the requests that come from a particular customer. The PHP engine and the web server can't do that without some extra steps. That's where *cookies* come in.

A cookie identifies a particular web client to the web server and PHP engine. Each time a web client makes a request, it sends the cookie along with the request. The engine reads the cookie and figures out that a particular request is coming from the same web client that made previous requests, which were accompanied by the same cookie.

If deli customers were faced with a memory-deprived clerk, they'd have to adopt the same strategy. Their requests for service would look like this:

"I'm customer 56 and I want a half pound of corned beef."
"I'm customer 29 and I want three knishes."
"I'm customer 56 and I want two pounds of pastrami."
"I'm customer 77 and I'm returning this rye bread—it's stale."
"I'm customer 29 and I want a salami."

The "I'm customer so-and-so" part of the requests is the cookie. It gives the clerk what she needs to be able to link a particular customer's requests together.

A cookie has a name (such as "customer") and a value (such as "77" or "ronald"). The following section shows you how to work with individual cookies in your programs: setting them, reading them, and deleting them.

One cookie is best at keeping track of one piece of information. Often, you need to keep track of more about a user (such as the contents of that user's shopping cart). Using multiple cookies for this is cumbersome. PHP's *session* capabilities solve this problem.

A session uses a cookie to distinguish users from one another and makes it easy to keep a temporary pile of data for each user on the server. This data persists across requests. On one request, you can add a variable to a user's session (such as putting something into the shopping cart). On a subsequent request, you can retrieve what's in the session (such as on the order checkout page when you need to list everything in the cart). "Activating Sessions" on page 213 describes how to get started with sessions, and "Storing and Retrieving Information" on page 214 provides the details on working with sessions.

Working with Cookies

To set a cookie, use the setcookie() function. This tells a web client to remember a cookie name and value and send them back to the server on subsequent requests. Example 10-1 sets a cookie named userid to the value ralph.

Example 10-1. Setting a cookie

```
setcookie('userid','ralph');
```

To read a previously set cookie from your PHP program, use the $_COOKIE auto-global array. Example 10-2 prints the value of the userid cookie.

Example 10-2. Printing a cookie value

```
print 'Hello, ' . $_COOKIE['userid'];
```

The value for a cookie that you provide to setcookie() can be a string or a number. It can't be an array or more complicated data structure.

The setcookie() function URL-encodes the cookie value before sending it to the web client. This means that a space is turned into a +, and everything else other than letters, digits, underscores, hyphens, and periods is turned into a percent sign followed by its ASCII value in hexadecimal. If you don't want PHP to monkey with your cookie value, use setrawcookie() instead of set cookie(). However, with setrawcookie(), your cookie value cannot contain =, ,, ;, or any whitespace.

When you call setcookie(), the response that the PHP engine generates to send back to the web client includes a special header that tells the web client about the new cookie. On subsequent requests, the web client sends that cookie name and value back to the server. This two-step conversation is illustrated in Figure 10-1.

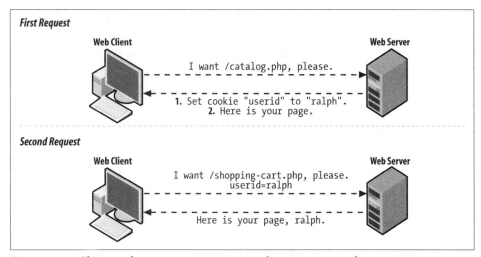

Figure 10-1. Client and server communication when setting a cookie

Usually, you must call setcookie() before the page generates any output. This means that setcookie() must come before any print statements. It also means that there can't be any text before the <?php start tag in the page that comes before the set cookie() function. Later in this chapter, "Why setcookie() and session_start() Want to Be at the Top of the Page" on page 226 explains why this requirement exists, and how, in some cases, you can get around it.

Example 10-3 shows the correct way to put a setcookie() call at the top of your page.

Example 10-3. Starting a page with setcookie()

```php
<?php
setcookie('userid','ralph');
?>
<html><head><title>Page with cookies</title><head>
<body>
This page sets a cookie properly, because the PHP block
with setcookie() in it comes before all of the HTML.
</body></html>
```

Cookies show up in $_COOKIE only when the web client sends them along with the request. This means that a name and value do not appear in $_COOKIE immediately after you call setcookie(). Only after that cookie-setting response is digested by the web client does the client know about the cookie. And only after the client sends the cookie back on a subsequent request does it appear in $_COOKIE.

The default lifetime for a cookie is the lifetime of the web client. When you quit Safari or Firefox, the cookie is deleted. To make a cookie live longer (or expire sooner), use the third argument to setcookie(). This is an optional cookie expiration time. Example 10-4 shows some cookies with different expiration times.

Example 10-4. Setting cookie expiration

```php
// The cookie expires one hour from now
setcookie('short-userid','ralph',time() + 60*60);

// The cookie expires one day from now
setcookie('longer-userid','ralph',time() + 60*60*24);

// The cookie expires at noon on October 1, 2019
$d = new DateTime("2019-10-01 12:00:00");
setcookie('much-longer-userid','ralph', $d->format('U'));
```

The cookie expiration time needs to be given to setcookie() expressed as the number of seconds elapsed since midnight on January 1, 1970. Two things make coming up with appropriate expiration values easier: time() and the U format character of DateTime::format().[1] The time() function returns the current number of elapsed seconds since January 1, 1970 (the Unix "epoch"). So, if you want the cookie expiration time to be a certain number of seconds from now, add that value to what time() returns. There are 60 seconds in a minute and 60 minutes in an hour, so 60*60 is the number of seconds in an hour. That makes time() + 60*60 equal to the "elapsed

---

[1] Chapter 15 has more detail about time() and DateTime.

seconds" value for an hour from now. Similarly, 60*60*24 is the number of seconds in a day, so `time()` + 60*60*24 is the "elapsed seconds" value for a day from now.

The `U` format character of `DateTime::format()` tells you the "elapsed seconds" value for the point in time represented by a `DateTime` object.

Setting a cookie with a specific expiration time makes the cookie last even if the web client exits and restarts.

Aside from expiration time, there are a few other cookie parameters that are helpful to adjust: the path, the domain, and two security-related parameters.

Normally, cookies are only sent back with requests for pages in the same directory (or below) as the page that set the cookie. A cookie set by *http://www.example.com/buy.php* is sent back with all requests to the server `www.example.com`, because *buy.php* is in the top-level directory of the web server. A cookie set by *http://www.example.com/catalog/list.php* is sent back with other requests in the *catalog* directory, such as *http://www.example.com/catalog/search.php*. It is also sent back with requests for pages in subdirectories of *catalog*, such as *http://www.example.com/catalog/detailed/search.php*. But it is not sent back with requests for pages above or outside the *catalog* directory, such as *http://www.example.com/sell.php* or *http://www.example.com/users/profile.php*.

The part of the URL after the hostname (such as */buy.php*, */catalog/list.php*, or */users/profile.php*) is called the *path*. To tell the web client to match against a different path when determining whether to send a cookie to the server, provide that path as the fourth argument to `setcookie()`. The most flexible path to provide is /, which means "send this cookie back with all requests to the server." Example 10-5 sets a cookie with the path set to /.

Example 10-5. Setting the cookie path

```
setcookie('short-userid','ralph',0,'/');
```

In Example 10-5, the expiration time argument to `setcookie()` is 0. This tells the `setcookie()` method to use the default expiration time (when the web client exits) for the cookie. When you specify a path to `setcookie()`, you have to fill in something for the expiration time argument. It can be a specific time value (such as `time()` + 60*60), or it can be 0 to use the default expiration time.

Setting the path to something other than / is a good idea if you are on a shared server and all of your pages are under a specific directory. For example, if your web space is under *http://students.example.edu/~alice/*, then you should set the cookie path to `/~alice/`, as shown in Example 10-6.

Example 10-6. Setting the cookie path to a specific directory

```
setcookie('short-userid','ralph',0,'/~alice/');
```

With a cookie path of */~alice/*, the short-userid cookie is sent with a request to *http://students.example.edu/~alice/search.php*, but not with requests to other students' web pages such as *http://students.example.edu/~bob/sneaky.php* or *http://students.example.edu/~charlie/search.php*.

The next argument that affects which requests the web client decides to send a particular cookie with is the domain. The default behavior is to send cookies only with requests to the same host that set the cookie. If *http://www.example.com/login.php* set a cookie, then that cookie is sent back with other requests to the server www.example.com—but not with requests to shop.example.com, www.yahoo.com, or www.example.org.

You can alter this behavior slightly. A fifth argument to setcookie() tells the web client to send the cookie with requests that have a hostname whose end matches the argument. The most common use of this feature is to set the cookie domain to something like .example.com (the period at the beginning is important for older web clients). This tells the web client that the cookie should accompany future requests to www.example.com, shop.example.com, testing.development.example.com, and any other server name that ends in .example.com. Example 10-7 shows how to set a cookie like this.

Example 10-7. Setting the cookie domain

```
setcookie('short-userid','ralph',0,'/','.example.com');
```

The cookie in Example 10-7 expires when the web client exits and is sent with requests in any directory (because the path is */*) on any server whose name ends with .example.com.

The path that you provide to setcookie() must match the end of the name of your server. If your PHP programs are hosted on the server students.example.edu, you can't supply .yahoo.com as a cookie path and have the cookie you set sent back to all servers in the yahoo.com domain. You can, however, specify .example.edu as a cookie domain to have your cookie sent with all requests to any server in the example.edu domain.

The last two optional arguments to setcookie() affect a cookie's security settings. A value of true for the sixth argument to setcookie() tells a web client to only return the cookie over a secure connection—one where the URL begins with https. It is still your responsibility to make sure to only call setcookie() like this when the request to the page executing setcookie() is done over a secure connection. But this instructs the client not to send the cookie back over a subsequent request to an insecure URL.

Finally, a value of true for the seventh argument to setcookie() tells the web client that this cookie is an *HttpOnly* cookie. An HttpOnly cookie gets sent back and forth between client and server as usual, but it is not accessible by client-side JavaScript. This can provide some protection from cross-site scripting attacks (described in "HTML and JavaScript" on page 138). Example 10-8 shows a cookie that expires in 24 hours, has no path or domain restrictions, should only be sent back over a secure connection, and is not available to client-side JavaScript.

Example 10-8. Setting a cookie with security parameters

```
// null for domain and path tell PHP not to put any
// domain or path in the cookie
setcookie('short-userid','ralph',0,null, null, true, true);
```

To delete a cookie, call setcookie() with the name of the cookie you want to delete and the empty string as the cookie value, as shown in Example 10-9.

Example 10-9. Deleting a cookie

```
setcookie('short-userid','');
```

If you've set a cookie with nondefault values for an expiration time, path, or domain, you must provide those same values again when you delete the cookie in order for the cookie to be deleted properly.

Most of the time, cookies you set will be fine with the default values for expiration time, path, or domain. But understanding how these values can be changed helps you understand how PHP's session behavior can be customized.

Activating Sessions

Sessions, by default, use a cookie called PHPSESSID. When you start a session on a page, the PHP engine checks for the presence of this cookie and sets it if it doesn't exist. The value of the PHPSESSID cookie is a random alphanumeric string. Each web client gets a different session ID. The session ID in the PHPSESSID cookie identifies that web client uniquely to the server. That lets the engine maintain separate piles of data for each web client.

The conversation between the web client and the server when starting up a session is illustrated in Figure 10-2.

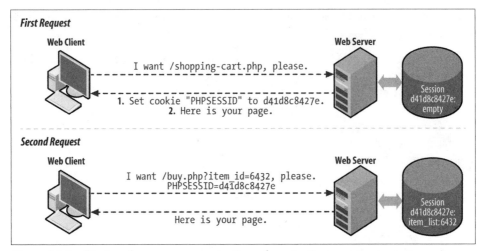

Figure 10-2. Client and server communication when starting a session

To use a session in a page, call `session_start()` at the beginning of your script. Like `setcookie()`, this function must be called before any output is sent. If you want to use sessions in all your pages, set the configuration directive `session.auto_start` to On. Appendix A explains how to change configuration settings. Once you do that, there's no need to call `session_start()` in each page.

Storing and Retrieving Information

Session data is stored in the `$_SESSION` auto-global array. Read and change elements of that array to manipulate the session data. Example 10-10 shows a page counter that uses the `$_SESSION` array to keep track of how many times a user has looked at the page.

Example 10-10. Counting page accesses with a session

```
session_start();

if (isset($_SESSION['count'])) {
    $_SESSION['count'] = $_SESSION['count'] + 1;
} else {
    $_SESSION['count'] = 1;
}
print "You've looked at this page " . $_SESSION['count'] . ' times.';
```

The first time a user accesses the page in Example 10-10, no PHPSESSID cookie is sent by the user's web client to the server. The `session_start()` function creates a new session for the user and sends a PHPSESSID cookie with the new session ID in it.

When the session is created, the $_SESSION array starts out empty. So, the code checks for a count key in the $_SESSION array. If it's there, then the value is incremented. If not, it's set to 1 to mark the first visit. The print statement outputs:

```
You've looked at this page 1 times.
```

At the end of the request, the information in $_SESSION is saved into a file on the web server associated with the appropriate session ID.

The next time the user accesses the page, the web client sends the PHPSESSID cookie. The session_start() function sees the session ID in the cookie and loads the file that contains the saved session information associated with that session ID. In this case, that saved information just says that $_SESSION['count'] is 1. Next, $_SESSION['count'] is incremented to 2 and You've looked at this page 2 times. is printed. Again, at the end of the request, the contents of $_SESSION (now with $_SESSION['count'] equal to 2) are saved to a file.

The PHP engine keeps track of the contents of $_SESSION separately for each session ID. When your program is running, $_SESSION contains the saved data for one session only—the active session corresponding to the ID that was sent in the PHPSESSID cookie. Each user's PHPSESSID cookie has a different value.

As long as you call session_start() at the top of a page (or if session.auto_start is On), you have access to a user's session data in your page. The $_SESSION array is a way of sharing information between pages.

Example 10-11 is a complete program that displays a form in which a user picks a dish and a quantity. That dish and quantity are added to the session variable order.

Example 10-11. Saving form data in a session

```
require 'FormHelper.php';

session_start();

$main_dishes = array('cuke' => 'Braised Sea Cucumber',
                     'stomach' => "Sauteed Pig's Stomach",
                     'tripe' => 'Sauteed Tripe with Wine Sauce',
                     'taro' => 'Stewed Pork with Taro',
                     'giblets' => 'Baked Giblets with Salt',
                     'abalone' => 'Abalone with Marrow and Duck Feet');

if ($_SERVER['REQUEST_METHOD'] == 'POST') {
    list($errors, $input) = validate_form();
    if ($errors) {
        show_form($errors);
    } else {
        process_form($input);
```

```
    }
} else {
    show_form();
}

function show_form($errors = array()) {
    // No defaults of our own, so nothing to pass to the
    // FormHelper constructor
    $form = new FormHelper();

    // Build up the error HTML to use later
    if ($errors) {
        $errorHtml = '<ul><li>';
        $errorHtml .= implode('</li><li>',$errors);
        $errorHtml .= '</li></ul>';
    } else {
        $errorHtml = '';
    }


    // This form is small, so we'll just print out its components
    // here
print <<<_FORM_
<form method="POST" action="{$form->encode($_SERVER['PHP_SELF'])}">
  $errorHtml
  Dish: {$form->select($GLOBALS['main_dishes'],['name' => 'dish'])} <br/>

  Quantity: {$form->input('text',['name' => 'quantity'])} <br/>

  {$form->input('submit',['value' => 'Order'])}
</form>
_FORM_;
}

function validate_form() {
    $input = array();
    $errors = array();

    // The dish selected in the menu must be valid
    $input['dish'] = $_POST['dish'] ?? '';
    if (! array_key_exists($input['dish'], $GLOBALS['main_dishes'])) {
        $errors[] = 'Please select a valid dish.';
    }

    $input['quantity'] = filter_input(INPUT_POST, 'quantity', FILTER_VALIDATE_INT,
                                  array('options' => array('min_range' => 1)));
    if (($input['quantity'] === false) || ($input['quantity'] === null)) {
        $errors[] = 'Please enter a quantity.';
    }
    return array($errors, $input);
}
```

```
function process_form($input) {
    $_SESSION['order'][] = array('dish'     => $input['dish'],
                                 'quantity' => $input['quantity']);

    print 'Thank you for your order.';
}
```

The form-handling code in Example 10-11 is mostly familiar. As in Examples 8-28 and 8-53, the form-element-printing helper class is loaded from the *FormHelper.php* file. The show_form(), validate_form(), and process_form() functions display, validate, and process the form data.

Where Example 10-11 takes advantage of sessions, however, is in process_form(). Each time the form is submitted with valid data, an element is added to the $_SESSION['order'] array. Session data isn't restricted to strings and numbers, like cookies. You can treat $_SESSION like any other array. The syntax $_SESSION['order'][ ] says, "Treat $_SESSION['order'] as an array and add a new element onto its end." In this case, what's being added to the end of $_SESSION['order'] is a two-element array containing information about the dish and quantity that were submitted in the form.

The program in Example 10-12 prints a list of dishes that have been ordered by accessing the information that's been stored in the session by Example 10-11.

Example 10-12. Printing session data

```
session_start();

$main_dishes = array('cuke' => 'Braised Sea Cucumber',
                     'stomach' => "Sauteed Pig's Stomach",
                     'tripe' => 'Sauteed Tripe with Wine Sauce',
                     'taro' => 'Stewed Pork with Taro',
                     'giblets' => 'Baked Giblets with Salt',
                     'abalone' => 'Abalone with Marrow and Duck Feet');

if (isset($_SESSION['order']) && (count($_SESSION['order']) > 0)) {
    print '<ul>';
    foreach ($_SESSION['order'] as $order) {
        $dish_name = $main_dishes[ $order['dish'] ];
        print "<li> $order[quantity] of $dish_name </li>";
    }
    print "</ul>";
} else {
    print "You haven't ordered anything.";
}
```

Example 10-12 has access to the data stored in the session by Example 10-11. It treats $_SESSION['order'] as an array: if there are elements in the array (because count()

returns a positive number), then it iterates through the array with `foreach()` and prints out a list element for each dish that has been ordered.

Configuring Sessions

Sessions work just fine with no additional tweaking. Turn them on with the `session_start()` function or the `session.auto_start` configuration directive, and the `$_SESSION` array is there for your enjoyment. However, if you're more particular about how you want sessions to function, there are a few helpful settings that can be changed.

Session data sticks around as long as the session is accessed at least once every 24 minutes. This is fine for most applications. Sessions aren't meant to be a permanent data store for user information—that's what the database is for. Sessions are for keeping track of recent user activity to make the browsing experience smoother.

Some situations may need a shorter session length, however. If you're developing a financial application, you may want to allow only 5 or 10 minutes of idle time to reduce the chance that an unattended computer can be used by an unauthorized person. Conversely, if your application doesn't work with critical data and you have easily distracted users, you may want to set the session length to longer than 24 minutes.

The `session.gc_maxlifetime` configuration directive controls how much idle time is allowed between requests to keep a session active. Its default value is `1440`—there are 1,440 seconds in 24 minutes. You can change `session.gc_maxlifetime` in your server configuration or by calling the `ini_set()` function from your program. If you use `ini_set()`, you must call it before `session_start()`. Example 10-13 shows how to use `ini_set()` to change the allowable session idle time to 10 minutes.

Example 10-13. Changing the allowable session idle time

```
ini_set('session.gc_maxlifetime',600); // 600 seconds == 10 minutes
session_start();
```

Expired sessions don't actually get wiped out instantly after 24 minutes elapse. Here's how it really works: at the beginning of any request that uses sessions (because the page calls `session_start()`, or `session.auto_start` is On), there is a 1% chance that the PHP engine scans through all of the sessions on the server and deletes any that are expired. "A 1% chance" sounds awfully unpredictable for a computer program. It is. But that randomness makes things more efficient. On a busy site, searching for expired sessions to destroy at the beginning of every request would consume too much server power.

You're not stuck with that 1% chance if you'd like expired sessions to be removed more promptly. The `session.gc_probability` configuration directive controls the percent chance that the "erase old sessions" routine runs at the start of a request. To have that happen on every request, set it to 100. Like with session.gc_maxlifetime, if you use ini_set() to change the value of session.gc_probability, you need to do it before session_start(). Example 10-14 demonstrates how to change session.gc_probability with ini_set().

Example 10-14. Changing the expired session cleanup probability

```
ini_set('session.gc_probability',100); // 100% : clean up on every request
session_start();
```

If you are activating sessions with the session.auto_start configuration directive and you want to change the value of session.gc_maxlifetime or session.gc_probability, you can't use ini_set() to change those values—you have to do it in your server configuration.

The cookie used to store a user's session ID can have its properties adjusted via configuration parameters as well. The properties you can adjust mirror the tweaks you can make to a regular cookie via the different arguments to setcookie() (except for the cookie value, of course). Table 10-1 describes the different cookie configuration parameters.

Table 10-1. Session cookie configuration parameters

Configuration parameter	Default value	Description
session.name	PHPSESSID	Name of the cookie. Letters and numbers only, with at least one letter.
session.cookie_lifetime	0	Seconds-since-1970 timestamp when the cookie should expire. 0 means "when the browser exits."
session.cookie_path	/	URL path prefix that must match for the cookie to be sent.
session.cookie_domain	None	Domain suffix that must match for the cookie to be sent. No value means the cookie is sent back only to the full hostname that sent it.
session.cookie_secure	Off	Set to On to have the cookie only sent back with HTTPS URLs.
session.cookie_httponly	Off	Set to On to tell browsers to prevent JavaScript from reading the cookie.

Login and User Identification

A session establishes an anonymous relationship with a particular user. Requiring users to log in to your website lets them tell you who they are. The login process typically requires users to provide you with two pieces of information: one that identifies them (a username or an email address) and one that proves that they are who they say they are (a secret password).

Once a user is logged in, he can access private data, submit message board posts with his name attached, or do anything else that the general public isn't allowed to do.

Adding user login on top of sessions has five parts:

1. Displaying a form asking for a username and password
2. Checking the form submission
3. Adding the username to the session (if the submitted password is correct)
4. Looking for the username in the session to do user-specific tasks
5. Removing the username from the session when the user logs out

The first three steps are handled in the context of regular form processing. The `validate_form()` function gets the responsibility of checking to make sure that the supplied username and password are acceptable. The `process_form()` function adds the username to the session. Example 10-15 displays a login form and adds the username to the session if the login is successful.

Example 10-15. Displaying a login form

```
require 'FormHelper.php';
session_start();

if ($_SERVER['REQUEST_METHOD'] == 'POST') {
    list($errors, $input) = validate_form();
    if ($errors) {
        show_form($errors);
    } else {
        process_form($input);
    }
} else {
    show_form();
}

function show_form($errors = array()) {
    // No defaults of our own, so nothing to pass to the
    // FormHelper constructor
    $form = new FormHelper();

    // Build up the error HTML to use later
    if ($errors) {
        $errorHtml = '<ul><li>';
        $errorHtml .= implode('</li><li>',$errors);
        $errorHtml .= '</li></ul>';
    } else {
        $errorHtml = '';
    }


    // This form is small, so we'll just print out its components
    // here
print <<<_FORM_
<form method="POST" action="{$form->encode($_SERVER['PHP_SELF'])}">
  $errorHtml
```

```
    Username: {$form->input('text', ['name' => 'username'])} <br/>
    Password: {$form->input('password', ['name' => 'password'])} <br/>
    {$form->input('submit', ['value' => 'Log In'])}
</form>
_FORM_;
}

function validate_form() {
    $input = array();
    $errors = array();

    // Some sample usernames and passwords
    $users = array('alice'   => 'dog123',
                   'bob'     => 'my^pwd',
                   'charlie' => '**fun**');

    // Make sure username is valid
    $input['username'] = $_POST['username'] ?? '';
    if (! array_key_exists($input['username'], $users)) {
        $errors[] = 'Please enter a valid username and password.';
    }
    // The else clause means we avoid checking the password if an invalid
    // username is entered
    else {
        // See if password is correct
        $saved_password = $users[ $input['username'] ];
        $submitted_password = $_POST['password'] ?? '';
        if ($saved_password != $submitted_password) {
            $errors[] = 'Please enter a valid username and password.';
        }
    }
    return array($errors, $input);
}


function process_form($input) {
    // Add the username to the session
    $_SESSION['username'] = $input['username'];

    print "Welcome, $_SESSION[username]";
}
?>
```

Figure 10-3 shows the form that Example 10-15 displays, Figure 10-4 shows what
happens when an incorrect password is entered, and Figure 10-5 shows what happens
when a correct password is entered.

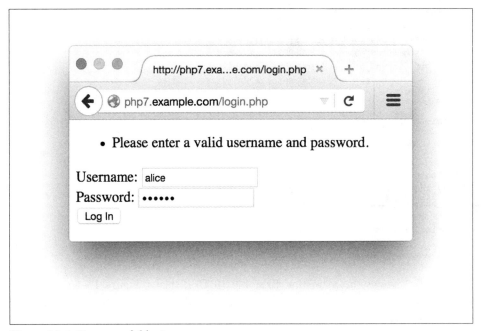

Figure 10-3. Login form

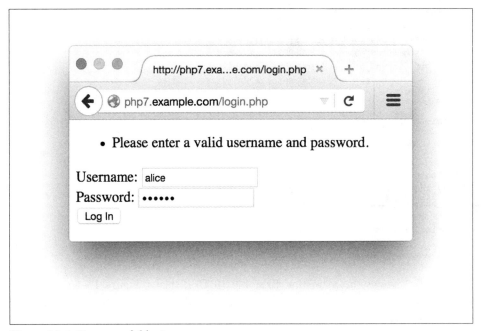

Figure 10-4. Unsuccessful login

Figure 10-5. Successful login

In Example 10-15, `validate_form()` checks two things: whether a valid username is entered and whether the correct password was supplied for that username. Note that the same error message is added to the `$errors` array in either case. If you use different error messages for a missing username (such as "Username not found") and bad passwords (such as "Password doesn't match"), you provide helpful information for someone trying to guess a valid username and password. Once this attacker stumbles on a valid username, she sees the "Password doesn't match" error message instead of the "Username not found" message. She then knows that she's working with a real username and has to guess the password only. When the error messages are the same in both cases, all the attacker knows is that something about the username/password combination she tried is not correct.

If the username is valid and the right password is submitted, `validate_form()` returns no errors. When this happens, tge `process_form()` function is called. This function adds the submitted username (`$input['username']`) to the session and prints out a welcome message for the user. This makes the username available in the session for other pages to use. Example 10-16 demonstrates how to check for a username in the session in another page.

Example 10-16. Doing something special for a logged-in user

```php
<?php
session_start();

if (array_key_exists('username', $_SESSION)) {
    print "Hello, $_SESSION[username].";
} else {
    print 'Howdy, stranger.';
}
?>
```

The only way a `username` element can be added to the `$_SESSION` array is by your program. So if it's there, you know that a user has logged in successfully.

The `validate_form()` function in Example 10-15 uses a sample array of usernames and passwords called `$users`. Storing passwords without hashing them is a bad idea. If the list of unhashed passwords is compromised, then an attacker can log in as any user. Storing hashed passwords prevents an attacker from getting the actual passwords even if she gets the list of hashed passwords, because there's no way to go from the hashed password back to the plain password she'd have to enter to log in. Operating systems that require you to log in with a password use this same technique.

A better `validate_form()` function is shown in Example 10-17. The `$users` array in this version of the function contains passwords that have been hashed with PHP's `password_hash()` function. Because the passwords are stored as hashed strings, they can't be compared directly with the plain password that the user enters. Instead, the submitted password in `$input['password']` is checked by the `password_verify()` function. This function uses the information in the saved hashed password to produce a hash of the submitted password in the same way. If the two hashes match, then the user has submitted the correct password and `password_verify()` returns `true`.

Example 10-17. Using hashed passwords

```php
function validate_form() {
    $input = array();
    $errors = array();

    // Sample users with hashed passwords
    $users = array('alice' =>
        '$2y$10$N47IXmT8C.sKUFXs1EBS9uJRuVV8bWxwqubcvNqYP9vcFmlSWEAbq',
                   'bob' =>
        '$2y$10$qCczYRc7S0llVRESMqUkGeWQT4V4OQ2qkSyhnx00c.fk.LulKwUwW',
                   'charlie' =>
        '$2y$10$nKfkdviOBONrzZkRq5pAgOCbaTFiFI6O2xFka9yzXpEBRAXMW5mYi');

    // Make sure username is valid
    if (! array_key_exists($_POST['username'], $users)) {
```

```
        $errors[ ] = 'Please enter a valid username and password.';
    }
    else {
        // See if password is correct
        $saved_password = $users[ $input['username'] ];
        $submitted_password = $_POST['password'] ?? '';
        if (! password_verify($submitted_password, $saved_password)) {
            $errors[ ] = 'Please enter a valid username and password.';
        }
    }

    return array($errors, $input);
}
```

Using password_hash() and password_verify() ensures that the passwords
are hashed in a sufficiently secure manner and gives you the ability to strengthen
that hash in the future if necessary. If you're interested in more details about how
they work, read the password_hash (*http://www.php.net/password_hash*) and pass
word_verify (*http://www.php.net/password_verify*) pages in the online PHP Manual,
or see Recipe 18.7 of *PHP Cookbook*, by David Sklar and Adam Trachtenberg
(O'Reilly).

 The password_hash()and password_verify() functions are available in PHP 5.5.0 and later. If you're using an earlier version of
PHP, use the password_compat library (*https://github.com/ircmax
ell/password_compat*), which provides versions of these functions.

Putting an array of users and passwords inside validate_form() makes these examples self-contained. However, more typically, your usernames and passwords are
stored in a database table. Example 10-18 is a version of validate_form() that
retrieves the username and hashed password from a database. It assumes that a database connection has already been set up outside the function and is available in the
global variable $db.

Example 10-18. Retrieving a username and password from a database

```
function validate_form() {
    global $db;
    $input = array();
    $errors = array();

    // This gets set to true only if the submitted password matches
    $password_ok = false;

    $input['username'] = $_POST['username'] ?? '';
    $submitted_password = $_POST['password'] ?? '';
```

```
$stmt = $db->prepare('SELECT password FROM users WHERE username = ?');
$stmt->execute($input['username']);
$row = $stmt->fetch();
// If there's no row, then the username didn't match any rows
if ($row) {
    $password_ok = password_verify($submitted_password, $row[0]);
}
if (! $password_ok) {
    $errors[] = 'Please enter a valid username and password.';
}

    return array($errors, $input);
}
```

The query that `prepare()` and `execute()` send to the database returns the hashed password for the user identified in `$input['username']`. If the username supplied doesn't match any rows in the database, then `$row` is `false`. If a row is returned, then `password_verify()` checks the submitted password against the hashed password retrieved from the database. Only if there is a row returned and the row contains a correct hashed password does `$password_ok` get set to `true`. Otherwise, an error message is added to the `$errors` array.

Just like with any other array, use `unset()` to remove a key and value from `$_SESSION`. This is how to log out a user. Example 10-19 shows a logout page.

Example 10-19. Logging out

```
session_start();
unset($_SESSION['username']);

print 'Bye-bye.';
```

When the `$_SESSION` array is saved at the end of the request that calls `unset()`, the username element isn't included in the saved data. The next time that session's data is loaded into `$_SESSION`, there is no username element, and the user is once again anonymous.

Why setcookie() and session_start() Want to Be at the Top of the Page

When a web server sends a response to a web client, most of that response is the HTML document that the browser renders into a web page on your screen: the soup of tags and text that Safari or Firefox formats into tables or changes the color or size of. But before that HTML is a section of the response that contains *headers*. These don't get displayed on your screen but are commands or information from the server for the web client. The headers say things such as "this page was generated at such-

and-such a time," "please don't cache this page," or the one that's relevant here, "please remember that the cookie named userid has the value ralph."

All of the headers in the response from the web server to the web client have to be at the beginning of the response, before the *response body*, which is the HTML that controls what the browser actually displays. Once some of the body is sent—even one line—no more headers can be sent.

Functions such as setcookie() and session_start() add headers to the response. In order for the added headers to be sent properly, they must be added before any output starts. That's why they must be called before any print statements or any HTML appearing outside <?php ?> PHP tags.

If any output has been sent before setcookie() or session_start() is called, the PHP engine prints an error message that looks like this:

```
Warning: Cannot modify header information - headers already sent by
(output started at /www/htdocs/catalog.php:2)
in /www/htdocs/catalog.php on line 4
```

This means that line 4 of *catalog.php* called a function that sends a header, but something was already printed by line 2 of *catalog.php*.

If you see the "headers already sent" error message, scrutinize your code for errant output. Make sure there are no print statements before you call setcookie() or session_start(). Check that there is nothing before the first <?php start tag in the page. Also, check that there is nothing outside the <?php and ?> tags in any included or required files—even blank lines.

An alternative to hunting down mischievous blank lines in your files is to use *output buffering*. This tells the PHP engine to wait to send *any* output until it's finished processing the whole request. Then, it sends any headers that have been set, followed by all the regular output. To enable output buffering, set the output_buffering configuration directive to On in your server configuration. Web clients will have to wait a few additional milliseconds to get the page content from your server, but you'll save megaseconds by not having to fix your code to have all output happen after calls to setcookie() or session_start().

With output buffering turned on, you can mix print statements, cookie and session functions, HTML outside of <?php and ?> tags, and regular PHP code without getting the "headers already sent" error. The program in Example 10-20 works only when output buffering is turned on. Without it, the HTML printed before the <?php start tag triggers the sending of headers, which prevents setcookie() from working properly.

Example 10-20. A program that needs output buffering to work

```
<html>
<head>Choose Your Site Version</head>
<body>
<?php
setcookie('seen_intro', 1);
?>
<a href="/basic.php">Basic</a>
 or
<a href="/advanced.php">Advanced</a>
</body>
</html>
```

Chapter Summary

This chapter covered:

- Understanding why cookies are necessary to identify a particular web browser to a web server
- Setting a cookie in a PHP program
- Reading a cookie value in a PHP program
- Modifying cookie parameters such as expiration time, path, and domain
- Deleting a cookie in a PHP program
- Turning on sessions from a PHP program or in the PHP engine configuration
- Storing information in a session
- Reading information from a session
- Saving form data in a session
- Removing information from a session
- Configuring session expiration and cleanup
- Displaying, validating, and processing a validation form
- Using hashed passwords
- Understanding why `setcookie()` and `session_start()` must be called before anything is printed

Exercises

1. Make a web page that uses a cookie to keep track of how many times a user has viewed the page. The first time a particular user looks at the page, it should print something like "Number of views: 1." The second time the user looks at the page, it should print "Number of views: 2," and so on.
2. Modify the web page from the first exercise so that it prints out a special message on the 5th, 10th, and 15th times the user looks at the page. Also modify it so that

on the 20th time the user looks at the page, it deletes the cookie and the page count starts over.

3. Write a PHP program that displays a form for a user to pick his favorite color from a list of colors. Make another page whose background color is set to the color that the user picks in the form. Store the color value in $_SESSION so that both pages can access it.

4. Write a PHP program that displays an order form. The order form should list six products. Next to each product name there should be a text box into which a user can enter how many of that product she wants to order. When the form is submitted, the submitted form data should be saved into the session. Make another page that displays the contents of the saved order, a link back to the order form page, and a Check Out button. If the link back to the order form page is clicked, the order form page should be displayed with the saved order quantities from the session in the text boxes. When the Check Out button is clicked, the order should be cleared from the session.

## CHAPTER 11

Talking to Other Websites and Services

Previous chapters discussed external sources of data such as databases and files. This chapter is about another important external source of data: other websites. PHP programs are often clients of other sites or APIs that offer up data that you need. Your website could itself serve up data to another site that needs it. This chapter shows how to retrieve external URLs and access APIs. It also explains what you need to do to serve API requests to others.

The first section shows how to use PHP's built-in file access functions with URLs instead of filenames. This is a convenient option for quick and easy remote URL access. For more power and flexibility, though, use PHP's cURL extension, discussed in "Comprehensive URL Access with cURL" on page 236. The cURL functions let you control many different aspects of the requests you're making.

Serving up API responses instead of web pages from your PHP program is the focus of "Serving API Requests" on page 244. These responses are similar to standard HTML pages but have some important differences.

Simple URL Access with File Functions

An extremely convenient aspect of file access functions like `file_get_contents()` is that they understand URLs in addition to local filenames. Grabbing a remote URL and putting it into a string is just a matter of handing that URL to `file_get_contents()`.

Example 11-1 uses `file_get_contents()` to display an interesting fact from the website *numbersapi.com* about September 27th.

Example 11-1. Retrieving a URL with file_get_contents()

```
Did you know that <?= file_get_contents('http://numbersapi.com/09/27') ?>
```

The Numbers API knows a lot of facts about each day, but for me the result of Example 11-1 looked like this:

```
Did you know that September 27th is the day in 1961 that Sierra Leone
joins the United Nations.
```

The `http_build_query()` function is useful when you need to build an API URL that includes query string parameters. Give `http_build_query()` an associative array of parameter names and values and it gives you back a string of *key=value* pairs joined by & and properly encoded—exactly what you need for a URL.

The United States Department of Agriculture has a nifty API on top of its National Nutrient Database. This NDB API is free and easy to use.

The NDB API used for examples in this chapter requires that requests have a parameter named `api_key` whose value is a distinct API key that you get by signing up for the API. To get your own API key, visit *https://api.data.gov/signup/*. It's free, quick, and requires you to provide minimal information—just your name and email address.

The examples in this chapter use the constant `NDB_API_KEY` in place of an actual API key. To run the examples on your own, you can either replace the `NDB_API_KEY` with a string containing your own API key, or use `define()` to set the `NDB_API_KEY` constant equal to the value of your API key. For example, if your API key were 273bqhebrfkhuebf, you'd put this line at the top of your code:

```
define('NDB_API_KEY','273bqhebrfkhuebf');
```

Example 11-2 uses the NDB search API to find some information about black pepper. This API returns information about each food in the database whose name matches what's in the q query string parameter.

Example 11-2. Putting query string parameters in an API URL

```
$params = array('api_key' => NDB_API_KEY,
                'q' => 'black pepper',
                'format' => 'json');

$url = "http://api.nal.usda.gov/ndb/search?" . http_build_query($params);
```

The `$url` variable in Example 11-2 is set to something like the following (the actual value depends on your API key):

```
http://api.nal.usda.gov/ndb/search?
api_key=j724nbefuy72n4&q=black+pepper&format=json
```

Each key and value in the $params array has been put together with = and &, and spe-
cial characters, such as the space in black pepper, have been encoded.

Passing such a URL to file_get_contents() makes the API call. In this case, the
API returns JSON, so the return value of file_get_contents() is this string:

```
{
    "list": {
        "q": "black pepper",
        "sr": "27",
        "start": 0,
        "end": 1,
        "total": 1,
        "group": "",
        "sort": "r",
        "item": [
            {
                "offset": 0,
                "group": "Spices and Herbs",
                "name": "Spices, pepper, black",
                "ndbno": "02030"
            }
        ]
    }
}
```

Because file_get_contents() returns the response from retrieving the URL as a
string, it's a snap to pass that string to other functions that further transform it. For
example, pass the API response above to json_decode() to transform the JSON into
a PHP data structure you can manipulate. Example 11-3 prints out the NDB ID number for each matching food item.

Example 11-3. Decoding a JSON API response

```
$params = array('api_key' => NDB_API_KEY,
                'q' => 'black pepper',
                'format' => 'json');

$url = "http://api.nal.usda.gov/ndb/search?" . http_build_query($params);
$response = file_get_contents($url);
$info = json_decode($response);

foreach ($info->list->item as $item) {
    print "The ndbno for {$item->name} is {$item->ndbno}.\n";
}
```

The json_decode() function turns JSON objects into PHP objects and JSON arrays into PHP arrays. The top-level item in the response is an object. This is the return value from json_decode() and is assigned to $info. That object has a list property that is another object. The list object can be referred to as $info->list. That list object has an array property named item whose elements hold the details about the matching foods. So, the array that foreach() iterates over is $info->list->item. Each $item inside the foreach() loop is one object from that array. Example 11-3 prints:

```
The ndbno for Spices, pepper, black is 02030.
```

The NDB API calls made so far return JSON because of the format=json query string parameter. The API also supports specifying the response format by sending a Content-Type header.[1] A header value of application/json tells the server to format the response as JSON.

To add headers to your HTTP request with file_get_contents(), you create a *stream context*. The PHP engine's underlying mechanisms for flowing data into and out of your programs are called *streams*. A stream can be a local file, a remote URL, or another exotic place that produces or consumes data. The first argument to file_get_contents() is the stream's *target*: the file or URL to read from or write to. Additional information about the reading or writing operation is expressed through the *stream context*, created by passing an associative array of the additional information to the stream_context_create() function.

Different kinds of streams support different kinds of options for their contexts. For the http stream, a header option gets a string value containing the names and values of any headers to send with the HTTP request. Example 11-4 shows how to create a stream context that includes an HTTP header and use it with file_get_contents().

Example 11-4. Sending HTTP headers with a stream context

```
// Just key and query term, no format specified in query string
$params = array('api_key' => NDB_API_KEY,
                'q' => 'black pepper');
$url = "http://api.nal.usda.gov/ndb/search?" . http_build_query($params);

// Options are to set a Content-Type request header
$options = array('header' => 'Content-Type: application/json');
// Create a context for an 'http' stream
$context = stream_context_create(array('http' => $options));
```

---

[1] The HTTP specification says to use an Accept header for this, but that's not how this particular API works.

```
// Pass the context as the third argument to file_get_contents
print file_get_contents($url, false, $context);
```

In Example 11-4, the `$options` array contains the key/value pairs of options to set. The `stream_context_create()` function needs to be told which kind of stream it's creating a context for, so its argument is an array whose key is the stream type (`http`) and the value is the options to set.

The second argument of `file_get_contents()` indicates whether the function should pay attention to the PHP engine's include path when looking for a file. This is irrelevant with HTTP, so `false` is supplied for a value. The context is the third argument to `file_get_contents()`.

The context is also how you send a `POST` request with `file_get_contents()`. The `method` context option controls the request method, and the `content` context option contains any request body to send. The content must be formatted properly for the content type you specify as a header.

We can't use the NDB API for `POST`, since it just tells us nutrition data via `GET`. It doesn't allow us to send new data in. Example 11-5 uses `file_get_contents()` to send a `POST` request to an example URL. This request acts just like a form submission sending two form variables: `name` and `smell`.

Example 11-5. Sending a POST request with file_get_contents()

```
$url = 'http://php7.example.com/post-server.php';

// Two variables to send via POST
$form_data = array('name' => 'black pepper',
                   'smell' => 'good');

// Set the method, content type, and content
$options = array('method' => 'POST',
                 'header' => 'Content-Type: application/x-www-form-urlencoded',
                 'content' => http_build_query($form_data));
// Create a context for an 'http' stream
$context = stream_context_create(array('http' => $options));

// Pass the context as the third argument to file_get_contents.
print file_get_contents($url, false, $context);
```

In Example 11-5, the `method` stream context option ensures that this is a `POST` request. The value you supply here is used verbatim by the PHP engine to make the request, so be sure to make it all capital letters. The value for the `Content-Type` header is the standard value that web browsers use for regular form data. It corresponds to data formatted like query string parameters but sent in the request body. Conveniently, this lets us use `http_build_query()` to construct the properly formatted request body.

 In Example 11-5, as in other examples in this section, php7.example.com is used as a sample hostname. You must change this to a real hostname (preferably of your own web server!) to make the code work.

If you need to send a different kind of data in your POST request, just change the value of the Content-Type header and how you format the request content. For example, to send JSON, change the header option to Content-Type: application/json and change the content option to json_encode($form_data).

More information about the PHP engine's different stream types and other supported context options is available at *http://www.php.net/context*.

Although the simplicity of retrieving URLs with built-in file access functions is fantastic, these functions do not make life simple if there is an error when making the request. When that happens, file_get_contents() returns false and the PHP engine generates an error message that looks like failed to open stream: HTTP request failed! HTTP/1.1 404 Not Found. Having more control over what to do when a request is not successful is one good reason to use the cURL functions instead.

Comprehensive URL Access with cURL

The file_get_contents() function, especially when combined with context options, lets you make a wide variety of HTTP requests. But when you really need control over the details of your HTTP requests and responses, turn to PHP's cURL functions. By using a powerful underlying library, libcurl, these functions give you access to all aspects of your HTTP requests and responses.

Retrieving URLs via GET

Accessing a URL with cURL begins by passing the URL you want to access to curl_init(). This function doesn't immediately go out and retrieve the URL; it returns a *handle*, which is a variable that you pass to other functions to set options and configure how cURL should work. You can have multiple handles in different variables at the same time. Each handle controls a different request.

The curl_setopt() function controls the PHP engine's behavior when retrieving the URL, and the curl_exec() function actually causes the request to be retrieved. Example 11-6 uses cURL to retrieve the *numbersapi.com* URL from Example 11-1.

Example 11-6. Retrieving a URL with cURL

```php
<?php

$c = curl_init('http://numbersapi.com/09/27');
// Tell cURL to return the response contents as a string
// rather then printing them out immediately
curl_setopt($c, CURLOPT_RETURNTRANSFER, true);
// Execute the request
$fact = curl_exec($c);

?>
Did you know that <?= $fact ?>
```

In Example 11-6, the call to `curl_setopt()` sets the `CURLOPT_RETURNTRANSFER` option. This tells cURL that when it makes the HTTP request, it should return the response as a string. Otherwise, it prints out the response as it is retrieved. The `curl_exec()` function makes the request and returns the result.

Other cURL options let you set headers. Example 11-7 uses cURL functions to make the request from Example 11-4.

Example 11-7. Using cURL with query string parameters and headers

```php
// Just key and query term, no format specified in query string
$params = array('api_key' => NDB_API_KEY,
                'q' => 'black pepper');
$url = "http://api.nal.usda.gov/ndb/search?" . http_build_query($params);

$c = curl_init($url);
curl_setopt($c, CURLOPT_RETURNTRANSFER, true);
curl_setopt($c, CURLOPT_HTTPHEADER, array('Content-Type: application/json'));
print curl_exec($c);
```

In Example 11-7, the URL is constructed in a familiar way with `http_build_query()`. The query string parameters are part of the URL, so they go into the URL string passed to `curl_init()`. The new `CURLOPT_HTTP_HEADER` option sets the HTTP header to be sent with the request. If you have multiple headers, put multiple items in this array.

There are two kinds of errors to deal with from cURL requests. The first is an error from cURL itself. This could be something such as not finding the hostname, or not being able to make a connection to the remote server. If this kind of thing happens, `curl_exec()` returns `false` and `curl_errno()` returns an error code. The `curl_error()` function returns the error message that corresponds to the code.

The second kind of error is an error from the remote server. This happens if the URL you ask for isn't found or the server has a problem producing a response to your request. cURL still considers this a successful request because the server returned something, so you need to check the HTTP response code to see if there's a problem. The curl_getinfo() function returns an array of information about the request. One of the elements in that array is the HTTP response code.

Example 11-8 shows cURL request-making code that handles both kinds of errors.

Example 11-8. Handling errors with cURL

```
// A pretend API endpoint that doesn't exist
$c = curl_init('http://api.example.com');
curl_setopt($c, CURLOPT_RETURNTRANSFER, true);
$result = curl_exec($c);
// Get all the connection info, whether or not it succeeded
$info = curl_getinfo($c);

// Something went wrong with the connection
if ($result === false) {
    print "Error #" . curl_errno($c) . "\n";
    print "Uh-oh! cURL says: " . curl_error($c) . "\n";
}
// HTTP response codes in the 400s and 500s mean errors
else if ($info['http_code'] >= 400) {
    print "The server says HTTP error {$info['http_code']}.\n";
}
else {
    print "A successful result!\n";
}
// The request info includes timing statistics as well
print "By the way, this request took {$info['total_time']} seconds.\n";
```

Example 11-8 starts out with a standard cURL request. After making the request, it stores the request info from curl_getinfo() into $info. The curl_getinfo() function needs to be passed the cURL handle it should operate on, just like curl_errno() and curl_error(). This is necessary in order to return information about the correct request.

The host api.example.com doesn't actually exist, so cURL can't connect to it to make a request. So, curl_exec() returns false. Example 11-8 prints:

```
Error #6
Uh-oh! cURL says: Could not resolve host: api.example.com
By the way, this request took 0.000146 seconds.
```

The PHP manual page (*http://www.php.net/curl_errno*) about curl_errno() has a list of all the cURL error codes.

If the request made it to the server but the server returned an error, then `$result` is not `false`, but holds whatever response the server sent back. This response code is in the `http_code` element of the `$info` array. If Example 11-8 encountered an HTTP 404 error, which means that the server couldn't find the page the request asked for, then the example would print:

```
The server says HTTP error 404.
By the way, this request took 0.00567 seconds.
```

Both outputs from the example also include the total time it took to make the request. This is another handy bit of request data in the `$info` array. The PHP manual page (*http://www.php.net/curl_getinfo*) for `curl_getinfo()` lists all the elements of this array.

Retrieving URLs via POST

To use the `POST` method with cURL, adjust the settings to change the request method and supply the request body data. The `CURLOPT_POST` setting tells cURL you want a `POST` request, and the `CURLOPT_POSTFIELDS` setting holds the data you want to send. Example 11-9 shows how to make a `POST` request with cURL.

Example 11-9. Making a POST request with cURL

```
$url = 'http://php7.example.com/post-server.php';

// Two variables to send via POST
$form_data = array('name' => 'black pepper',
                   'smell' => 'good');

$c = curl_init($url);
curl_setopt($c, CURLOPT_RETURNTRANSFER, true);
// This should be a POST request
curl_setopt($c, CURLOPT_POST, true);
// This is the data to send
curl_setopt($c, CURLOPT_POSTFIELDS, $form_data);

print curl_exec($c);
```

In Example 11-9, you don't need to set the `Content-Type` header or format the data you're sending. cURL takes care of that for you.

However, if you want to send a different content type than regular form data, you need to do a little more work. Example 11-10 shows how to send JSON via a `POST` request with cURL.

Example 11-10. Sending JSON via POST with cURL

```
$url = 'http://php7.example.com/post-server.php';

// Two variables to send as JSON via POST
$form_data = array('name' => 'black pepper',
                   'smell' => 'good');

$c = curl_init($url);
curl_setopt($c, CURLOPT_RETURNTRANSFER, true);
// This should be a POST request
curl_setopt($c, CURLOPT_POST, true);
// This is a request containing JSON
curl_setopt($c, CURLOPT_HTTPHEADER, array('Content-Type: application/json'));
// This is the data to send, formatted appropriately
curl_setopt($c, CURLOPT_POSTFIELDS, json_encode($form_data));

print curl_exec($c);
```

In Example 11-10, the CURLOPT_HTTPHEADER setting tells the server that the request body is JSON, not regular form data. Then, the value of CURLOPT_POSTFIELDS is set to json_encode($form_data) so that the request body is indeed JSON.

Using Cookies

If the response to a cURL request includes a header that sets a cookie, cURL doesn't do anything special with that header by default. But cURL does give you a few configuration settings that let you track cookies, even across different PHP programs or executions of the same program.

Example 11-11 is a simple page that maintains a cookie, c. Each time the page is requested, the response includes a c cookie whose value is one greater than whatever value is supplied for the c cookie in the request. If no c cookie is sent, then the response sets the c cookie to 1.

Example 11-11. Simple cookie-setting server

```
// Use the value sent in the cookie, if any, or 0 if no cookie supplied
$value = $_COOKIE['c'] ?? 0;
// Increment the value by 1
$value++;
// Set the new cookie in the response
setcookie('c', $value);
// Tell the user what cookies we saw
print "Cookies: " . count($_COOKIE) . "\n";
foreach ($_COOKIE as $k => $v) {
    print "$k: $v\n";
}
```

With no additional configuration, cURL doesn't keep track of the cookie sent back in Example 11-11. In Example 11-12, curl_exec() is called twice on the same handle, but the cookie sent back in the response to the first request is not sent on the second request.

Example 11-12. cURL's default cookie-handling behavior

```
// Retrieve the cookie server page, sending no cookies
$c = curl_init('http://php7.example.com/cookie-server.php');
curl_setopt($c, CURLOPT_RETURNTRANSFER, true);
// The first time, there are no cookies
$res = curl_exec($c);
print $res;

// The second time, there are still no cookies
$res = curl_exec($c);
print $res;
```

 In Example 11-12, as in the other client examples in this section, the program is accessible at *http://php7.example.com/cookie-server.php*. To run the code yourself, change the URL to point to your PHP server.

Example 11-12 prints:

```
Cookies: 0
Cookies: 0
```

Both requests get a response of Cookies: 0 because cURL sent no Cookie header with the request.

Enabling cURL's *cookie jar* tells it to keep track of cookies. To keep track of cookies within the lifetime of a specific cURL handle, set CURLOPT_COOKIEJAR to true, as in Example 11-13.

Example 11-13. Enabling cURL's cookie jar

```
// Retrieve the cookie server page, sending no cookies
$c = curl_init('http://php7.example.com/cookie-server.php');
curl_setopt($c, CURLOPT_RETURNTRANSFER, true);
// Turn on the cookie jar
curl_setopt($c, CURLOPT_COOKIEJAR, true);

// The first time, there are no cookies
$res = curl_exec($c);
print $res;

// The second time, there are cookies from the first request
```

```
$res = curl_exec($c);
print $res;
```

Example 11-13 prints:

```
Cookies: 0
Cookies: 1
c: 1
```

In Example 11-13, cURL keeps track of cookies sent in response to a request as long as the handle for that cURL request exists in your program. The second time `curl_exec()` is called for the handle `$c`, the cookie set in the first response is used.

In this mode, the cookie jar only tracks cookies within a handle. Changing the value of `CURLOPT_COOKIEJAR` to a filename tells cURL to write the cookie values to that file. Then you can also provide that filename as the value for `CURLOPT_COOKIEFILE`. Before sending a request, cURL reads in any cookies from the `CURLOPT_COOKIEFILE` file and uses them in subsequent requests. Example 11-14 shows the cookie jar and cookie file in action.

Example 11-14. Tracking cookies across requests

```
// Retrieve the cookie server page
$c = curl_init('http://php7.example.com/cookie-server.php');
curl_setopt($c, CURLOPT_RETURNTRANSFER, true);
// Save cookies to a 'saved.cookies' file in the same directory
// as this program
curl_setopt($c, CURLOPT_COOKIEJAR, __DIR__ . '/saved.cookies');
// Load cookies (if any have been previously saved) from the
// 'saved.cookies' file in this directory
curl_setopt($c, CURLOPT_COOKIEFILE, __DIR__ . '/saved.cookies');

// This request includes cookies from the file (if any)
$res = curl_exec($c);
print $res;
```

The first time Example 11-14 is run, it prints:

```
Cookies: 0
```

The second time Example 11-14 is run, it prints:

```
Cookies: 1
c: 1
```

The third time Example 11-14 is run, it prints:

```
Cookies: 1
c: 2
```

And so forth. Each time the program runs, it looks for a *saved.cookies* file, loads up any cookies stored in the file, and uses them for the request. After the request, it saves any cookies back to the same file because the CURLOPT_COOKIEFILE setting has the same value as the CURLOPT_COOKIEJAR setting. This updates the saved cookies file so it's ready with the new value the next time the program runs.

If you're writing a program that mimics a user logging in with a web browser and then making requests, the cookie jar is a very convenient way to have all of the server-sent cookies accompany the requests cURL makes.

Retrieving HTTPS URLs

To retrieve URLs that use the https protocol, you do all the same things with cURL that you'd do with regular http URLs. However, there are some security settings that are important to get right. Usually, your defaults will be OK. This section explains those values so you can be sure they're correct and understand why you shouldn't change them.

When a web client retrieves an https URL, the security provided has two separate features. One is identity verification: the server asserts that it is really the server that should be handling the URL (based on the hostname). The other is protection from eavesdropping: anybody who scoops up the conversation between the client and the server sees just a meaningless jumble of characters instead of the real request and response.

The CURLOPT_SSL_VERIFYPEER and CURLOPT_SSL_VERIFYHOST settings control whether cURL is strict about identify verification. If CURLOPT_SSL_VERIFYPEER is set to false, or CURLOPT_SSL_VERIFYHOST is set to something other than 2, then cURL will skip essential steps that make sure the server is who it says it is.

If you're using cURL version 7.10 or later, then CURLOPT_SSL_VERIFYPEER is turned on by default. If you're using cURL version 7.28.1 or later, then cURL won't let you change CURLOPT_SSL_VERIFYHOST to a value other than 2.

Use the curl_version() function to find out what version your PHP installation has. This function returns an associative array of information about the installed version of cURL's capabilities. The version element of the array contains the version of cURL that the PHP engine is relying on.

There are also different versions of the secure protocol that web clients and servers use to implement HTTPS URLs. Which protocol version cURL uses is controlled by the CURLOPT_SSLVERSION setting. There should be no need to change this value. The default value (which you can explicitly set with the constant CURL_SSLVERSION_DEFAULT) uses the most up-to-date and secure version of the protocol available to the version of cURL you have.

Serving API Requests

Your PHP program can serve API requests to clients as well. Instead of generating a plain HTML page, you generate whatever data is appropriate to the API call. Additionally, you may need to manipulate the HTTP response code and response headers you send.

To send an HTTP header along with your response, use the `header()` function. Example 11-15 is a tiny clock API in PHP. It serves up the current time in JSON format.

Example 11-15. Serving a JSON response

```
$response_data = array('now' => time());
header('Content-Type: application/json');
print json_encode($response_data);
```

The call to `header()` in Example 11-15 adds a header line to the HTTP response that the PHP engine generates. The header line is whatever you pass to the function. The code uses the `json_encode()` function to generate the JSON that makes up the response. This function is the opposite of `json_decode()`. You give it a PHP data type (string, number, object, array, etc.) and it returns a string containing the JSON representation of what was passed in. Example 11-15 generates an HTTP response that looks like this:

```
HTTP/1.1 200 OK
Host: www.example.com
Connection: close
Content-Type: application/json

{"now":1962258300}
```

The first four lines are the response headers. A few get added automatically by your web server. The `Content-Type: application/json` line is from the call to `header()`. After the blank line comes the request body. This is the stuff you see in your web browser (or, if it's HTML, you see the results of your web browser rendering the HTML). In this case, the request body is a JSON object with one property, `now`, whose value is a timestamp corresponding to the current time. The value you get when you run this code will almost certainly be different because you are almost certainly running this code at a different time than the timestamp printed here. For more details on time handling in PHP, see Chapter 15.

The first line of the response headers contains the response code, which in this case is 200—which is HTTP-speak for "everything was fine." To send a different response code, use the `http_response_code()` function. Example 11-16 is like Example 11-15 except it sends back a 403 status code ("Forbidden") and an error response body unless a query string parameter named key is supplied with a value of pineapple.

Example 11-16. Changing the response code

```php
if (! (isset($_GET['key']) && ($_GET['key'] == 'pineapple'))) {
    http_response_code(403);
    $response_data = array('error' => 'bad key');
}
else {
    $response_data = array('now' => time());
}
header('Content-Type: application/json');
print json_encode($response_data);
```

Without the proper query string parameter supplied, Example 11-16's response looks like this:

```
HTTP/1.1 403 Forbidden
Host: www.example.com
Connection: close
Content-Type: application/json
```

```
{"error":"bad key"}
```

Example 11-4 used a Content-Type header to tell the NDB API to send back a response as JSON. To access incoming request headers from your PHP program, look in the $_SERVER array. Each incoming header is there. A header's array key is HTTP_ followed by the header's name in all uppercase and with any dashes (-) converted to underscores (_). For example, the value of an incoming Content-Type header would be in $_SERVER['HTTP_CONTENT_TYPE']. Example 11-17 examines the value of an incoming Accept header to determine how to format the output data.

Example 11-17. Examining a request header

```php
<?php

// Formats we want to support
$formats = array('application/json','text/html','text/plain');
// Response format if not specified
$default_format = 'application/json';

// Was a response format supplied?
if (isset($_SERVER['HTTP_ACCEPT'])) {
    // If a supported format is supplied, use it
    if (in_array($_SERVER['HTTP_ACCEPT'], $formats)) {
        $format = $_SERVER['HTTP_ACCEPT'];
    }
    // An unsupported format was supplied, so return an error
```

```php
    else {
        // 406 means "You want a response in a format I can't generate"
        http_response_code(406);
        // Exiting now means no response body, which is OK
        exit();
    }
} else {
    $format = $default_format;
}


// Figure out what time it is
$response_data = array('now' => time());
// Tell the client what kind of content we're sending
header("Content-Type: $format");
// Print the time in a format-appropriate way
if ($format == 'application/json') {
    print json_encode($response_data);
}
else if ($format == 'text/html') { ?>
<!doctype html>
  <html>
    <head><title>Clock</title></head>
    <body><time><?= date('c', $response_data['now']) ?></time></body>
  </html>
<?php
} else if ($format == 'text/plain') {
    print $response_data['now'];
}
```

If the incoming `Accept` header is `application/json`, `text/html`, or `text/plain`, then `$format` is set to the proper format to use. This value gets put in the `Content-Type` header of the response and is used to generate a format-appropriate output. If no `Accept` header is supplied, a default of `application/json` is used. If any other value is supplied in the `Accept` header, then the program returns an empty body with a `406` error code. This tells the client that an invalid format was asked for.[2]

The `$_SERVER` array is also where you look to determine if the current request is a secure request; that is, if it was made with HTTPS. If the current request is secure, then `$_SERVER['HTTPS']` is set to on. Example 11-18 checks if the current request was made over HTTPS and redirects to an HTTPS version of the current request's URL if not.

---

2 Parsing real Accept headers is a bit more complicated because clients are allowed to send multiple formats and indicate which one they prefer. Look on GitHub (*https://github.com/willdurand/Negotiation*) for a complete solution to this process, which is called *content negotiation*.

Example 11-18. Checking for HTTPS

```
$is_https = (isset($_SERVER['HTTPS']) && ($_SERVER['HTTPS'] == 'on'));
if (! $is_https) {
    $newUrl = 'https://' . $_SERVER['HTTP_HOST'] . $_SERVER['REQUEST_URI'];
    header("Location: $newUrl");
    exit();
}
print "You accessed this page over HTTPS. Yay!";
```

In Example 11-18, the first line determines whether the current request was over HTTPS by ensuring two things: first, that there is a value set for $_SERVER['HTTPS'] and second, that the value is on. If both of those things are not true, then an HTTPS version of the current URL is built by combining the right protocol (https://) with the current request's hostname (the value of $_SERVER['HTTP_HOST']) and the current request's path (the value of $_SERVER['REQUEST_URI']). If the request included any query string parameters, those are included in $_SERVER['REQUEST_URI'] as well. The Location header, sent by the header() function, redirects a web client to a new URL.

Chapter Summary

This chapter covered:

- Retrieving URLs with file_get_contents()
- Retrieving a URL that includes query string parameters
- Decoding a JSON HTTP response
- Understanding PHP's stream contexts
- Including additional headers when retrieving a URL
- Retrieving URLs via the POST method with file_get_contents()
- Retrieving URLs with cURL
- Using query string parameters with cURL
- Adding request headers with cURL
- Handling errors from cURL requests
- Retrieving URLs via the POST method with cURL
- Keeping track of HTTP cookies with cURL
- Using cURL securely with HTTPS
- Serving non-HTML responses
- Changing the HTTP response code
- Using values from HTTP request headers
- Checking if a request is made with HTTPS

Exercises

1. *http://php.net/releases/?json* is a JSON feed of the latest PHP releases. Write a program that uses `file_get_contents()` to retrieve this feed and print out the latest version of PHP released.
2. Modify your program from the previous exercise to use cURL instead of `file_get_contents()`.
3. Write a web page that uses a cookie to tell the user when he last looked at the web page (you may find the date-and-time-handling functions described in Chapter 15 useful).
4. A GitHub *gist* is a snippet of text or code that is easy to share. The GitHub API (*https://developer.github.com/v3/gists/#create-a-gist*) allows you to create gists without logging in. Write a program that creates a gist whose contents are the program you're writing to create a gist. Note that the GitHub API requires you to set a `User-Agent` header in your HTTP API requests. The `CURLOPT_USERAGENT` setting can be used to set this header.

## CHAPTER 12

Debugging

Programs rarely work correctly the first time you run them. This chapter shows you some techniques for finding and fixing the problems in your programs. When you're just learning PHP, your programs are probably simpler than the programs that PHP wizards write. The errors you get, however, generally aren't much simpler, and you have to use the same tools and techniques to find and fix those errors.

Controlling Where Errors Appear

Many things can go wrong in your program that cause the PHP engine to generate an error message. You have a choice about where those error messages go. The messages can be sent along with other program output to the web browser. They can also be included in the web server error log.

A useful way to configure an error message display is to have the errors displayed on screen while you're developing a PHP program, and then when you're done with development and people are actually using the program, send error messages to the error log. While you're working on a program, it's helpful to see immediately that there was a parse error on a particular line, for example. But once the program is (supposedly) working and your coworkers and customers are using it, such an error message would be confusing to them.

To make error messages display in the browser, set the `display_errors` configuration directive to `On`. Set it to `Off` to prevent error messages from displaying in the browser. To make sure errors end up in the web server error log, keep `log_errors` set to `On`.

An error message that the PHP engine generates will fall into one of five different categories:

Parse error
> A problem with the syntax of your program, such as leaving a semicolon off of the end of a statement. The engine stops running your program when it encounters a parse error.

Fatal error
> A severe problem with the content of your program, such as calling a function that hasn't been defined. The engine stops running your program when it encounters a fatal error.

Warning
> An advisory from the engine that something is fishy in your program, but the engine can keep going. Using the wrong number of arguments when you call a function causes a warning.

Notice
> A tip from the PHP engine playing the role of Miss Manners. For example, printing a variable without first initializing it to some value generates a notice.

Strict notices or deprecation warning
> An admonishment from the PHP engine about your coding style, or that something you're doing will stop working in a future version of PHP.

You don't have to be notified about all the error categories. The `error_reporting` configuration directive controls which kinds of errors the PHP engine reports. The default value for `error_reporting` is `E_ALL & ~E_NOTICE & ~E_DEPRECATED`, which tells the engine to report all errors except notices and deprecation warnings. Appendix A explains what the `&` and `~` mean in configuration directive values.

PHP defines some constants you can use to set the value of `error_reporting` such that only errors of certain types get reported:

- `E_ALL` (for all errors)
- `E_PARSE` (parse errors)
- `E_ERROR` (fatal errors)
- `E_WARNING` (warnings)
- `E_NOTICE` (notices)
- `E_STRICT` (strict notices, in versions of PHP before 7.0.0)

Because strict notices were new to PHP 5, they are not included in `E_ALL` in versions of PHP before 5.4.0. To tell an older version of the PHP engine that you want to hear about everything that could possibly be an error, set `error_reporting` to `E_ALL | E_STRICT`.

Fixing Parse Errors

The PHP engine is really picky but not very chatty. If you leave out a necessary semicolon, or start a string with a single quote but end it with a double quote, the engine doesn't run your program. It throws up its (virtual) hands, complains about a "parse error," and leaves you stuck in the debugging wilderness.

This can be one of the most frustrating things about programming when you're getting started. Everything has to be phrased and punctuated *just so* in order for the PHP engine to accept it. One thing that helps this process along is writing your programs in an editor that is PHP-aware. This is a program that, when you tell it that you are editing a PHP program, turns on some special features that make programming easier.

One of these special features is *syntax highlighting*. It changes the color of different parts of your program based on what those parts are. For example, strings would be pink, keywords such as if and while would be blue, comments would be grey, and variables would be black. Syntax highlighting makes it easier to detect things such as a string that's missing its closing quote: the pink text continues past the line that the string is on, all the way to the end of the file (or the next quote that appears later in the program).

Another feature is *quote and bracket matching*, which helps to make sure that your pairs of quotes and brackets are balanced. When you type a closing delimiter such as }, the editor highlights the opening { that it matches. Different editors do this in different ways, but typical methods are to flash the cursor at the location of the opening {, or to bold the { } pair for a short time. This behavior is helpful for pairs of punctuation that go together: single and double quotes that delimit strings, parentheses, square brackets, and curly braces.

These editors also show the line numbers of your program files. When you get an error message from the PHP engine complaining about a parse error in line 35 in your program, you know where to look for your error.

Table 12-1 lists some PHP-aware editors. Prices are in USD and accurate at the time of writing.

Table 12-1. PHP-aware text editors

Name	URL	Cost
PhpStorm	https://www.jetbrains.com/phpstorm	$89
NetBeans	https://netbeans.org	Free
Zend Studio	http://www.zend.com/en/products/studio	$89
Eclipse + PDT	http://www.eclipse.org/pdt	Free
Sublime Text	http://www.sublimetext.com	$70

Name	URL	Cost
Emacs	http://ergoemacs.org/emacs/which_emacs.html	Free
Vim	http://vim.wikia.com/wiki/Where_to_download_Vim	Free

PhpStorm, NetBeans, Zend Studio, and Eclipse + PDT are more like traditional integrated development environments (IDEs), whereas Sublime Text, Emacs, and Vim are more like traditional text editors—though they can easily be customized with plugins that help them understand PHP. PhpStorm and Zend Studio are the most PHP-specific of these editors, while the others are made to work with many other programming languages as well. All of the non-free editors in Table 12-1 have free evaluation periods, so you can try them out to see which one is most comfortable for you.

Parse errors happen when the PHP engine comes upon something unexpected in your program. Consider the broken program in Example 12-1.

Example 12-1. A parse error

```php
<?php
if $logged_in) {
        print "Welcome, user.";
    }
?>
```

When told to run the code in Example 12-1, the PHP engine produces the following error message:

```
PHP Parse error:  syntax error, unexpected '$logged_in' (T_VARIABLE),
expecting '(' in welcome.php on line 2
```

That error message means that in line 2 of the file, the PHP engine was expecting to see an open parenthesis but instead encountered $logged_in, which it thinks is something called a T_VARIABLE. The T_VARIABLE is a *token*. Tokens are the PHP engine's way of expressing different fundamental parts of programs. When the engine reads in a program, it translates what you've written into a list of tokens. Wherever you put a variable in your program, there is a T_VARIABLE token in the engine's list.

So, what the PHP engine is trying to tell you with the error message is "I was reading line 2 and saw a variable named $logged_in where I was expecting an open parenthesis." Looking at line 2 of Example 12-1, you can see why this is so: the open parenthesis that should start the if() test expression is missing. After seeing if, PHP expects a (to start the test expression. Since that's not there, it sees $logged_in, a variable, instead.

A list of all the tokens that the PHP engine uses (and therefore that may show up in an error message) can be found in the online PHP Manual (*http://www.php.net/ tokens*).

The insidious thing about parse errors, though, is that the line number reported in the error message is often not the line where the error actually is. Example 12-2 has such an error in it.

Example 12-2. A trickier parse error

```php
<?php
$first_name = "David';
if ($logged_in) {
    print "Welcome, $first_name";
} else {
    print "Howdy, Stranger.";
}
?>
```

When it tries to run the code in Example 12-2, the PHP engine says:

```
PHP Parse error:  syntax error, unexpected 'Welcome' (T_STRING)
in trickier.php on line 4
```

That error makes it seem like line 4 contains a string (Welcome) in a place where it shouldn't. But you can scrutinize line 4 all you want to find a problem with it, and you still won't find one. That line, print "Welcome, $first_name";, is perfectly correct—the string is correctly delimited with double quotes and the line appropriately ends with a semicolon.

The real problem in Example 12-2 is in line 2. The string being assigned to $first_name starts with a double quote but "ends" with a single quote. As the PHP engine reads line 2, it sees the double quote and thinks, "OK, here comes a string. I'll read everything until the next (unescaped) double quote as the contents of this string." That makes the engine fly right over the single quote in line 2 and keep going all the way until the first double quote in line 4. When it sees that double quote, the engine thinks it's found the end of the string. So then it considers what happens after the double quote to be a new command or statement. But what's after the double quote is Welcome, $first_name";. This doesn't make any sense to the engine. It's expecting an immediate semicolon to end a statement, or maybe a period to concatenate the just-defined string with another string. But Welcome, $first_name"; is just an undelimited string sitting where it doesn't belong. So the engine gives up and shouts out a parse error.

Imagine you're running down the streets of Manhattan at supersonic speed. The sidewalk on 35th Street has some cracks in it, so you trip. But you're going so fast that you land on 39th Street and dirty the pavement with your blood and guts. Then a traffic safety officer comes over and says, "Hey! There's a problem with 39th Street! Someone's soiled the sidewalk with their innards!"

That's what the PHP engine is doing in this case. The line number in the parse error is where the engine sees something it doesn't expect, which is not always the same as the line number where the actual error is.

When you get a parse error from the engine, first take a look at the line reported in the parse error. Check for the basics, such as making sure that you've got a semicolon at the end of the statement. If the line seems OK, work your way forward and back a few lines in the program to hunt down the actual error. Pay special attention to punctuation that goes in pairs: single or double quotes that delimit strings, parentheses in function calls or test expressions, square brackets in array elements, and curly braces in code blocks. Count that the number of opening punctuation marks (such as (, [, and {) matches the number of closing punctuation marks (such as),], and }).

Situations such as this one are where a PHP-aware editor is really helpful. With syntax highlighting or bracket matching, the editor can tell you about the problem without making you have to hunt around for it. For example, if you're reading a digital version of this book, the syntax highlighting and color coding of Example 12-2 probably made it very easy to spot the error.

Inspecting Program Data

Once you clear the parse error hurdle, you still may have some work to do before you reach the finish line. A program can be syntactically correct but logically flawed. Just as the sentence "The tugboat chewed apoplectically with six subtle buffaloes" is grammatically correct but meaningless nonsense, you can write a program that the PHP engine doesn't find any problems with but that doesn't do what you expect.

Finding and fixing parts of a programs that don't behave as you expect is a big part of programming. The specifics of how you'd diagnose and explore particular situations vary greatly depending on what you're trying to fix. This section shows you two techniques for investigating what's going on in your PHP program. The first, adding debugging output, is easy, but requires modifying your program and may not be suitable for a production environment where regular users can also see the output. The second, using a debugger, requires more work to set up properly, but gives you more runtime flexibility as to how you inspect the running program.

Adding Debug Output

If your program is acting funny, add some checkpoints that display the values of variables. That way, you can see where the program's behavior diverges from your expectations. Example 12-3 shows a program that incorrectly attempts to calculate the total cost of a few items.

Example 12-3. A broken program

```
$prices = array(5.95, 3.00, 12.50);
$total_price = 0;
$tax_rate = 1.08; // 8% tax

foreach ($prices as $price) {
    $total_price = $price * $tax_rate;
}

printf('Total price (with tax): $%.2f', $total_price);
```

Example 12-3 doesn't do the right thing. It prints:

```
Total price (with tax): $13.50
```

The total price of the items should be at least $20. What's wrong with Example 12-3? One way you can try to find out is to insert a line in the foreach() loop that prints the value of $total_price before and after it changes. That should provide some insight into why the math is wrong. Example 12-4 annotates Example 12-3 with some diagnostic print statements.

Example 12-4. A broken program with debugging output

```
$prices = array(5.95, 3.00, 12.50);
$total_price = 0;
$tax_rate = 1.08; // 8% tax

foreach ($prices as $price) {
    print "[before: $total_price]";
    $total_price = $price * $tax_rate;
    print "[after: $total_price]";
}

printf('Total price (with tax): $%.2f', $total_price);
```

Example 12-4 prints:

```
[before: 0][after: 6.426][before: 6.426][after: 3.24][before: 3.24]
[after: 13.5]Total price (with tax): $13.50
```

From analyzing the debugging output from Example 12-4, you can see that $total_price isn't increasing on each trip through the foreach() loop. Scrutinizing the code further leads you to the conclusion that the line:

```
$total_price = $price * $tax_rate;
```

should be:

```
$total_price += $price * $tax_rate;
```

Instead of the assignment operator (=), the code needs the increment-and-assign operator (+=).

Editing the Right File

If you make changes to a program while debugging it but don't see those changes reflected when you reload the program in your web browser, make sure you're editing the right file. When working with a local copy of the program but loading it in the browser from a remote server, be sure to copy the changed file to the server before you reload the page.

One way to make sure that the file you're editing and the page you're looking at in the web browser are in sync is to temporarily add a line at the top of the program that calls die(), as in the following.

```
die('This is: ' . __FILE__);
```

The special constant __FILE__ holds the name of the file being run. So, when you load a PHP page in your browser with a URL such as *http://www.example.com/catalog.php*, which has the code just shown at the top, all you should see is something like:

```
This is: /usr/local/htdocs/catalog.php
```

When you see the results of die() in your web browser, you know you're editing the right file. Remove the call to die() from your program and continue debugging.

Example 12-5. Printing all submitted form parameters with var_dump()

```
print '<pre>';
var_dump($_POST);
print '</pre>';
```

To include an array in debugging output, use var_dump(). It prints all the elements in an array. Surround the output of var_dump() with HTML <pre> and </pre> tags to have it nicely formatted in your web browser. Example 12-5 prints the contents of all submitted form parameters with var_dump().

Debugging messages are informative but can be confusing or disruptive when mixed in with the regular page output. To send debugging messages to the web server error log instead of the web browser, use the `error_log()` function instead of `print`. Example 12-6 shows the program from Example 12-4 but uses `error_log()` to send the diagnostic messages to the web server error log.

Example 12-6. A broken program with error log debugging output

```
$prices = array(5.95, 3.00, 12.50);
$total_price = 0;
$tax_rate = 1.08; // 8% tax

foreach ($prices as $price) {
    error_log("[before: $total_price]");
    $total_price = $price * $tax_rate;
    error_log("[after: $total_price]");
}

printf('Total price (with tax): $%.2f', $total_price);
```

Example 12-6 prints just the total price line:

```
Total price (with tax): $13.50
```

However, it sends lines to the web server error log that look like this:

```
[before: 0]
[after: 6.426]
[before: 6.426]
[after: 3.24]
[before: 3.24]
[after: 13.5]
```

The exact location of your web server error log varies based on how your web server is configured. If you're using Apache, the error log location is specified by the `ErrorLog` Apache configuration setting.

Because the `var_dump()` function itself prints information, you need to do a little fancy footwork to send its output to the error log, similar to the output buffering functionality discussed at the end of "Why setcookie() and session_start() Want to Be at the Top of the Page" on page 226. You surround the call to `var_dump()` with functions that temporarily suspend output, as shown in Example 12-7.

Example 12-7. Sending all submitted form parameters to the error log with var_dump()

```
// Capture output instead of printing it
ob_start();
// Call var_dump() as usual
var_dump($_POST);
// Store in $output the output generated since calling ob_start()
$output = ob_get_contents();
// Go back to regular printing of output
ob_end_clean();
// Send $output to the error log
error_log($output);
```

The ob_start(), ob_get_contents(), and ob_end_clean() functions in Example 12-7 manipulate how the PHP engine generates output. The ob_start() function tells the engine, "Don't print anything from now on. Just accumulate anything you would print in an internal buffer." When var_dump() is called, the engine is under the spell of ob_start(), so the output goes into that internal buffer. The ob_get_contents() function returns the contents of the internal buffer. Since var_dump() is the only thing that generated output since ob_start() was called, this puts the output of var_dump() into $output. The ob_end_clean() function undoes the work of ob_start(): it tells the PHP engine to go back to its regular behavior with regard to printing. Finally, error_log() sends $output (which holds what var_dump() "printed") to the web server error log.

Using a Debugger

The printing and logging approach described in the previous section is easy to use. But because it requires modifying your program, you can't use it in a production environment where regular users might see the debugging output. Also, you need to decide what information you want to print or log before you start running your program. If you haven't added any code to print a value you're interested in, you have to modify your program again and rerun it.

Examining your program with a debugger solves these problems. A debugger lets you inspect your program while it is running so you can see the values of variables and which functions call which other functions. It doesn't require any changes to your program, but it does require some separate setup.

There are a few debuggers that work with PHP, and many of the editors listed in Table 12-1 integrate well with a debugger to allow you to inspect a running PHP program from within your editor. This section shows program inspection with the phpdbg debugger, which comes with PHP.

The phpdbg debugger is part of PHP versions 5.6 and later, but your installation of the PHP engine may not be configured to include it. If you don't have a `phpdbg` program on your system that you can run, check (or ask your system administrator to check) that your PHP installation was built with the `--enable-phpdbg` option.

The Xdebug debugger (*http://www.xdebug.org*) is powerful and full-featured. It can communicate with editors and IDEs using a protocol but does not come with an easy-to-use client on its own. Xdebug is free.

The Zend Debugger is part of Zend Studio (*http://www.zend.com/ Studio*). It uses its own protocol to communicate with Zend Studio, but some other IDEs, such as PhpStorm, work with it as well.

To start a debugging session with phpdbg, run the `phpdbg` program with a `-e` argument indicating what program you want to debug:

```
phpdbg -e broken.php
```

phpdbg responds with:

```
Welcome to phpdbg, the interactive PHP debugger, v0.4.0]
To get help using phpdbg type "help" and press enter
[Please report bugs to <http://github.com/krakjoe/phpdbg/issues>]
[Successful compilation of broken.php]
```

This means that phpdbg has read *broken.php*, has digested the commands in it, and is ready to run it for you. First, we're going to set a *breakpoint*. This tells phpdbg to pause whenever it reaches a certain place in the program. When phpdbg pauses, we can inspect the program's innards. Line 7 is the line where `$total_price` gets its value assigned within the loop, so let's break there:

```
prompt> break 7
```

The `prompt>` part is not something to type. phpdbg prints that on its own as a prompt telling you it is ready for a command. The `break 7` command tells phpdbg to pause execution when it reaches line 7 of the program. phpdbg responds with:

```
[Breakpoint #0 added at broken.php:7]
```

We're ready to go, so tell phpdbg to start running the program:

```
prompt> run
```

It starts from the beginning, running each line of the program until it gets to the breakpoint at line 7. At that point, phpdbg says:

```
[Breakpoint #0 at broken.php:7, hits: 1]
>00007:      $total_price = $price * $tax_rate;
```

```
00008: }
00009:
```

Now we can add a *watch point* for $total_price. This tells phpdbg to pause program execution each time the value of $total_price changes. This is exactly what we need to diagnose our problem, since it's the value of $total_price that's not getting set to what we expect. The watch command adds a watch point:

```
prompt> watch $total_price
```

phpdbg responds with:

```
[Set watchpoint on $total_price]
```

Now that we have our watch point, we don't need the breakpoint on line 7 any more. The break del command deletes a breakpoint:

```
prompt> break del 0
```

This tells phpdbg to remove the first breakpoint we set (like PHP with array elements, phpdbg starts numbering things with 0, not 1). phpdbg acknowledges the breakpoint deletion with:

```
[Deleted breakpoint #0]
```

We are all set to continue running the program and have it pause whenever the value of $total_price changes. The continue command tells phpdbg to keep going:

```
prompt> continue
```

phpdbg starts running the program. The first commands that now get executed are the ones in line 7, which change the value of $total_price. So right away program execution is paused, and phpdbg says:

```
[Breaking on watchpoint $total_price]
Old value: 0
New value: 6.426
>00007:       $total_price = $price * $tax_rate;
 00008: }
 00009:
```

This is useful—we see that the code is changing $total_price from 0 to 6.426. Let's see what happens next. The continue command tells phpdbg to get things going again:

```
prompt> continue
```

And then the program stops again:

```
[Breaking on watchpoint $total_price]
Old value: 6.426
New value: 3.24
>00007:       $total_price = $price * $tax_rate;
```

```
00008: }
00009:
```

Back again on line 7 in the loop, `$total_price` goes from 6.426 to 3.24. That definitely doesn't look right—`$total_price` should be increasing! Let's keep going:

```
prompt> continue
```

One last time, the value of `$total_price` gets changed:

```
[Breaking on watchpoint $total_price]
Old value: 3.24
New value: 13.5
>00007:      $total_price = $price * $tax_rate;
 00008: }
 00009:
```

This time it increases to 13.5. And a final continue to finish out the program:

```
prompt> continue
```

phpdbg keeps running the program, and we get the actual program output:

```
Total price (with tax): $13.50
[$total_price was removed, removing watchpoint]
[Script ended normally]
```

The second time phpdbg pauses at the watch point, it is clear that there is a problem with how the value of `$total_price` is being calculated. This is the same conclusion that the debugging output introduced in the previous section shows.

The specific syntax to type (or places to click in a GUI) may vary with a different debugger or IDE, but the basic idea is the same: the debugger runs your program with special oversight. You get to pause your program execution in the places of your choosing and inspect the program's guts when it pauses.

Handling Uncaught Exceptions

"Indicating a Problem with Exceptions" on page 108 explained the basics of how PHP uses exceptions, and Example 6-8 showed what happens if an exception is thrown but not caught: your PHP program stops running and the PHP engine prints out error information and a stack trace (the list of functions that have called one another at the point where the program has stopped).

While you should always include `try`/`catch` blocks around any code that might throw an exception, in practice it can be difficult to meet that goal perfectly. You might be using a third-party library and unaware of exceptions it throws, or you might just make a mistake and forget a situation where your own code can throw an exception. For these situations, PHP gives you a way to specify a special exception handler that will get called if your code doesn't handle an exception. This exception handler is a good place to log information about the exception and present information to your program's user that is friendlier than a stack trace.

To use a custom exception handler for otherwise uncaught exceptions, do two things:

1. Write a function that will handle the exception. It takes one argument: the exception.
2. Use `set_exception_handler()` to tell the PHP engine about your function.

Example 12-8 sets up an exception handler that prints a nice error message for a user and logs more detailed information about the exception.

Example 12-8. Setting up a custom exception handler

```
function niceExceptionHandler($ex) {
    // Tell the user something unthreatening
    print "Sorry! Something unexpected happened. Please try again later.";
    // Log more detailed information for a sysadmin to review
    error_log("{$ex->getMessage()} in {$ex->getFile()} @ {$ex->getLine()}");
    error_log($ex->getTraceAsString());
}

set_exception_handler('niceExceptionHandler');

print "I'm about to connect to a made up, pretend, broken database!\n";

// The DSN given to the PDO constructor does not specify a valid database
// or connection parameters, so the constructor will throw an exception
$db = new PDO('garbage:this is obviously not going to work!');

print "This is not going to get printed.";
```

In Example 12-8, the `niceExceptionHandler()` function uses `print` to give the user a simple message and `error_log()`, along with methods on the `Exception` object, to log more detailed technical information for review. The call to `set_exception_handler()` with the `niceExceptionHandler` argument (as a string) tells the PHP engine to give any unhandled exceptions to that function.

The output from Example 12-8 is:

```
I'm about to connect to a made up, pretend, broken database!
Sorry! Something unexpected happened. Please try again later.
```

And the logged error information is:

```
could not find driver in exception-handler.php @ 17
#0 exception-handler.php(17): PDO->__construct('garbage:this is...')
#1 {main}
```

This prevents the user from seeing confusing technical details that could potentially leak secure information (such as database credentials or file paths) but stores that information in the error log for review.

A custom exception handler doesn't prevent your program from stopping after the exception is handled. After the exception handler runs, your program is done. That's why, in Example 12-8, the `This is not going to get printed.` line is never printed.

Chapter Summary

This chapter covered:

- Configuring error display for a web browser, a web server error log, or both
- Configuring the PHP engine's error-reporting level
- Getting the benefits of a PHP-aware text editor
- Deciphering parse error messages
- Finding and fixing parse errors
- Printing debugging information with `print`, `var_dump()`, and `error_log()`
- Sending `var_dump()` output to the error log with output buffering functions
- Inspecting a running program with a debugger
- Handling exceptions not caught by any other code

Exercises

1. This program has a syntax error in it:

```php
<?php
$name = 'Umberto';
function say_hello() {
    print 'Hello, ';
    print global $name;
}
say_hello();
?>
```

   Without running the program through the PHP engine, figure out what the parse error that gets printed when the engine tries to run the program looks like. What change must you make to the program to get it to run properly and print `Hello, Umberto`?

2. Modify the `validate_form()` function in your answer to Exercise 3 in Chapter 7 (see "Exercise 3" on page 345) so that it prints in the web server error log the names and values of all of the submitted form parameters.

3. Modify your answer to Exercise 4 in Chapter 8 (see "Exercise 4" on page 357) to use a custom database error-handling function that prints out different messages in the web browser and in the web server error log. The error-handling function should make the program exit after it prints the error messages.

4. The following program is supposed to print out an alphabetical list of all the customers in the table from Exercise 4 in Chapter 8 (see "Exercise 4" on page 357). Find and fix the errors in it.

```php
<?php
// Connect to the database
try {
    $db = new PDO('sqlite::/tmp/restaurant.db');
} catch ($e) {
    die("Can't connect: " . $e->getMessage());
}
// Set up exception error handling
$db->setAttribute(PDO::ATTR_ERRMODE, PDO::ERRMODE_EXCEPTION);
// Set up fetch mode: rows as arrays
$db->setAttribute(PDO::ATTR_DEFAULT_FETCH_MODE, PDO::FETCH_ASSOC);
// Get the array of dish names from the database
$dish_names = array();
$res = $db->query('SELECT dish_id,dish_name FROM dishes');
foreach ($res->fetchAll() as $row) {
    $dish_names[ $row['dish_id']]] = $row['dish_name'];
}
$res = $db->query('SELECT ** FROM customers ORDER BY phone DESC');
$customers = $res->fetchAll();
if (count($customers) = 0) {
    print "No customers.";
} else {
    print '<table>';
    print '<tr><th>ID</th><th>Name</th><th>Phone</th>
    <th>Favorite Dish</th></tr>';
    foreach ($customers as $customer) {
        printf("<tr><td>%d</td><td>%s</td><td>%f</td><td>%s</td></tr>\n",
                $customer['customer_id'],
                htmlentities($customer['customer_name']),
                $customer['phone'],
                $customer['favorite_dish_id']);
    }
    print '</table>';
}
?>
```

## CHAPTER 13

Testing: Ensuring Your Program Does the Right Thing

How do you know your program does what you think it does? Even with your careful attention to detail, are you sure that sales tax calculation function works properly? How do you know?

This chapter is about giving you the peace of mind that comes with answers to those questions. *Unit testing* is a way of making assertions about small bits of your code— "If I put these values into this function, I should get this other value out." By creating tests that check the behavior of your code in appropriate situations, you can have confidence in how your program behaves.

PHPUnit is the de facto standard for writing tests for PHP code. Your tests are themselves little bits of PHP code. The following section describes how to install PHPUnit. "Writing a Test" shows some code and a first test for it. Use and run this code to make sure you've got PHPUnit installed properly and understand the basic pieces of a test.

Then, "Isolating What You Test" on page 270 looks at how to narrow the focus of what you're testing for maximum efficiency.

"Test-Driven Development" on page 273 extends the tested code by adding some tests for code that doesn't exist yet, and then adding the code to make the tests pass. This technique can be a handy way to ensure you're writing code that is tested properly.

At the end of this chapter, "More Information About Testing" on page 275 provides details on where to find more information about PHPUnit and testing in general.

Installing PHPUnit

The quickest way to get PHPUnit running is to download a self-contained PHP Archive of the entire PHPUnit package and make it executable. As described at the PHPUnit website (*https://phpunit.de/getting-started.html*), the PHPUnit project makes this archive available at *https://phar.phpunit.de/phpunit.phar*. You can download this file and make it executable to run it directly as in Example 13-1, or just run it through the php command-line program, as in Example 13-2.

Example 13-1. Running PHPUnit as an executable PHAR file

```
# Assuming phpunit.phar is in the current directory, this
# makes it executable
chmod a+x phpunit.phar
# And this runs it
./phpunit.phar --version
```

Example 13-2. Running PHPUnit with the php command-line program

```
php ./phpunit.phar --version
```

However you run PHPUnit, if things are working properly, the output of `phpunit.phar --version` should look something like this:

```
PHPUnit 4.7.6 by Sebastian Bergmann and contributors.
```

If you decide to use PHPUnit for testing in a larger project that relies on Composer to manage packages and dependencies, add a reference to it in the `require-dev` section of your *composer.json* file by running the following command:

```
composer require-dev phpunit/phpunit
```

Writing a Test

The `restaurant_check()` function from Example 5-11 calculates the total bill for a restaurant meal, given the cost of the meal itself, the tax rate, and the tip rate. Example 13-3 shows the function again to refresh your memory.

Example 13-3. restaurant_check()

```
function restaurant_check($meal, $tax, $tip) {
    $tax_amount = $meal * ($tax / 100);
    $tip_amount = $meal * ($tip / 100);
    $total_amount = $meal + $tax_amount + $tip_amount;
```

```
        return $total_amount;
}
```

Tests in PHPUnit are organized as methods inside a class. The class you write to contain your tests must extend the `PHPUnit_Framework_TestCase` class. The name of each method that implements a test must begin with `test`. Example 13-4 shows a class with a test in it for `restaurant_check()`.

Example 13-4. Testing restaurant check calculation

```
include 'restaurant-check.php';

class RestaurantCheckTest extends PHPUnit_Framework_TestCase {

    public function testWithTaxAndTip() {
        $meal = 100;
        $tax = 10;
        $tip = 20;
        $result = restaurant_check($meal, $tax, $tip);
        $this->assertEquals(130, $result);
    }

}
```

Note that Example 13-4 assumes that the `restaurant_check()` function is defined in a file named *restaurant-check.php*, which it includes before defining the test class. It is your responsibility to make sure that the code that your tests are testing is loaded and available for your test class to invoke.

To run the test, give the filename you've saved the code in as an argument to the PHPUnit program:

```
phpunit.phar RestaurantCheckTest.php
```

That produces output like the following:

```
PHPUnit 4.8.11 by Sebastian Bergmann and contributors.

.

Time: 121 ms, Memory: 13.50Mb

OK (1 test, 1 assertion)
```

Each . before the `Time:` line represents one test that was run. The last line (`OK (1 test, 1 assertion)`) tells you the status of all the tests, how many tests were run, and how many assertions all those tests contained. An `OK` status means no tests failed. This example had one test method, `testWithTaxAndTip()`, and inside that test method there was one assertion: the call to `assertEquals()` that checked that the return value from the function equaled 130.

A test method is generally structured like the preceding example. It has a name beginning with `test` that describes what behavior the method is testing. It does any variable initialization or setup necessary to exercise the code to test. It invokes the code to test. Then it makes some assertions about what happened. Assertions are available as instance methods on the `PHPUnit_Framework_TestCase` class, so they are available in our test subclass.

The assertion method names each begin with `assert`. These methods let you check all sorts of aspects of how your code works, such as whether values are equal, elements are present in an array, or an object is an instance of a certain class. Appendix A (*https://phpunit.de/manual/current/en/appendixes.assertions.html*) of the PHPUnit manual lists all the assertion methods available.

PHPUnit's output looks different when a test fails. Example 13-5 adds a second test method to the `RestaurantCheckTest` class.

Example 13-5. A test with a failing assertion

```
include 'restaurant-check.php';

class RestaurantCheckTest extends PHPUnit_Framework_TestCase {

    public function testWithTaxAndTip() {
        $meal = 100;
        $tax = 10;
        $tip = 20;
        $result = restaurant_check($meal, $tax, $tip);
        $this->assertEquals(130, $result);
    }

    public function testWithNoTip() {
        $meal = 100;
        $tax = 10;
        $tip = 0;
        $result = restaurant_check($meal, $tax, $tip);
        $this->assertEquals(120, $result);
    }
}
```

In Example 13-5, the `testWithNoTip()` test method asserts that the total check on a $100 meal with 10% tax and no tip should equal $120. This is wrong—the total should be $110. PHPUnit's output in this case looks like this:

```
PHPUnit 4.8.11 by Sebastian Bergmann and contributors.

.F
```

```
Time: 129 ms, Memory: 13.50Mb

There was 1 failure:

1) RestaurantCheckTest::testWithNoTip
Failed asserting that 110.0 matches expected 120.

RestaurantCheckTest.php:20

FAILURES!
Tests: 2, Assertions: 2, Failures: 1.
```

Because the test fails, it gets an F instead of a . in the initial part of the output. PHPUnit also reports more details on the failure. It tells you what test class and test method contained the failure, and what the failed assertion was. The test code expected 120 (the first argument to assertEquals()) but instead got 110 (the second argument to assertEquals()).

If you change the assertion in testWithNoTip() to expect 110 instead, the test passes.

Some deliberation and creativity is usually required to ensure that your tests cover an adequate variety of situations so that you have confidence in how your code behaves. For example, how should restaurant_check() calculate the tip? Some people calculate the tip just on the meal amount, and some on the meal amount plus tax. A test is a good way to be explicit about your function's behavior. Example 13-6 adds tests that verify the function's existing behavior: the tip is calculated only on the meal, not on the tax.

Example 13-6. Testing how tip is calculated

```php
include 'restaurant-check.php';

class RestaurantCheckTest extends PHPUnit_Framework_TestCase {

    public function testWithTaxAndTip() {
        $meal = 100;
        $tax = 10;
        $tip = 20;
        $result = restaurant_check($meal, $tax, $tip);
        $this->assertEquals(130, $result);
    }

    public function testWithNoTip() {
        $meal = 100;
        $tax = 10;
        $tip = 0;
        $result = restaurant_check($meal, $tax, $tip);
        $this->assertEquals(110, $result);
    }
```

```
public function testTipIsNotOnTax() {
    $meal = 100;
    $tax = 10;
    $tip = 10;
    $checkWithTax = restaurant_check($meal, $tax, $tip);
    $checkWithoutTax = restaurant_check($meal, 0, $tip);
    $expectedTax = $meal * ($tax / 100);
    $this->assertEquals($checkWithTax, $checkWithoutTax + $expectedTax);
}

}
```

The `testTipIsNotOnTax()` method calculates two different restaurant checks: one with the provided tax rate and one with a tax rate of 0. The difference between these two should just be the expected amount of tax. There should not also be a difference in the tip. The assertion in this test method checks that the check with tax is equal to the check without tax, plus the expected tax amount. This ensures that the function is not calculating the tip on the tax amount, too.

Isolating What You Test

An important principle of productive testing is that the thing you're testing should be as isolated as possible. Ideally, there is no global state or long-lived resource outside of your test function whose contents or behavior could change the results of the test function. Your test functions should produce the same result regardless of the order in which they are run.

Consider the `validate_form()` function from Example 7-13. To validate incoming data, it examines the `$_POST` array and uses `filter_input()` to operate directly on INPUT_POST. This is a concise way to access the data that needs validating. However, in order to test this function, it looks like we'd have to adjust values in the auto-global `$_POST` array. What's more, that wouldn't even help `filter_input()` work properly. It always looks at the underlying, unmodified submitted form data, even if you change the values in `$_POST`.

To make this function testable, it needs to be passed the submitted form data to validate as an argument. Then this array can be referenced instead of `$_POST`, and `filter_var()` can examine the array's elements. Example 13-7 shows this isolated version of the `validate_form()` function.

Example 13-7. Validating form data in isolation

```
function validate_form($submitted) {
    $errors = array();
    $input = array();
```

```
$input['age'] = filter_var($submitted['age'] ?? NULL, FILTER_VALIDATE_INT);
if ($input['age'] === false) {
    $errors[] = 'Please enter a valid age.';
}

$input['price'] = filter_var($submitted['price'] ?? NULL,
                             FILTER_VALIDATE_FLOAT);
if ($input['price'] === false) {
    $errors[] = 'Please enter a valid price.';
}

$input['name'] = trim($submitted['name'] ?? '');
if (strlen($input['name']) == 0) {
    $errors[] = "Your name is required.";
}

    return array($errors, $input);
}
```

The first argument to filter_var() is the variable to filter. PHP's normal rules about undefined variables and undefined array indices apply here, so the null coalesce operator is used ($submitted['age'] ?? NULL) to provide NULL as the value being filtered if it's not present in the array. Since NULL is not a valid integer or float, filter_var() returns false in those cases, just as it would if an invalid number was provided.

When the modified validate_form() function is called in your application, pass $_POST as an argument:

```
list ($form_errors, $input) = validate_form($_POST);
```

In your test code, pass it an array of pretend form input that exercises the situation you want to test and then verify the results with assertions. Example 13-8 shows a few tests for validate_form(): one that makes sure decimal ages are not allowed; one that makes sure prices with dollar signs are not allowed; and one that makes sure values are returned properly if a valid price, age, and name are provided.

Example 13-8. Testing isolated form data validation

```
// validate_form() is defined in this file
include 'isolate-validation.php';

class IsolateValidationTest extends PHPUnit_Framework_TestCase {

    public function testDecimalAgeNotValid() {
        $submitted = array('age' => '6.7',
                           'price' => '100',
                           'name' => 'Julia');
        list($errors, $input) = validate_form($submitted);
        // Expecting only one error -- about age
```

```
        $this->assertContains('Please enter a valid age.', $errors);
        $this->assertCount(1, $errors);
    }

    public function testDollarSignPriceNotValid() {
        $submitted = array('age' => '6',
                           'price' => '$52',
                           'name' => 'Julia');
        list($errors, $input) = validate_form($submitted);
        // Expecting only one error -- about age
        $this->assertContains('Please enter a valid price.', $errors);
        $this->assertCount(1, $errors);
    }

    public function testValidDataOK() {
        $submitted = array('age' => '15',
                           'price' => '39.95',
                           // Some whitespace around name that
                           // should be trimmed
                           'name' => '  Julia  ');
        list($errors, $input) = validate_form($submitted);
        // Expecting no errors
        $this->assertCount(0, $errors);
        // Expecting 3 things in input
        $this->assertCount(3, $input);
        $this->assertSame(15, $input['age']);
        $this->assertSame(39.95, $input['price']);
        $this->assertSame('Julia', $input['name']);
    }
}
```

Example 13-8 uses a few new assertions: `assertContains()`, `assertCount()`, and `assertSame()`. The `assertContains()` and `assertCount()` assertions are useful with arrays. The first tests whether a certain element is in an array and the second checks the size of the array. These two assertions express the expected condition about the `$errors` array in the tests and about the `$input` array in the third test.

The `assertSame()` assertion is similar to `assertEquals()` but goes one step further. In addition to testing that two values are equal, it also tests that the types of the two values are the same. The `assertEquals()` assertion passes if given the string `'130'` and the integer `130`, but `assertSame()` fails. Using `assertSame()` in `testValidDataOK()` checks that the input data variable types are being set properly by `filter_var()`.

Test-Driven Development

A popular programming technique that makes extensive use of tests is called *test-driven development* (TDD). The big idea of TDD is that when you have a new feature to implement, you write a test for the feature *before* you write the code. The test is your expression of what you expect the code to do. Then you write the code for the new feature so that the test passes.

While not ideal for every situation, TDD can be helpful for providing clarity on what you need to do and helping you build a comprehensive set of tests that cover your code. As an example, we can use TDD to add an optional feature to the `restaurant_check()` function that tells it to include the tax in the total amount when calculating the tip. This feature is implemented as an optional fourth argument to the function. A `true` value tells `restaurant_check()` to include the tax in the tip-calculation amount. A `false` value tells it not to. If no value is provided, the function should behave as it already does.

First, the test. We need a test that tells `restaurant_check()` to include the tax in the tip-calculation amount and then ensures that the total check amount is correct. We also need a test that makes sure the function works properly when it is explicitly told not to include the tax in the tip-calculation amount. These two new test methods are shown in Example 13-9. (For clarity, just the two new methods are shown, not the whole test class.)

Example 13-9. Adding tests for new tip-calculation logic

```
public function testTipShouldIncludeTax() {
    $meal = 100;
    $tax = 10;
    $tip = 10;
    // 4th argument of true says that the tax should be included
    // in the tip-calculation amount
    $result = restaurant_check($meal, $tax, $tip, true);
    $this->assertEquals(121, $result);
}

public function testTipShouldNotIncludeTax() {
    $meal = 100;
    $tax = 10;
    $tip = 10;
    // 4th argument of false says that the tax should explicitly
    // NOT be included in the tip-calculation amount
    $result = restaurant_check($meal, $tax, $tip, false);
    $this->assertEquals(120, $result);
}
```

It should not be surprising that the new test testTipShouldIncludeTax() fails:

```
PHPUnit 4.8.11 by Sebastian Bergmann and contributors.

...F.

Time: 138 ms, Memory: 13.50Mb

There was 1 failure:

1) RestaurantCheckTest::testTipShouldIncludeTax
Failed asserting that 120.0 matches expected 121.

RestaurantCheckTest.php:40

FAILURES!
Tests: 5, Assertions: 5, Failures: 1.
```

To get that test to pass, restaurant_check() needs to handle a fourth argument that controls the tip-calculation behavior, as shown in Example 13-10.

Example 13-10. Changing tip calculation logic

```
function restaurant_check($meal, $tax, $tip, $include_tax_in_tip = false) {
    $tax_amount = $meal * ($tax / 100);
    if ($include_tax_in_tip) {
        $tip_base = $meal + $tax_amount;
    } else {
        $tip_base = $meal;
    }
    $tip_amount = $tip_base * ($tip / 100);
    $total_amount = $meal + $tax_amount + $tip_amount;

    return $total_amount;
}
```

With the new logic in Example 13-10, the restaurant_check() function reacts to its fourth argument and changes the base of what the tip is calculated on accordingly. This version of restaurant_check() lets all the tests pass:

```
PHPUnit 4.8.11 by Sebastian Bergmann and contributors.

.....

Time: 120 ms, Memory: 13.50Mb

OK (5 tests, 5 assertions)
```

Because the test class includes not just the new tests for this new functionality but all of the old tests as well, it ensures that existing code using restaurant_check() before this new feature was added continues to work. A comprehensive set of tests provides reassurance that changes made to the code don't break existing functionality.

More Information About Testing

As your projects grow larger, the benefits of comprehensive testing increase as well. At first, it feels like a drag to write a bunch of seemingly extra code to verify something obvious, such as the basic mathematical operations in `restaurant_check()`. But as your project accumulates more and more functionality (and perhaps more and more people working on it), the accumulated tests are invaluable.

Absent some fancy-pants computer science formal methods, which rarely find their way into modern PHP applications, the results of your tests are the evidence you have to answer the question "How do you know your program does what you think it does?" With tests, you know what the program does because you run it in various ways and ensure the results are what you expect.

This chapter shows the basics for integrating PHPUnit into your project and writing some simple tests. To go further, here are a few additional resources about PHPUnit and testing in general:

- The PHPUnit manual (*https://phpunit.de/manual/current/en/index.html*) is helpful and comprehensive. It includes tutorial-style information on common PHPUnit tasks as well as reference material on PHPUnit's features.
- There is a great list of presentations about PHPUnit at *https://phpunit.de/presentations.html*.
- Browsing the *test* directory of popular PHP packages to see how those packages do their tests is instructive as well. In the Zend Framework, you can find the tests for the `zend-form` (*https://github.com/zendframework/zend-form/tree/master/test*) component and the `zend-validator` (*https://github.com/zendframework/zend-validator/tree/master/test*) component on GitHub. The popular Monolog (*https://github.com/Seldaek/monolog/tree/master/tests/Monolog*) package has its tests on on GitHub as well.
- Naturally, PHPUnit has numerous tests (*https://github.com/sebastianbergmann/phpunit/tree/master/tests*) that verify its behavior. And those tests are PHPUnit tests!

Chapter Summary

This chapter covered:

- Understanding the benefits of code testing
- Installing and running PHPUnit

- Understanding how test case classes, test methods, and assertions work together in PHPUnit
- Writing a test that verifies a function's behavior
- Running your test in PHPUnit
- Understanding PHPUnit's output when tests succeed and fail
- Understanding why to isolate the code you are testing
- Removing global variables from code to make it more testable
- Learning about test-driven development
- Writing a test for a new feature before the feature's code is written
- Writing code to make the new test pass
- Where to go to find more information about PHPUnit and testing

Exercises

1. Follow the instructions in "Installing PHPUnit " on page 266 to install PHPUnit, write a test class with a single test containing a single simple assertion that passes (such as `$this->assertEquals(2, 1 + 1);`) and run PHPUnit on your test class.
2. Add a test case to Example 13-8 that ensures an error is returned when no name is submitted.
3. Write tests to verify the behavior of the `select()` function from Example 7-29. Be sure to consider the following situations:

   - If an associative array of options is provided, then each `<option>` tag should be rendered with the array key as the `value` attribute of the `<option>` tag and the array value as the text between `<option>` and `</option>`.
   - If a numeric array of options is provided, then each `<option>` tag should be rendered with the array index as the `value` attribute of the `<option>` tag and the array value as the text between `<option>` and `</option>`.
   - If no attributes are provided, then the opening tag should be `<select>`.
   - If an attribute is provided with a boolean `true` value, then only the attribute's name should be included inside the opening `<select>` tag.
   - If an attribute is provided with a boolean `false` value, then the attribute should not be included inside the opening `<select>` tag.
   - If an attribute is provided with any other value, then the attribute and its value should be included inside the opening `<select>` tag as an *attribute*=*value* pair.
   - If the `multiple` attribute is set, `[ ]` should be appended to the value of the `name` attribute in the opening `<select>` tag.
   - Any attribute values or option text that contains special characters such as `<` or `&` should be rendered with encoded HTML entities such as `&lt;` or `&amp;`.

4. The HTML5 forms specification (*http://www.w3.org/TR/html5/forms.html*) lists, in great detail, the specific attributes that are allowed for each form element. The complete set of possible attributes is mighty and numerous. Some attributes are relatively constrained, though. For example, the <button> tag supports only three possible values for its type attribute: submit, reset, and button.

Without first modifying FormHelper, write some new tests that check the value of a type attribute provided for a <button> tag. The attribute is optional, but if it's provided, it must be one of the three allowable values.

After you've completed your tests, write the new code for FormHelper that makes the tests pass.

## CHAPTER 14

Software Engineering Practices
You Should Be Aware Of

Unlike previous chapters, this chapter is not a detailed look at how to do something in a PHP program. Instead, it looks at a few tools and topics that apply to software development in general. These techniques are especially useful when coordinating with other people but can also be valuable when you're working on a project all by yourself.

The PHP code you write to make the computer do something specific isn't the entirety of your software project. You also need to keep track of how your code has changed so you can go back to an earlier version if a bug creeps in or reconcile changes that two people have made to the same parts of the code. If bugs do come up or users make requests for new features, how do you keep track of those tasks? Has a bug been fixed? What code was changed to fix that bug? Who fixed it? Is the version of the code with the bug fix live for users to see yet? Source control systems (discussed in "Source Control" on page 280) and issue tracking systems (discussed in "Issue Tracking" on page 281) give you the information you need to answer these questions.

On all but the smallest projects, when you make changes, you don't want to edit the code that is running on the actual website that users interact with. Doing that exposes potential problems to your users. Your users will not be happy if you accidentally save a file with a typo in it, or you make a change that bogs down your server with time-consuming calculations.

Instead, work on a set of files that gets released to the servers that users interact with only when you're happy with how the program works. "Environments and Deployment" on page 282 discusses how to do this and how to make your PHP programs run smoothly in different contexts.

The chapter concludes with "Scaling Eventually" on page 283, a brief discussion of when to worry about your website's performance and how to optimize it when necessary.

Source Control

A source control system keeps track of changes to your files. It lets you review the history of how your code has changed, see who made what changes, and compare versions. With a source control system, two developers can work independently on changes and then combine them with ease.

A source control system is essential when more than one person is working on a project, but it is also useful for projects that you're working on alone. Being able to "go back in time" and see what your code contained at a previous point is a lifesaver when you're trying to figure out when a bug was introduced.

There are many popular source control systems, and which one you use will either be a matter of personal preference (for your own projects) or a foregone conclusion (when you're working on an existing project that already has one). The code for the PHP engine itself is managed using the Git source control system. You can browse the PHP engine's source code at *http://git.php.net*. Other popular source control systems include Mercurial (*https://www.mercurial-scm.org*) and Subversion (*http://subversion.apache.org*).

Learning About Git

Git is popular, powerful, and comprehensive. If you've never used it (or any source control system), spend a few minutes with the excellent tutorial at *https://try.github.io*. With a simulated terminal prompt in your browser, it guides you through the basics. You'll learn how to tell Git to keep track of the changes to files, make changes, undo changes, and show the list of changes you've made.

Source control systems excel at handling text files. Since your PHP code is essentially a collection of text files, there's nothing special you need to do to make it play nicely with any popular source control system. Still, following some conventions will make your code easier to manage.

One convention is how to organize classes in files. If you're writing object-oriented code, define only one class per file and make the filename the same as the class name (plus the *.php* extension). If you define classes inside namespaces, make a directory that corresponds to each namespace component, and arrange your files under those directories.

For example, a class named CheeseGrater goes in the file *CheeseGrater.php*. If you've defined that class in a Utensils namespace, then *CheeseGrater.php* goes in a *Utensils* subdirectory. Multiple levels of namespace mean multiple subdirectories. A class whose fully qualified name is \Kitchen\Utensils\CheeseGrater goes in the path *Kitchen/Utensils/CheeseGrater.php*.

This convention is known as *PSR-4*. *PSR* means *PHP Standard Recommendation*. The PHP Standard Recommendations (*http://www.php-fig.org/psr/*) are conventions on coding style and organization that most major PHP projects use.

Issue Tracking

Methods abound for keeping track of what you should be working on. Formal issue tracking systems are a reliable way to keep lists of bugs, feature requests, and other work that needs to be done. These systems ensure that each task is assigned to a person responsible for it. Each task is associated with relevant metadata, such as priority, estimated length of time to do it, progress and completion status, and comments. This metadata makes it a breeze to sort, search, and understand the background of each issue.

There are lots of issue tracking systems out there, and, like with source control systems, which one you use may be dictated by whatever's already in use in the project you're joining or the company you work for. If you're looking for a free system to try out, one worth mentioning is MantisBT (*http://www.mantisbt.org*), because it is open source and itself written in PHP.

Issue tracking systems are agnostic about what programming language you're using, so no special work is required to get your PHP programs to play nicely with them. A helpful convention, though, is to refer to issue IDs liberally in your program when you're writing code relevant to a particular issue.

Each issue tracked by the system gets an ID. It might be numbers, letters, or a combination, and it provides a short and unique way to reference an issue. For example, imagine a bug with the description "Login doesn't work when there's a + in email address" that, when entered into the system, gets assigned the ID MXH-26. When you write the code to fix the problem, reference that issue ID in a comment. For example:

```
// MXH-26: URL-encode email address to prevent problems with +
$email = urlencode($email);
```

This way, when another developer is looking at the code, she can see the issue number and look it up in the issue tracking system for context and an explanation of why your code is there.

Environments and Deployment

Ideally, the files you're editing when you're writing your PHP program are not the same files your web server is reading when it is responding to user requests. Editing those "live" files directly can cause many problems:

- Your users will immediately see errors if you save a file with a typo.
- Bad guys may be able to access backup copies that your editor saves automatically.
- You don't have a good way to test changes before real users see them.

Avoid these problems by maintaining different *environments*—separate contexts where your code can run. At a minimum, you need a *development* environment and a *production* environment. The development environment is where you do your work and the production environment is where you run the code that real users interact with. A typical setup is that the development environment is on your own computer and the production environment is on a server in a data center or cloud hosting provider such as Amazon Web Services or Google Cloud Platform.

Like the other aspects of software engineering discussed in this chapter, there are many ways of setting up different environments, moving code between environments, and managing all the different computers involved. These tools and techniques are typically not language-specific. There are things you can do in your PHP code, however, to make it easier to run seamlessly in different environments.

The most important thing is to separate environment-specific configuration information from your code so the configuration can be swapped without changing the code itself. This information includes data such as database hostnames and login credentials, locations of log files, other filesystem paths, and verbosity of logging. Once this information is in a separate file, PHP gives you a few methods for getting it into your program.

The `parse_ini_file()` function turns the contents of a *key=value* config file (the same format that the PHP engine's *php.ini* file uses) into an associative array. For example, consider the following configuration file:

```
;
; Comment lines in a config file start with semicolon
;

; Database Information
; Need quotes around the dsn value because of the = inside it
dsn="mysql:host=db.dev.example.com;dbname=devsnacks"
dbuser=devuser
dbpassword=raisins
```

Example 14-1 reads that configuration file (assuming it's been saved into *config.ini*) and uses the configuration data to establish a database connection.

Example 14-1. Reading a configuration file

```
$config = parse_ini_file('config.ini');
$db = new PDO($config['dsn'], $config['dbuser'], $config['dbpassword']);
```

In Example 14-1, the array returned by `parse_ini_file()` contains keys and values that correspond to each *key=value* line in *config.ini*. In a different environment with different database connection information, nothing has to change in the PHP program. The only thing necessary to establish the right connection is a new *config.ini* file.

Scaling Eventually

If you spend time around software engineers or businesspeople interested in building or running big systems, you'll hear them ask questions like "Does this scale?" or "Is this system scalable?" They are not talking about cleaning fish. They are wondering, sometimes imprecisely, what happens when this system gets big and busy? Does the website that is speedy with 3 people using it get slow when 3,000 people are using it? What about 3,000,000 people?

The best advice about making a scalable system for a beginning programmer is "don't worry about it for now." It is far more important to get things (mostly) working at first with just a light burden on your application than it is to ensure up front that everything will be OK with a heavy burden.

PHP at Scale

Because PHP is easy to get started with, it's used on zillions of small websites. But it handles plenty of giants as well. Facebook even built its own version of the PHP engine, HHVM (*http://hhvm.com*), to run the PHP code that powers its infrastructure even more efficiently. Baidu, Wikipedia, and Etsy use that engine, too.

What's more, when you do start to notice performance issues in your application, your PHP code is probably not the biggest problem. Many things can affect an application's performance. An inefficient database query that takes a few seconds to run makes a web page load very slowly, even if the PHP program sending the query to the database and generating HTML from the database's response only takes a few milliseconds to do its part. A web page that the server quickly sends to a client still feels slow to a human user if the HTML loads hundreds of images that take a long time to display in a web browser.

When you do get to the point of ensuring that the PHP-specific parts of your application are speedy, use a *profiler* to gather data on how the PHP engine performs when running your code. The two most popular open source profilers are Xdebug (*http://www.xdebug.org*) and XHProf (*http://www.php.net/xhprof*). XHProf has not been updated to work with PHP 7. Xdebug supports PHP 7 as of its 2.4.0rc1 release in November 2015.

As discussed in Chapter 12, Xdebug integrates with several IDEs, including PhpStorm and NetBeans. To learn about profiling in PhpStorm, read the JetBrains article about it (*http://bit.ly/profiling-phpstorm*). If you're not using PhpStorm, check out the Xdebug docs (*http://xdebug.org/docs/profiler*) for generic information on getting Xdebug's profiler up and running and then viewing the profiling output.

Chapter Summary

This chapter covered:

- Understanding what a source control system is
- Organizing classes into files with the PSR-4 convention
- Using an issue tracking system
- Referencing issue IDs in code comments
- Working in separate environments for development and production
- Putting environment-specific information in a configuration file
- Reading a configuration file with `parse_ini_file()`
- Being comfortable with not worrying about scalability at first
- Learning where to find more information on using the Xdebug and XHProf profilers

## CHAPTER 15

Handling Dates and Times

Dates and times are all over the place in a web application. In a shopping cart, you need to handle shipping dates of products. In a forum, you need to keep track of when messages are posted. In all sorts of applications, you need to keep track of the last time each user logged in so that you can tell them things like "15 new messages were posted since you last logged in."

Handling dates and times properly in your programs is more complicated than handling strings or numbers. A date or a time is not a single value but a collection of values—month, day, and year, for example, or hour, minute, and second. Because of this, doing math with them can be tricky. Instead of just adding or subtracting entire dates and times, you have to consider their component parts and what the allowable values for each part are. Hours go up to 12 (or 24), minutes and seconds go up to 59, and not all months have the same number of days.

To ease this burden, PHP provides you with a class, DateTime, that encapsulates all the information about a specific point in time. With the methods of this class, you can print out a date or time in the format of your choice, add or subtract two dates, and work with time intervals.

In this book, the phrase *time parts* (or *date parts* or *time-and-date parts*) means an array or group of time-and-date components such as day, month, year, hour, minute, and second. *Formatted time string* (or *formatted date string*, etc.) means a string that contains some particular grouping of time-and-date parts—for example "Thursday, October 20, 2016" or "3:54 p.m."

Displaying the Date or Time

The simplest display of date or time is telling your users what time it is. For this, use the format() method of a DateTime object, as shown in Example 15-1.

Example 15-1. What time is it?

```
$d = new DateTime();
print 'It is now: ';
print $d->format('r');
print "\n";
```

 If you get a warning that "It is not safe to rely on the system's timezone settings" from the PHP engine when you run the code in Example 15-1, peek ahead at "Working with Timezones" on page 291 to find out what that means and how to make it go away.

At noon on October 20, 2016, Example 15-1 would print:

```
It is now: Thu, 20 Oct 2016 12:00:00 +0000
```

When you create a `DateTime` object, the time or date to store inside it is provided to the object constructor. If no argument is provided, as in Example 15-1, the current date and time are used. The format string passed to the `format()` method controls how the date and time are formatted for printing.

Individual letters in the format string translate into certain time values. Example 15-2 prints out a month, day, and year.

Example 15-2. Printing a formatted date string

```
$d = new DateTime();
print $d->format('m/d/y');
```

At noon on October 20, 2016, Example 15-2 would print:

```
10/20/16
```

In Example 15-2, the m becomes the month (`10`), the d becomes the day of the month (`20`), and the y becomes the two-digit year (`04`). Because the slash is not a format character that `format()` understands, it is left alone in the string that `format()` returns.

Table 15-1 lists all of the special characters that `DateTime::format()` understands.

Table 15-1. Date/time formatting characters

Type	Format character	Description	Range/example
Day	j	Day of the month; numeric	1–31
Day	d	Day of the month; numeric; leading zeros	01–31
Day	S	English ordinal suffix for day of month, text	st, th, nd, rd

Type	Format character	Description	Range/example
Day	z	Day of the year; numeric	0–365
Day	w	Day of the week; numeric; 0 == Sunday	0–6
Day	N	Day of the week; numeric; 1 == Monday	1–7
Day	D	Abbreviated weekday name; text	Mon–Sun
Day	l	Full weekday name; text	Monday–Sunday
Week	W	Week number in the year (ISO-8601); numeric; leading zeros; week 01 is the first week that has at least four days in the current year; Monday is the first day of the week	01-53
Month	M	Abbreviated month name; text	Jan-Dec
Month	F	Full month name; text	January–December
Month	n	Month; numeric	1–12
Month	m	Month; numeric; leading zeros	01–12
Month	t	Month length in days; numeric	28–31
Year	y	Year; without century; numeric	00–99
Year	Y	Year; including century; numeric	0000–9999
Year	o	Year (ISO-8601); including century; numeric; year that the current week number (W) belongs to	0000–9999
Year	L	Leap year flag; 1 == yes	0,1
Hour	g	Hour; 12-hour clock; numeric	1–12
Hour	h	Hour; 12-hour clock; numeric; leading zeros	01–12
Hour	G	Hour; 24-hour clock; numeric	0–23
Hour	H	Hour; 24-hour clock; numeric; leading zeros	00–23
Hour	a	a.m. or p.m. designation	am, pm
Hour	A	A.M. or P.M. designation	AM, PM
Minute	i	Minutes; numeric; leading zeros	00–59
Second	s	Seconds; numeric; leading zeros	00–59
Second	u	Microseconds; numeric; leading zeros	000000–999999
Timezone	e	Timezone identifier; text	From supported timezones (*http://www.php.net/timezones*)
Timezone	T	Timezone abbreviation; text	GMT, CEST, MDT, etc.
Timezone	O	Timezone difference to UTC in hours with sign; text	-1100 – +1400
Timezone	P	Timezone difference to UTC in hours with sign and colon; text	-11:00 – +14:00
Timezone	Z	Timezone difference to UTC in seconds; numeric	-39600–50400
Other	I	Daylight Saving Time flag; 1 == yes	0,1
Other	B	Swatch Internet Time; numeric	000–999
Other	c	ISO-8601 formatted date; text	2016-10-20T12:33:56+06:00

Type	Format character	Description	Range/example
Other	r	RFC-2822 formatted date; text	Thu, 20 Oct 2016 12:33:56 +0600
Other	U	Seconds since 12:00:00 a.m. UTC on Jan 1, 1970	1476945236

Parsing a Date or Time

To create a DateTime object that represents a specific time, pass that time as a first argument to the constructor. This argument is a string indicating the date and time you want the object to represent. A DateTime object understands a very wide variety of format strings. Whatever you are dealing with probably works, but an exhaustive list of all the possible formats is available at *http://www.php.net/datetime.formats*.

Example 15-3 shows a few date-and-time formats that the DateTime constructor understands.

Example 15-3. Formatted date/time strings that DateTime understands

```
// If only a time is supplied, the current date is used for day/month/year
$a = new DateTime('10:36 am');
// If only a date is supplied, the current time is used for hour/minute/second
$b = new DateTime('5/11');
$c = new DateTime('March 5th 2017');
$d = new DateTime('3/10/2018');
$e = new DateTime('2015-03-10 17:34:45');
// DateTime understands microseconds
$f = new DateTime('2015-03-10 17:34:45.326425');
// Epoch timestamp must be prefixed with @
$g = new DateTime('@381718923');
// Common log format
$h = new DateTime('3/Mar/2015:17:34:45 +0400');

// Relative formats, too!
$i = new DateTime('next Tuesday');
$j = new DateTime("last day of April 2015");
$k = new DateTime("November 1, 2012 + 2 weeks");
```

At noon on October 20, 2016, the full dates and times that would end up in the variables in Example 15-3 would be:

```
Thu, 20 Oct 2016 10:36:00 +0000
Wed, 11 May 2016 00:00:00 +0000
Sun, 05 Mar 2017 00:00:00 +0000
Sat, 10 Mar 2018 00:00:00 +0000
Tue, 10 Mar 2015 17:34:45 +0000
Tue, 10 Mar 2015 17:34:45 +0000
Fri, 05 Feb 1982 01:02:03 +0000
Tue, 03 Mar 2015 17:34:45 +0400
```

```
Tue, 25 Oct 2016 00:00:00 +0000
Thu, 30 Apr 2015 00:00:00 +0000
Thu, 15 Nov 2012 00:00:00 +0000
```

If you have discrete date-and-time parts, such as those submitted from form elements in which a user can specify month, day, and year or hour, minute, and second, you can also pass them to the the `setTime()` and `setDate()` methods to adjust the time and date stored inside the `DateTime` object.

Example 15-4 shows `setTime()` and `setDate()` at work.

Example 15-4. Setting date or time parts

```
// $_POST['mo'], $_POST['dy'], and $_POST['yr']
// contain month number, day, and year submitted
// from a form
//
// $_POST['hr'], $_POST['mn'] contain
// hour and minute submitted from a form

// $d contains the current time, but soon that will
// be overridden
$d = new DateTime();

$d->setDate($_POST['yr'], $_POST['mo'], $_POST['dy']);
$d->setTime($_POST['hr'], $_POST['mn']);

print $d->format('r');
```

If `$_POST['yr']` is 2016, `$_POST['mo']` is 5, `$_POST['dy']` is 12, `$_POST['hr']` is 4, and `$_POST['mn']` is 15, then Example 15-4 prints:

```
Thu, 12 May 2016 04:15:00 +0000
```

Even though `$d` is initialized to the current date and time when Example 15-4 is run, the calls to `setDate()` and `setTime()` change what's stored inside the object.

The `DateTime` object tries to be as accommodating as possible when parsing incoming data. Sometimes this is helpful, but sometimes it is not. For example, consider what you think should happen if, in Example 15-4, `$_POST['mo']` is 3 and `$_POST['dy']` is 35. It can never be the 35th of March. That doesn't bother `DateTime`, though. It considers March 35 to be the same as April 4 (March 31 is the last day of March, so March 32 is the next day (April 1), March 33 is April 2, March 34 is April 3, and March 35 is April 4). Calling `$d->setDate(2016, 3, 35)` gives you a `DateTime` object set to April 4, 2016.

For stricter validation of days and months, use `checkdate()` on the month, day, and year first. It tells you whether the provided month and day are valid for the provided year, as shown in Example 15-5.

Example 15-5. Verifying months and days

```
if (checkdate(3, 35, 2016)) {
    print "March 35, 2016 is OK";
}
if (checkdate(2, 29, 2016)) {
    print "February 29, 2016 is OK";
}
if (checkdate(2, 29, 2017)) {
    print "February 29, 2017 is OK";
}
```

In Example 15-5, only the second call to checkdate() returns true. The first fails because March always has fewer than 35 days, and the third fails because 2017 is not a leap year.

Calculating Dates and Times

Once you've got a DateTime object that represents a particular point in time, it's straightforward to do date or time calculations. You might want to give a user a set of dates or times to choose from in a menu. Example 15-6 displays an HTML <select> menu where each choice is a day. The first choice is the date corresponding to the first Tuesday after the program is run. The subsequent choices are every other day after that.

Example 15-6. Displaying a range of days

```
$daysToPrint = 4;
$d = new DateTime('next Tuesday');
print "<select name='day'>\n";
for ($i = 0; $i < $daysToPrint; $i++) {
    print " <option>" . $d->format('l F jS') . "</option>\n";
    // Add 2 days to the date
    $d->modify("+2 day");
}
print "</select>";
```

In Example 15-6, the modify() method changes the date inside the DateTime object at each pass through the loop. The modify() method accepts a string holding one of the relative date/time formats described at *http://www.php.net/ datetime.formats.relative* and adjusts the object accordingly. In this case, +2 day bumps it forward two days each time.

On October 20, 2016, Example 15-6 would print:

```
<select name='day'>
  <option>Tuesday October 25th</option>
  <option>Thursday October 27th</option>
```

```
<option>Saturday October 29th</option>
<option>Monday October 31st</option>
</select>
```

The `DateTime` object's `diff()` method tells you the difference between two dates. It returns a `DateInterval` object, which encapsulates the interval between the dates. Example 15-7 checks whether a given birthdate means someone is over 13 years old.

Example 15-7. Computing a date interval

```
$now = new DateTime();
$birthdate = new DateTime('1990-05-12');
$diff = $birthdate->diff($now);

if (($diff->y > 13) && ($diff->invert == 0)) {
    print "You are more than 13 years old.";
} else {
    print "Sorry, too young.";
}
```

In Example 15-7, the call to `$birthdate->diff($now)` returns a new `DateInterval` object. This object's properties describe the interval between `$birthdate` and `$now`. The `y` property is the number of years and the `invert` property is 0 when the difference is a positive amount (the `invert` property would be 1 if `$birthdate` were after `$now`). The other properties are `m` (months), `d` (days in the month), `h` (hours), `i` (minutes), `s` (seconds), and `days` (total number of days between the two dates).

Working with Timezones

Dates and times are, unfortunately, not just collections of hours, minutes, seconds, months, days, and years. To be complete, they must also include a timezone. "Noon on October 20, 2016" is not the same instant in time in New York City as it is in London.

The PHP engine must be configured with a default timezone to use. The easiest way to do this is to set the `date.timezone` configuration parameter in your PHP configuration file.[1] If you can't adjust the file, call the `date_default_timezone_set()` function in your program before you do any date or time manipulation. In PHP 7, the engine defaults to the UTC timezone if you don't specify your own default value.

There is a big list of possible timezone values that the PHP engine understands (*http://www.php.net/timezones*). Instead of using your local timezone, however, a convention that often makes software development easier is to set the timezone to UTC,

---

[1] "Modifying PHP Configuration Directives" on page 328 explains how to adjust configuration parameters.

the code for Coordinated Universal Time. This is the time at zero degrees longitude and doesn't adjust in the summer for a Daylight Saving Time setting. Although you have to do a little mental math to convert a UTC timestamp that appears, say, in a log file to your local time, using UTC makes it easier to work with time data that could be coming from multiple servers located in different timezones. It also avoids confusion during the switch to and from Daylight Saving Time because the apparent "clock time" doesn't change.

Chapter Summary

This chapter covered:

- Defining some time- and date-handling vocabulary such as *time-and-date parts* and *formatted time-and-date string*
- Getting the current time and date
- Printing formatted time-and-date strings with the `DateTime` object's `format()` method
- Exploring the format characters that `format()` understands
- Parsing a date or time from an absolute or relative format
- Calculating a date or time relative to another date or time
- Computing the difference between two dates
- Understanding why `UTC` is a convenient default timezone

## CHAPTER 16

Package Management

Take the virtuous laziness introduced in Chapter 5 to a powerful new level by relying on entire packages of code that other people have written. This chapter shows you how to use the Composer package management system to find existing libraries and integrate them into your programs.

If you've tried to integrate third-party libraries without a package manager before, you're probably familiar with all the steps that entails: downloading an archive file containing the library, unpacking it, putting the unpacked files in a special place, and then modifying your program so it can find the new files.

With Composer, all of that is reduced to a single command. Plus, when newer versions of the packages you use are released, Composer can upgrade them in a snap.

If you've used a package manager in another language (such as npm with JavaScript, gem with Ruby, or cpan with Perl) you'll find the Composer experience familiar and pleasant.

Installing Composer

Download and run Composer's installer by running this command at a shell prompt in your terminal:

```
curl -sS https://getcomposer.org/installer | php
```

On Windows, download and run the Composer installer (*https://getcomposer.org/ Composer-Setup.exe*) and then run *Composer-Setup.exe*.

If you've installed Composer successfully, when you run it from the command line (by typing php composer.phar, or just composer on Windows, you should see a help screen listing the commands that Composer supports.

Adding a Package to Your Program

The `require` command adds a package to your program. At a minimum, `require` must be told the name of the package to add. Example 16-1 adds the Swift Mailer library to your program.

Example 16-1. Adding a package with require

```
php composer.phar require swiftmailer/swiftmailer
```

This command downloads the package, installs its files under a directory named *vendor* in your current project directory, and updates the *composer.json* file. The *composer.json* file tracks the packages you've installed as well as other Composer-managed settings about your project. Composer also maintains a *composer.lock* file, which tracks the specific versions of packages you've installed.

Once Composer has installed a package, all you have to do to make it available to your program is to reference the Composer autoload file with this simple line of PHP code: `require "vendor/autoload.php;"`. The logic in this file contains a mapping from class names to filenames. When you reference a class in an installed package, it ensures that the files that define the class are loaded.

You only need to load the *vendor/autoload.php* file once, no matter how many packages you have installed. Programs that rely on Composer-installed packages generally make the `require "vendor/autoload.php";` statement one of the first things in the program. Example 16-2 shows that statement in the context of using Swift Mailer to create a message (as discussed in Chapter 17).

Example 16-2. Using a Composer-installed library

```
// Tell PHP to load Composer's class-finding logic
require 'vendor/autoload.php';
// The Swift_Message class is now automatically available
$message = Swift_Message::newInstance();
$message->setFrom('julia@example.com');
$message->setTo(array('james@example.com' => 'James Beard'));
$message->setSubject('Delicious New Recipe');
$message->setBody(<<<_TEXT_
Dear James,

You should try this: puree 1 pound of chicken with two pounds
of asparagus in the blender, then drop small balls of the mixture
into a deep fryer. Yummy!

Love,
Julia
```

```
_TEXT_
);
```

If your program is being checked into a source control system (see Chapter 14), you need to take a few steps to make sure things play nicely with Composer. First, make sure that you include both *composer.json* and *composer.lock* in the files that are tracked by the source control system. These are necessary for somebody else who checks out the program from the source control system to be able to install the same packages and the same package versions as you have. Second, make sure that the *vendor* directory is *not* tracked by the source control system. All the code in *vendor* is managed by Composer. When you upgrade a package version, the only files you want to track changes in are the *composer.json* and *composer.lock* files—not all of the individual files under *vendor* that may have changed.

With *composer.json* and *composer.lock* but not *vendor* in source control, another person who checks out your code from the source control system just has to run the command `php composer.phar install` and they will have all of the right versions of the right packages in the right place.

Finding Packages

The real utility of a package management system such as Composer, of course, depends on the utility of the packages you can install. So how do you find great packages to install that solve the problems you have? The most popular Composer package repository (a site that indexes the packages for you to browse and download) is Packagist (*https://packagist.org*).

For example, perhaps you need to geocode some addresses—i.e., find the longitude and latitude that correspond to each particular address. Type `geocode` into the search box at the top of the Packagist website, click the arrow next to the search box to sort the results by number of downloads, and you instantly see a bunch of results, as shown in Figure 16-1.

Adding one of those packages to your project is now as easy as typing either `php composer.phar require willdurand/geocoder` or `php composer.phar require league/geotools`. Figure 16-2 shows what happens at the terminal prompt when `willdurand/geocoder` is installed.

In Figure 16-2, `php composer.phar require willdurand/geocoder` kicks things off at the top. Composer then figures out the most recent stable version to use (3.2) and what dependencies also need to be installed, and then downloads and installs those packages. One of the dependencies (`http-adapter`) suggests, but doesn't require, that a number of other packages could be installed, so Composer prints out messages about those packages instead of installing them.

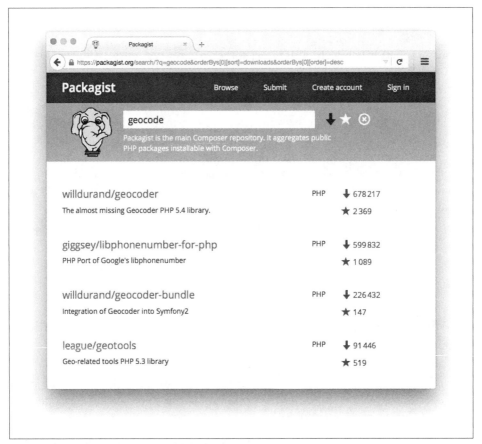

Figure 16-1. Finding packages on packagist.org

Getting More Information on Composer

The overview of Composer in this chapter is all about using code that other people have written in your project. If you are interested in making your code available as a library for other people to install via Composer, read the "Libraries" chapter of the documentation. Publishing a package on Packagist is free and easy.

There are other Composer repositories as well. For example, WordPress Packagist (*http://wpackagist.org*) is a repository of WordPress themes and plugins set up so you can install the themes and plugins with Composer. Drupal packages are available via Composer from Packagist.

Figure 16-2. Installing the willdurand/geocoder package

Chapter Summary

This chapter covered:

- Installing the Composer package management tool
- Downloading and installing a package for use in your program
- Making sure your code has access to the package files by loading the Composer *autoload.php* file
- Integrating your Composer-using program with your source control system
- Finding packages to install
- Getting more information about using Composer

## CHAPTER 17

Sending Email

Most of your interaction with users will be via web pages, but sending or receiving an email message every now and then is useful, too. Email is a great way send updates, order confirmations, and links that let users reset their passwords.

This chapter explains the basics of using the Swift Mailer library to send email messages.

Swift Mailer

First, use Composer to install Swift Mailer:

```
php composer.phar require swiftmailer/swiftmailer
```

As long as you've got the standard `require "vendor/autoload.php";` statement in your program, Swift Mailer is now available to use.

Swift Mailer represents messages as `Swift_Message` objects. To create an email message, you create one of these objects and then call methods on it to build the message. Then you hand the message object to an instance of the `Swift_Mailer` class so that the message can be sent. The `Swift_Mailer` instance, in turn, is configured with a particular kind of `Swift_Transport` class. This transport class embodies the logic of how the message is actually sent—either by connecting to a remote server or by using mail utilities on the local server.

Example 17-1 creates a simple email message with a subject, from address, to address, and plain-text body.

Example 17-1. Creating an email message

```
$message = Swift_Message::newInstance();
$message->setFrom('julia@example.com');
$message->setTo(array('james@example.com' => 'James Bard'));
$message->setSubject('Delicious New Recipe');
$message->setBody(<<<_TEXT_
Dear James,

You should try this: puree 1 pound of chicken with two pounds
of asparagus in the blender, then drop small balls of the mixture
into a deep fryer. Yummy!

Love,
Julia

_TEXT_
);
```

The arguments to setFrom() and setTo() can be email addresses as strings or email addresses and full names as key/value pairs. To specify multiple recipients, pass an array that contains any mix of strings (addresses) and key/value pairs (addresses and full names).

The setBody() method sets the plain-text body of the message. To add an HTML version of the message body, call addPart() with the alternative message body as a first argument and the right MIME type as the second argument. For example:

```
$message->addPart(<<<_HTML_
<p>Dear James,</p>
<p>You should try this:</p>
<ul>
<li>puree 1 pound of chicken with two pounds of asparagus in the blender</li>
<li>drop small balls of the mixture into a deep fryer.</li>
</ul>

<p><em>Yummy!</em></p>

<p>Love,</p>
<p>Julia</p>

_HTML_
    // MIME type as second argument
    , "text/html");
```

A message needs a mailer to send it, and a mailer needs a transport to know how to send the message. This chapter shows the Simple Mail Transfer Protocol (SMTP) transport, which connects to a standard email server to send the message. Creating an instance of the Swift_SmtpTransport class requires you to know the hostname and port (and maybe username and password) of your mail server. Ask your system administrator or check the account settings in your email program to find this information.

Example 17-2 creates a `Swift_SmtpTransport` object that uses an example SMTP server at port 25 of host `smtp.example.com` and then creates a `Swift_Mailer` object which uses that transport.

Example 17-2. Creating an SMTP transport

```
$transport = Swift_SmtpTransport::newInstance('smtp.example.com', 25);
$mailer = Swift_Mailer::newInstance($transport);
```

Once you've got a `Swift_Mailer`, pass your `Swift_Message` object to its `send()` method and your message is sent:

```
$mailer->send($message);
```

Swift Mailer supports a lot more functionality than what's described here. You can attach files to messages, add arbitrary headers to messages, request read receipts, connect to mail servers over SSL, and more. The Swift Mailer documentation (*http://swiftmailer.org/docs/introduction.html*) is the place to start to find out the details of these features.

Chapter Summary

This chapter covered:

- Installing Swift Mailer
- Understanding Swift Mailer message, mailer, and transport objects
- Creating a `Swift_Message` and adjusting its contents
- Creating a `Swift_SmtpTransport` and using it with a `Swift_Mailer`
- Sending a message
- Finding Swift Mailer documentation to learn more

## CHAPTER 18

Frameworks

An application *framework* is a set of functions, classes, and conventions that make it easier to accomplish common tasks. Lots of programming languages have popular frameworks, and PHP is no exception. This chapter provides an overview of three popular PHP frameworks. These frameworks speed your journey from nothing to a functioning web application.

Frameworks aimed at web development generally provide standard ways to accomplish at least the following tasks:

Routing
> Translating user-requested URLs to specific methods or functions that are responsible for generating a response

Object-relational mapping
> Letting you treat rows in your database as objects in your code and providing methods on those objects that modify the database

User management
> Standard mechanisms for maintaining information about your app's users and deciding which users have permission to do which operations

By using a framework, you save time compared to implementing all of the framework's functionality yourself. You may also be able to jump-start new developers coming to work with you if they are familiar with the framework. The trade-off is that you must invest time in learning the framework and adapting to its conventions of how to accomplish things.

The three frameworks explored in this chapter are Laravel, Symfony, and Zend Framework. Each provides a very different kind of solution to the "framework" question. They differ in how they are installed, what their documentation explains, how they balance simplicity and capability, and what you do to find more information when you're stumped.

There are many other PHP frameworks out there. The three in this chapter are included because they are some of the most popular and most capable, but the exclusion of other frameworks should not be taken as an injunction against trying something else. The Internet abounds with guides that attempt to answer the question "What PHP framework should I use?" For up-to-date information, check out the PHP Frameworks (*https://www.quora.com/PHP-Frameworks*) topic on Quora or search for php framework on Hacker News (*http://news.ycombinator.com*) or Site-Point (*http://www.sitepoint.com*).

Laravel

Laravel's (*http://laravel.com*) creator describes it as a framework for people who value "elegance, simplicity, and readability." It has well-thought-out documentation, a vibrant ecosystem of users, and available hosting providers and tutorials.

To install Laravel, run the command php composer.phar global require laravel/installer=~1.1". Then, to create a new web project that uses Laravel, run laravel new *project-name*,[1] substituting your project name for *project-name*. For example, running laravel new menu creates a directory called *menu* and populates it with the necessary code and configuration scaffolding for Laravel to work properly.

To see the scaffolding in action, fire up the built-in PHP web server by pointing it at *server.php* in your project directory. For example, php -S localhost:8000 -t menu2/public menu/server.php lets you access the new Laravel project in the *menu* subdirectory at *http://localhost:8000*.

Laravel's routing is controlled by the code in *app/Http/routes.php*. Each call to a static method in the Route class tells Laravel what to do when an HTTP request comes in with a certain method and URL path. The code in Example 18-1 tells Laravel to respond to a GET request for /show.

---

1 This requires that the global composer binary directory be in your system's $PATH. See "Running a PHP REPL" on page 314 for more information.

Example 18-1. Adding a Laravel route

```
Route::get('/show', function() {
    $now = new DateTime();
    $items = [ "Fried Potatoes", "Boiled Potatoes", "Baked Potatoes" ];
    return view('show-menu', [ 'when' => $now,
                               'what' => $items ]);
});
```

In Example 18-1, the call to `Route::get()` tells Laravel that it should be responding to HTTP GET (not POST) requests, and the first argument of /show tells Laravel that this `Route::get()` call provides information on what to do when the URL /show is visited. The second argument to `Route::get()` is the function that Laravel runs to compute the response to GET /show. This function sets up two variables, $now and $items, and then passes them to the show-menu view as keys when and what.

A *view* is a template that contains presentation logic—what your application should display. The view() function in Laravel looks for a file in a predefined location and then runs the PHP code in that file to generate a response. The call to view('show-menu') tells Laravel to look for a file named *show-menu.php* in the *resources/views* directory. Example 18-2 contains the code for this view.

Example 18-2. A Laravel view

```
<p> At <?php echo $when->format('g:i a') ?>, here is what's available: </p>
<ul>
<?php foreach ($what as $item) { ?>
<li><?php echo $item ?></li>
<?php } ?>
</ul>
```

The view is just plain PHP. Any data coming from an external source such as a user or database should be properly escaped to prevent cross-site scripting problems, as discussed in "HTML and JavaScript" on page 138. Laravel includes support for the Blade templating engine, which makes many things easier, including escaping output by default.

Symfony

Symfony (*https://symfony.com*) describes itself as both a set of reusable components and a framework for web projects. This means that even if you don't use its framework for request routing or other web-related tasks, you can still use its individual components for tasks such as templating, managing configuration files, or debugging.

Like Laravel, Symfony has a command-line program used to create and manage projects. Install the symfony program (*http://symfony.com/installer*) and rename the downloaded *installer* file to *symfony*. Move it into a directory in your system path. On Linux or OS X, make the symfony program executable by typing chmod a +x /path/to/symfony (where /path/to/symfony is the full path of the place you've put the symfony program).

Then, to create a new web project that uses Symfony, run symfony new *project-name*, substituting your project name for *project-name*. For example, running the command symfony new menu creates a directory called *menu* and populates it with the code and configuration scaffolding necessary for Symfony to work properly.

Symfony includes some glue that makes it easy to run your project in PHP's built-in web server. Just change your current directory to your project directory (e.g., cd menu) and then run php app/console server:run. Then visit *http://localhost:8000/* in your web browser, and you'll see a "Welcome to Symfony" page complete with lots of interesting diagnostic information at the bottom.

With Symfony, routes are not specified in one central place. Instead, individual classes in the *src/AppBundle/Controller* directory define the methods that are triggered by the routes that the app handles. A special annotation in a comment next to a method indicates what route the method handles. Example 18-3 defines a handler for a GET /show request. Put it in *MenuController.php* in *src/AppBundle/Controllers*.

Example 18-3. Specifying a route with Symfony

```
namespace AppBundle\Controller;

use Symfony\Bundle\FrameworkBundle\Controller\Controller;
use Sensio\Bundle\FrameworkExtraBundle\Configuration\Route;
use Sensio\Bundle\FrameworkExtraBundle\Configuration\Method;
use Symfony\Component\HttpFoundation\Response;

class MenuController extends Controller
{
    /**
     * @Route("/show")
     * @Method("GET")
     */
    public function showAction()
    {
        $now = new \DateTime();
        $items = [ "Fried Potatoes", "Boiled Potatoes", "Baked Potatoes" ];

        return $this->render("show-menu.html.twig",
                             [ 'when' => $now,
                               'what' => $items ]);
```

```
        }
}
```

In Example 18-3, the items in the comment before the showAction() method indicate the route that showAction() handles: URL path /show with method GET. The render() method returns a Symfony data structure that holds the contents of the response. Its first argument is the name of a view template file to use, and the second argument is data to pass to the template. It is possible to use plain PHP as a template language with Symfony, but its default setup is to use the Twig templating engine (*http://twig.sensiolabs.org/*), so that's what's specified here.

Symfony's view directory is *app/Resources/views*. This means that passing show-menu.html.twig to render() tells Symfony to look for *app/Resources/views/ show-menu.html.twig* in your project directory. Save the contents of Example 18-4 in that place.

Example 18-4. Defining a Symfony view

```
{% extends 'base.html.twig' %}

{% block body %}
<p> At {{ when|date("g:i a") }}, here is what's available: </p>
<ul>
{% for item in what %}
<li>{{ item }}</li>
{% endfor %}
</ul>
{% endblock %}
```

In Twig, {% %} indicates a templating language command and {{ }} indicates a variable whose value (with proper HTML escaping) should be included in the output. Its syntax may take some getting used to, but Twig is a powerful and speedy templating language.

Zend Framework

More so than the other two frameworks reviewed in this chapter, Zend Framework (*http://framework.zend.com/*) takes a "collection of components" approach. While this makes it easy to drop a component or two into an existing project without conforming to a particular file structure or request routing convention, it also means starting from scratch is a little more complicated.

To install a Zend Framework "skeleton" app into the *menu* directory that contains the basics necessary to get up and running, run the following Composer command all on one line:

```
composer create-project --no-interaction --stability="dev"
zendframework/skeleton-application menu
```

Then, to make the built-in PHP web server serve up your new Zend Framework application, change into the project directory and run php -S localhost:8000 -t public/ public/index.php. Visit *http://localhost:8000* to see the default front page of your new application.

Zend Framework organizes related application code into *modules*. In a big application, you can create separate modules for separate high-level parts of your program. For this small sample application, we'll add code to the base Application module that's already there. This module contains some default routing logic that maps paths under */Application* to code in controller classes in a specific place in the filesystem. Example 18-5 shows a new *MenuController.php*. Save it in the *module/Application/src/ Application/Controller* directory of your Zend Framework project.

Example 18-5. A Zend Framework controller

```
namespace Application\Controller;
use Zend\Mvc\Controller\AbstractActionController;
use Zend\View\Model\ViewModel;

class MenuController extends AbstractActionController
{
    public function showAction()
    {
        $now = new \DateTime();
        $items = [ "Fried Potatoes", "Boiled Potatoes", "Baked Potatoes" ];

        return new ViewModel(array('when' => $now, 'what' => $items));
    }
}
```

Then, to tell the framework about your new class, find the section of *module/Application/config/module.config.php* that looks like this:

```
'controllers' => array(
        'invokables' => array(
            'Application\Controller\Index' =>
            'Application\Controller\IndexController'
        ),
    ),
```

And add this line as a second element in the invokables array:

```
'Application\Controller\Menu' => 'Application\Controller\MenuController'
```

Don't forget to add a comma after `'Application\Controller\IndexController'` so that the array elements have the proper syntax. When you're done, this section of the config file should look like this:

```
'controllers' => array(
     'invokables' => array(
         'Application\Controller\Index' =>
         'Application\Controller\IndexController',
         'Application\Controller\Menu' =>
         'Application\Controller\MenuController'
     ),
),
```

Now you've got a new controller and the framework knows how to use it. The last step is to add a view so the time and items information can be rendered. With Zend Framework, the default template language is just plain PHP. Save the code in Example 18-6 in *module/Application/view/application/menu/show.phtml* under your project directory.

Example 18-6. A Zend Framework view

```
<p> At <?php echo $when->format("g:i a") ?>, here is what's available: </p>
<ul>
<?php foreach ($what as $item) { ?>
<li><?php echo $this->escapeHtml($item) ?></li>
<?php } ?>
</ul>
```

The keys in the array passed to `new ViewModel()` in the controller are local variable names in the view. This makes accessing these values very straightforward. However, because the template language is plain PHP, HTML entities and other special characters are not escaped by default. Example 18-6 uses the `escapeHtml()` helper method to escape special characters in each item name.

Chapter Summary

This chapter covered:

- Understanding what an application framework is and why you might want to use one
- Installing Laravel
- Creating a new Laravel project
- Adding a route with Laravel
- Adding a view for a route with Laravel
- Installing Symfony
- Creating a new Symfony project

- Adding a route with Symfony
- Adding a view for a route with Symfony
- Installing Zend Framework
- Creating a new Zend Framework project
- Adding a route with Zend Framework
- Adding a view for a route with Zend Framework

## CHAPTER 19

Command-Line PHP

Usually, the PHP engine is invoked by a web server in response to a request from a web client. However, the PHP engine can also be run as a command-line utility on your computer. If you've been running all of the code examples in the book so far, you've run PHP as a command-line program when you used PHPUnit and Composer.

Writing a PHP program intended for use on the command line is a little different than writing a PHP program intended for use in a website. You have access to all the same functions for string manipulation, JSON and XML handling, working with files, and so forth, but there's no incoming form or URL data. Instead, you get information from command-line arguments. The standard `print` statement prints data to the console. The next section, "Writing Command-Line PHP Programs", shows you the basics of writing a command-line PHP program.

The PHP engine also comes with a mini web server that you can invoke by running PHP on the command line. "Using PHP's Built-in Web Server" on page 313 explains how this works. The built-in web server is handy for quick testing.

One other handy use for PHP on the command line is as an interactive shell, otherwise known as a *Read-Eval-Print Loop* (REPL). This is a program that gives you a prompt to type in some PHP code, and then runs that PHP code and tells you the results. For exploration of how a PHP function works and quick gratification, nothing beats a REPL. "Running a PHP REPL" on page 314 explains PHP's built-in REPL, and provides information about one others.

Writing Command-Line PHP Programs

A simple PHP program that outputs data works fine from the command line. Consider Example 19-1, which uses the Yahoo! Weather API to print out the current weather conditions for a zip code.

Example 19-1. Finding the weather

```
// Zip code to look up weather for
$zip = "98052";

// YQL query to find the weather
// See https://developer.yahoo.com/weather/ for more info
$yql = 'select item.condition from weather.forecast where woeid in '.
       '(select woeid from geo.places(1) where text="'.$zip.'")';

// The params that the Yahoo! YQL query endpoint expects
$params = array("q" => $yql,
                "format" => "json",
                "env" => "store://datatables.org/alltableswithkeys");

// Build the YQL URL, appending the query parameters
$url = "https://query.yahooapis.com/v1/public/yql?" . http_build_query($params);
// Make the request
$response = file_get_contents($url);
// Decode the response as JSON
$json = json_decode($response);
// Select the object in the nested JSON response that contains the info
$conditions = $json->query->results->channel->item->condition;
// Print out the weather
print "At {$conditions->date} it is {$conditions->temp} degrees " .
      "and {$conditions->text} in $zip\n";
```

If you save Example 19-1 in a file called *weather.php*, you can run it with a command such as php weather.php and be told the current weather. But it's only accurate if you want the weather for zip code 98052. Otherwise you have to edit the file. This is not very useful. It would be better if you could provide a zip code as an argument to the program when you run it. Example 19-2 is an updated version of the program that looks in the $_SERVER['argv'] array for command-line arguments. The command-line version of the PHP engine automatically populates this array with provided arguments.

Example 19-2. Accessing command-line arguments

```
// Zip code to look up weather for
if (isset($_SERVER['argv'][1])) {
    $zip = $_SERVER['argv'][1];
} else {
```

```
        print "Please specify a zip code.\n";
        exit();
}

// YQL query to find the weather
// See https://developer.yahoo.com/weather/ for more info
$yql = 'select item.condition from weather.forecast where woeid in ' .
        '(select woeid from geo.places(1) where text="'.$zip.'")';

// The params that the Yahoo! YQL query endpoint expects
$params = array("q" => $yql,
                "format" => "json",
                "env" => "store://datatables.org/alltableswithkeys");

// Build the YQL URL, appending the query parameters
$url = "https://query.yahooapis.com/v1/public/yql?" . http_build_query($params);
// Make the request
$response = file_get_contents($url);
// Decode the response as JSON
$json = json_decode($response);
// Select the object in the nested JSON response that contains the info
$conditions = $json->query->results->channel->item->condition;
// Print out the weather
print "At {$conditions->date} it is {$conditions->temp} degrees " .
        "and {$conditions->text} in $zip\n";
```

Assuming you save Example 19-2 in *weather2.php*, you can run php weather2 19096 to get the weather for zip code 19096.

Note that the first argument is at $_SERVER['argv'][1], even though, as mentioned in "Creating a Numeric Array" on page 60, PHP arrays start with index 0. This is because $_SERVER['argv'][0] contains the name of the program you've run. In the case of running php weather2.php 19096, $_SERVER['argv'][0] is weather2.php.

Using PHP's Built-in Web Server

If you want to check out how some PHP code you're writing behaves with real requests from a web browser, a quick way to dive in is to use the PHP engine's built-in web server.

 The built-in web server is available in PHP 5.4.0 and later.

Run php with a -S argument that provides a hostname and port number, and you've got a running web server providing access to the files in whatever directory you ran php in. For example, to run the web server on port 8000 of your local machine, run `php -S localhost:8000`. With that server running, visiting *http://localhost:8000/pizza.php* causes the web server to execute the code in *pizza.php* and send the results back to your web browser.

If the web server is not finding files that you think it should, check what directory you were in when you ran the `php -S` command. By default, the PHP web server serves up files in the directory that you ran `php -S` in (and below). To provide an alternate document root directory, add a `-t` argument. For example, `php -S localhost:8000 -t /home/mario/web` serves up the files under */home/mario/web* at *http://localhost:8000*.

The PHP web server doesn't do anything fancy to map URLs to files. It just looks for a filename under its base directory as specified in the URL. If you leave a filename out of the URL, it looks for *index.php* and *index.html* before returning a "file not found" error.

The built-in web server only handles one request at a time. It is best for testing functionality and experiments on a development machine. It's much easier to get up and running than a big Apache or nginx installation that you'd need to configure, but it also is not as full-featured. When it's time to deploy your code to a production environment, use a web server that can handle the scale and security requirements of general usage.

Running a PHP REPL

The built-in web server is a great way to quickly see your PHP code in action. Another handy tool for exploration and testing is the PHP REPL. Run `php -a` and you get a `php >` prompt at which you can type in some PHP code and immediately see the results, as shown in Example 19-3.

Example 19-3. Using the PHP REPL

```
% php -a
Interactive shell

php > print strlen("mushrooms");
9
php > $releases = simplexml_load_file("https://secure.php.net/releases/feed.php");
php > print $releases->entry[0]->title;
PHP 7.0.5 released!
php >
```

In Example 19-3, the initial % is a Unix shell prompt and `php -a` is what you type to run the PHP REPL. The REPL then prints `Interactive shell` and a `php >` prompt.

It executes what you type when you press the Return key and prints any results. Typing `print strlen("mushrooms");` (and then Return) tells the REPL to run `strlen("mushrooms")` and pass the results to `print`, so it prints 9. Don't forget the trailing `;`—PHP code typed into the REPL follows the same syntax rules as PHP code you write in a regular program.

If you just typed `strlen("mushrooms");` the code would execute without any errors, but you wouldn't see any output before the next `php >` prompt. The PHP REPL only displays something if the PHP code you enter creates output.

The REPL remembers variables between commands. Entering `$releases = simplexml_load_file("https://secure.php.net/releases/feed.php");` uses the `simplexml_load_file()` function to retrieve the XML from the provided URL and store the results, as a SimpleXML object, in `$releases`.[1] SimpleXML provides a hierarchy of objects corresponding to the structure of the returned XML, so the value of the `title` element under the first `entry` element under the top-level XML element is `$releases->entry[0]->title`. When the code in Example 19-3 was run, the first element in the releases feed was PHP 7.0.5.

There are other REPLs aside from the built-in one. A nifty example is PsySH (*http://psysh.org*). You can install it with Composer: `php composer.phar global require psy/psysh`.

That `global` before `require` tells Composer to install PsySH not in any package-specific directory but in a systemwide Composer directory. On OS X and Linux, this is the *.composer* directory under your home directory. On Windows, it's *AppData \Roaming\Composer* under your home directory. For example, if you log in to your computer with username `squidsy`, then the Composer directory is */Users/ squidsy/.composer* on OS X, */home/squidsy/.composer* on Linux, and *C:\Users\squidsy \AppData\Roaming\Composer* on Windows.

The actual `psysh` program is put in a *vendor/bin* directory under the Composer directory. So, to run it from the command line, you either need to type out the full path (e.g., `/Users/squidsy/.composer/vendor/bin/psysh`) or add that *vendor/bin* directory to your system's `$PATH`, the default set of directories it looks in for program names that you type.

Once you run `psysh`, you get a prompt at which you can type in some PHP code. Unlike the built-in REPL, it prints the value a statement evaluates to (even if you don't include a `print` command) and uses different colors of text for different kinds of variables.

---

1 SimpleXML (*http://www.php.net/simplexml*) is a speedy way of doing XML processing in PHP.

Chapter Summary

This chapter covered:

- Running from the command line a PHP program you've written
- Accessing command-line arguments from a PHP program
- Running your PHP programs via the built-in web server
- Executing commands in the built-in PHP REPL
- Installing PsySH and running it from the global Composer directory

## CHAPTER 20

Internationalization and Localization

As mentioned in "Text" on page 19, strings in PHP are sequences of bytes. A byte can have up to 256 possible values. This means that representing text that only uses English characters (the US-ASCII character set) is straightforward in PHP, but you must take extra steps to ensure that processing text that contains other kinds of characters works properly.

The Unicode standard defines how computers encode the thousands and thousands of possible characters you can use. In addition to letters such as ä, ñ, ž, λ, כ ,ٮ, and ʢ , the standard also includes a variety of symbols and icons. The *UTF-8* encoding defines what bytes represent each character. The easy English characters are each represented by only one byte. But other characters may require two, three, or four bytes.

You probably don't have to do anything special to ensure your PHP installation uses UTF-8 for text processing. The `default_charset` configuration variable controls what encoding is used, and its default value is `UTF-8`. If you are having problems, make sure `default_charset` is set to `UTF-8`.

This chapter tours the basics of successfully working with multibyte UTF-8 characters in your PHP programs. The next section, "Manipulating Text", explains basic text manipulations, such as calculating length and extracting substrings. "Sorting and Comparing" on page 320 shows how to sort and compare strings in ways that respect different languages' rules for the proper order of characters. "Localizing Output" on page 321 provides examples of how to use PHP's message formatting features so your program can display information in a user's preferred language.

The code in this chapter relies on PHP functions in the `mbstring` and `intl` extensions. The functions in "Manipulating Text" whose names begin with `mb_` require the `mbstring` extension. The `Collator` and `MessageFormatter` classes referenced in "Sorting and Comparing" on page 320 and "Localizing Output" on page 321 require the `intl` extension. The `intl` extension in turn relies on the third-party ICU library (*http://site.icu-project.org/*). If these extensions aren't available, ask your system administrator or hosting provider to install them, or follow the instructions in Appendix A.

Manipulating Text

Since the `strlen()` function only counts bytes, it reports incorrect results when a character requires more than one byte. To count the characters in a string, independent of how many bytes each character requires, use `mb_strlen()`, as shown in Example 20-1.

Example 20-1. Measuring string length

```
$english = "cheese";
$greek = "τυρί";

print "strlen() says " . strlen($english) . " for $english and " .
    strlen($greek) . " for $greek.\n";

print "mb_strlen() says " . mb_strlen($english) . " for $english and " .
    mb_strlen($greek) . " for $greek.\n";
```

Since each of the Greek characters requires two bytes, the output of Example 20-1 is:

```
strlen() says 6 for cheese and 8 for τυρί.
mb_strlen() says 6 for cheese and 4 for τυρί.
```

Operations that depend on string positions, such as finding substrings, must also be done in a character-aware instead of byte-aware way when multibyte characters are used. Example 2-12 used `substr()` to extract the first 30 bytes of a user-submitted message. To extract the first 30 characters, use `mb_substr()` instead, as shown in Example 20-2.

Example 20-2. Extracting a substring

```
$message = "In Russia, I like to eat каша and drink квас.";

print "substr() says: " . substr($message, 0, 30) . "\n";
print "mb_substr() says: " . mb_substr($message, 0, 30) . "\n";
```

Example 20-2 prints:

```
substr() says: In Russia, I like to eat ка◆
mb_substr() says: In Russia, I like to eat каша
```

The line of output from `substr()` is totally bungled! Each Cyrillic character requires more than one byte, and 30 bytes into the string is midway through the byte sequence for a particular character. The output from `mb_substr()` stops properly on the correct character boundary.

What "uppercase" and "lowercase" mean is also different in different character sets. The `mb_strtolower()` and `mb_strtoupper()` functions provide character-aware versions of `strtolower()` and `strtoupper()`. Example 20-3 shows these functions at work.

Example 20-3. Changing case

```
$english = "Please stop shouting.";
$danish = "Venligst stoppe råben.";
$vietnamese = "Hãy dừng la hét.";

print "strtolower() says: \n";
print "    " . strtolower($english) . "\n";
print "    " . strtolower($danish) . "\n";
print "    " . strtolower($vietnamese) . "\n";

print "mb_strtolower() says: \n";
print "    " . mb_strtolower($english) . "\n";
print "    " . mb_strtolower($danish) . "\n";
print "    " . mb_strtolower($vietnamese) . "\n";

print "strtoupper() says: \n";
print "    " . strtoupper($english) . "\n";
print "    " . strtoupper($danish) . "\n";
print "    " . strtoupper($vietnamese) . "\n";

print "mb_strtoupper() says: \n";
print "    " . mb_strtoupper($english) . "\n";
print "    " . mb_strtoupper($danish) . "\n";
print "    " . mb_strtoupper($vietnamese) . "\n";
```

Example 20-3 prints:

```
strtolower() says:
    please stop shouting.
    venligst stoppe r♦ben.
    h♦y dừng la h♦t.
mb_strtolower() says:
    please stop shouting.
    venligst stoppe råben.
    hãy dừng la hét.
strtoupper() says:
    PLEASE STOP SHOUTING.
    VENLIGST STOPPE RåBEN.
    HãY D{NG LA HéT.
mb_strtoupper() says:
    PLEASE STOP SHOUTING.
```

VENLIGST STOPPE RÅBEN.
HÃY DỪNG LA HÉT.

Because strtoupper() and strtolower() work on individual bytes, they don't replace whole multibyte characters with the correct equivalents like mb_strtoupper() and mb_strtolower() do.

Sorting and Comparing

PHP's built-in text sorting and comparison functions also operate on a byte-by-byte basis following the order of letters in the English alphabet. Turn to the Collator class to do these operations in a character-aware manner.

First, construct a Collator object, passing its constructor a *locale string*. This string references a particular country and language and tells the Collator what rules to use. There are lots of finicky details (*http://userguide.icu-project.org/locale*) about what can go into a locale string, but usually it's a two-letter language code, then _, then a two-letter country code. For example, en_US for US English, or fr_BE for Belgian French, or ko_KR for South Korean. Both a language code and a country code are provided to allow for the different ways a language may be used in different countries.

The sort() method does the same thing as the built-in sort() function, but in a language-aware way: it sorts array values in place. Example 20-4 shows how this function works.

Example 20-4. Sorting arrays

```
// US English
$en = new Collator('en_US');
// Danish
$da = new Collator('da_DK');

$words = array('absent','åben','zero');

print "Before sorting: " . implode(', ', $words) . "\n";

$en->sort($words);
print "en_US sorting: " . implode(', ', $words) . "\n";

$da->sort($words);
print "da_DK sorting: " . implode(', ', $words) . "\n";
```

In Example 20-4, the US English rules put the Danish word åben before the English word absent, but in Danish, the å character sorts at the end of the alphabet, so åben goes at the end of the array.

The Collator class has an asort() method too that parallels the built-in asort() method. Also, the compare() method works like strcmp(). It returns -1 if the first string sorts before the second, 0 if they are equal, and 1 if the first string sorts after the second.

Localizing Output

An application used by people all over the world not only has to handle different character sets properly, but also has to produce messages in different languages. One person's "Click here" is another's "Cliquez ici" or "اضغط هنا" The MessageFormatter class helps you generate messages that are appropriately localized for different places.

First, you need to build a message catalog. This is a list of translated messages for each of the locales you support. They could be simple strings such as Click here, or they may contain markers for values to be interpolated, such as My favorite food is {0}, in which {0} should be replaced with a word.

In a big application, you may have hundreds of different items in your message catalog for each locale. To explain how MessageFormatter works, Example 20-5 shows a few entries in a sample catalog.

Example 20-5. Defining a message catalog

```
$messages = array();
$messages['en_US'] = array('FAVORITE_FOODS' => 'My favorite food is {0}',
                           'COOKIE' => 'cookie',
                           'SQUASH' => 'squash');
$messages['en_GB'] = array('FAVORITE_FOODS' => 'My favourite food is {0}',
                           'COOKIE' => 'biscuit',
                           'SQUASH' => 'marrow');
```

The keys in the $messages array are locale strings. The values are the messages appropriately translated for each locale, indexed by a key that is used to refer to the message later.

To create a locale-specific message, create a new MessageFormatter object by providing a locale and a message format to its constructor, as shown in Example 20-6.

Example 20-6. Formatting a message

```
$fmtfavs = new MessageFormatter('en_GB', $messages['en_GB']['FAVORITE_FOODS']);
$fmtcookie = new MessageFormatter('en_GB', $messages['en_GB']['COOKIE']);

// This returns "biscuit"
$cookie = $fmtcookie->format(array());
```

```
// This prints the sentence with "biscuit" substituted
print $fmtfavs->format(array($cookie));
```

Example 20-6 prints:

```
My favourite food is biscuit
```

When a message format has curly braces, the elements in the array passed as an argument to format() are substituted for the curly braces.

In Example 20-6, we had to do most of the work to figure out the right en_GB strings to use, so MessageFormatter didn't add much. It really helps, though, when you need locale-specific formatting of numbers and other data. Example 20-7 shows how MessageFormatter can properly handle numbers and money amounts in different locales.

Example 20-7. Formatting numbers in a message

```
$msg = "The cost is {0,number,currency}.";

$fmtUS = new MessageFormatter('en_US', $msg);
$fmtGB = new MessageFormatter('en_GB', $msg);

print $fmtUS->format(array(4.21)) . "\n";
print $fmtGB->format(array(4.21)) . "\n";
```

Example 20-7 prints:

```
The cost is $4.21.
The cost is £4.21.
```

Because MessageFormatter relies on the powerful ICU library, it uses its internal database of currency symbols, number formatting, and other rules about how different places and languages organize information to produce proper output.

The MessageFormatter class can do lots more than what's described here, such as format text properly for singular and plural, handle languages where the gender of a word affects how it's written, and format dates and times. If you want to learn more, check out the ICU User Guide to Formatting and Parsing (*http://userguide.icu-project.org/formatparse*).

Chapter Summary

This chapter covered:

- Understanding why some characters need more than one byte to represent them
- Measuring string length in characters instead of bytes
- Extracting substrings by character position
- Safely changing the case of characters
- Sorting text in a locale-aware manner
- Comparing strings in a locale-aware manner
- Localizing output for different locales

Installing and Configuring the PHP Engine

If you want to write some PHP programs, you need a PHP engine to turn them from punctuation-studded text files into actual interactive web pages. The easiest way to get up and running with PHP is to sign up with a cheap or free web-hosting provider that offers PHP—but you can run the PHP engine on your own computer, too.

Using PHP with a Web-Hosting Provider

If you already have an account with a web-hosting provider, you probably have access to a PHP-enabled server. These days, it is the odd web-hosting provider that *doesn't* have PHP support. Usually, hosting providers configure their servers so that files whose names end in *.php* are treated as PHP programs. To see whether your hosted website supports PHP, first save the file in Example A-1 on your server as *phptest.php*.

Example A-1. PHP test program

```
<?php print "PHP enabled"; ?>
```

Load the file in your browser by visiting the URL for your site (e.g., *http://www.example.com/phptest.php*). If you see just the message PHP enabled, then your website host supports PHP. If you see the entire contents of the page (<?php print "PHP enabled"; ?>), then your hosting provider probably doesn't support PHP. Check with them, however, to make sure that they haven't turned on PHP for a different file extension or made some other nonstandard configuration choice.

Installing the PHP Engine

Installing the PHP engine on your own computer is a good idea if you don't have an account with a hosting provider, or you just want to experiment with PHP without exposing your programs to the entire Internet. If you're not using a hosting provider and want to install the PHP engine on your own computer, follow the instructions in this section. After you've installed the engine, you'll be able to run your own PHP programs.

Installing the PHP engine is a matter of downloading some files and putting them in the right places on your computer. You may also need to configure your web server so that it knows about PHP. This section contains instructions on how to do this for computers running Linux and OS X, and also includes some references for how to install PHP on Windows. If you get stuck, check out the *php.net* installation FAQ (*http://www.php.net/manual/faq.installation*).

Installing on OS X

OS X comes with PHP 5.5 installed. However, to install a newer version of PHP and be able to easily manage add-ons and extensions, you'll want to install your own PHP engine using the Homebrew package manager. Homebrew helps you install OS X programs and the libraries those programs depend on.

First, install Homebrew if you don't already have it installed. Visit *http://brew.sh/* for all the nitty-gritty details, or just type the following into a Terminal prompt (on a single line):

```
ruby -e "$(curl -fsSL
https://raw.githubusercontent.com/Homebrew/install/master/install)"
```

If that's too much to type, visit the Homebrew site, from which you can copy the command to the clipboard and paste it into Terminal.

Once Homebrew is installed, you need to tell it where to find the latest and greatest PHP. Run these commands to do so:

```
brew tap homebrew/dupes
brew tap homebrew/versions
brew tap homebrew/homebrew-php
```

Then, to install PHP 7, run `brew install php70`. That's it!

At the end of installation, Homebrew prints out a bunch of stuff about configuring your setup. Pay attention to those instructions, since you need to follow them to tell your Mac's copy of the Apache web server where to find PHP.

Homebrew includes a number of extensions (including `intl` and `mbstring`, used in Chapter 20), but also offers other PHP extensions for installation. Run `brew search php70-` to see a list of extension packages. Installing one of those extensions and its dependent libraries is as easy as running `brew install` with the extension package name. For example, `brew install php70-gmp` installs the GMP (GNU Multiple Precision) extension for doing arbitrary-precision math with huge numbers.

Justin Hileman (*http://bit.ly/hileman-php/*) has more details on installing PHP with Homebrew.

Installing on Linux

Most Linux distributions come with PHP already installed or with binary PHP packages that you can install. For example, if you're using Fedora Linux (*https://getfe dora.org*), use `yum` to install the `php` package. If you're using Ubuntu (*http://www.ubuntu.com/*), use `apt-get` to install the package. The most up-to-date PHP 5 package is `php5`, and at the time of writing, an official `php7` package is not available yet. A well-supported PHP 7 package for Ubuntu is available from an alternate source. First, run `sudo add-apt-repository ppa:ondrej/php` and `sudo apt-get update`, and then you can install the `php7.0` package with `apt-get`.

If those packages are out of date, you can build PHP yourself. Download (*http://www.php.net/downloads.php*) the Current Stable *.tar.gz* package. From a shell prompt, uncompress and unpack the archive:

```
gunzip php-7.0.5.tar.gz
tar xvf php-7.0.5.tar
```

This creates a directory, *php-7.0.5*, that contains the PHP engine source code. Read the file *INSTALL* at the top level of the source code directory for detailed installation instructions. There is also an overview of PHP installation on Linux and Unix on *php.net* (*http://www.php.net/manual/install.unix*), as well as instructions for installing PHP with Apache 2.0 (*http://www.php.net/manual/install.unix.apache2*).

Installing on Windows

Installing PHP on Windows is a little different than on OS X or Linux. The assumptions that the PHP engine can make about the things it needs when it's being installed are different, as well as the tools that might be available for it to compile itself.

Fortunately, there are several good all-in-one packages that combine PHP, Apache, and MySQL for Windows. These include WampServer (*http://www.wampserver.com/en/*), the Bitnami WAMP Stack (*https://bitnami.com/stack/wamp*), and Apache Friends XAMPP (*https://www.apachefriends.org/index.html*).

Microsoft maintains a website devoted to running PHP with IIS (*http://php.iis.net/*). Additionally, the official PHP For Windows website (*http://windows.php.net/*) has different versions of PHP for Windows available for download.

Modifying PHP Configuration Directives

Earlier chapters in the book mention various PHP *configuration directives*. These are settings that affect the behavior of the PHP engine, such as how errors are reported, where the PHP engine looks for included files and extensions, and much more.

Read this section when you encounter a configuration directive you want to alter or are curious about how you can tweak the PHP engine's settings (whether you are using PHP on your own computer or with a hosting provider). For example, changing the `output_buffering` directive (as discussed in "Why setcookie() and session_start() Want to Be at the Top of the Page" on page 226) makes your life much easier if you are working with cookies and sessions.

The values of configuration directives can be changed in a few places: in the PHP engine's *php.ini* configuration file, in Apache's *httpd.conf* or *.htaccess* configuration files, and in your PHP programs. Not all configuration directives can be changed in all places. If you can edit your *php.ini* or *httpd.conf* file, it's easiest to set PHP configuration directives there. But if you can't change those files because of server permissions, then you can still change some settings in your PHP programs.

If your web server talks to the PHP engine using CGI or FastCGI, you can also set configuration directives in *.user.ini* files. In PHP 5.3.0 and later, the PHP engine looks for a file called *.user.ini* in the same directory as the PHP program it's running. If the PHP program is inside the web server's document root, the PHP engine also looks in the program's parent directory, and that directory's parent, and so on, up to the document root. The syntax for *.user.ini* files is the same as for the main *php.ini* file.

The *php.ini* file holds systemwide configuration for the PHP engine. When the web server process starts up, the PHP engine reads the *php.ini* file and adjusts its configuration accordingly. To find the location of your system's *php.ini* file, examine the output from the `phpinfo()` function. This function prints a report of the PHP engine's configuration. The tiny program in Example A-2 produces a page that looks like the one in Figure A-1.

Example A-2. Getting configuration details with phpinfo()

```
<?php phpinfo(); ?>
```

In Figure A-1, the sixth line (`Configuration File (php.ini) Path`) shows that the *php.ini* file is located at */php7/etc/php.ini*. Your *php.ini* file may be in a different place.

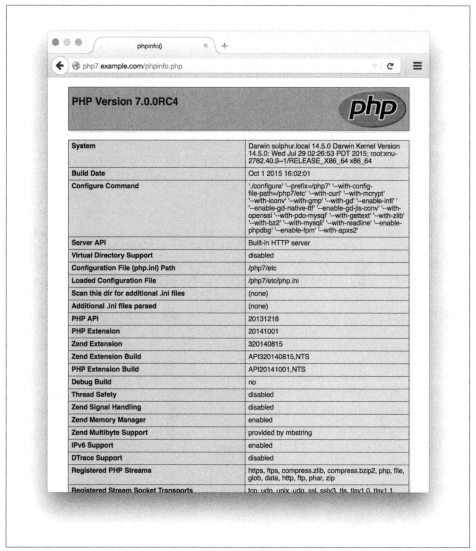

Figure A-1. Output of phpinfo()

In the *php.ini* file, lines that begin with a semicolon (;) are comments. Lines that set values for configuration directives look like those shown in Example A-3.

Example A-3. Sample lines in php.ini

```
; How to specify directories on Unix: forward slash for a separator
; and a colon between the directory names
include_path = ".:/usr/local/lib/php/includes"
```

```
; How to specify directories on Windows: backslash for a separator
; and a semicolon between the directory names
; Windows: "\path1;\path2"
include_path = ".;c:\php\includes"

; Report all errors except notices
error_reporting = E_ALL & ~E_NOTICE

; Record errors in the error log
log_errors = On

; An uploaded file can't be more than 2 megabytes
upload_max_filesize = 2M

; Sessions expire after 1440 seconds
session.gc_maxlifetime = 1440
```

The error_reporting configuration directive is set by combining built-in constants with logical operators. For example, the line error_reporting = E_ALL & ~E_NOTICE sets error_reporting to E_ALL but not E_NOTICE. The operators you can use are & ("and"), | ("either ... or"), and ~ ("not"). So, to the PHP engine, E_ALL & ~E_NOTICE means E_ALL and not E_NOTICE. You may find it easier to read "and not" as "but not," as in E_ALL but not E_NOTICE. The setting E_ALL | E_NOTICE means either E_ALL or E_NOTICE.

When setting a configuration directive whose value is a number (such as upload_max_filesize), you can use M (for megabyte) or K (for kilobyte) at the end of the number to multiply by 1,048,576 or 1,024. Setting upload_max_filesize=2M is the same as setting upload_max_filesize=2097152. There are 1,048,576 bytes in a megabyte, and 2,097,152 = 2 * 1,048,576.

To change a configuration directive in Apache's *httpd.conf* or *.htaccess* file, you must use a slightly different syntax, shown in Example A-4.

Example A-4. Sample PHP configuration lines in httpd.conf

```
; How to specify directories on Unix: forward slash for a separator
; and a colon between the directory names
php_value include_path ".:/usr/local/lib/php/includes"

; How to specify directories on Windows: backslash for a separator
; and a semicolon between the directory names
; Windows: "\path1;\path2"
php_value include_path ".;c:\php\includes"

; Report all errors but notices
php_value error_reporting "E_ALL & ~E_NOTICE"

; Record errors in the error log
```

```
php_flag log_errors On

; An uploaded file can't be more than 2 megabytes
php_value upload_max_filesize 2M

; Sessions expire after 1440 seconds
php_value session.gc_maxlifetime 1440
```

The php_flag and php_value words in Example A-4 tell Apache that the rest of the line is a PHP configuration directive. After php_flag, put the name of the configuration directive and then On or Off. After php_value, put the name of the directive and then its value. If the value has spaces in it (such as E_ALL & ~E_NOTICE), you must put it in quotes. There is no equals sign between the name of the configuration directive and the value.

To change a configuration directive from within a PHP program, use the ini_set() function. Example A-5 sets error_reporting from within a PHP program.

Example A-5. Changing a configuration directive with ini_set()

```
ini_set('error_reporting',E_ALL & ~E_NOTICE);
```

The first argument to ini_set() is the name of the configuration directive to set. The second argument is the value to which you want to set the configuration directive. For error_reporting, that value is the same logical expression as you'd put in *php.ini*. For configuration directives whose values are strings or integers, pass the string or integer to ini_set(). For configuration directives whose values are On or Off, pass 1 (for On) or 0 (for Off) to ini_set().

To find the value of a configuration directive from within a program, use ini_get( ). Pass it the name of the configuration directive, and it returns the value. This is useful for adding a directory to the include_path, as shown in Example A-6.

Example A-6. Changing include_path with ini_get() and ini_set()

```
// These lines add /home/ireneo/php to the end of the include_path
$include_path = ini_get('include_path');
ini_set('include_path',$include_path . ':/home/ireneo/php');
```

As mentioned earlier, not all configuration directives can be set in all places. There are some configuration directives that cannot be set from within your PHP programs. These are directives that the PHP engine must know about before it starts reading your program, such as output_buffering. The output_buffering directive makes a change to the engine's behavior that must be active before the engine gets a look at your program, so you can't set output_buffering with ini_set(). In addition, some configuration directives are prohibited from being set in Apache *.htaccess* files and some from being set in the Apache *httpd.conf* file. All configuration directives can be set in the *php.ini* file.

The PHP Manual (*http://www.php.net/ini.list*) has a big list of all the configuration directives and the contexts in which they can be changed. Some useful configuration directives to know about are listed in Table A-1.

Table A-1. Useful configuration directives

Directive	Recommended value	Description
allow_url_fopen	On	Whether to allow functions such as file_get_contents() to work with URLs in addition to local files.
auto_append_file		Set this to a filename to have the PHP code in that file run after the PHP engine runs a program. This is useful for printing out a common page footer.
auto_prepend_file		Set this to a filename to have the PHP code in that file run before the PHP engine runs a program. This is useful for defining functions or including files that you use in your entire site.
date.timezone	UTC	The PHP engine needs a default timezone set before you call any date or time functions. Using UTC, as discussed in "Working with Timezones" on page 291, makes many time-related tasks easier.
display_errors	On for debugging, Off for production	When this is on, the PHP engine prints errors as part of your program output.
error_reporting	E_ALL	This controls what kinds of errors the PHP engine reports. See "Controlling Where Errors Appear" on page 249.
extension		Each extension line in *php.ini* loads a PHP extension. The extension library must be present on your system to load it.
extension_dir		The directory the PHP engine looks in to find extensions specified by the extension directive.
file_uploads	On	Whether to allow file uploads via forms.
include_path		A list of directories that the PHP engine looks in for files loaded via include, require, include_once, and require_once.
log_errors	On	When this is on, the PHP engine puts program errors in the web server error log.
output_buffering	On	When this is on, the PHP engine waits until your script runs before it sends HTTP headers, making it easier to use cookies and sessions. See "Why setcookie() and session_start() Want to Be at the Top of the Page" on page 226 in Chapter 10.
session.auto_start	On (if you're using sessions)	When this is on, the PHP engine starts a session at the beginning of each page, so you don't have to call session_start().
session.gc_maxlifetime	1440	The number of seconds that a session should last. The default value of 1440 is fine for most applications.

Directive	Recommended value	Description
session.gc_probability	1	The likelihood (out of 100) that expired sessions are cleaned up at the beginning of any request. The default value of 1 is fine for most applications.
short_open_tag	Off	When this is on, you can start a PHP block with <? as well as <?php. Since not all servers are configured to accept short tags, it's good practice to leave this off and always use the <?php start tag.
track_errors	On for debugging, Off for production	When this is on, the PHP engine stores an error message in the global variable $php_errormsg when it encounters a problem. See "Checking for Errors" on page 199.
upload_max_filesize	2M	The maximum permitted size for a file uploaded via a form. Unless you are building an application that requires users to upload very large files, don't increase this value. Lots of large uploaded files can clog your server.

Appendix Summary

This appendix covered:

- Using PHP with a web-hosting provider
- Installing the PHP engine on OS X, Linux, or Windows
- Using phpinfo() to see the PHP engine's configuration
- Understanding the structure of the *php.ini* configuration file
- Configuring the PHP engine in the *httpd.conf* configuration file
- Reading and writing configuration directive values with ini_get() and ini_set()
- Using common configuration directives

Answers to Exercises

Chapter 2

Exercise 1

1. The opening PHP tag should be just <?php with no space between the <? and php.
2. Because the string I'm fine contains a ', it should be surrounded by double quotes ("I'm fine") or the ' should be escaped ('I\'m fine').
3. The closing PHP tag should be ?>, not ??>. Or, if this code were the last thing in its file, the closing PHP tag could be omitted.

Exercise 2

```
$hamburger = 4.95;
$shake = 1.95;
$cola = 0.85;

$tip_rate = 0.16;
$tax_rate = 0.075;

$food = (2 * $hamburger) + $shake + $cola;
$tip = $food * $tip_rate;
$tax = $food * $tax_rate;

$total = $food + $tip + $tax;

print 'The total cost of the meal is $' . $total;
```

Exercise 3

```
$hamburger = 4.95;
$shake = 1.95;
$cola = 0.85;

$tip_rate = 0.16;
$tax_rate = 0.075;

$food = (2 * $hamburger) + $shake + $cola;
$tip = $food * $tip_rate;
$tax = $food * $tax_rate;

$total = $food + $tip + $tax;

printf("%d %-9s at \$%.2f each: \$%5.2f\n", 2, 'Hamburger', $hamburger,
        2 * $hamburger);
printf("%d %-9s at \$%.2f each: \$%5.2f\n", 1, 'Shake', $shake, $hamburger);
printf("%d %-9s at \$%.2f each: \$%5.2f\n", 1, 'Cola', $cola, $cola);
printf("%25s: \$%5.2f\n", 'Food Total', $food);
printf("%25s: \$%5.2f\n", 'Food and Tax Total', $food + $tax);
printf("%25s: \$%5.2f\n", 'Food, Tax, and Tip Total', $total);
```

Exercise 4

```
$first_name = 'Srinivasa';
$last_name = 'Ramanujan';
$name = "$first_name $last_name";
print $name;
print strlen($name);
```

Exercise 5

```
$n = 1; $p = 2;
print "$n, $p\n";

$n++; $p *= 2;
print "$n, $p\n";

$n++; $p *= 2;
print "$n, $p\n";

$n++; $p *= 2;
print "$n, $p\n";

$n++; $p *= 2;
print "$n, $p\n";
```

Chapter 3

Exercise 1

1. false
2. true
3. true
4. false
5. false
6. true
7. true
8. false

Exercise 2

Message 3.Age: 12. Shoe Size: 14

Exercise 3

```
$f = -50;
while ($f <= 50) {
    $c = ($f - 32) * (5/9);
    printf("%d degrees F = %d degrees C\n", $f, $c);
    $f += 5;
}
```

Exercise 4

```
for ($f = -50; $f <= 50; $f += 5) {
    $c = ($f - 32) * (5/9);
    printf("%d degrees F = %d degrees C\n", $f, $c);
}
```

Chapter 4

Exercise 1

```
<table>
<tr><th>City</th><th>Population</th></tr>
<?php
$census = ['New York, NY' => 8175133,
           'Los Angeles, CA' => 3792621,
           'Chicago, IL' => 2695598,
           'Houston, TX' => 2100263,
           'Philadelphia, PA' => 1526006,
           'Phoenix, AZ' => 1445632,
```

```
                    'San Antonio, TX' => 1327407,
                    'San Diego, CA' => 1307402,
                    'Dallas, TX' => 1197816,
                    'San Jose, CA' => 945942];

$total = 0;
foreach ($census as $city => $population) {
    $total += $population;
    print "<tr><td>$city</td><td>$population</td></tr>\n";
}
print "<tr><td>Total</td><td>$total</td></tr>\n";
print "</table>";
```

Exercise 2

```
$census = ['New York, NY' => 8175133,
           'Los Angeles, CA' => 3792621,
           'Chicago, IL' => 2695598,
           'Houston, TX' => 2100263,
           'Philadelphia, PA' => 1526006,
           'Phoenix, AZ' => 1445632,
           'San Antonio, TX' => 1327407,
           'San Diego, CA' => 1307402,
           'Dallas, TX' => 1197816,
           'San Jose, CA' => 945942];

// Sort the associative array by value
asort($census);

print "<table>\n";
print "<tr><th>City</th><th>Population</th></tr>\n";
$total = 0;
foreach ($census as $city => $population) {
    $total += $population;
    print "<tr><td>$city</td><td>$population</td></tr>\n";
}
print "<tr><td>Total</td><td>$total</td></tr>\n";
print "</table>";

// Sort the associative array by key
ksort($census);

print "<table>\n";
print "<tr><th>City</th><th>Population</th></tr>\n";
$total = 0;
foreach ($census as $city => $population) {
    $total += $population;
    print "<tr><td>$city</td><td>$population</td></tr>\n";
}
print "<tr><td>Total</td><td>$total</td></tr>\n";
print "</table>";
```

Exercise 3

```
<table>
<tr><th>City</th><th>Population</th></tr>
<?php
// Each element in $census is a three-element array
// containing city name, state, and population
$census = [ ['New York', 'NY', 8175133],
            ['Los Angeles', 'CA' , 3792621],
            ['Chicago', 'IL' , 2695598],
            ['Houston', 'TX' , 2100263],
            ['Philadelphia', 'PA' , 1526006],
            ['Phoenix', 'AZ' , 1445632],
            ['San Antonio', 'TX' , 1327407],
            ['San Diego', 'CA' , 1307402],
            ['Dallas', 'TX' , 1197816],
            ['San Jose', 'CA' , 945942] ];

$total = 0;
$state_totals = array();
foreach ($census as $city_info) {
    // Update the total population
    $total += $city_info[2];
    // If we haven't seen this state yet, initialize its
    // population total to 0
    if (! array_key_exists($city_info[1], $state_totals)) {
        $state_totals[$city_info[1]] = 0;
    }
    // Update the per-state population
    $state_totals[$city_info[1]] += $city_info[2];
    print "<tr><td>$city_info[0], $city_info[1]</td><td>
        $city_info[2]</td></tr>\n";
}
print "<tr><td>Total</td><td>$total</td></tr>\n";
// Print the per-state totals
foreach ($state_totals as $state => $population) {
    print "<tr><td>$state</td><td>$population</td></tr>\n";
}
print "</table>";
```

Exercise 4

```
/* The grades and ID numbers of students in a class:
   An associative array whose key is the student's name and whose value is
   an associative array of grade and ID number
*/
$students = [ 'James D. McCawley' => [ 'grade' => 'A+','id' => 271231 ],
              'Buwei Yang Chao' => [ 'grade' => 'A', 'id' => 818211 ] ];

/* How many of each item in a store inventory are in stock:
   An associative array whose key is the item name and whose value is the
   number in stock
*/
```

```
*/
$inventory = [ 'Wok' => 5, 'Steamer' => 3, 'Heavy Cleaver' => 3,
               'Light Cleaver' => 0 ];

/* School lunches for a week — the different parts of each meal
   (entree, side dish, drink, etc.) and the cost for each day:
   An associative array whose key is the day and whose value is an
   associative array describing the meal. This associative array has a key/value
   pair for cost and a key/value pair for each part of the meal.
*/
$lunches = [ 'Monday' => [ 'cost' => 1.50,
                           'entree' => 'Beef Shu-Mai',
                           'side' => 'Salty Fried Cake',
                           'drink' => 'Black Tea' ],
             'Tuesday' => [ 'cost' => 2.50,
                            'entree' => 'Clear-steamed Fish',
                            'side' => 'Turnip Cake',
                            'drink' => 'Bubble Tea' ],
             'Wednesday' => [ 'cost' => 2.00,
                              'entree' => 'Braised Sea Cucumber',
                              'side' => 'Turnip Cake',
                              'drink' => 'Green Tea' ],
             'Thursday' => [ 'cost' => 1.35,
                             'entree' => 'Stir-fried Two Winters',
                             'side' => 'Egg Puff',
                             'drink' => 'Black Tea' ],
             'Friday' => [ 'cost' => 3.25,
                           'entree' => 'Stewed Pork with Taro',
                           'side' => 'Duck Feet',
                           'drink' => 'Jasmine Tea' ] ];


/* The names of people in your family:
   A numeric array whose indices are implicit and whose values are the names
   of family members
 */
$family = [ 'Bart', 'Lisa', 'Homer', 'Marge', 'Maggie' ];

/* The names, ages, and relationship to you of people in your family:
   An associative array whose keys are the names of family members and whose
   values are associative arrays with age and relationship key/value pairs
 */
$family = [ 'Bart' => [ 'age' => 10,
                        'relation' => 'brother' ],
            'Lisa' => [ 'age' => 7,
                        'relation' => 'sister' ],
            'Homer' => [ 'age' => 36,
                         'relation' => 'father' ],
            'Marge' => [ 'age' => 34,
                         'relation' => 'mother' ],
            'Maggie' => [ 'age' => 1,
                          'relation' => 'self' ] ];
```

Chapter 5

Exercise 1

```php
function html_img($url, $alt = null, $height = null, $width = null) {
    $html = '<img src="' . $url . '"';
    if (isset($alt)) {
        $html .= ' alt="' . $alt . '"';
    }
    if (isset($height)) {
        $html .= ' height="' . $height . '"';
    }
    if (isset($width)) {
        $html .= ' width="' . $width . '"';
    }
    $html .= '/>';
    return $html;
}
```

Exercise 2

```php
function html_img2($file, $alt = null, $height = null, $width = null) {
    if (isset($GLOBALS['image_path'])) {
        $file = $GLOBALS['image_path'] . $file;
    }
    $html = '<img src="' . $file . '"';
    if (isset($alt)) {
        $html .= ' alt="' . $alt . '"';
    }
    if (isset($height)) {
        $html .= ' height="' . $height . '"';
    }
    if (isset($width)) {
        $html .= ' width="' . $width . '"';
    }
    $html .= '/>';
    return $html;
}
```

Exercise 3

```php
// The html_img2() function from the previous exercise is saved in this file
include "html-img2.php";

$image_path = '/images/';

print html_img2('puppy.png');
print html_img2('kitten.png','fuzzy');
print html_img2('dragon.png',null,640,480);
```

Exercise 4

```
I can afford a tip of 11% (30)
I can afford a tip of 12% (30.25)
I can afford a tip of 13% (30.5)
I can afford a tip of 14% (30.75)
```

Exercise 5

```php
/* Using dechex(): */
function web_color1($red, $green, $blue) {
    $hex = [ dechex($red), dechex($green), dechex($blue) ];
    // Prepend a leading 0 if necessary to 1-digit hex values
    foreach ($hex as $i => $val) {
        if (strlen($i) == 1) {
            $hex[$i] = "0$val";
        }
    }
    return '#' . implode('', $hex);
}

/* You can also rely on sprintf()'s %x format character to do
   hex-to-decimal conversion: */
function web_color2($red, $green, $blue) {
    return sprintf('#%02x%02x%02x', $red, $green, $blue);
}
```

Chapter 6

Exercise 1

```php
class Ingredient {
    protected $name;
    protected $cost;

    public function __construct($name, $cost) {
        $this->name = $name;
        $this->cost = $cost;
    }

    public function getName() {
        return $this->name;
    }

    public function getCost() {
        return $this->cost;
    }
}
```

Exercise 2

```php
class Ingredient {
    protected $name;
    protected $cost;

    public function __construct($name, $cost) {
        $this->name = $name;
        $this->cost = $cost;
    }

    public function getName() {
        return $this->name;
    }

    public function getCost() {
        return $this->cost;
    }

    // This method sets the cost to a new value
    public function setCost($cost) {
        $this->cost = $cost;
    }

}
```

Exercise 3

```php
class PricedEntree extends Entree {
    public function __construct($name, $ingredients) {
        parent::__construct($name, $ingredients);
        foreach ($this->ingredients as $ingredient) {
            if (! $ingredient instanceof Ingredient) {
                throw new Exception('Elements of $ingredients must be
                Ingredient objects');
            }
        }
    }

    public function getCost() {
        $cost = 0;
        foreach ($this->ingredients as $ingredient) {
            $cost += $ingredient->getCost();
        }
        return $cost;
    }
}
```

Exercise 4

The `Ingredient` class in its own namespace:

```php
namespace Meals;

class Ingredient {
    protected $name;
    protected $cost;

    public function __construct($name, $cost) {
        $this->name = $name;
        $this->cost = $cost;
    }

    public function getName() {
        return $this->name;
    }

    public function getCost() {
        return $this->cost;
    }

    // This method sets the cost to a new value
    public function setCost($cost) {
        $this->cost = $cost;
    }

}
```

The `PricedEntree` class referencing that namespace:

```php
class PricedEntree extends Entree {
    public function __construct($name, $ingredients) {
        parent::__construct($name, $ingredients);
        foreach ($this->ingredients as $ingredient) {
            if (! $ingredient instanceof \Meals\Ingredient) {
                throw new Exception('Elements of $ingredients must be
                Ingredient objects');
            }
        }
    }

    public function getCost() {
        $cost = 0;
        foreach ($this->ingredients as $ingredient) {
            $cost += $ingredient->getCost();
        }
        return $cost;
    }
}
```

Chapter 7

Exercise 1

```
$_POST['noodle'] = 'barbecued pork';
$_POST['sweet'] = [ 'puff', 'ricemeat' ];
$_POST['sweet_q'] = '4';
$_POST['submit'] = 'Order';
```

Exercise 2

```
/* Since this is operating on form data, it looks directly at $_POST
   instead of a validated $input array */
function process_form() {
    print '<ul>';
    foreach ($_POST as $k => $v) {
        print '<li>' . htmlentities($k) .'=' . htmlentities($v) . '</li>';
    }
    print '</ul>';
}
```

Exercise 3

```
<?php

// This assumes FormHelper.php is in the same directory as
// this file.
require 'FormHelper.php';

// Set up the arrays of choices in the select menu.
// This is needed in display_form(), validate_form(),
// and process_form(), so it is declared in the global scope.
$ops = array('+','-','*','/');

// The main page logic:
// - If the form is submitted, validate and then process or redisplay
// - If it's not submitted, display
if ($_SERVER['REQUEST_METHOD'] == 'POST') {
    // If validate_form() returns errors, pass them to show_form()
    list($errors, $input) = validate_form();
    if ($errors) {
        show_form($errors);
    } else {
        // The submitted data is valid, so process it
        process_form($input);
        // And then show the form again to do another calculation
        show_form();
    }
} else {
    // The form wasn't submitted, so display
    show_form();
```

```
}

function show_form($errors = array()) {
    $defaults = array('num1' => 2,
                      'op' => 2, // the index of '*' in $ops
                      'num2' => 8);
    // Set up the $form object with proper defaults
    $form = new FormHelper($defaults);

    // All the HTML and form display is in a separate file for clarity
    include 'math-form.php';
}

function validate_form() {
    $input = array();
    $errors = array();

    // op is required
    $input['op'] = $GLOBALS['ops'][$_POST['op']] ?? '';
    if (! in_array($input['op'], $GLOBALS['ops'])) {
        $errors[] = 'Please select a valid operation.';
    }
    // num1 and num2 must be numbers
    $input['num1'] = filter_input(INPUT_POST, 'num1', FILTER_VALIDATE_FLOAT);
    if (is_null($input['num1']) || ($input['num1'] === false)) {
        $errors[] = 'Please enter a valid first number.';
    }

    $input['num2'] = filter_input(INPUT_POST, 'num2', FILTER_VALIDATE_FLOAT);
    if (is_null($input['num2']) || ($input['num2'] === false)) {
        $errors[] = 'Please enter a valid second number.';
    }

    // Can't divide by zero
    if (($input['op'] == '/') && ($input['num2'] == 0)) {
        $errors[] = 'Division by zero is not allowed.';
    }

    return array($errors, $input);
}

function process_form($input) {
    $result = 0;
    if ($input['op'] == '+') {
        $result = $input['num1'] + $input['num2'];
    }
    else if ($input['op'] == '-') {
        $result = $input['num1'] - $input['num2'];
    }
    else if ($input['op'] == '*') {
        $result = $input['num1'] * $input['num2'];
    }
```

```php
    else if ($input['op'] == '/') {
        $result = $input['num1'] / $input['num2'];
    }
    $message = "{$input['num1']} {$input['op']} {$input['num2']} = $result";

    print "<h3>$message</h3>";
}
?>
```

The code relies on the *FormHelper.php* file discussed in Chapter 7. The *math-form.php* file referenced, which displays the form HTML, contains:

```php
<form method="POST" action="<?= $form->encode($_SERVER['PHP_SELF']) ?>">
<table>
    <?php if ($errors) { ?>
        <tr>
            <td>You need to correct the following errors:</td>
            <td><ul>
                <?php foreach ($errors as $error) { ?>
                    <li><?= $form->encode($error) ?></li>
                <?php } ?>
            </ul></td>
    <?php }  ?>

    <tr><td>First Number:</td>
        <td><?= $form->input('text', ['name' => 'num1']) ?></td>
    </tr>
    <tr><td>Operation:</td>
        <td><?= $form->select($GLOBALS['ops'], ['name' => 'op']) ?></td>
    </tr>
    <tr><td>Second Number:</td>
        <td><?= $form->input('text', ['name' => 'num2']) ?></td>
    </tr>

    <tr><td colspan="2" align="center"><?= $form->input('submit',
    ['value' => 'Calculate']) ?>
    </td></tr>

</table>
</form>
```

Exercise 4

```php
<?php

// This assumes FormHelper.php is in the same directory as
// this file.
require 'FormHelper.php';

// Set up the array of choices in the select menu.
// This is needed in display_form(), validate_form(),
// and process_form(), so it is declared in the global scope.
```

```php
$states = [ 'AL', 'AK', 'AZ', 'AR', 'CA', 'CO', 'CT', 'DC', 'DE', 'FL', 'GA',
'HI', 'ID', 'IL', 'IN', 'IA', 'KS', 'KY', 'LA', 'ME', 'MD', 'MA', 'MI', 'MN',
'MS', 'MO', 'MT', 'NE', 'NV', 'NH', 'NJ', 'NM', 'NY', 'NC', 'ND', 'OH', 'OK',
'OR', 'PA', 'RI', 'SC', 'SD', 'TN', 'TX', 'UT', 'VT', 'VA', 'WA', 'WV', 'WI',
'WY' ];

// The main page logic:
// - If the form is submitted, validate and then process or redisplay
// - If it's not submitted, display
if ($_SERVER['REQUEST_METHOD'] == 'POST') {
    // If validate_form() returns errors, pass them to show_form()
    list($errors, $input) = validate_form();
    if ($errors) {
        show_form($errors);
    } else {
        // The submitted data is valid, so process it
        process_form($input);
    }
} else {
    // The form wasn't submitted, so display
    show_form();
}

function show_form($errors = array()) {
    // Set up the $form object with proper defaults
    $form = new FormHelper();

    // All the HTML and form display is in a separate file for clarity
    include 'shipping-form.php';
}

function validate_form() {
    $input = array();
    $errors = array();

    foreach (['from','to'] as $addr) {
        // Check required fields
        foreach (['Name' => 'name', 'Address 1' => 'address1',
                'City' => 'city', 'State' => 'state'] as $label => $field){
            $input[$addr.'_'.$field] = $_POST[$addr.'_'.$field] ?? '';
            if (strlen($input[$addr.'_'.$field]) == 0) {
                $errors[] = "Please enter a value for $addr $label.";
            }
        }
        // Check state
        $input[$addr.'_state'] =
        $GLOBALS['states'][$input[$addr.'_state']] ?? '';
        if (! in_array($input[$addr.'_state'], $GLOBALS['states'])) {
            $errors[] = "Please select a valid $addr state.";
        }
        // Check zip code
        $input[$addr.'_zip'] = filter_input(INPUT_POST, $addr.'_zip',
```

```
                                FILTER_VALIDATE_INT,
                                ['options' => ['min_range'=>10000,
                                              'max_range'=>99999]]);
        if (is_null($input[$addr.'_zip']) || ($input[$addr.'_zip']===false)) {
            $errors[] = "Please enter a valid $addr ZIP";
        }
        // Don't forget about address2!
        $input[$addr.'_address2'] = $_POST[$addr.'_address2'] ?? '';
    }

    // height, width, depth, weight must all be numbers > 0
    foreach(['height','width','depth','weight'] as $field) {
        $input[$field] =filter_input(INPUT_POST, $field, FILTER_VALIDATE_FLOAT);
        // Since 0 is not valid, we can just test for truth rather than
        // null or exactly false
        if (! ($input[$field] && ($input[$field] > 0))) {
            $errors[] = "Please enter a valid $field.";
        }
    }
    // Check weight
    if ($input['weight'] > 150) {
        $errors[] = "The package must weigh no more than 150 lbs.";
    }
    // Check dimensions
    foreach(['height','width','depth'] as $dim) {
        if ($input[$dim] > 36) {
            $errors[] = "The package $dim must be no more than 36 inches.";
        }
    }

    return array($errors, $input);
}

function process_form($input) {
    // Make a template for the report
    $tpl=<<<HTML
<p>Your package is {height}" x {width}" x {depth}" and weighs {weight} lbs.</p>

<p>It is coming from:</p>
<pre>
{from_name}
{from_address}
{from_city}, {from_state} {from_zip}
</pre>

<p>It is going to:</p>
<pre>
{to_name}
{to_address}
{to_city}, {to_state} {to_zip}
</pre>
HTML;
```

```
    // Adjust addresses in $input for easier output
    foreach(['from','to'] as $addr) {
        $input[$addr.'_address'] = $input[$addr.'_address1'];
        if (strlen($input[$addr.'_address2'])) {
            $input[$addr.'_address'] .= "\n" . $input[$addr.'_address2'];
        }
    }

    // Replace each template variable with the corresponding value
    // in $input
    $html = $tpl;
    foreach($input as $k => $v) {
        $html = str_replace('{'.$k.'}', $v, $html);
    }

    // Print the report
    print $html;
}
?>
```

The code relies on the *FormHelper.php* file discussed in Chapter 7. The *shipping-form.php* file referenced, which displays the form HTML, contains:

```
<form method="POST" action="<?= $form->encode($_SERVER['PHP_SELF']) ?>">
<table>
    <?php if ($errors) { ?>
        <tr>
            <td>You need to correct the following errors:</td>
            <td><ul>
                <?php foreach ($errors as $error) { ?>
                    <li><?= $form->encode($error) ?></li>
                <?php } ?>
            </ul></td>
    <?php } ?>

    <tr><th>From:</th><td></td></tr>
    <tr><td>Name:</td>
        <td><?= $form->input('text', ['name' => 'from_name']) ?></td></tr>
    <tr><td>Address 1:</td>
        <td><?= $form->input('text', ['name' => 'from_address1']) ?></td></tr>
    <tr><td>Address 2:</td>
        <td><?= $form->input('text', ['name' => 'from_address2']) ?></td></tr>
    <tr><td>City:</td>
        <td><?= $form->input('text', ['name' => 'from_city']) ?></td></tr>
    <tr><td>State:</td>
        <td><?= $form->select($GLOBALS['states'], ['name' => 'from_state']) ?>
        </td></tr>
    <tr><td>ZIP:</td>
        <td><?= $form->input('text', ['name' => 'from_zip', 'size' => 5]) ?>
        </td></tr>

    <tr><th>To:</th><td></td></tr>
```

```
    <tr><td>Name:</td>
        <td><?= $form->input('text', ['name' => 'to_name']) ?></td></tr>
    <tr><td>Address 1:</td>
        <td><?= $form->input('text', ['name' => 'to_address1']) ?></td></tr>
    <tr><td>Address 2:</td>
        <td><?= $form->input('text', ['name' => 'to_address2']) ?></td></tr>
    <tr><td>City:</td>
        <td><?= $form->input('text', ['name' => 'to_city']) ?></td></tr>
    <tr><td>State:</td>
        <td><?= $form->select($GLOBALS['states'], ['name' => 'to_state']) ?>
        </td></tr>
    <tr><td>ZIP:</td>
        <td><?= $form->input('text', ['name' => 'to_zip', 'size' => 5]) ?>
        </td></tr>

    <tr><th>Package:</th><td></td></tr>
    <tr><td>Weight:</td>
        <td><?= $form->input('text', ['name' => 'weight']) ?></td></tr>
    <tr><td>Height:</td>
        <td><?= $form->input('text', ['name' => 'height']) ?></td></tr>
    <tr><td>Width:</td>
        <td><?= $form->input('text', ['name' => 'width']) ?></td></tr>
    <tr><td>Depth:</td>
        <td><?= $form->input('text', ['name' => 'depth']) ?></td></tr>

    <tr><td colspan="2" align="center">
    <?= $form->input('submit', ['value' => 'Ship!']) ?>
    </td></tr>

</table>
</form>
```

Exercise 5

```
function print_array($ar) {
    print '<ul>';
    foreach ($ar as $k => $v) {
        if (is_array($v)) {
            print '<li>' . htmlentities($k) .':</li>';
            print_array($v);
        } else {
            print '<li>' . htmlentities($k) .'=' . htmlentities($v) . '</li>';
        }
    }
    print '</ul>';
}

/* Since this is operating on form data, it looks directly at $_POST
   instead of a validated $input array */
function process_form() {
    print_array($_POST);
}
```

Chapter 8

Exercise 1

```php
try {
    // Connect
    $db = new PDO('sqlite:/tmp/restaurant.db');
    // Set up exceptions on DB errors
    $db->setAttribute(PDO::ATTR_ERRMODE, PDO::ERRMODE_EXCEPTION);
    $stmt = $db->query('SELECT * FROM dishes ORDER BY price');
    $dishes = $stmt->fetchAll();
    if (count($dishes) == 0) {
        $html = '<p>No dishes to display</p>';
    } else {
        $html = "<table>\n";
        $html .= "<tr><th>Dish Name</th><th>Price</th><th>Spicy?</th></tr>\n";
        foreach ($dishes as $dish) {
            $html .= '<tr><td>' .
                    htmlentities($dish['dish_name']) . '</td><td>$' .
                    sprintf('%.02f', $dish['price']) . '</td><td>' .
                    ($dish['is_spicy'] ? 'Yes' : 'No') . "</td></tr>\n";
        }
        $html .= "</table>";
    }
} catch (PDOException $e) {
    $html = "Can't show dishes: " . $e->getMessage();
}
print $html;
```

Exercise 2

```php
<?php

// Load the form helper class
require 'FormHelper.php';

// Connect to the database
try {
    $db = new PDO('sqlite:/tmp/restaurant.db');
} catch (PDOException $e) {
    print "Can't connect: " . $e->getMessage();
    exit();
}
// Set up exceptions on DB errors
$db->setAttribute(PDO::ATTR_ERRMODE, PDO::ERRMODE_EXCEPTION);

// Set up fetch mode: rows as objects
$db->setAttribute(PDO::ATTR_DEFAULT_FETCH_MODE, PDO::FETCH_OBJ);

// The main page logic:
// - If the form is submitted, validate and then process or redisplay
```

```php
// - If it's not submitted, display
if ($_SERVER['REQUEST_METHOD'] == 'POST') {
    // If validate_form() returns errors, pass them to show_form()
    list($errors, $input) = validate_form();
    if ($errors) {
        show_form($errors);
    } else {
        // The submitted data is valid, so process it
        process_form($input);
    }
} else {
    // The form wasn't submitted, so display
    show_form();
}

function show_form($errors = array()) {
    // Set up the $form object with proper defaults
    $form = new FormHelper();
    // All the HTML and form display is in a separate file for clarity
    include 'price-form.php';
}

function validate_form() {
    $input = array();
    $errors = array();

    // Minimum price must be a valid floating-point number
    $input['min_price'] = filter_input(INPUT_POST,'min_price',
    FILTER_VALIDATE_FLOAT);
    if ($input['min_price'] === null || $input['min_price'] === false) {
        $errors[] = 'Please enter a valid minimum price.';
    }
    return array($errors, $input);
}

function process_form($input) {
    // Access the global variable $db inside this function
    global $db;

    // Build up the query
    $sql = 'SELECT dish_name, price, is_spicy FROM dishes WHERE
            price >= ?';

    // Send the query to the database program and get all the rows back
    $stmt = $db->prepare($sql);
    $stmt->execute(array($input['min_price']));
    $dishes = $stmt->fetchAll();

    if (count($dishes) == 0) {
        print 'No dishes matched.';
    } else {
        print '<table>';
```

```
            print '<tr><th>Dish Name</th><th>Price</th><th>Spicy?</th></tr>';
            foreach ($dishes as $dish) {
                if ($dish->is_spicy == 1) {
                    $spicy = 'Yes';
                } else {
                    $spicy = 'No';
                }
                printf('<tr><td>%s</td><td>$%.02f</td><td>%s</td></tr>',
                        htmlentities($dish->dish_name), $dish->price, $spicy);
            }
            print '</table>';
        }
    }
?>
```

The code relies on the *FormHelper.php* file discussed in Chapter 7. The *price-form.php* file referenced, which displays the form HTML, contains:

```
<form method="POST" action="<?= $form->encode($_SERVER['PHP_SELF']) ?>">
<table>
    <?php if ($errors) { ?>
        <tr>
            <td>You need to correct the following errors:</td>
            <td><ul>
                <?php foreach ($errors as $error) { ?>
                    <li><?= $form->encode($error) ?></li>
                <?php } ?>
            </ul></td>
    <?php } ?>
    <tr>
        <td>Minimum Price:</td>
        <td><?= $form->input('text',['name' => 'min_price']) ?></td>
    </tr>
    <tr>
        <td colspan="2" align="center">
            <?= $form->input('submit', ['name' => 'search',
                                        'value' => 'Search']) ?></td>
    </tr>
</table>
</form>
```

Exercise 3

```
<?php

// Load the form helper class
require 'FormHelper.php';

// Connect to the database
try {
    $db = new PDO('sqlite:/tmp/restaurant.db');
} catch (PDOException $e) {
```

```php
        print "Can't connect: " . $e->getMessage();
        exit();
}
// Set up exceptions on DB errors
$db->setAttribute(PDO::ATTR_ERRMODE, PDO::ERRMODE_EXCEPTION);

// Set up fetch mode: rows as objects
$db->setAttribute(PDO::ATTR_DEFAULT_FETCH_MODE, PDO::FETCH_OBJ);

// The main page logic:
// - If the form is submitted, validate and then process or redisplay
// - If it's not submitted, display
if ($_SERVER['REQUEST_METHOD'] == 'POST') {
    // If validate_form() returns errors, pass them to show_form()
    list($errors, $input) = validate_form();
    if ($errors) {
        show_form($errors);
    } else {
        // The submitted data is valid, so process it
        process_form($input);
    }
} else {
    // The form wasn't submitted, so display
    show_form();
}

function show_form($errors = array()) {
    global $db;

    // Set up the $form object with proper defaults
    $form = new FormHelper();

    // Retrieve the list of dish names to use from the database
    $sql = 'SELECT dish_id, dish_name FROM dishes ORDER BY dish_name';
    $stmt = $db->query($sql);
    $dishes = array();
    while ($row = $stmt->fetch()) {
        $dishes[$row->dish_id] = $row->dish_name;
    }

    // All the HTML and form display is in a separate file for clarity
    include 'dish-form.php';
}

function validate_form() {
    $input = array();
    $errors = array();

    // As long as some dish_id value is submitted, we'll consider it OK.
    // If it doesn't match any dishes in the database, process_form()
    // can report that.
    if (isset($_POST['dish_id'])) {
```

```
        $input['dish_id'] = $_POST['dish_id'];
    } else {
        $errors[] = 'Please select a dish.';
    }
    return array($errors, $input);
}

function process_form($input) {
    // Access the global variable $db inside this function
    global $db;

    // Build up the query
    $sql = 'SELECT dish_id, dish_name, price, is_spicy FROM dishes WHERE
            dish_id = ?';

    // Send the query to the database program and get all the rows back
    $stmt = $db->prepare($sql);
    $stmt->execute(array($input['dish_id']));
    $dish = $stmt->fetch();

    if (count($dish) == 0) {
        print 'No dishes matched.';
    } else {
        print '<table>';
        print '<tr><th>ID</th><th>Dish Name</th><th>Price</th>';
        print '<th>Spicy?</th></tr>';
        if ($dish->is_spicy == 1) {
            $spicy = 'Yes';
        } else {
            $spicy = 'No';
        }
        printf('<tr><td>%d</td><td>%s</td><td>$%.02f</td><td>%s</td></tr>',
                $dish->dish_id,
                htmlentities($dish->dish_name), $dish->price, $spicy);
        print '</table>';
    }
}
?>
```

The code relies on the *FormHelper.php* file discussed in Chapter 7. The *dish-form.php* file referenced, which displays the form HTML, contains:

```
<form method="POST" action="<?= $form->encode($_SERVER['PHP_SELF']) ?>">
<table>
    <?php if ($errors) { ?>
        <tr>
            <td>You need to correct the following errors:</td>
            <td><ul>
                <?php foreach ($errors as $error) { ?>
                    <li><?= $form->encode($error) ?></li>
                <?php } ?>
            </ul></td>
    <?php }  ?>
```

```
        <tr>
            <td>Dish:</td>
            <td><?= $form->select($dishes,['name' => 'dish_id']) ?></td>
        </tr>
        <tr>
            <td colspan="2" align="center">
                <?= $form->input('submit', ['name' => 'info',
                                    'value' => 'Get Dish Info']) ?></td>
        </tr>
</table>
</form>
```

Exercise 4

```php
<?php

// Load the form helper class
require 'FormHelper.php';

// Connect to the database
try {
    $db = new PDO('sqlite:/tmp/restaurant.db');
} catch (PDOException $e) {
    print "Can't connect: " . $e->getMessage();
    exit();
}
// Set up exceptions on DB errors
$db->setAttribute(PDO::ATTR_ERRMODE, PDO::ERRMODE_EXCEPTION);

// Set up fetch mode: rows as objects
$db->setAttribute(PDO::ATTR_DEFAULT_FETCH_MODE, PDO::FETCH_OBJ);

// Put the list of dish IDs and names in a global array because
// we'll need it in show_form() and validate_form()
$dishes = array();
$sql = 'SELECT dish_id, dish_name FROM dishes ORDER BY dish_name';
$stmt = $db->query($sql);
while ($row = $stmt->fetch()) {
    $dishes[$row->dish_id] = $row->dish_name;
}


// The main page logic:
// - If the form is submitted, validate and then process or redisplay
// - If it's not submitted, display
if ($_SERVER['REQUEST_METHOD'] == 'POST') {
    // If validate_form() returns errors, pass them to show_form()
    list($errors, $input) = validate_form();
    if ($errors) {
        show_form($errors);
    } else {
        // The submitted data is valid, so process it
        process_form($input);
```

```
    }
} else {
    // The form wasn't submitted, so display
    show_form();
}

function show_form($errors = array()) {
    global $db, $dishes;

    // Set up the $form object with proper defaults
    $form = new FormHelper();

    // All the HTML and form display is in a separate file for clarity
    include 'customer-form.php';
}

function validate_form() {
    global $dishes;
    $input = array();
    $errors = array();

    // Make sure a dish_id valid is submitted and in $dishes.
    // As long as some dish_id value is submitted, we'll consider it OK.
    // If it doesn't match any dishes in the database, process_form()
    // can report that.
    $input['dish_id'] = $_POST['dish_id'] ?? '';
    if (! array_key_exists($input['dish_id'], $dishes)) {
        $errors[] = 'Please select a valid dish.';
    }

    // Name is required
    $input['name'] = trim($_POST['name'] ?? '');
    if (0 == strlen($input['name'])) {
        $errors[] = 'Please enter a name.';
    }

    // Phone number is required
    $input['phone'] = trim($_POST['phone'] ?? '');
    if (0 == strlen($input['phone'])) {
        $errors[] = 'Please enter a phone number.';
    } else {
        // Be US-centric and ensure that the phone number contains
        // at least 10 digits. Using ctype_digit() on each
        // character is not the most efficient way to do this,
        // but is logically straightforward and avoids
        // regular expressions.
        $digits = 0;
        for ($i = 0; $i < strlen($input['phone']); $i++) {
            if (ctype_digit($input['phone'][$i])) {
                $digits++;
            }
        }
```

```
            if ($digits < 10) {
                $errors[] = 'Phone number needs at least ten digits.';
            }
        }

        return array($errors, $input);
    }

    function process_form($input) {
        // Access the global variable $db inside this function
        global $db;

        // Build up the query. No need to specify customer_id because
        // the database will automatically assign a unique one.
        $sql = 'INSERT INTO customers (name,phone,favorite_dish_id) ' .
               'VALUES (?,?,?)';

        // Send the query to the database program and get all the rows back
        try {
            $stmt = $db->prepare($sql);
            $stmt->execute(array($input['name'],$input['phone'],$input['dish_id']));
            print '<p>Inserted new customer.</p>';
        } catch (Exception $e) {
            print "<p>Couldn't insert customer: {$e->getMessage()}.</p>";
        }
    }
?>
```

The code relies on the *FormHelper.php* file discussed in Chapter 7. The *customer-form.php* file referenced, which displays the form HTML, contains:

```
<form method="POST" action="<?= $form->encode($_SERVER['PHP_SELF']) ?>">
<table>
    <?php if ($errors) { ?>
        <tr>
            <td>You need to correct the following errors:</td>
            <td><ul>
                <?php foreach ($errors as $error) { ?>
                    <li><?= $form->encode($error) ?></li>
                <?php } ?>
            </ul></td>
    <?php }  ?>
    <tr>
    <tr><td>Name:</td><td><?= $form->input('text', ['name' => 'name']) ?>
    </td></tr>
    <tr><td>Phone Number:</td>
        <td><?= $form->input('text', ['name' => 'phone']) ?></td></tr>
    <tr><td>Favorite Dish:</td>
        <td><?= $form->select($dishes,['name' => 'dish_id']) ?></td>
    </tr>
    <tr>
        <td colspan="2" align="center">
            <?= $form->input('submit', ['name' => 'add',
```

```
                                'value' => 'Add Customer']) ?></td>
    </tr>
</table>
</form>
```

Chapter 9

Exercise 1

The template file, *template.html*:

```
<html>
    <head><title>{title}</title></head>
    <body>
        <h1>{headline}</h1>
        <h2>By {byline}</h2>
        <div class="article">{article}</div>
        <p><small>Page generated: {date}</small></p>
    </body>
</html>
```

The PHP program to replace template variables:

```
$now = new DateTime();
// Express the vars as simply as possible, just key => value
$vars = array('title' => 'Man Bites Dog',
                'headline' => 'Man and Dog Trapped in Biting Fiasco',
                'byline' => 'Ireneo Funes',
                'article' => <<<_HTML_
<p>While walking in the park today, Bioy Casares took a big juicy
bite out of his dog, Santa's Little Helper. When asked why he did
it, Mr. Casares said, "I was hungry."</p>
_HTML_
                ,
                'date' => $now->format('l, F j, Y'));

// Make a version of $vars to match the templating syntax, with
// {} around the keys
$template_vars = array();
foreach ($vars as $k => $v) {
    $template_vars['{'.$k.'}'] = $v;
}
// Load the template
$template = file_get_contents('template.html');
if ($template === false) {
    die("Can't read template.html: $php_errormsg");
}
// If given an array of strings to look for and an array of replacements,
// str_replace() does all the replacements at once for you
$html = str_replace(array_keys($template_vars),
                    array_values($template_vars),
                    $template);
```

```
// Write out the new HTML page
$result = file_put_contents('article.html', $html);
if ($result === false) {
    die("Can't write article.html: $php_errormsg");
}
```

Exercise 2

```
// The array to accumulate address counts
$addresses = array();

$fh = fopen('addresses.txt','rb');
if (! $fh) {
    die("Can't open addresses.txt: $php_errormsg");
}
while ((! feof($fh)) && ($line = fgets($fh))) {
    $line = trim($line);
    // Use the address as the key in $addresses. The value is the number
    // of times the address has appeared.
    if (! isset($addresses[$line])) {
        $addresses[$line] = 0;
    }
    $addresses[$line] = $addresses[$line] + 1;
}
if (! fclose($fh)) {
    die("Can't close addresses.txt: $php_errormsg");
}

// Reverse sort (biggest first) $addresses by element value
arsort($addresses);

$fh = fopen('addresses-count.txt','wb');
if (! $fh) {
    die("Can't open addresses-count.txt: $php_errormsg");
}
foreach ($addresses as $address => $count) {
    // Don't forget the newline at the end
    if (fwrite($fh, "$count,$address\n") === false) {
        die("Can't write $count,$address: $php_errormsg");
    }
}
if (! fclose($fh)) {
    die("Can't close addresses-count.txt: $php_errormsg");
}
```

Here is a sample *addresses.txt* to use:

```
brilling@tweedledee.example.com
slithy@unicorn.example.com
uffish@knight.example.net
slithy@unicorn.example.com
jubjub@sheep.example.com
tumtum@queen.example.org
```

slithy@unicorn.example.com
uffish@knight.example.net
manxome@king.example.net
beamish@lion.example.org
uffish@knight.example.net
frumious@tweedledum.example.com
tulgey@carpenter.example.com
vorpal@crow.example.org
beamish@lion.example.org
mimsy@walrus.example.com
frumious@tweedledum.example.com
raths@owl.example.net
frumious@tweedledum.example.com

Exercise 3

```php
$fh = fopen('dishes.csv','rb');
if (! $fh) {
    die("Can't open dishes.csv: $php_errormsg");
}
print "<table>\n";
while ((! feof($fh)) && ($line = fgetcsv($fh))) {
    // Using implode() as in Chapter 4
    print "<tr><td>" . implode("</td><td>", $line) . "</td></tr>\n";
}
print "</table>";
```

Exercise 4

```php
<?php

// Load the form helper class
require 'FormHelper.php';

// The main page logic:
// - If the form is submitted, validate and then process or redisplay
// - If it's not submitted, display
if ($_SERVER['REQUEST_METHOD'] == 'POST') {
    // If validate_form() returns errors, pass them to show_form()
    list($errors, $input) = validate_form();
    if ($errors) {
        show_form($errors);
    } else {
        // The submitted data is valid, so process it
        process_form($input);
    }
} else {
    // The form wasn't submitted, so display
    show_form();
}

function show_form($errors = array()) {
```

```php
        // Set up the $form object with proper defaults
        $form = new FormHelper();

        // All the HTML and form display is in a separate file for clarity
        include 'filename-form.php';
}

function validate_form() {
        $input = array();
        $errors = array();

        // Make sure a filename is specified
        $input['file'] = trim($_POST['file'] ?? '');
        if (0 == strlen($input['file'])) {
            $errors[] = 'Please enter a filename.';
        } else {
            // Make sure the full filename is under the web
            // server's document root
            $full = $_SERVER['DOCUMENT_ROOT'] . '/' . $input['file'];
            // Use realpath() to resolve any .. sequences or
            // symbolic links
            $full = realpath($full);
            if ($full === false) {
                $errors[] = "Please enter a valid filename.";
            } else {
                // Make sure $full begins with the document root directory
                $docroot_len = strlen($_SERVER['DOCUMENT_ROOT']);
                if (substr($full, 0, $docroot_len) != $_SERVER['DOCUMENT_ROOT']) {
                    $errors[] = 'File must be under document root.';
                } else {
                    // If it's OK, put the full path in $input so we can use
                    // it in process_form()
                    $input['full'] = $full;
                }
            }
        }

        return array($errors, $input);
}


        function process_form($input) {
        if (is_readable($input['full'])) {
            print htmlentities(file_get_contents($input['full']));
        } else {
            print "Can't read {$input['file']}.";
        }
}
?>
```

The code relies on the *FormHelper.php* file discussed in Chapter 7. The *filename-form.php* file referenced, which displays the form HTML, contains:

```
<form method="POST" action="<?= $form->encode($_SERVER['PHP_SELF']) ?>">
<table>
    <?php if ($errors) { ?>
        <tr>
            <td>You need to correct the following errors:</td>
            <td><ul>
                <?php foreach ($errors as $error) { ?>
                    <li><?= $form->encode($error) ?></li>
                <?php } ?>
            </ul></td>
    <?php }  ?>

    <tr><td>File:</td>
        <td><?= $form->input('text', ['name' => 'file']) ?></td></tr>
    <tr><td colspan="2"
        align="center"><?= $form->input('submit', ['value' => 'Display']) ?>
    </td></tr>

</table>
</form>
```

Exercise 5

Here is the new `validate_form()` function that implements the additional test using `strcasecmp()`:

```
function validate_form() {
    $input = array();
    $errors = array();

    // Make sure a filename is specified
    $input['file'] = trim($_POST['file'] ?? '');
    if (0 == strlen($input['file'])) {
        $errors[] = 'Please enter a filename.';
    } else {
        // Make sure the full filename is under the web
        // server's document root
        $full = $_SERVER['DOCUMENT_ROOT'] . '/' . $input['file'];
        // Use realpath() to resolve any .. sequences or
        // symbolic links
        $full = realpath($full);
        if ($full === false) {
            $errors[] = "Please enter a valid filename.";
        } else {
            // Make sure $full begins with the document root directory
            $docroot_len = strlen($_SERVER['DOCUMENT_ROOT']);
            if (substr($full, 0, $docroot_len) != $_SERVER['DOCUMENT_ROOT']) {
                $errors[] = 'File must be under document root.';
            } else if (strcasecmp(substr($full, -5), '.html') != 0) {
```

```
            $errors[] = 'File name must end in .html';
        } else {
            // If it's OK, put the full path in $input so we can use
            // it in process_form()
            $input['full'] = $full;
        }
    }
}

return array($errors, $input);
}
```

Chapter 10

Exercise 1

```
$view_count = 1 + ($_COOKIE['view_count'] ?? 0);
setcookie('view_count', $view_count);
print "<p>Hi! Number of times you've viewed this page: $view_count.</p>";
```

Exercise 2

```
$view_count = 1 + ($_COOKIE['view_count'] ?? 0);

if ($view_count == 20) {
    // An empty value for setcookie() removes the cookie
    setcookie('view_count', '');
    $msg = "<p>Time to start over.</p>";
} else {
    setcookie('view_count', $view_count);
    $msg = "<p>Hi! Number of times you've viewed this page: $view_count.</p>";
    if ($view_count == 5) {
        $msg .= "<p>This is your fifth visit.</p>";
    } elseif ($view_count == 10) {
        $msg .= "<p>This is your tenth visit. You must like this page.</p>";
    } elseif ($view_count == 15) {
        $msg .= "<p>This is your fifteenth visit. " .
                "Don't you have anything else to do?</p>";
    }
}
print $msg;
```

Exercise 3

The color-picking page:

```
<?php
// Start sessions first thing so we can use $_SESSION freely later
session_start();

// Load the form helper class
```

```php
require 'FormHelper.php';

$colors = array('ff0000' => 'Red',
                'ffa500' => 'Orange',
                'ffffff' => 'Yellow',
                '008000' => 'Green',
                '0000ff' => 'Blue',
                '4b0082' => 'Indigo',
                '663399' => 'Rebecca Purple');

// The main page logic:
// - If the form is submitted, validate and then process or redisplay
// - If it's not submitted, display
if ($_SERVER['REQUEST_METHOD'] == 'POST') {
    // If validate_form() returns errors, pass them to show_form()
    list($errors, $input) = validate_form();
    if ($errors) {
        show_form($errors);
    } else {
        // The submitted data is valid, so process it
        process_form($input);
    }
} else {
    // The form wasn't submitted, so display
    show_form();
}

function show_form($errors = array()) {
    global $colors;

    // Set up the $form object with proper defaults
    $form = new FormHelper();
    // All the HTML and form display is in a separate file for clarity
    include 'color-form.php';
}

function validate_form() {
    $input = array();
    $errors = array();

    // color must be a valid color
    $input['color'] = $_POST['color'] ?? '';
    if (! array_key_exists($input['color'], $GLOBALS['colors'])) {
        $errors[] = 'Please select a valid color.';
    }

    return array($errors, $input);
}

function process_form($input) {
    global $colors;
```

```
    $_SESSION['background_color'] = $input['color'];
    print '<p>Your color has been set.</p>';
}
?>
```

The code relies on the *FormHelper.php* file discussed in Chapter 7. The *color-form.php* file referenced, which displays the form HTML, contains:

```
<form method="POST" action="<?= $form->encode($_SERVER['PHP_SELF']) ?>">
<table>
    <?php if ($errors) { ?>
        <tr>
            <td>You need to correct the following errors:</td>
            <td><ul>
                <?php foreach ($errors as $error) { ?>
                    <li><?= $form->encode($error) ?></li>
                <?php } ?>
            </ul></td>
    <?php } ?>
    <tr>
        <td>Favorite Color:</td>
        <td><?= $form->select($colors,['name' => 'color']) ?></td>
    </tr>
    <tr>
        <td colspan="2" align="center">
            <?= $form->input('submit', ['name' => 'set',
                                        'value' => 'Set Color']) ?></td>
    </tr>
</table>
</form>
```

The page with background color set:

```
<?php
// Start sessions first thing so we can use $_SESSION freely later
session_start();
?>
<html>
  <head><title>Background Color Example</title>
  <body style="background-color:<?= $_SESSION['background_color'] ?>">
    <p>What color did you pick?</p>
  </body>
</html>
```

Exercise 4

The ordering page:

```
session_start();

// This assumes FormHelper.php is in the same directory as
// this file.
require 'FormHelper.php';
```

```php
// Set up the array of choices in the select menu.
// This is needed in display_form(), validate_form(),
// and process_form(), so it is declared in the global scope.
$products = [ 'cuke'    => 'Braised Sea Cucumber',
              'stomach' => "Sauteed Pig's Stomach",
              'tripe'   => 'Sauteed Tripe with Wine Sauce',
              'taro'    => 'Stewed Pork with Taro',
              'giblets' => 'Baked Giblets with Salt',
              'abalone' => 'Abalone with Marrow and Duck Feet'];

// The main page logic:
// - If the form is submitted, validate and then process or redisplay
// - If it's not submitted, display
if ($_SERVER['REQUEST_METHOD'] == 'POST') {
    // If validate_form() returns errors, pass them to show_form()
    list($errors, $input) = validate_form();
    if ($errors) {
        show_form($errors);
    } else {
        // The submitted data is valid, so process it
        process_form($input);
    }
} else {
    // The form wasn't submitted, so display
    show_form();
}

function show_form($errors = array()) {
    global $products;
    $defaults = array();
    // Start out with 0 as a default
    foreach ($products as $code => $label) {
        $defaults["quantity_$code"] = 0;
    }
    // If quantities are in the session, use those
    if (isset($_SESSION['quantities'])) {
        foreach ($_SESSION['quantities'] as $field => $quantity) {
            $defaults[$field] = $quantity;
        }
    }
    $form = new FormHelper($defaults);
    // All the HTML and form display is in a separate file for clarity
    include 'order-form.php';
}

function validate_form() {
    global $products;

    $input = array();
    $errors = array();
```

```
    // For each quantity box, make sure the value is
    // a valid integer >= 0
    foreach ($products as $code => $name) {
        $field = "quantity_$code";
        $input[$field] = filter_input(INPUT_POST, $field,
                                FILTER_VALIDATE_INT,
                                ['options' => ['min_range'=>0]]);
        if (is_null($input[$field]) || ($input[$field] === false)) {
            $errors[] = "Please enter a valid quantity for $name.";
        }
    }
}

    return array($errors, $input);
}

function process_form($input) {
    $_SESSION['quantities'] = $input;

    print "Thank you for your order.";
}
```

The code relies on the *FormHelper.php* file discussed in Chapter 7. The *order-form.php* file referenced, which displays the form HTML, contains:

```
<form method="POST" action="<?= $form->encode($_SERVER['PHP_SELF']) ?>">
<table>
    <?php if ($errors) { ?>
        <tr>
            <td>You need to correct the following errors:</td>
            <td><ul>
                <?php foreach ($errors as $error) { ?>
                    <li><?= $form->encode($error) ?></li>
                <?php } ?>
            </ul></td>
    <?php }  ?>

    <tr><th>Product</th><td>Quantity</td></tr>
<?php foreach ($products as $code => $name) { ?>
    <tr><td><?= htmlentities($name) ?>:</td>
        <td><?= $form->input('text', ['name' => "quantity_$code"]) ?></td></tr>
<?php } ?>
    <tr><td colspan="2"
        align="center"><?= $form->input('submit', ['value' => 'Order']) ?>
    </td></tr>

</table>
</form>
```

The checkout page:

```
session_start();

// The same products from the order page
```

```
$products = ['cuke'    => 'Braised Sea Cucumber',
             'stomach' => "Sauteed Pig's Stomach",
             'tripe'   => 'Sauteed Tripe with Wine Sauce',
             'taro'    => 'Stewed Pork with Taro',
             'giblets' => 'Baked Giblets with Salt',
             'abalone' => 'Abalone with Marrow and Duck Feet'];

// Simplified main page logic without form validation
if ($_SERVER['REQUEST_METHOD'] == 'POST') {
    process_form();
} else {
    // The form wasn't submitted, so display
    show_form();
}

function show_form() {
    global $products;

    // The "form" is just a single submit button, so we won't use
    // FormHelper and just inline all the HTML here
    if (isset($_SESSION['quantities']) && (count($_SESSION['quantities'])>0)) {
        print "<p>Your order:</p><ul>";
        foreach ($_SESSION['quantities'] as $field => $amount) {
            list($junk, $code) = explode('_', $field);
            $product = $products[$code];
            print "<li>$amount $product</li>";
        }
        print "</ul>";
        print '<form method="POST" action=' .
            htmlentities($_SERVER['PHP_SELF']) . '>';
        print '<input type="submit" value="Check Out" />';
        print '</form>';
    } else {
        print "<p>You don't have a saved order.</p>";
    }
    // This assumes the order form page is saved as "order.php"
    print '<a href="order.php">Return to Order page</a>';
}

function process_form() {
    // This removes the data from the session
    unset($_SESSION['quantities']);
    print "<p>Thanks for your order.</p>";
}
```

Chapter 11

Exercise 1

```
$json = file_get_contents("http://php.net/releases/?json");
if ($json === false) {
```

```
        print "Can't retrieve feed.";
}
else {
    $feed = json_decode($json, true);
    // $feed is an array whose top-level keys are major release
    // numbers. First we need to pick the biggest one.
    $major_numbers = array_keys($feed);
    rsort($major_numbers);
    $biggest_major_number = $major_numbers[0];
    // The "version" element in the array under the major number
    // key is the latest release for that major version number
    $version = $feed[$biggest_major_number]['version'];
    print "The latest version of PHP released is $version.";
}
```

Exercise 2

```
$c = curl_init("http://php.net/releases/?json");
curl_setopt($c, CURLOPT_RETURNTRANSFER, true);
$json = curl_exec($c);
if ($json === false) {
    print "Can't retrieve feed.";
}
else {
    $feed = json_decode($json, true);
    // $feed is an array whose top-level keys are major release
    // numbers. First we need to pick the biggest one.
    $major_numbers = array_keys($feed);
    rsort($major_numbers);
    $biggest_major_number = $major_numbers[0];
    // The "version" element in the array under the major number
    // key is the latest release for that major version number
    $version = $feed[$biggest_major_number]['version'];
    print "The latest version of PHP released is $version.";
}
```

Exercise 3

```
// Seconds from Jan 1, 1970 until now
$now = time();
setcookie('last_access', $now);
if (isset($_COOKIE['last_access'])) {
    // To create a DateTime from a seconds-since-1970 value,
    // prefix it with @.
    $d = new DateTime('@'. $_COOKIE['last_access']);
    $msg = '<p>You last visited this page at ' .
        $d->format('g:i a') . ' on ' .
        $d->format('F j, Y') . '</p>';
} else {
    $msg = '<p>This is your first visit to this page.</p>';
}
```

```
print $msg;
```

Exercise 4

```
$url = 'https://api.github.com/gists';
$data = ['public' => true,
        'description' => "This program a gist of itself.",
        // As the API docs say:
        // The keys in the files object are the string filename,
        // and the value is another object with a key of content
        // and a value of the file contents.
        'files' => [ basename(__FILE__) =>
                     [ 'content' => file_get_contents(__FILE__) ] ] ];

$c = curl_init($url);
curl_setopt($c, CURLOPT_RETURNTRANSFER, true);
curl_setopt($c, CURLOPT_POST, true);
curl_setopt($c, CURLOPT_HTTPHEADER, array('Content-Type: application/json'));
curl_setopt($c, CURLOPT_POSTFIELDS, json_encode($data));
curl_setopt($c, CURLOPT_USERAGENT, 'learning-php-7/exercise');

$response = curl_exec($c);
if ($response === false) {
    print "Couldn't make request.";
} else {
    $info = curl_getinfo($c);
    if ($info['http_code'] != 201) {
        print "Couldn't create gist, got {$info['http_code']}\n";
        print $response;
    } else {
        $body = json_decode($response);
        print "Created gist at {$body->html_url}\n";
    }
}
```

Chapter 12

Exercise 1

The keyword global should not be in line 5, so the parse error should report that unexpected keyword. The actual parse error is:

```
PHP Parse error:  syntax error, unexpected 'global' (T_GLOBAL)
in debugging-12.php on line 5
```

To make the program run properly, change the line print global $name; to print $GLOBALS['name'];. Or, you can add global name; as the first line of the function and then change print global $name; to print $name;.

Exercise 2

```
function validate_form() {
    $input = array();
    $errors = array();

    // turn on output buffering
    ob_start();
    // dump all the submitted data
    var_dump($_POST);
    // capture the generated "output"
    $output = ob_get_contents();
    // turn off output buffering
    ob_end_clean();
    // send the variable dump to the error log
    error_log($output);

    // op is required
    $input['op'] = $GLOBALS['ops'][$_POST['op']] ?? '';
    if (! in_array($input['op'], $GLOBALS['ops'])) {
        $errors[] = 'Please select a valid operation.';
    }
    // num1 and num2 must be numbers
    $input['num1'] = filter_input(INPUT_POST, 'num1', FILTER_VALIDATE_FLOAT);
    if (is_null($input['num1']) || ($input['num1'] === false)) {
        $errors[] = 'Please enter a valid first number.';
    }

    $input['num2'] = filter_input(INPUT_POST, 'num2', FILTER_VALIDATE_FLOAT);
    if (is_null($input['num2']) || ($input['num2'] === false)) {
        $errors[] = 'Please enter a valid second number.';
    }

    // can't divide by zero
    if (($input['op'] == '/') && ($input['num2'] == 0)) {
        $errors[] = 'Division by zero is not allowed.';
    }

    return array($errors, $input);
}
```

Exercise 3

At the top of the program, this code defines an exception handler and sets it up to be called on unhandled exceptions:

```
function exceptionHandler($ex) {
    // Log the specifics to the error log
    error_log("ERROR: " . $ex->getMessage());
    // Print something less specific for users to see
    // and exit
    die("<p>Sorry, something went wrong.</p>");
}
set_exception_handler('exceptionHandler');
```

Then the try/catch blocks can be removed from the two places they are used (once around creating the PDO object and once in process_form()) because the exceptions will be handled by the exception handler.

Exercise 4

- Line 4: Change :: to : in the DSN.
- Line 5: Change catch ($e) to catch (Exception $e).
- Line 16: Change $row['dish_id']] to $row['dish_id'] as the key to look up in the $dish_names array.
- Line 18: Change ** to * in the SQL query.
- Line 20: Change = to ==.
- Line 26: Change the third format specifier from %f to %s—$customer['phone'] is a string.
- Line 30: Change $customer['favorite_dish_id'] to $dish_names[$customer['favorite_dish_id']] so that the dish ID is translated into the name of the corresponding dish.
- Line 33: Insert a } to match the opening { in line 22.

The complete corrected program is:

```
<?php
// Connect to the database
try {
    $db = new PDO('sqlite:/tmp/restaurant.db');
} catch (Exception $e) {
    die("Can't connect: " . $e->getMessage());
}
// Set up exception error handling
$db->setAttribute(PDO::ATTR_ERRMODE, PDO::ERRMODE_EXCEPTION);
// Set up fetch mode: rows as arrays
$db->setAttribute(PDO::ATTR_DEFAULT_FETCH_MODE, PDO::FETCH_ASSOC);
// Get the array of dish names from the database
$dish_names = array();
$res = $db->query('SELECT dish_id,dish_name FROM dishes');
foreach ($res->fetchAll() as $row) {
    $dish_names[ $row['dish_id'] ] = $row['dish_name'];
}
$res = $db->query('SELECT * FROM customers ORDER BY phone DESC');
```

```
$customers = $res->fetchAll();
if (count($customers) == 0) {
    print "No customers.";
} else {
    print '<table>';
    print '<tr><th>ID</th><th>Name</th>
            <th>Phone</th><th>Favorite Dish</th></tr>';
    foreach ($customers as $customer) {
        printf("<tr><td>%d</td><td>%s</td><td>%s</td><td>%s</td></tr>\n",
                $customer['customer_id'],
                htmlentities($customer['customer_name']),
                $customer['phone'],
                $dish_names[$customer['favorite_dish_id']]);
    }
    print '</table>';
}
?>
```

Chapter 13

Exercise 2

```
public function testNameMustBeSubmitted() {
        $submitted = array('age' => '15',
                            'price' => '39.95');
        list($errors, $input) = validate_form($submitted);
        $this->assertContains('Your name is required.', $errors);
        $this->assertCount(1, $errors);

    }
```

Exercise 3

```
include 'FormHelper.php';

class FormHelperTest extends PHPUnit_Framework_TestCase {

    public $products = [ 'cu&ke'    => 'Braised <Sea> Cucumber',
                         'stomach' => "Sauteed Pig's Stomach",
                         'tripe'   => 'Sauteed Tripe with Wine Sauce',
                         'taro'    => 'Stewed Pork with Taro',
                         'giblets' => 'Baked Giblets with Salt',
                         'abalone' => 'Abalone with Marrow and Duck Feet'];
    public $stooges = ['Larry','Moe','Curly','Shemp'];

    // This code gets run before each test. Putting it in
    // the special setUp() method is more concise than having
    // to repeat it in each test method.
    public function setUp() {
        $_SERVER['REQUEST_METHOD'] = 'GET';
    }
```

```php
    public function testAssociativeOptions() {
        $form = new FormHelper();
        $html = $form->select($this->products);
        $this->assertEquals($html,<<<_HTML_
<select ><option  value="cu&amp;ke">Braised &lt;Sea&gt; Cucumber</option>
<option  value="stomach">Sauteed Pig's Stomach</option>
<option  value="tripe">Sauteed Tripe with Wine Sauce</option>
<option  value="taro">Stewed Pork with Taro</option>
<option  value="giblets">Baked Giblets with Salt</option>
<option  value="abalone">Abalone with Marrow and Duck Feet</option></select>
_HTML_
        );
    }

    public function testNumericOptions() {
        $form = new FormHelper();
        $html = $form->select($this->stooges);
        $this->assertEquals($html,<<<_HTML_
<select ><option  value="0">Larry</option>
<option  value="1">Moe</option>
<option  value="2">Curly</option>
<option  value="3">Shemp</option></select>
_HTML_
        );
    }

    public function testNoOptions() {
        $form = new FormHelper();
        $html = $form->select([]);
        $this->assertEquals('<select ></select>', $html);
    }

    public function testBooleanTrueAttributes() {
        $form = new FormHelper();
        $html = $form->select([],['np' => true]);
        $this->assertEquals('<select np></select>', $html);

    }

    public function testBooleanFalseAttributes() {
        $form = new FormHelper();
        $html = $form->select([],['np' => false, 'onion' => 'red']);
        $this->assertEquals('<select onion="red"></select>', $html);
    }

    public function testNonBooleanAttributes() {
        $form = new FormHelper();
        $html = $form->select([],['spaceship'=>'<=>']);
        $this->assertEquals('<select spaceship="&lt;=&gt;"></select>', $html);
    }
```

```
    public function testMultipleAttribute() {
        $form = new FormHelper();
        $html = $form->select([],["name" => "menu",
                              "q" => 1, "multiple" => true]);
        $this->assertEquals('<select name="menu[]" q="1" multiple></select>',
        $html);
    }
}
```

Exercise 4

The additional test methods for `FormHelperTest`:

```
public function testButtonNoTypeOK() {
        $form = new FormHelper();
        $html = $form->tag('button');
        $this->assertEquals('<button  />',$html);
    }
    public function testButtonTypeSubmitOK() {
        $form = new FormHelper();
        $html = $form->tag('button',['type'=>'submit']);
        $this->assertEquals('<button type="submit" />',$html);
    }
    public function testButtonTypeResetOK() {
        $form = new FormHelper();
        $html = $form->tag('button',['type'=>'reset']);
        $this->assertEquals('<button type="reset" />',$html);
    }
    public function testButtonTypeButtonOK() {
        $form = new FormHelper();
        $html = $form->tag('button',['type'=>'button']);
        $this->assertEquals('<button type="button" />',$html);
    }
    public function testButtonTypeOtherFails() {
        $form = new FormHelper();
        // FormHelper should throw an InvalidArgumentException
        // when an invalid attribute is provided
        $this->setExpectedException('InvalidArgumentException');
        $html = $form->tag('button',['type'=>'other']);
    }
```

The necessary modifications for `FormHelper` that make the tests pass are:

```
// This code goes just after the "class FormHelper" declaration
    // This array expresses, for the specified elements,
    // what attribute names have what allowed values
    protected $allowedAttributes = ['button' => ['type' => ['submit',
                                                            'reset',
                                                            'button' ] ] ];



    // tag() is modified to pass $tag as the first argument to
    // $this->attributes()
```

```php
    public function tag($tag, $attributes = array(), $isMultiple = false) {
        return "<$tag {$this->attributes($tag, $attributes, $isMultiple)} />";
    }

    // start() is also modified to pass $tag as the first argument to
    // $this->attributes()
    public function start($tag, $attributes = array(), $isMultiple = false) {
        // <select> and <textarea> tags don't get value attributes on them
        $valueAttribute = (! (($tag == 'select')||($tag == 'textarea')));
        $attrs = $this->attributes($tag, $attributes, $isMultiple,
                                   $valueAttribute);
        return "<$tag $attrs>";
    }


    // attributes() is modified to accept $tag as a first argument,
    // set up $attributeCheck if allowed attributes for the tag have
    // been defined in $this->allowedAttributes, and then, if allowed
    // attributes have been defined, see if the provided value is
    // allowed and throw an exception if not
    protected function attributes($tag, $attributes, $isMultiple,
                                  $valueAttribute = true) {
        $tmp = array();
        // If this tag could include a value attribute and it
        // has a name and there's an entry for the name
        // in the values array, then set a value attribute
        if ($valueAttribute && isset($attributes['name']) &&
            array_key_exists($attributes['name'], $this->values)) {
            $attributes['value'] = $this->values[$attributes['name']];
        }
        if (isset($this->allowedAttributes[$tag])) {
            $attributeCheck = $this->allowedAttributes[$tag];
        } else {
            $attributeCheck = array();
        }
        foreach ($attributes as $k => $v) {
            // Check if the attribute's value is allowed
            if (isset($attributeCheck[$k]) &&
                (! in_array($v, $attributeCheck[$k]))) {
                throw new
                InvalidArgumentException("$v is not allowed as value for $k");
            }
            // True boolean value means boolean attribute
            if (is_bool($v)) {
                if ($v) { $tmp[] = $this->encode($k); }
            }
            // Otherwise k=v
            else {
                $value = $this->encode($v);
                // If this is an element that might have multiple values,
                // tack [] onto its name
                if ($isMultiple && ($k == 'name')) {
```

```
                $value .= '[]';
            }
            $tmp[] = "$k=\"$value\"";
        }
    }
    return implode(' ', $tmp);
}
```

Index

Symbols

! (negation) operator, 50
!= (not equal) operator, 45
" " (quotation marks, double)
   debugging, 251
   interpolating array elements in double-
     quoted strings, 68
   string delimiter in PHP, 22
(octothorpe) character, introducing com-
   ments, 16
$ (dollar sign), denoting variables, 12
$GLOBALS array, 93
   modifying global variable with, 94
   recommended use versus global keyword,
     95
$params array, 233
$this variable, 104
   example of, 105
$_COOKIE array, 208, 210
$_GET array, 124
$_POST array, 122, 124
$_SERVER array, 122
   accessing incoming request headers, 245
   argv, 312
   HTTPS, 246
   HTTP_HOST, 247
   PHP_SELF element, 122
   REQUEST_METHOD element, 122
   REQUEST_URI, 247
   useful elements, 123
$_SESSION array, 214
   removing a key and value from, 226
   usernames in, 224
% (percent sign)
   beginning format string rules, 26
   literal, matching with LIKE, 180
   modulus operator, 30
   Unix shell prompt, 314
   wildcard character in SQL, 180
&& (logical and) operator, 51
' ' (quotation marks, single)
   debugging, 251
   escaping in PHP strings, 20
   string delimiter in PHP, 20
' (apostrophe), in SQL queries, 169
   escaping, 169
() (parentheses)
   following function names, 82
   grouping operations with, 31, 51
* (asterisk)
   ** (exponentiation) operator, 30
   multiplication operator, 30
   wildcard character, using with SELECT, 175
+ (plus sign)
   ++ (increment) operator, 34
   += (addition and assignment) operator, 34,
     256
   addition operator, 30
- (subtraction) operator, 30
-- (decrement) operator, 34
-> (arrow) operator, 105
. (period)
   .. in filenames, 202
   string concatenation operator, 23
. (string concatenation) operator
   combining with assignment operator, 34
/ (slash)
   /* and */ delimiting multiline comments, 16

asort() function, 72
asort() method (Collator), 321
assertion methods, 268
assertions, 267
    IsolateValidationTest (example), 272
assignment
    assigning value to properties, 105
    chaining assignment operations, 41
    comparison versus, 44
    using with function call in test expression, 91
associative arrays, 61, 178
    multidimensional, iterating through, 75
    sorting by element value, 72
auto-globals, 95

B

backslash (\)
    escape character in PHP, 20
    escaping in PHP strings, 21
    top-level namespace, 115
booleans, 39, 96, 200
    in type comparisons, 132
    truth values, 40
browsers (see web browsers)
buffering (output), 227
    data written with fwrite(), 200
    output_buffering directive, 331
    sending var_dump() output to error log, 257
bytes (PHP string representation), 20

C

case
    case-sensitivity in variable names, 33
    in string comparisons, 25
    keywords and function names in PHP, 15
    manipulating for strings, 27
    SQL and, 157
    uppercase and lowercase in different character sets, 319
case sensitivity in PHP, 15
catch blocks, 110
catching exceptions, 109
character sets, 317
    default_charset configuration variable, 317
class keyword, 104
classes, 103
    (see also objects)

constructors, 107
    defining, 104
    extending, 110
    organizing into files, 280
    static methods, 106
client-side languages, 3
client/server commuications
    initiating sessions, 213
    when setting a cookie, 209
Collator class, 320
columns
    common types for database columns, 161
    defining in a database table, 160
command line, PHP on, 311-316
    running a PHP REPL, 314
    using as interactive shell, 311
    writing a program for, 312
        accessing command-line arguments, 312
        using PHP built-in web server, 314
comments, 8
    in config files, 282, 329
    multiline, 16
    single-line, styles for, 16
    SQL, 166
compare() method (Collator), 321
comparison operators, 40, 43
comparisons, 40
    comparing text, 320
Composer, 266, 293-298
    adding a package with, 294
    information resources on, 296
    installing, 293
    installing Laravel, 304
    installing PsySH, 315
    installing Swift Mailer with, 299
    using a Composer-installed library, 294
    using with source control systems, 295
configuration directives, 328-333
    changing in php.ini file, 328
    changing within PHP program with ini_set(), 331
    summary listing of useful directives, 332
configuration files, 282, 328
    reading, 283
__construct() method, 107
constructors, 104, 107
    calling, 107
    putting in a subclass, 112
    throwing exceptions, 108

About the Author

David Sklar works as a Staff Software Engineer at Google. Before that, he built platforms, APIs, and sandboxed PHP execution runtimes at Ning. He lives in New York City, where he enjoys eating and walking, sometimes simultaneously. Read David's blog at *www.sklar.com/blog*.

Colophon

The animal on the cover of *Learning PHP* is an eagle. Eagles fall into the category of bird known as "raptors," a category that also includes falcons and hawks. There are two types of raptor: grasping killers, with beaks shaped for tearing and cutting, and short toes with curved claws designed for killing; and grasping holders, with beaks shaped for tearing and biting, and longer toes designed for holding. Eagles are grasping killers. Sea eagles have special adaptations to their toes that enable them to grasp smooth prey such as fish. Their excellent vision enables all eagles to spot prey from the air or a high perch. The eagle then swoops down, grabs its prey, and takes off in flight again, in one graceful movement. Eagles often eat their victims while still flying, breaking them apart and discarding the nonedible parts to lighten their load. Eagles, like most raptors, often dine on sick or wounded animals.

There are more than 50 species of eagle spread throughout the world, with the exception of New Zealand and Antarctica. All species of eagles build nests, known as aeries, high above the ground, in trees or on rocky ledges. A pair of eagles will use the same nest year after year, lining it with green leaves and grass, fur, turf, or other soft materials. The eagle will add to its nest each year. The largest eagle nest ever found was 20 feet deep and 10 feet across.

Hunting, increased use of pesticides, and the diminishment of their natural environment, with the attendant reduction in food sources, have endangered many species of eagle.

Many of the animals on O'Reilly covers are endangered; all of them are important to the world. To learn more about how you can help, go to *animals.oreilly.com*.

The cover image is a 19th-century engraving from the Dover Pictorial Archive. The cover fonts are URW Typewriter and Guardian Sans. The text font is Adobe Minion Pro; the heading font is Adobe Myriad Condensed; and the code font is Dalton Maag's Ubuntu Mono.

Have it your way.

Get even more for your money.

Join the O'Reilly Community, and register the O'Reilly books you own. It's free, and you'll get:

- $4.99 ebook upgrade offer
- 40% upgrade offer on O'Reilly print books
- Membership discounts on books and events
- Free lifetime updates to ebooks and videos
- Multiple ebook formats, DRM FREE
- Participation in the O'Reilly community
- Newsletters
- Account management
- 100% Satisfaction Guarantee

Signing up is easy:

1. Go to: oreilly.com/go/register
2. Create an O'Reilly login.
3. Provide your address.
4. Register your books.

Note: English-language books only

To order books online:
oreilly.com/store

For questions about products or an order:
orders@oreilly.com

To sign up to get topic-specific email announcements and/or news about upcoming books, conferences, special offers, and new technologies:
elists@oreilly.com

For technical questions about book content:
booktech@oreilly.com

To submit new book proposals to our editors:
proposals@oreilly.com

O'Reilly books are available in multiple DRM-free ebook formats. For more information:
oreilly.com/ebooks